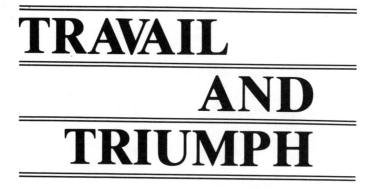

TRAVAIL
AND
TRIUMPH

RECENT TITLES IN
CONTRIBUTIONS IN AFRO-AMERICAN AND AFRICAN STUDIES

Series Advisor: Hollis R. Lynch

The Black Infantry in the West, 1869-1891
Arlen L. Fowler

The Decline and Abolition of Negro Slavery in Venezuela, 1820-1854
John V. Lombardi

Political Philosophy of Martin Luther King, Jr.
Hanes Walton

The American Slave, Series 1, Vols. 1-7; Series 2, Vols. 8-19
George P. Rawick

Nigeria, Dilemma of Nationhood
Joseph Okpaku, editor

Private Black Colleges at the Crossroads
Daniel Thompson

Ebony Kinship: Africa, Africans, and the Afro-American
Robert G. Weisbord

Slavery and Race Relations in Latin America
Robert Brent Toplin, editor

Good Time Coming?: Black Nevadans in the Nineteenth Century
Elmer R. Rusco

Race First: The Ideological and Organizational Struggles of Marcus Garvey and the Universal Negro Improvement Association
Tony Martin

Silence to the Drums: A Survey of the Literature of the Harlem Renaissance
Margaret Perry

Internal Combustion: The Races in Detroit, 1915-1926
David Allan Levine

Henry Sylvester Williams and the Origins of the Pan-African Movement, 1869-1911
Owen Charles Mathurin

Periodic Markets, Urbanization, and Regional Planning: A Case Study from Western Kenya
Robert A. Obudho and *Peter P. Waller*

Frederick Douglass on Women's Rights
Philip S. Foner, editor

Arnold H. Taylor

TRAVAIL
AND
TRIUMPH

Black Life and Culture in the South Since the Civil War

**Contributions in Afro-American and African Studies,
Number 26**

GREENWOOD PRESS
Westport, Connecticut • London, England

Library of Congress Cataloging in Publication Data

Taylor, Arnold H
  Travail and triumph.

  (Contributions in Afro-American and African studies ; no. 26)
  Bibliography: p.
  Includes index.
  1. Afro-Americans—Southern States. 2. Afro-Americans—Social conditions. 3. Southern States—History—1865-   I. Title.   II. Series.
E185.6.T28   301.45'19'6073075   76-5264
ISBN 0-8371-8912-8

The poem "Go Down Death" is from *God's Trombones* by James Weldon Johnson. Copyright 1927 by the Viking Press, Inc., Copyright © renewed 1955 by Grace Nail Johnson. Reprinted by permission of The Viking Press.

The poem "We Wear the Mask" is from *The Complete Poems of Paul Laurence Dunbar.* Published in 1900 by Dodd, Mead, and Company. Reprinted by permission of Dodd, Mead.

The poem "Legacy: My South" by Dudley Randall is from *Poem Counterpoem* by Margaret Danner and Dudley Randall. Published in 1969 by Broadside Press. Reprinted by permission of Broadside Press.

To my son, Brad

Library of Congress Catalog Card Number: 76-5264
ISBN 0-8371-8912-8

First published in 1976

Greenwood Press, Inc.
51 Riverside Avenue, Westport, Connecticut 06880

Printed in the United States of America

CONTENTS

PREFACE

At the close of the Civil War approximately eleven out of twelve Afro-Americans resided in the South. Thirty-five years later, at the beginning of the twentieth century, the regional distribution of black Americans had not substantially changed. Moreover, despite the Northern migration of large numbers of black Southerners during World War I and the 1920s, seven out of nine Afro-Americans still lived in the South on the eve of America's entry into World War II. While the proportion of Southern blacks in the Afro-American population declined rather dramatically as a result of the heavy migration to the North and West during the next three decades, they continued to comprise 68 percent of the black populace in 1950, 60 percent in 1960, and 53 percent in 1970. Since 1970 a remarkable development has occurred. Apparently attracted by an improved racial climate and growing economic opportunities, 276,000 blacks have moved into the South while only 241,000 have left. The majority of the former are probably natives of the South, including some retirees who are returning to the region of their youth to live out their remaining days.

Although partially obscured by the recent popular, scholarly, and governmental interest in the Northern ghettos, an interest inspired in part by the urban riots of the 1960s, these developments serve to remind us that since the days of slavery and even for most of the twentieth century, the overwhelming majority of black Americans have been Southerners. Moreover, most black residents of other sections of the nation have deep Southern roots and are either the direct carriers of Southern black culture or have inherited it atavistically.

Thus, rather than being a specialized treatment of a limited segment of the black historical experience in America, this study purports to illumine what may validly be regarded as the quintessential Afro-American experience. It represents an attempt to synthesize information about and refocus attention on a regional community in which the most significant, the most representative, and the most dynamic patterns of Afro-American life have evolved over the past three and a half centuries.

Because the main purpose of this study is to provide students on several levels with a body of basic information that will enhance their understanding of the historical circumstances of Southern black life and the evolution and functioning of the Southern black community, the subjects chosen for discussion are fairly traditional and are treated, for the most part, in a traditional way. No attempt has been made, therefore, to impose an overall abstract and complex conceptual framework upon the issues discussed. There is, however, a dominant theme: throughout their history, black Southerners have been more than merely passive victims of an oppressive social order. Whether deliberately pursuing the goals of freedom and human dignity or simply seeking to meet the challenge of daily existence, they have responded variously to their social and physical environment and have frequently seized the intitiative in shaping their individual lives and in developing a viable community life and a rich expressive culture. In light of the forces with which they have had to contend, their perseverance is a testament to the strength, resiliency, and triumph of the human spirit.

Because this book is largely a work of synthesis, my debt to other scholars is large. For the most part, however, I have limited footnotes to primary sources, quoted material, the works of authors mentioned in the text, and a few selected books and articles upon which I have relied heavily. Because certain works of fiction, drama, and poetry are often more readily accessible in anthologies than in the original publication, I have frequently cited the anthologies in which they are reprinted.

I am deeply grateful for assistance from Professors Thomas Holt and Okon Uya, former colleagues and Ms. Sharon Harley, a Howard University graduate student, who read portions of the manuscript and offered constructive and useful criticism. A grant from the Howard University history department enabled me to use briefly the services of Ms. Harley and Mrs. Evelyn Barnett as research assistants and also helped to finance the typing of the manuscript. By remaining engrossed in his own "research" during the many times that he accompanied me to the library, my eight-year-old son Brad, to whom this book is dedicated, considerably lightened my own task of research and synthesis.

PART ONE

DEFERRED FREEDOM

ONE

Black Reconstruction: The Quest for Equality and Status

THE DREAM

The role and status of former slaves in the social order of the South was the central issue of the Reconstruction era, the period in American history beginning near the end of the Civil War and lasting until 1877 in some states. Perceptive blacks in the South early understood what the issue of the postwar period would be. Two and a half months before Lee surrendered to Grant at Appomattox, the New Orleans *Tribune,* a black newspaper, expressed grave concern that the freedom being obtained by the slaves might have little substance, and that the status of black men in the South would lie in some nebulous sphere "between slavery and freedom" where "he possesses neither the right to live according to his wishes, nor the power to act by himself. . . ." "Emancipation," declared the *Tribune,* "is one fact, effective liberty is another. Man does not have all his rights and privileges, he does not have free exercise of his faculties and skills by the simple consequence of the abolition of slavery." The *Tribune* went on to insist that there should be "No pariahs in America" and that the liberties of the black community should not be circumscribed, but should be the same for all people. In order to be truly free, the *Tribune* declared, the former slaves must enjoy the same status and possess the same rights as all other citizens. They must have freedom of movement, the right to vote and hold public office, the right to education at public expense, and the "right to be judged, treated and governed according to the common law."[1]

During the first year following the end of the war, black people throughout the South, individually and collectively, in informal discussions and through formal pronouncements, made similar comments. A group of black ex-soldiers in North Carolina asserted in May 1865 that "men who are willing on the field of danger to carry the muskets of Republics, in days of peace ought to be permitted to carry its ballots. . . ."[2] In August 1865, a black assembly at Alexandria, Virginia, demanded that the freedmen be accorded recognition as the equals of all other men and be granted full political and civil rights as citizens. And blacks in Louisiana, in order to stress their determination to gain full rights as citizens, staged a mock election in August 1865 in which their gubernatorial candidate received more votes than the officially elected governor.

In other ways, too, black people in the South early exhibited their resolve to enjoy "effective freedom." As the Civil War drew to a close, and particularly after formal emancipation, the former slaves tested their freedom in various ways. Many abruptly left the plantations, farms, and other slave habitations, and either moved about the countryside or migrated to the cities and towns of the South. Some left with mixed emotions. A Virginia planter who had treated his slaves kindly reported that "some of them came up with tears in their eyes to shake hands with me and say good-bye." When he reminded them that they had been well-treated and inquired why they were leaving they merely responded politely that "we 'bleege to go, sah . . . , we 'bleege to go, massa." All but four or five of his 115 slaves departed when they heard that they were free. Only the old and the infirm remained.[3]

For the most part, the former slaves who left the plantations engaged in no aimless wandering, but went out seeking new economic and social opportunities and relationships. Many looked for wives, husbands, children, and parents from whom they had been separated during slavery. Others sought land. Some searched for jobs in the cities. And some, as Charley Davenport, a Mississippi ex-slave, recalled in the 1930s, simply wanted to experience the joy of unrestricted movement:

> Lak all de fool Niggers o' dat time, I was right smart bit by the freedom bug for awhile.
> It sounded pow'ful nice to be tol': you don't have to chop cotton no more. You can th'ow dat hoe down an' go fishin' whensoever de notion strikes you. An' you can roam roun' at night an' court gals jus' as late as you please. Ain't no master gwine a-say to you, "Charlie, you's got to be back when de clock strikes nine."
> . . . Freedom meant too us could leave where us'd been born an' bred, but it meant too, dat us had to scratch for us ownse'fs.[4]

Charles Moses, another Mississippi ex-slave, put the matter more succinctly: "I didn' spec nothin' out o' freedom 'ceptin peace an' happiness, an' the right to go my way as I pleased."[5]

Despite the seductiveness of freedom, many ex-slaves, like Charley Daven-port, remained at the homesteads of their former masters, and some who went away eventually returned. They were inspired less by affection for "old Massa," however, than by the hope of finding some means of livelihood in familiar surroundings or among familiar people. Some were also moved by an instinctive feeling that the old cabin in which they had spent so much of their lives and the land on which they had labored so long ought by right to belong to them. Whatever their motives, they were no longer prepared to tolerate the old economic and social arrangements. They demanded a new dispensation—either wages for work or the opportunity to cultivate under just arrangements a portion of the former master's land. They protested, and sometimes resisted, the efforts of their former masters to physically discipline them, their wives, and their children. In short, most ex-slaves consciously or intuitively desired a new social order in the South in which they could exercise the rights, duties, and privileges of a free people.

White allegations to the contrary then, the exhilaration, and even in some cases the trepidation, confusion, or indifference with which the former slaves greeted freedom was mixed with the realization that, as Charley Daven-port recalled, "us now had to scratch for us ownse'f's." In declaration after declaration, assemblages of freedmen asserted that freedom meant respon-sibility. "We scorn and treat with contempt the allegation that we under-stand freedom to mean idleness and indolence," declared blacks in Peters-burg, Virginia, in 1865, "but we do understand freedom to mean industry and the enjoyment of the fruits thereof." A year later, black Kentuckians echoed the sentiments of their Virginia brethren in almost the same language when they asserted that ". . . freedom does not mean idleness . . . ; that with all its blessings it confers upon us new duties, new obligations, new responsibilities, and we trust, new energies and purposes."[6]

OBSTACLES TO FREEDOM

In their efforts to assume the rights, obligations, and responsibilities of freedom, the recently freed blacks also realized that they would face formid-able obstacles. They knew they were handicapped by their own ignorance and inexperience. As the black Kentuckians acknowledged they were ". . . not unmindful of the fact that we have just been released from bondage; that we are just stepping out of the dark into the full beauty of God's bright day. . . ." Yet these Kentuckians undoubtedly endorsed the views of their Virginia counterparts who emphatically maintained "that our comparative ignorance is not just reason for our disfranchisement, as we can compare favorably with a large number of our white fellow citizens . . . in intelli-gence . . . many of whom can neither read or write, and know nothing of the institutions of the country."[7]

But as an assembly of blacks in Charleston, South Carolina, recognized in the fall of 1865, white prejudice was the principal obstacle to real freedom. "We fully understand what prejudices and preconceived notions must be overcome before out prayers can be granted," they explained, "but we try to believe that the people of South Carolina are capable of rising superior to the prejudices of habit and education. . . ."[8]

Black Charlestonians were soon to learn, however, that not only were the whites of South Carolina disinclined to rise above their deeply ingrained prejudices, but that neither President Lincoln nor his successor, Andrew Johnson, was able to envisage a place of equality and dignity for black people in American society. Both believed that America was preeminently a white man's country and would and should remain that way. During the course of the Civil War, Lincoln investigated and encouraged projects aimed at colonizing the black population abroad—in Haiti and in other parts of Latin America. Although he mildly expressed the view that the highly intelligent blacks and those who had fought on the side of the Union should be accorded the right to vote, his plan for restoring the Southern states to their proper place within the Union contained no provisions for extending citizenship rights to the freedmen.

President Andrew Johnson privately suggested that the right of suffrage be extended to literate and propertied blacks as a means of facilitating Northern acceptance of his lenient Reconstruction program. He was adamantly opposed, however, to elevating the mass of blacks to civil and political equality in the South. Such a development, he maintained, would lead to the dreaded "Africanization" of the region. Thus, encouraged by Johnson's attitude, the Southern state governments that were reorganized under the Lincoln and Johnson Reconstruction plans refused to consider seriously the extension of the vote to any black person. Instead, most of these governments enacted laws in 1865 and 1866 that came perilously close to reinstituting the system of slavery.

The black codes, passed by the governments organized under the Lincoln and Johnson plans (governments composed largely of the same people who had just recently fought against the United States) provided for just that nebulous suspension of the freedmen between slavery and freedom that the New Orleans *Tribune* had feared. By recognizing the legitimacy of black marriages and the resulting offspring, and by allowing blacks to own certain types of property and to bring suit in the courts, the codes gave a passing nod to the Emancipation Proclamation and the Thirteenth Amendment. More importantly, however, by severely circumscribing the degree of liberty that the former slaves were to enjoy, the codes attempted to transform the freedmen into a socially proscribed caste and an economically subservient proletariat. In the social and civil realms, for example, the codes and related legislation prohibited interracial marriage (at the risk in Mississippi, for example, of imprisonment for life), barred blacks from serving on juries and testifying in court in cases involving whites only, and increased penalties for crimes which blacks were thought most likely to commit. In the economic realm some states prohibited blacks from buying or renting farmland, while other states barred blacks from ownership of real estate in towns or cities. Mississippi and South Carolina prohibited blacks from engaging in any form of employment other than agricultural labor without a special license. Nearly all of the ex-Confederate states required blacks to enter contracts for employment on pain of being arrested, convicted of vagrancy, and farmed out to labor on public works or for private employers until the sentence imposed had been satisfied. Those who did sign contracts but who failed to fulfill the terms of labor, could be arrested and returned to their place of employment or assigned to forced labor on public works. Some codes specified that black minors without parents, or with parents unable to properly care for them, were to be apprenticed to white guardians, preferably their former masters, who were to have essentially the same authority over them as masters had over their slaves.

Supplementing the black codes as means of assuring the subordinate status of the black population, the Lincoln-Johnson state governments restricted the suffrage and public education to whites. Many towns, too, passed ordinances severely limiting the social, economic, and political freedom of former slaves.

Many Southern whites were not content to depend on legislation alone to keep the freedmen in their place. While the Lincoln-Johnson governments were in power (and later), the freedmen, no longer having the status of property and, consequently, no longer enjoying the protection of their former masters against physical abuse by other whites, were frequently the victims of violence. Blacks were beaten, maimed, killed; their schools, churches, and personal property were destroyed. During his tour of the South for the *Nation* from July 1865 to March 1866 Richard Dennett, a white Northerner, heard numerous accounts from black and white Southerners of the manner in which the freedmen were ill-treated. Many former slaveholders attempted to continue to discipline their black workers with the lash. Whites of all classes, in an effort to assure that the old social order remained intact, tended to respond violently to the slightest hint of black insubordination, real or imagined. They assaulted blacks with fist, club, whip, and gun for failing to address whites as master or mistress, to respond obsequiously to questions, to yield the right of way on a street, or for having the audacity to leave a plantation or farm without permission or to complain to the Freedmen's Bureau or military officers about the ill-treatment they received.[9] Some Southern whites, whose disappointment and resentment at the outcome of the war was transformed into hatred of the freedmen, undoubtedly shared this view expressed by one woman: "I wish they'd shoot 'em all. . . . If I could get up tomorrow morning and hear that every nigger in the country was dead, I'd just jump up and down."[10]

Not all white Southerners hated the freedmen or wished them harm, however. There were ex-slaveholders who, out of a commixture of altruistic and selfish motives, of feelings of paternalism and a desire to maintain the old economic and social arrangements, went to extra lengths to assure the former slaves a means of securing a living. A few white Southerners were even prepared to accord the freedmen the right to testify in court in cases involving whites, and a rare few, such as James Lusk Alcorn of Mississippi, were not averse as early as 1865 to granting a limited number of freedmen the suffrage. Undoubtedly there were white Southerners who sympathized with most of the ex-slaves' aspirations but were not prepared to brave community censure by expressing their views openly. Dennett reported that he found one such person in North Carolina "who was in favor of equal suffrage for whites and blacks. As he told me so he lowered his voice and looked carefully to the fastening of the door. If the fact was known, his village would be no place for him, he said. . . ."[11]

On the whole, however, during the early postwar years, as historian John Hope Franklin has aptly stated, "There was an open season on Negroes; groups like the Regulators, Jayhawkers and the Black Horse Cavalry were committing the 'most fiendish and diabolical outrages.'"[12] During these years, too, while Southern whites were in political power, and blacks had no power whatsoever, the Ku Klux Klan was formed and soon evolved into the premier terrorist organization of the Reconstruction period.

The black codes and the denial of the suffrage and education to the freedmen received the endorsement of most white Southerners. Even the anti-black atrocities received substantial approval. Many shared the view of Edmund Rhett of South Carolina that "the general interest of both the white man and of the negroes requires that he should be kept as near to the condition of slavery as possible, and as far from the condition of the white man as is practicable. . . ."[13]

ACQUISITION OF CITIZENSHIP

The black people of the South vigorously protested the restrictions placed on them. They were joined in their protests by many whites such as Freedmen's Bureau officials in the South and humanitarians and Republican politicians in the North. Eventually the very obstacles which Southern whites erected against the freedmen became a factor in the white South's undoing. Genuinely disturbed by what they regarded as a bold attempt on the part of the South to maintain slavery by another name, angered at the South's audacity in returning ex-Confederate leaders to power in the state governments and in the U.S. Congress, and fearing the loss of their national political dominance to the Democrats, Northern Republicans in Congress nullified presidential Reconstruction plans, dismantled the Southern state governments, and enacted their own program for restoring the Southern states to the Union.

The Republicans' program was designed not merely to permit the Southern states to reenter the Union but was aimed also at restructuring them socially politically, and, to some extent, economically. Their Reconstruction plan went into effect in March 1867 and was subsequently perfected. Its central feature was the bestowal of citizenship and political rights upon the black people of the South. As part of the process of resuming their place in the Union, the Southern states, under military supervision, enrolled blacks and whites as voters, held constitutional conventions in which white and black delegates participated, formed new state governments in which blacks and whites held office, and ratified the Fourteenth Amendment which made blacks citizens and forbade the states to deny them equal protection of the law or to deprive them of life, liberty, or property without due process of law.

PREPARATION FOR RESPONSIBILITY

How prepared were black Southerners for their new status? A superficial first glance might lead one to conclude that the freedmen, having just emerged from slavery, mostly illiterate and ignorant of public affairs and lacking experience in making basic decisions even about their own affairs, were clearly unqualified for their new rights and responsibilities. To a more careful observer, however, it should be clear that the former slaves were less naïve and less helpless than they may have appeared. Aside from the fact that the best way for the freedmen to learn to enjoy their new rights and perform their new duties responsibly was that they exercise and perform them, the ex-slaves had made some progress by 1867 toward understanding the issues that affected them.

First, black Southerners were fortunate in having the services of a small cadre of intelligent and capable black leaders. Some of these leaders were from the North, having come into the South during the war or shortly thereafter. Most were well educated by the standards of the day, surpassing many of their white colleagues in this respect. Conspicuous among such Northern natives who were political leaders in South Carolina were Jonathan J. Wright, an associate justice of the South Carolina Supreme Court, 1870-1877; Robert Brown Elliot, a member of the state legislature, 1868-1870, U.S. Congressman, 1870-1874, and speaker of the South Carolina House of Representatives, 1874-1876; Richard H. Gleaves, president of the state Republican party convention of July 1867 and lieutenant governor from 1872 to 1877; and

William J. Whipper, a member of the state legislature and elected in 1875, but prevented from serving, to the Circuit Court in Charleston.

Wright, a native of Pennsylvania, attended college in New York, read law in Pennsylvania, and was the first black person admitted to the Pennsylvania bar. Elliot, who came to South Carolina in 1867 from Boston, may have been born and reared in England. Despite the dubiousness of his claims of having been educated at a High Holborn Academy in London, at Eton, and at the Massachusetts School of Law, he was well educated, highly intelligent, and an able lawyer. Whipper, a Michigan native, had served as a clerk in a law office before going to South Carolina.

In Mississippi perhaps the most influential black carpetbagger was James D. Lynch, a native of Pennsylvania, who was elected secretary of state in 1869. He was described by a politically hostile Democratic newspaper in Mississippi as "the best educated man" among the carpetbaggers in the state. Jonathan C. Gibbs, who served as secretary of state and superintendent of public instruction of Florida during the Reconstruction period, was born in Philadelphia and educated at Kimball Union Academy, Dartmouth College, and Princeton Theological Seminary.

Several black leaders had been born free in the South but had been educated in the North or abroad. Among the most prominent of this group in South Carolina were Francis L. Cardozo, Richard H. Cain, and Martin R. Delany.

Cardozo was born in Charleston, South Carolina, and received his early education there. He completed his education at the University of Glasgow and at a London theological school. Before entering politics in South Carolina, where he served as secretary of state from 1868 to 1872 and as treasurer from 1872 to 1876, he was first a Presbyterian minister in New Haven, Connecticut, and then principal of Avery Institute, a black school in Charleston.

Richard H. Cain was born free in Virginia but was reared in Ohio. He became a minister and later, at the age of 35, entered Wilberforce University. He subsequently became a leading figure in the African Methodist Episcopal Church, pastoring churches in Brooklyn, New York, and later in Charleston, South Carolina. He was a member of the South Carolina constitutional convention of 1868, served a term in the state senate, and was elected to two nonconsecutive terms in Congress.

Although he held no major political office, Martin R. Delany was an influential black leader in Reconstruction in South Carolina. Before coming to the state as a major in the Union army, Delany had had varied experiences. He spent the first ten years of his life in Charleston, in western Virginia, where he learned to read and write from Northern book salesmen. His family moved to Chambersburg, Pennsylvania, in 1822. His further formal education was received at a black private school in Pittsburgh. After having edited and published his own newspaper for nearly four years and serving a brief stint as coeditor of Frederick Douglass's *North Star,* Delany enrolled in

Harvard Medical School in 1851 at the age of thirty-nine. Before the outbreak of the Civil War, Delany practiced medicine, visited Africa, and was a leader of a movement to colonize black Americans in Central America.

Mississippi's most prominent free-born black leader during Reconstruction was Hiram Revels, who completed the unexpired term of Jefferson Davis in the U.S. Senate. Revels was born in Fayetteville, North Carolina. He attended a school for blacks in North Carolina, a Quaker seminary in Indiana, a black seminary in Ohio, and Knox College in Galesburg, Illinois. During the Civil War he served in Mississippi as chaplain of a black regiment of the Union army.

In Louisiana, a large number of black leaders came from the long and well-established "free colored class," which numbered nearly 19,000 in 1860. P.B.S. Pinchback, who served as Louisiana's lieutenant governor and acted as governor for a brief period, was born in Georgia and attended high school in Cincinnati, Ohio. He went to New Orleans in 1862 to raise a company of volunteers, the Corps d'Afrique, for the Union army. Another black leader, C. C. Antoine, had been a businessman in Shreveport before becoming involved in Reconstruction politics.

Notable among the black leadership elite in several states were former slaves who through fortunate circumstances or personal effort had developed their talents far beyond the ordinary. Mississippi's principal leaders came from this class. Blanche K. Bruce, who represented Mississippi for a full term in the U.S. Senate from 1875 to 1881, was born a slave in Prince Edward County, Virginia. While still a slave he receive private tutoring. Later he was carried to Missouri where he learned the printing trade. Shortly after the war he organized, in Hannibal, Missouri's first school for blacks. After the war Bruce studied for two years at Oberlin College.

John R. Lynch represented Mississippi for three terms in the U.S. House of Representatives. Born a slave near Vidalia, Louisiana, he was later carried to Natchez, Mississippi. Like Bruce, Lynch received favored treatment as a slave. Most of his education was achieved on his own initiative, however. After Natchez fell to Union troops, Lynch attended school at night. He educated himself further by engaging private tutors and by reading extensively.

Similarly favored as a slave was James Hill, Mississippi's secretary of state. Born near Holly Springs, Mississippi, Hill was taught to read and write by his master's two daughters. He acquired most of his subsequent education through self-study rather than formal training.

Robert Smalls and Beverly Nash, former slaves, were prominent leaders in South Carolina. Smalls, a Civil War hero and the intrepid captain of the *Planter,* reputedly had been tutored intensively by professional educators while stationed at the Philadelphia naval yard. Nash had no formal training and was basically self-taught.

Among Louisiana's black elite, Oscar J. Dunn, who served as lieutenant governor, was a former slave. Dunn ran away from slavery, educated himself, and finally purchased his freedom. One of his most distinguished attributes, according to his contemporaries, was his incorruptibility.

Black leaders in other states had similar backgrounds as natives of the North, free black natives of the South, and as former slaves. Their experiences lead to several observations. Despite crippling restrictions on the black population in both the North and South, some individuals had been able to rise above these restrictions and develop their talents. In the North a large proportion of the black population was literate. Even in the South many free blacks had been able to secure an education before the Civil War. In 1850 a reported 1,129 black students were enrolled in schools in New Orleans, Charleston, and Mobile. Moreover, despite stringent laws against teaching slaves to read and write, many slaves had managed to obtain a rudimentary education; some 200,000 slaves were literate when the Civil War began.

Enlarging the group from which black leadership came were those who were educated by the Union army, the Freedmen's Bureau, and religious and philanthropic organizations during and immediately after the Civil War. The army taught many black enlistees not only how to read and write but also what their rights and duties were as men and as future citizens. Moreover, two months after the war ended, some 24,440 black children and adults were attending schools established by army commanders in Louisiana and Mississippi alone. It is not surprising, then, that as a result of these various developments, that at least 82 percent of the black delegates to the South Carolina constitutional convention of 1868 were literate, and that only 7 percent were known to have been illiterate.[14]

Despite the substantial progress made in providing education for the freedmen during the Civil War and Reconstruction period, the mass of blacks in the South remained illiterate. Their illiteracy, however, did not preclude them from comprehending the existing conditions and from perceiving which persons and what policies best represented their interests. At an 1865 convention of freedmen in Raleigh, North Carolina, one speaker, after acknowledging that he and his colleagues were ignorant and were charged with not knowing "what the word constitution means," went on to assert that:

> But if we don't know enough to know what the Constitution is, we know what justice is. I can see for myself down at my own court-house. If they makes a white man pay five dollars for doing something today, and makes a nigger pay ten dollars for doing that thing tomorrow, don't I know that ain't justice.[15]

Thus Richard H. Cain was not speaking exclusively of his own South Carolina constituents when he maintained in 1868 that "He [the freedman] may not understand a great deal of the knowledge that is derived from books; he may not be generally familiar with the ways of the world, but he can, nevertheless, judge between right and wrong, and to this extent he has as much ability to cast his vote and declare his opinion as any other man, no matter what his station in life."[16]

In determining right from wrong in political affairs, the freedmen did not have to rely solely on intuition, for they were given an intense, realistic, although patently biased, political education by the Union League, an organization of the Radical Republicans, and by other organs of the Republican party in the various Southern states. The Union League helped to elevate the political consciousness of the black community by holding political meetings and discussions; sponsoring rallies, parades, and picnics; teaching blacks their rights and duties as citizens; and organizing blacks into political clubs. Their advice to the freedmen to vote the Republican ticket was preeminently sound. Black voters easily perceived that the only alternative to voting Republican was to vote for conservative Southern Democrats who, as former slaveholders, authors of black codes, and opponents of civil and political rights for blacks, were fundamentally opposed to black interests.

Black political consciousness and education were further advanced by service in the Union army and in the state militias after the Civil War, and through the educational work of Northern missionaries and officials of the Freedmen's Bureau, an agency of the federal government established in 1865 to assist the ex-slaves. The black church also played a major role, despite the view of some clergymen that politics was the devil's work. Many leading black politicians, as well as lesser political figures and officeholders, were clergymen in the black Baptist and Methodist churches. Henry M. Turner of Georgia, Richard H. Cain of South Carolina, and Hiram Revels of Mississippi, for example, were all ministers in the African Methodist Episcopal Church. Four of the eight black delegates to the 1868 Arkansas constitutional convention were ministers. And if one accepts the findings of Richard L. Hume, 27 percent of the black members of all the Reconstruction constitutional conventions of 1867-1868 whose occupational backgrounds (excluding ex-servicemen) are known were ministers. Moreover, Thomas Holt has found that forty-three of the 255 blacks who sat in the South Carolina legislature from 1868 to 1876 were also ministers.[17]

Other black leaders came from the ranks of teachers, lawyers, businessmen, and artisans. However, the largest, single occupational category was artisans—carpenters, mechanics, bricklayers, blacksmiths, shoemakers, stonemasons, wheelwrights, tailors, and barbers. When ex-servicemen are excluded, artisans constituted about one third of the black membership (whose occupations are known) of the constitutional conventions of 1867-1868. Of the 186 South Carolina black legislators whose primary occupations are known thirty-six (20 percent) were artisans. As Edward Magdol has shown, those of the artisan class in rural areas were prime targets of Ku Klux Klan violence because of their community and political activities.[18]

These black leaders, then, were men who had had some training or experience in community organizations and affairs or had occupations which gave them a measure of independence. Thus, when the black voter went to the polls, he generally was sufficiently aware of the outstanding political issues and personalities to avoid voting blindly and perfunctorily. And initial confusion over issues and the election process gradually yielded to political experience.

BLACK POLITICAL PARTICIPATION

Black Southerners took their new rights and responsibilities seriously. Freedmen of St. Helena Island in South Carolina were so determined to exercise the right to vote that in the election in 1867 for delegates to the state constitutional convention they carried their weapons with them to the polls. In North Carolina one black man went to the polls to vote immediately after his leg had been amputated; others walked nearly forty miles to reach the polls. In Tennessee a group of blacks, after having been threatened with reprisals if they voted, went to the polls in a body so that the illiterate among them would vote for the right candidates.[19]

The blacks' desire to exercise their political rights is also reflected in the representative number who registered to vote in the various states in 1867 (see Table 1).

Table 1.

**POPULATION AND REGISTRATION
IN THE RECONSTRUCTED STATES**

State	Population 1860		Registration 1867	
	Negro	*White*	*Negro*	*White*
Alabama	437,770	526,271	104,518	61,295
Arkansas	111,259	324,143	17,109	49,722
Florida	62,677	77,746	16,089	11,914
Georgia	465,698	591,550	95,168	96,333
Louisiana	350,373	357,456	84,436	45,218
Mississippi	437,404	353,899	77,328	62,362
North Carolina	361,544	629,942	72,932	106,721
South Carolina	412,320	291,300	80,550	46,882
Texas	182,921	420,891	49,497	59,633
Virginia	548,000	1,000,000	105,832	120,101

SOURCE: Lerone Bennett, Jr., *Black Power U.S.A.: The Human Side of Reconstruction, 1867-1877*
(Chicago: Johnson Publishing Co., 1967), p. 75.

In some states a considerable number of those who registered also voted.

In South Carolina, 85 percent of the 81,000 registered black voters cast their ballots in the election of 1867 for delegates to the state constitutional convention. In 1868, in the general election, some 80 percent of the 84,000 eligible black voters went to the polls.

The extent to which blacks participated in the state governments varied from state to state. In the constitutional conventions of 1867 and 1868 black membership ranged from a high of 61 percent in South Carolina to a low of 10 percent in Texas. (See Table 2.)[20]

Table 2.
MEMBERSHIP OF STATE CONVENTIONS, 1867-1868

State	Negro	White		Total	Percentage		
					Negro	White	
		Native	North-ern	Total		Native	North-ern
Alabama	18	59	31	90	108	17	55	28
Arkansas	8	35	23	58	66	13	52	35
Florida	18	12	15	27	45	40	27	33
Georgia	33	128	9	137	170	19	74	7
Louisiana	49	*	*	49	98	50	*	*
Mississippi	17	29	54	83	100	17	29	54
North Carolina	15	100	18	118	133	11	75	14
South Carolina	76	27	21	48	124	61	22	17
Virginia	25	33	47	80	105	24	31	45
Texas	9	*	*	81	90	10	*	*

*Further breakdown unavailable.
SOURCE: John H. Franklin, *Reconstruction After the Civil War*
(Chicago: Unviersity of Chicago Press, 1963), p. 102.

Black membership in the first state legislature elected under the Radical plan of Reconstruction similarly varied. South Carolina was again first as eighty-five of the 155 members of its legislature were black. The 115-member Mississippi legislature contained forty blacks. Approximately forty-nine of Louisiana's 137 legislators were black; because many members of the Louisiana legislature were light-skinned mulattoes, it is difficult to discern their racial identity. The Alabama legislature of eighty-four members contained twenty-six blacks. In a legislature of 180 in Virginia there were only twenty-seven black members. Georgia's thirty-two black legislators were overwhelmingly outnumbered in the 216-member legislature. Similarly, the nineteen black members of North Carolina's legislature could hardly hope to dominate a body of 136 members. Texas had 107 members in its legislature of whom only thirteen were black. The Florida legislature had nineteen black members out of a total of seventy-six. None of Tennessee's legislators were black.

Blacks also served in the executive and judicial branches of state governments. Some lieutenant governors—the highest office reached by blacks on the state level—in their respective states were Alonzo J. Ransier and Richard H. Gleaves in South Carolina; Oscar J. Dunn, P.B.S. Pinchback (who also served as acting governor for 43 days in 1872), and C. C. Antoine in Louisiana, and A. K. Davis in Mississippi. The office of secretary of state was held in South Carolina by Francis L. Cardozo, in Mississippi by James Hill, in Louisiana by P. G. Deslonde, and in Florida by Jonathan C. Gibbs. Serving as state treasurer were Francis L. Cardozo of South Carolina and Antoine Dubuclet of Louisiana. J. C. Corbin in Arkansas, Jonathan C. Gibbs in Florida, W. G. Brown in Louisiana, and Thomas W. Cardozo in Mississippi held the very important office, from the point of view of black interests, of superintendent of public instruction. James W. Hood served as assistant superintendent of public instruction in North Carolina. Jonathan J. Wright, associate justice of the supreme court of South Carolina for seven years, was the only black man in any state to hold a high judicial post.

Holding prominent positions in state legislatures were Samuel J. Lee and Robert Brown Elliot, both of whom served as speaker in the South Carolina House of Representatives. John R. Lynch served in the same capacity in Mississippi.

Between 1868 and 1901, twenty-two blacks served in the U.S. Congress, sixteen of them during the Reconstruction period. Revels and Bruce represented Mississippi in the Senate, and P.B.S. Pinchback was elected to that body from Louisiana but was refused his seat. During Reconstruction six blacks represented South Carolina in the lower house of Congress, three represented Alabama, and Georgia, Florida, Mississippi, North Carolina, and Louisiana were each represented by one black congressman.

Blacks also held minor state and local positions. There were at least twelve black county sheriffs in Mississippi during the Reconstruction period. Blacks also held such offices as superintendent of schools, county auditor, county supervisor, and justice of the peace.

The black political leaders and officeholders sought to serve not only their black constituents but their entire state populations. In the beginning many cautiously exercised their power and influence, and sometimes deferred to their white colleagues, the carpetbaggers and scalawags, with respect to the leading offices. As time passed, however, the black leaders and their constituents became more aggressive and demanded positions in accordance with their numbers in the electorate. In some states such increasing black aggressiveness contributed to the breakup of the uneasy political alliance among blacks and white carpetbaggers and scalawags as some among the latter two groups found black assertiveness unpalatable.

It is difficult to measure the extent of black influence in the Reconstruction governments of the Southern states. One fact is indisputable: blacks controlled the government of no state. Consequently, the long prevailing popular myth that they were substantially responsible for the corruption and extravagance that existed to some degree in several state governments is without foundation. Even in South Carolina's first legislature after 1867, blacks had a majority only in the House of Representatives. Whites outnumbered blacks by a substantial margin in the state Senate. In addition, no state had a black governor, only one a state supreme court justice, and in only three states—Louisiana, South Carolina, and Mississippi—did any substantial number of blacks hold more than minor offices.

Furthermore, the potential power that blacks did possess was often offset by the racism and timidity of their white Republican allies. Many white Republicans, the majority of whom were natives of the South, while desiring to exploit the black vote to keep themselves in power, were nevertheless opposed to extensive officeholding by blacks. They feared, correctly, that too conspicuous a black presence in the higher echelons of government and of the Republican party would cost them white support. Therefore, when blacks began to rebel against their minority status within party councils in such states as South Carolina, Louisiana, and Mississippi, several white Republican leaders tried to counteract this movement by seeking the support of conservative white Southerners through subtle appeals to racism.

Indeed the very composition of the Republican party in the South argued against a permanent coalition between blacks and whites, for the constituent elements within the party were themselves divided internally. The carpetbaggers (Northern Yankees) consisted of blacks and whites, and of humanitarians and the self-interested. Scalawags consisted of pre-Civil War Whigs and Democrats devoted to the interests of the planter and business class as well as of poorer Southern whites seeking relief from debt, unfair contract laws, and discriminatory taxes, and desiring educational opportunities for their children.

Factional quarrels within and among these groups often split black ranks as well. But there were also some intrinsic divisions within the black leadership group. Some black leaders, like a relatively well-to-do and well-educated mulatto element in South Carolina of pre-Civil War free black lineage, while strong advocates of civil rights, were inclined to be economically conservative. They were thus reluctant or unable to support the kinds of economic measures (land confiscation, for example) that the black masses wanted. Similar divisions existed within other states. In Alabama, the poorer black leaders in the constitutional convention of 1867 took a more radical position on political issues than their more prominent mulatto colleagues. And in relatively few states were most black legislators united on all important questions. Some black leaders were inclined to play a subordinate role to their white colleagues; they were content to practice the kind of clientage politics that came to characterize black politics in several Northern cities in the twentieth century. Other more independent and assertive black politicians insisted on strong leadership roles in the political process.

Among the black leaders there were also those who were in varying degrees corrupt. T. W. Cardozo, as superintendent of education in Mississippi, embezzled funds allotted to Tougaloo University, and parish officials in Louisiana embezzled funds appropriated for the public schools. Legislators in South Carolina and Mississippi accepted gratuities for voting "right" on legislation designed to benefit special economic interest groups. Other black leaders, however, like Oscar Dunn of Louisiana and John R. Lynch of Mississippi, even in an era when white Democrats sought to pin the label of corruptionist on virtually all Republicans, had reputations for impeccable honesty.

In addition to the differences among black leaders certain internal weaknesses of the black community also limited black influence. A major defect in Reconstruction policy was the failure of the Republicans to buttress black political power with an independent black economic base. Adherents of nineteenth-century liberal conceptions of the sanctity of private property, white Republicans (and some blacks as well) were disinclined to formulate and push through effective measures that would result in the transfer of property from the former slave holders to the former slaves. Thus the bulk of black voters, unable to purchase land because they lacked money or credit or because white landowners refused to sell to them, found themselves vulnerable to brutal economic pressure from their white employers.

Within the black community, too, there were the ignorant, the apathetic, the apolitical, as well as those who were seduced by the arguments that whites of the planter class were their best friends. Nor was the black community without members who were prepared to mislead it for their own personal gain. Such a person was Sydenham Porter of Livingstone, Alabama. Porter, a well-to-do man with no visible source of income other than the sale of liquor, was a hireling of the Democrats. In 1868 he urged his fellow black Alabamians to ". . . let politics alone, go to work, and cherish good and kind feeling toward our old friends. . . ." He warned that ". . . if we do not work and attend to our business and do our duty, but go to public meetings all the time, and stir up bad feelings, ourselves, our families, and our country will be ruined."[21]

Moreover, in certain areas of the South subtle and overt divisions along class lines probably contributed in a small way to the debilitation of the black community as a political force. As Thomas Holt has shown, blacks in South Carolina of slave background and dark of color were sometimes skeptical of the efficacy of the leadership offered by the comparatively well-educated, well-to-do mulattoes who had been free before the war.[22] Despite the conscientious efforts of the black elite to promote the uplift of the whole race, lower-class blacks in other localities as well were sometimes inclined to be suspicious of them. Upper-class blacks undoubtedly contributed to this tendency by seeking to remain socially aloof from the poor and illiterate masses while at the same time trying to lead them.

Finally circumscribing black power and influence was the unrelenting opposition of conservative Southern whites who used every means at their disposal, from anti-black propaganda to murder, to eliminate blacks from the political process and to deny them equality of rights and status in Southern society.

After all the foregoing facts are taken into consideration, an adequate assessment of the extent of black political power during Reconstruction still remains elusive. A simple calculation of the ratio of black and white voters and officeholders is manifestly insufficient. In every Southern state the black vote was important to white officeholders as well as black. In several states it was crucial in determining which party or which faction of the Republican party was elevated to or remained in power. For example, scalawag Franklin K. Moses owed his election to the governorship of South Carolina over carpetbagger Reuben Tomlinson in 1872 to black votes. Similarly, carpetbagger Adelbert Ames was elected governor of Mississippi over scalawag James L. Alcorn in 1873 because of black support. Moreover, in South Carolina blacks were not only in a majority in the House of Representatives from 1868 to 1876, but after 1872 they also held a majority of the committee chairmanships in both houses of the legislature, including several of the more influential ones.[23] On the local level, too, many white officeholders owed their positions to black voters, and in varying degrees they were held accountable to their constituents. Even in states where the black vote was small, there were occasions when whites were divided among themselves on a particular candidate or issue and blacks held the balance of power. Indeed, after the Reconstruction era was over black voters were an essential element in the victories of the Readjusters in Virginia. Nevertheless, in the final analysis, because of the prevailing racial climate and the resultant vulnerability of the black community, in every Southern state which underwent Reconstruction, white power, not black power, was dominant.

GOALS AND ACHIEVEMENTS

Although black Southerners did not dominate the political process in the South, they did influence it to some extent in every state. Black officeholders and voters, representing an economically and socially subordinate class, in cooperation with similar elements in the Southern white community, and with the assistance of Yankee migrants from the North, made an enormous impact on the social and political character of the South. Black people were naturally in the vanguard of those demanding reform and change in the Southern social order.

Black voters wanted land, education, equal political and civil rights, and law and order. In response to the demand for land the federal government passed the Southern Homestead Act in 1866, but failed to take or carry through the far-reaching measures that many whites and blacks had urged and that were necessary to transform the ex-slaves into independent farmers. One state, South Carolina, where blacks had the greatest political power, through the establishment of a land commission and tax policies designed to make available land that was not in use, attempted to meet the freedmen's demands. However, because much of the land made available under the federal and state programs was poor, or because most blacks lacked the financial resources to take advantage of them, the best land ended up in the hands of well-to-do whites, including land speculators. For the great majority of freedmen, then, these programs were of little value.

The freedmen's zeal for education as a functional necessity and as a key to success and status, combined with the desire of poor whites to receive an education free of the stigma of pauperism and with the tradition of universal public education that Northern whites brought with them to the South, produced the regions's first true system of public education.

In the state constitutional conventions of 1867 and 1868, most black leaders insisted on the principle of integrated schools. They feared that separate schools for the races would mean inadequate funding and inferior facilities for black pupils. However, only in Louisiana was the practice of integrated schools begun. Other state constitutions were silent on the issue, and separate schools became the custom. Most blacks were not unduly disturbed by this development, however, for the social imperative of a good system of public education for their children took strong precedence over the desire for integrated schools.

Black Southerners were equally insistent in their demands for political and civil rights. The demands were succinctly expressed in May 1867 by a convention of black people in Mobile, Alabama, "as a claim for . . . exactly the same rights, privileges and immunities as are enjoyed by white men—we ask for nothing more and will be content with nothing less."[24]

On the national level, adoption of the Fourteenth and Fifteenth Amendments and passage of the Civil Rights Act of 1875 prohibiting discrimination in places of public accommodation and on public conveyances met, in principle, black insistence on equal rights. On the state level the black codes were repealed, and the judicial system was opened to the participation of blacks as witnesses, jurors, attorneys, judges, and law enforcement officers. In states where blacks had substantial power universal male suffrage was prescribed. In addition progress was made toward providing equal educational facilities for blacks and whites, and efforts were made to eliminate discrimination in public accommodations.

The black hope for law and order was scarcely fulfilled, however, despite some effort to that effect. Violence pervaded the whole Reconsturction era. The adoption of the Fourteenth and Fifteenth Amendments, passage and enforcement of the Federal Enforcement Acts of 1870 and 1871, the enactment of state laws between 1868 and 1871 outlawing terrorist organizations and their activities, and the creation of state militias with a large component of blacks failed to provide the security of life, property, and freedom that black Southerners so earnestly desired. White violence combined with economic intimidation was largely responsible for the eventual disappearance of blacks from the political arena.

While seeking to promote their own interests, as all political groups do, black voters and officeholders were by no means unmindful of the interests of the general population. Black leaders advocated and supported social welfare measures for the physically and mentally handicapped, orphans, the poverty-strickened, and the aged. They supported legislation to abolish imprisonment for debt, to give workers some chance to recover unpaid wages from bankrupt employers, and to enable defaulting landowners to protect their property from foreclosure. They promoted road repair and building projects, financial and tax measures to encourage railroad construction and industrial expansion, projects to renovate public buildings, and other measures to promote the physical rehabilitation and economic progress of the respective states. Rather than being vengeful, they advocated the removal of the political disabilities imposed on ex-Confederate leaders by the national and state governments. On the national level black Congressmen like Senator Bruce of Mississippi worked for better treatment of the Indian and control of the liquor traffic. He opposed measures restricting Chinese immigration to the United States. On both the state and national levels some black leaders were far in advance of their times in advocating women's suffrage and full equality for women in the American social order. Their progressive spirit was also reflected in their support of equitable representation of poor districts and groups in the state legislatures and in their advocacy of penal reform.

Through these various measures blacks and their white allies played a major role in making the South more prosperous, more democratic, and more sensitive to human needs. The white South was not inclined to acknowledge the black contribution, however, and throughout the Reconstruction period Southern whites waged a relentless campaign, employing a variety of methods, designed to discredit the governments in which blacks participated and to reestablish white supremacy in the South.

TWO

Apartheid: Southern Style

OVERTHROW OF RADICAL RECONSTRUCTION

Between 1870 and 1877 white Democrats (also called Conservatives) regained control of the governments of the former Confederate states. Their return to power occurred at different times in different states. Virginia, for example, never truly experienced civilian rule by the Radicals, for its first civilian government after readmission to the Union in 1870 was controlled by the Democrats. Similarly, as early as 1869, the Georgia legislature came under the control of the Democrats, who promptly proceeded to expel the black members of the legislature. After a brief reimposition of military rule to rectify the injustice, the Conservatives returned to power and captured control of the governorship in 1871. The Democrats returned permanently to power in North Carolina and Tennessee in 1870, in Texas in 1873, in Alabama and Arkansas in 1874, in Mississippi in 1875, and in Florida, Louisiana, and South Carolina in 1877.

The return of Southern white Democrats to power meant the reestablishment of white supremacy in the South. Conservative whites had been adamantly opposed to the Radical Reconstruction regimes primarily because these governments depended largely on black votes or because blacks participated in them. Many whites wanted to drive blacks from the political arena altogether. Others, particularly those of the old planter class, were willing to allow blacks to vote provided they were prepared to take dictation from the white Conservatives. Consequently, while the overthrow of Radical Reconstruction severely diminished black political activity, the divided view among Southern whites enabled substantial numbers of blacks to continue to vote in many Southern states until the late 1890s. In that decade, however, increasing numbers of Southern whites of all political persuasions became convinced that white progress and security required black degradation, that white supremacy must be made secure by reducing blacks to social pariahs and political nonentities in Southern society.

CONSERVATIVE POLITICAL TACTICS

Despite the time gaps between the return of Southern Democrats to power and the full-scale reestablishment of white supremacy, the principles and processes involved in the two movements were so similar and related as to make them continuous developments. Anti-black propaganda, economic intimidation, violence, electoral frauds, divide and conquer tactics, and Northern acquiescence in these activities were common features of both movements. In the first instance these tactics were aimed at reestablishing Southern white dominance. In the second movement they were designed to institutionalize and preserve that dominance.

In several states the overthrow of Radical Reconstruction was relatively easy. In states where black voters were in a distinct minority, white voters, upon being restored to the franchise or abandoning their self-imposed boycott of the electoral process, simply outvoted blacks and their allies. In other states white Conservatives reduced the black-white Radical majority to a minority in a variety of ways. To deny legitimacy to the Republican governments in the South, white Democrats waged a relentless propaganda campaign against them. Placing total blame for the corruption that existed in some states on the Republicans and exaggerating its extent, the Democrats depicted the Radical regimes as hopelessly corrupt, extravagant, and undemocratic. They referred to them epithetically as "negro governments" under which white Southerners were oppressed and subjected to extreme forms of indignity by depraved and bestial men. The propaganda was eminently successful in inducing Southern whites to withhold and Northern whites to abandon support for the Radical governments. Unfortunately, much of the propaganda was later accepted at face value by historians and other scholars and came to dominate both academic and popular views about the Reconstruction period. In turn these views have served to influence the political and social behavior of Southern whites even down to the present.

Although they severely condemned the Radicals as corrupt and extravagant, political corruption and chicanery was an integral element of the white Conservatives' campaign. Ballot boxes were stuffed; polling places were located far beyond black communities or changed at the last moment; votes were purchased or obtained by coercion; and ballots were miscounted. In some districts the votes counted exceeded the number of registered voters. As Republicans responded with similar tactics, the whole electoral process became practically meaningless in some areas, and the ultimate decision rested on the application of force.

Southern Conservatives also employed the strategy of divide and conquer to dissolve the unstable coalition of blacks, scalawags, and carpetbaggers. They made subtle and overt appeals to the latent and overt racism among the white elements in the coalition. In response to such appeals, many scalawags and some carpetbaggers abandoned the Radical alliance and joined white Democrats. The Conservatives also appealed to the black electorate on the grounds that the better class of Southern whites were the blacks' best friends and would protect them in their rights in return for Conservative control over the black vote. Some black leaders, disillusioned with factional disputes within the Republican party and by the insincerity and corruption of their Republican allies, succumbed to such appeals. For example, after whites in Mississippi had invited blacks to join the Democratic clubs, Hiram Revels supported the white Conservatives in the campaign of 1875, claiming disillusionment with Republican corruption. P.B.S. Pinchback similarly joined the Conservative element in Louisiana as factional disputes destroyed the Radical coalition. In other states where the black vote was substantial, Democrats made similar overtures to the black electorate. Their success in wooing the black vote varied, however, and was often related to the economic and physical pressures to which blacks were subjected.

Economic intimidation was widely used by Southern whites in the effort to overthrow Radical Reconstruction. White landlords and employers threatened black tenants and workers with the loss of their jobs if they voted the Republican ticket. If blacks voted at all they must cast their ballots for the Democrats. White physicians warned blacks that they would be denied medical treatment if they continued to support Republican candidates.

WHITE TERRORISM, BLACK RESISTANCE

Economic intimidation was supplemented by violence and the threat of violence. As previously indicated, blacks were victimized by violence even before they began to participate in politics. During Radical Reconstruction the violence was intensified. Terrorist organizations like the Ku Klux Klan, the Knights of the White Camelia, the Pale Faces, the White Line, the Knights of the Rising Sun, the White Brotherhood, the Constitutional Union Guards, the White League, the Council of Safety, the Red Shirts, and countless other groups committed many and varied atrocities against blacks and their white allies, ranging from threats to the destruction of property, and from whippings to murder. As early as the presidential campaign of 1868, for example, whites in Opelousas and Caddo and Bouvier parishes in Louisiana systematically "hunted down" and exterminated over 400 black people within one month. Later in the same year, in Moore County, North Carolina, the Ku Klux Klan, while in the process of terrorizing black and white Republicans, murdered a black woman and all five of her children and then set their house afire.[1] The violence became so extensive in the early 1870s that Congress was moved to pass the Enforcement Acts of 1870 and 1871 to crush it. President Grant, by invoking martial law in several counties in South Carolina, and by threatening similar action elsewhere, also tried to deal with the violence. The violence did subside temporarily, but soon flared up again in many forms.

Mississippi Democrats led the way in employing violence as a specific and deliberate weapon against the Radical state regime. Adopting the slogan in the state election campaign of 1875 of "Carry the election peaceably if we can, forcibly if we must," the Democrats waged a systematic campaign of intimidation and terrorism which Democrats in other states where the Radicals were still in power soon copied. Political meetings of black Republicans were broken up; black leaders, particularly on the local level, were systematically assassinated; black militiamen were assaulted; black voters lynched; and race riots instigated. White Republicans who continued to cooperate with blacks were also victimized.

Race riots were nothing new in the American experience, of course, having occurred in the North during the Civil War. They were precipitated in the South during the Reconstruction period not only by passion-inflamed incidents but as a deliberate method of keeping the black population cowed and subordinate. As early as 1866 riots occurred in New Orleans and Memphis. In the former city, the riots were caused by white resentment of black demands for the suffrage. In Memphis the rescue of a black man by black soldiers from the custody of the police precipitated the riot. Major riots also occurred in Meridian, Mississippi, in 1871; Savannah, Georgia, in 1872; and in Hamburg and Charleston, South Carolina, in 1876. Most of the riots were characterized by white assaults on blacks and severe losses among the latter. Blacks in Charleston, however, incensed by a score of indignities, including anger at the attack upon blacks in Hamburg, were the aggressors. They first assaulted a group of black Democrats and then went on to attack whites and their property in various parts of the city.

Black resistance to and retaliation against violence was not uncommon. When the Conservative white press and other elements in Wilmington, North Carolina, attempted to create a Klan scare in April 1868 in order to discourage blacks from voting on the recently drafted state constitution, groups of blacks responded by patrolling the streets for four days armed with such weapons as guns and fence rails. As a result of this demonstration the Ku Klux Klan disappeared from the Wilmington area for the remainder of the

Reconstruction period. During the same month a group of about 200 blacks in Alexandria, Louisiana, armed with clubs, routed a band of Klansmen who had been parading throughout the community threatening to kill any black man who dared to vote on that state's new constitution.[2] And on the night of July 4, 1868, some twenty to thirty black men in Columbia, Tennessee, where the Klan was extremely active, attacked a group of about 250 Klansmen.

> With closed ranks and steady aim they fired a volley among their fantastically dressed enemy. Several [Klansmen] fell from their horses, uttering cries of pain. They immediatley formed in line and charged upon the blacks who had fallen back to some old breastworks, where they received the charge with another volley, the best they had.

The blacks, who eventually retreated to the safety of the camp of an army infantry company, suffered no losses in this encounter. At least one Klansman, however, was killed and several others seriously wounded.[3]

Blacks also retaliated against white abuse of individual blacks. In 1867, in Hale County, Alabama, a white man named John Orick killed Alex Webb because of the latter's objection to Orick's attempts to seduce a female member of Webb's family. Only with great difficulty were white leaders able to persuade "a band of infuriated Negroes" from burning down the town in which the incident occurred. The blacks scoured the woods for Orick, captured him, and brought him to town for trial. In a similar incident in January 1868, a group of black men in the Orangeburg district of South Carolina captured a white man who had shot a black man, "with the avowed intention of hanging him in case the wounded negro should die."[4]

During the early 1870s, when violence by the Klan and similar terrorist organizations reached its peak, black resistance and retaliation continued. In the mid-summer of 1870, in the town of Belmont in Sumter County, Alabama, the angry friends of a black man who had been whipped by a band of whites assembled at the victim's home. They shot and wounded a member of a party of whites who were keeping the house under surveillance. Shortly thereafter they killed the leader and wounded two other members of another group of whites sent to arrest them. Incensed and frightened by these developments, "a large number of whites, from various parts of the county, flocked to Belmont." The blacks, in turn, with their numbers augmented, took refuge in a swamp and prepared to resist the impending white onslaught. They carried the body of the white man whom they had killed with them. When the white community sent a deputation of two unarmed men to the swamp to demand that the man's body be given up, the blacks replied that if the whites wanted it, they would have to fight for it. On the next day, however, as a huge aggregation of whites prepared to launch an attack, the blacks surrendered the body with the sarcastic claim that they only gave it up "because it smelled so bad." By the time the indignant whites reached the swamp the blacks had dispersed, and the enraged whites had to return home with their thirst for revenge unsatiated.[5]

Similar incidents occurred in other states. In July 1871, in Barnwell County, South Carolina, the home of a white man who had mistreated a black man was attacked by the black man's friends. A visitor to the home was killed and the homeowner, his wife, and his mother were wounded. Similarly, in 1871, a white man in Selma, Alabama, who had been arrested for killing a black man, was taken from the authorities by an estimated crowd of 400 to 500 blacks. They "beat him over the head, dragged him up and down the public streets by the heels and cut his throat, and stabbed him in several places." When an armed group of whites went to the man's rescue the blacks "drew off a short distance, ready for a fight. . . ."[6]

While in the foregoing confrontations between blacks and whites, blacks were the victors, in the majority of the reported incidents, whites ultimately prevailed. More importantly, black resistance and retaliation usually became part of a cycle of interracial violence, as whites retaliated in turn against the black community. For example, in 1871, a black militia unit at Chester, South Carolina, although grossly outnumbered, successfully repelled an attack by an aggregation of at least 200 Klansmen. In fleeing, the terrorists left behind a number of white sheets and mealbags with which they had covered their horses. Although they did not return to attack the militia, it is highly probable that the atrocities that were committed against blacks in the countryside in subsequent weeks represented an attempt by the Klan to reestablish its credibility. In March 1871 another black militia company defeated the Klan in two pitched engagements in Chester County. Armed whites then poured into the county from surrounding areas and from as far away as North Carolina. In a third battle the militiamen were defeated and forced to flee.[7]

In the same month the Meridian, Mississippi, riot occurred. Wearied of the activities of white terrorists, armed black men from the countryside joined their brothers in Meridian on March 4 in preparation for a showdown. "If the whites want war," they declared, "let it come." A clash was averted, however, and the blacks dispersed. But in succeeding days gangs of armed whites confiscated guns from black homes and killed or drove black leaders and their white allies from the community.[8]

Most Southerners at the time, despite the frequent white talk of an impending black uprising, probably realized that in a confrontation between blacks and whites, blacks would be at a disadvantage. James L. Orr, governor of South Carolina from 1865 to 1868, made that point clear in the following exchange with Congressman Job Stevenson of Ohio during the Congressional hearings on the Ku Klux Klan in 1871:

Question. I would like to have your opinion on a question that has been somewhat mooted, and that is, why, in a State like South Carolina, where the negroes are largely in the majority, they have not

resisted and retaliated when outraged? Why have they not done somewhat as the white race would do if attacked in the same way?

Answer. I think the moral power of the white race over the colored
race, which was acquired during two hundred years of slavery, exists
to a very great extent yet. I think you may take colored men and train
them and make good soldiers of them, if you have officers who will
lead them. But if you trust to their individuality in resisting aggression
and outrage upon them, it would be an exceptional case where the
white race would be resisted.

Question. Do you believe that, having the numerical majority, as
they have there, if they would make an organized and determined effort at resistance and retaliation, they would be successful?

Answer. No Sir; I do not.

Question. Why not?

Answer. For the very reasons that I have assigned to you. Nearly all
the white element of South Carolina from twenty to sixty years of age,
was, more or less, during the war, trained to bear arms; they are familiar
with the use of arms and have always been. And when you put what
would practically be an organized mass against an unorganized mob
you will at once perceive what the result would be. I have no doubt
that great damage would be done by them.

Question. You mean the whites would be organized and the negroes
unorganized?

Answer. Yes sir; and they could not be organized to such an extent
as to accomplish the end you seem to indicate.[9]

While Orr's comments are instructive, they provide only a partial explanation for the failure of blacks to retaliate more frequently or to win
more of the encounters with whites. He failed to note, for example, that the
violence in South Carolina was concentrated not in the black belt counties
of the low country where blacks outnumbered whites, but in the middle and
upper counties of the state where whites were in a substantial majority. He
also neglected to observe that throughout the Reconstruction period bands
of whites such as the Klan, as well as legal authorities, made a concerted
effort to disarm the black population by confiscating their weapons.

Black Southerners had one weapon at their disposal that was not subject
to confiscation, however. This was incendiarism. During the Klan hearings
one planter in Chester, South Carolina, testified that "I think there has
been more burning done since the war than ever before the settlement of the
country." Happy that he had not yet been victimized, he went on to recount
that "Along last summer when so much cotton was burned, I said to my
man, 'George, remove that cotton from under the screw; it might be burned.'
George laughed, and said, 'No danger of burning your cotton. You treat the

colored people with justice. It is only when they don't get justice that they burn it.'"[10]

The arson about which the planter spoke was particularly extensive during the first half of 1871, as blacks retaliated against the wave of Klan violence in Chester and York counties. By the summer of that year they were suspected of burning at least twenty-four barns and other farm buildings owned by whites. Similar incidents of incendiarism occurred in other states. In retaliation against atrocities committed by the Constitutional Union Guard in Jones and Lenoir counties in North Carolina in 1869, the freedmen burned the homes of the best known members of the organization. In Chatham and surrounding counties in the middle of the state a secret organization of blacks, bound together by oath, similarly resorted to arson in the winter of 1870-1871 after the guns of many of its members had been confiscated by the Klan.[11] Unlike armed resistance, arson could be employed as easily by a single person with a grievance as it could be used as an instrument of group retaliation. Nevertheless, to the extent that it, too, inspired white counter-violence, its contribution to the security of the black community was limited.

While clashes between groups of blacks and whites were likely to attract the most attention, the individual black man or woman and the individual black family, while walking along the road, working in the fields, or sleeping in the home, was the principal victim of white violence. Because they were almost invariably grossly outnumbered by their attackers, the alternatives open to them were limited. They could submit, hoping to receive at most no more than a beating. They could attempt to flee, an option usually limited by the suddenness of the attack and the size of the attacking party. Or they could resist, hoping to repel their attackers and, if failing, resolve to sell their lives as dearly as possible.

Many black Southerners did resist. In March 1869 a woman in Alamance County, North Carolina, beat a Klansman attempting to break into her home so severely with an ax that he soon left the state. In Winston County, Mississippi, William Coleman, a relatively prosperous farmer, with nothing but an ax handle battled eight Klansmen who shot their way into his home just before daybreak on an April morning in 1871. After shooting and cutting him several times and beating him with their guns, fists, and feet, they finally left him for dead. Coleman survived, however, and subsequently vowed that "I will never vote the conservative ticket if I die."[12]

Willis Johnson, a laborer on the estate of a white planter in Newberry County, South Carolina, made a similar vow after he was beaten for his political activities by the Klan in June 1871. When Klansmen burst into his house shortly after midnight, Johnson reported that

> I raised my pistol quickly, right up to one's back, and shot, and he fell and hallooed, and the other tried to pull him out. As he pulled him I shot

again. As they were pulling, others ran up and pulled him out in the yard, and when the whole party was out in the yard I stepped to the door and shot again, and then jumped to the back door and ran. I got off. I staid away until the next morning; then I came back and tracked them half a mile where they had toted this man and laid him down. I was afraid to go further.

When Johnson was later advised by the Democratic candidate for the state legislature that in order to avoid white retaliation he should go to the home of each white person in the community and promise that he would "never vote the radical ticket again," Johnson told him "I would not do that."[13]

In their commitments to the Republican cause despite the violence and intimidation directed against them, Johnson and Coleman were by no means unique. Even in the states where violence was widespread blacks continued to vote the Republican ticket in large numbers throughout the 1870s. Ultimately, however, the combined tactics of the Conservatives proved to be too great an obstacle for them to overcome. Thus by 1877 the process of white "redemption" was virtually completed.

NORTHERN ACQUIESCENCE IN REDEMPTION

The native white Conservatives could not have "redeemed" their states in the manner described had not the North and the federal government acquiesced in what they were doing. By the mid-1870s, many humanitarian reformers had lost their zeal in behalf of black rights and had turned their attention to other issues, notably political corruption. The ranks of white champions of the black cause had also been thinned by death. Thaddeus Stevens died in 1868 and, as he had requested, was buried in a black cemetery. Charles Sumner died in 1874. Many Republicans in the North had begun to perceive their political future and the interest of their constituents, especially businessmen, as lying in an alliance with Southern Conservatives. And the average white Northerner was inclined on the whole to sympathize with the white Southerners' views on race.

These changing attitudes and circumstances were reflected by President Grant's increasing reluctance after 1874 to use federal power to curb violence in the South, and in the refusal of Congress after 1871 to pass legislation to ensure fair and free elections in the region. The Supreme Court, too, reflected the prevailing climate in its decisions. In 1876 the Court, in *United States v. Reese,* held that inasmuch as the suffrage was a state matter, Congress did not have the authority under the Fifteenth Amendment to punish anyone for interfering with the right to vote except in those cases where the infringement was on account of race, color, and previous condition of servitude. In the same year, in *United States v. Cruikshank,* the Court maintained that the Fourteenth Amendment merely provided federal protection of the private rights of citizens against state interference and not against interference by private persons. On the basis of the latter principle the Court in 1883 in the Civil Rights Cases voided the Civil Rights Act of 1875, which had barred discrimination on public conveyances and in places of public accommodations, on the grounds that the act forbade private rather than state discrimination.

The climax came in 1877, when President-elect Rutherford B. Hayes, in order to ensure his acceptance as president, struck a bargain with Southern Conservatives. In return for Southern acquiescence in his election and Southern promises of fair treatment for Southern blacks, Hayes' advisers implied that he would secure federal subsidies for the construction of a Southern transcontinental railroad and other internal improvements projects in the South, and Hayes agreed to appoint ex-Confederates to high national office and to withdraw federal troops from Florida, Louisiana, and South Carolina, thus bringing to an end the Reconstruction era. Thereafter, the role and status of blacks in Southern society was to be left up to the South and to be solved in the inimitable Southern fashion.

POLITICS DURING THE INTERREGNUM

As previously indicated, the return of Southern whites to power was not followed immediately by complete black disfranchisement. Blacks continued to vote in most states, although in reduced numbers. J. Morgan Kousser estimates that in the presidential election of 1880 the percentage of adult black males voting in the various states was a follows: Alabama, 59; Arkansas, 70; Florida, 88; Georgia, 39; Louisiana, 57; Mississippi, 34; North Carolina, 84; South Carolina, 68; Tennessee, 91; Texas, 72; and Virginia, 66. The low black voter turnout in Mississippi was due primarily to anti-black violence while that in Georgia reflected the disfranchising effects of the poll tax. Indicative of continuing black resistance to the pressure and cajolery of the Democrats, a majority of the black votes in all the states except Louisiana, despite Democratic fraud at the polls, were counted for the Republicans. In Alabama, South Carolina, Tennessee, and to a lesser extent Arkansas, however, a sizable proportion of the black votes was counted for the Democrats. This phenomenon indicated that while some blacks voluntarily defected to the Democrats, others, like those in Louisiana, were either coerced or were counted as voting Democratic whether they did so or not.[14]

After Reconstruction, blacks also continued to hold a decreasing number of offices in several states. In Mississippi, for example, in 1876, the year after Southern Democrats regained political control of the state, twenty-one blacks sat in the state legislature. The number declined thereafter, however, reaching a high of eleven in 1882 and then declining to six in 1890, the year Mississippi framed a new constitution designed to eliminate blacks completely from politics. As a result of the election of 1878 twelve blacks sat in the legislature of South Carolina. During his administration as governor, Wade Hampton, keeping campaign promises and practicing the politics of paternalism, appointed some eighty-six blacks to various local offices. In other states with large black populations blacks also continued to hold office, and between 1877 and 1901 six blacks represented Southern states in Congress.

Although six states surpassed Virginia in the percentage of adult blacks voting in the presidential election of 1880, Virginia was the state in which blacks enjoyed the greatest political success between the end of the Reconstruction era and 1890. As a result of disfranchising measures employed by the Democrats, black Virginians had seen their representation in the state legislature decline from thirty members in 1870 to five in 1878. Between 1879 and 1883, however, they staged a political comeback. Taking advantage of the defection of white agrarians (called Readjusters) from the Democratic party, blacks won twelve seats in the House of Delegates and two in the state Senate in the 1879 election. In the subsequent organization of the General Assembly the black legislators threw their support to the Readjusters, giving the latter control of both houses.

Under the leadership of William Mahone, the fusion of black Republicans and defecting Democrats around a platform calling for the scaling down of the state debt, tax reform, increased expenditures for public education and other social services, and repeal of the poll tax made the Readjusters politically dominant in Virginia from 1879 to 1883. The black and white members of the coalition had much in common. According to Carl Degler's apt description, "the Readjusters were generally poor farm people, fairly prosperous yeomen farmers in the Shenandoah valley, 'hillbillies' in the Southwestern part of the state, together with a large number of Negroes and a few poor whites in the eastern plantation counties."[15] As James T. Moore has shown blacks were indeed a vital and independent force within the Readjuster movement; they comprised about one-third of the delegates at the Readjuster state convention of June 1881. And in the state election of that year, they supplied 67 percent of the votes which gave the Readjusters control of the governorship as well as the legislature.[16]

As a result of their crucial role blacks won a number of concessions of particular importance to the black community. They cooperated with their white allies in securing the abolition of the whipping post for crimes, the poll tax for voting, and unequal salaries for black and white teachers. They secured the establishment of both a state college and an insane asylum for their race in Petersburg. As a result of increased state appropriations for public education, the number of black schools increased from 675 in 1879 to

1,715 in 1883, and black public school enrollment rose from 36,000 to 91,000 over the same period. Black teachers replaced white teachers in black public schools, and a limited number of blacks found jobs with the state government. In time blacks demanded more political offices and in some localities won control of the party machinery.[17]

These black successes eventually contributed to the Readjusters' undoing. Whites began to defect from the movement in the face of a Conservative Democratic counterattack which branded the Readjusters with the label of a Negro party. In 1883 the Readjusters lost control of the legislature. Two years later they lost the governorship as well.

Although blacks in Virginia and in other states continued their political activity, they did so in the face of severe obstacles. Violence and intimidation continued, and every conceivable device was employed to make it difficult for them to get to the polls and have their votes counted. Election districts were gerrymandered so as to create white majorities, more states levied the poll tax, black voters were disfranchised on conviction for minor offenses, and complex registration and election procedures were introduced. These developments were harbingers of worse things to come.

BLACK POPULISM

Many blacks who continued to vote did not do so freely. By controlling their black tenants and laborers and stuffing ballot boxes, white Conservatives in counties with large black populations were able to keep themselves in power on the state level against the challenge of more radical political forces. Other blacks, disturbed by the lily-white Southern strategy of the national Republican party, which saw its continued influence on the national level requiring dissociation from the blacks in the South, voted Democratic as an alternative. Still other blacks saw their most promising course as lying in a coalition with the more radical Southern whites who had begun to organize Farmers Alliances in the late 1880s to combat the combination of conservative economic and political forces which they felt were exploiting them.

Black farmers, too, became organized in the South. The Colored Farmers' Alliance and Cooperative Union, formed in 1886, claimed over a million members at the peak of its existence. The organization rapidly declined after 1891, however, as a result of its defeat in a cotton pickers strike in that year.[18] By that time black and white farmers in the West and South were joining together in the Populist movement.

Populism was the political response in the 1890s of farmers in the South and West to a decline in their standard of living brought on by falling prices for farm commodities accompanied by a rise in the cost of agricultural production, stemming in part from high interest rates and transportation costs.

For example, the average market price for cotton declined from about $.11 per pound between 1874 and 1877 to less than $.06 between 1894 and 1897 while the price per bushel for corn declined from $.41 to a little less than $.30. Prior to 1892 farmers had attempted to rectify this problem through such organizations as the Farmers' Alliance, formed in Texas in 1875, and the Agricultural Wheel, founded in Arkansas in 1882, and through such political movements as the Grangers, Greenbackers, and other independent agrarian groups. When the Democratic party in the South and the Republican party in the West failed to respond to the farmers' demands in the early 1890s, leaders of agrarian, labor, and reform organizations met at St. Louis in February 1892 and formed the Populist party.

To raise farm prices the Populists demanded an expanded money supply through the free and unlimited coinage of silver. To gain cheap credit they advocated the subtreasury system, under which farmers would store their nonperishable commodities in government warehouses until prices rose and receive in the meantime government loans with the stored crops serving as collateral. To lower the costs of transporting their products to market they advocated government ownership or control of the railroads. The national platform of the party also contained planks recommending a graduated income tax and government ownership or control of the telegraph and telephone systems. In several Southern states, due to their heavy reliance on black votes or the need to prevent white Democrats in black belt counties from stuffing ballot boxes, the Populist demanded free ballots and honest elections.

In the South the rank-and-file members and supporters of the Populist party tended to be small farmers and tenants, although several leaders of the party were quite well-to-do. Black supporters obviously fell within the former category, concentrated, however, at the lower socio economic scales as tenants, sharecroppers, and farm laborers. As well as sharing the economic ills of white farmers, blacks had certain problems of their own. Indicative of their plight were the average wages which black and white cotton workers in the South received. Even in the best of times their income was low, ranging from $.50 to $.75 a day, $6 to $15 per month, and from $60 to $125 per year in 1880. In the face of the agricultural depression in the 1890s these workers undoubtedly received even lower wages during the first half of that decade.

Yet, in supporting Populism, black Southerners seemed to be as much concerned with the right to vote, to sit on juries, to be free from the convict lease system, and to be secure against violence as they were with mainly economic problems. Therefore, while adhering to the rhetoric of the commonality of black-white economic interests, their support of the Populists varied in accordance with their perception of the commitment of the latter to black civil and political rights. At a meeting of representatives of the Colored Farmers' Alliance, the Northern Farmers' Alliance, and the Southern Farmers' Alliance in Ocala, Florida, in 1890, in anticipation of the formation of the Populist party two years later, the black delegates insistently stressed the need for a "free vote and an honest count." Therefore, in spite of the vigorous opposition of the Southern Alliance, the Colored Alliance adopted resolutions urging Congress to pass the Lodge Federal Elections Bill, a proposal designed to give the federal government a positive role in assuring blacks access to the polls. The Reverend J. L. Moore of the Putnam County, Florida, Colored Farmers' Alliance subsequently explained that:

> Our object was to have the protection of the ballot boxes, because none sees the need of reform more than we do. . . .
> We want protection at the ballot box, so that the laboring man may have an equal showing. . . . We are aware of the fact that the laboring colored man's interests and the laboring white man's interests are one and the same. Especially is this true at the South. . . . So I for one have fully decided to vote with and work for that party, or those who favor the workingman, let them belong to the Democrats, or Republican, or the People's Party.[19]

In many Southern states black-white cooperation through Populism offered black citizens a refreshing and promising alternative to supporting Conservative Democrats who, even if inspired by the best sentiments of noblesse oblige (most were not) toward blacks, elicited black support largely because they were the blacks' employers, creditors, and landlords. The Populists offered blacks the possibility of a politically respectable coalition that was based not on paternalism and intimidation but on common interests. Going beyond the traditional overtures made by such Populist forerunners as the Readjusters, Independents, and Greenbackers of the 1870s and 1880s to black voters and leaders through the aegis of white Republican leaders, the Populists made a direct appeal to blacks for political cooperation on the grounds that poor white and poor black farmers shared "common grievances and a common oppressor." To woo black voters, Populists in some states included planks against lynchings and the convict lease system in the party platforms, arranged various forms of entertainment for potential supporters, organized black Populist clubs, and worked to see that blacks were allowed to vote. In several states blacks participated fully in the party's functions by serving as members of its state and local committees and as delegates to its national convention.

Indeed blacks were among the vanguard of Alliance men at the Ocala meeting in 1890 and the Cincinnati meeting in 1891 urging the formation of a national third party. Of the seven Louisianians present at the former meeting, for example, only the three black Alliance men voted for a third-party movement. John B. Rayner of Texas, as a political orator and organizer, was a principal promoter of the People's cause in that state. Elected to the state executive committee of the party in 1895, he was one of the leading six Populist leaders in Texas. Rayner advised his party colleagues that ". . . if you want the negro to vote a straight people's party ticket you must put men on the precinct or county tickets whom he likes. Kind words and just treatment go further with the negro than money or promises."[20] In Grimes County, Texas, the People's movement survived to 1900 as a vibrant coalition of black Republicans led by Jim Kennard, Jack Haynes, and Morris Carrington and white agrarians led by Garrett Scott. Its demise was brought about by the assassination in 1900 of Kennard and Haynes and the near assassination of Scott by a Democratic organization known as the White Man's Union. In Georgia, Henry S. Doyle performed yeoman service as a speaker and organizer for the Populist cause, narrowly escaping being lynched by irate Democrats by fleeing to the protection of Tom Watson, the leading white Populist in that state.

The most promising coalitions of black and white agrarians existed in such states as North Carolina, Georgia, Texas, and Louisiana. In South Carolina, Alabama, Mississippi, and other Southern states the agrarians were active but ambivalent about courting black support. Virginia Populists discouraged black support for fear that they would be designated the "Negro party." Nevertheless, in the election of 1893 many blacks cast their ballots for the Populist gubernatorial candidate. Probably one-fifth of the black vote went to the Democrats, however, on the expedient principle that the Democratic party was composed of "that class of people that own and control everything."

The Populists failed to win major victories in the South in the 1892 elections. In many cases they were cheated out of victories by fraudulent practices of Conservative Democrats. In several states the Democrats bribed or coerced blacks to vote the Democratic ticket or in black belt counties simply counted blacks as having voted whether they actually voted or not. On the other hand many blacks probably voted for white Conservatives rather than the Populists because they perceived the former to be less prejudiced.

In 1894 the Populists were more successful. Their greatest victory occurred in North Carolina where under a fusionist ticket of Populist and Republican candidates, they captured control of the state legislature. Two black men, James Young and William H. Crews, were among the Fusionists elected to the legislature, despite the fact that many black votes under Democratic control in the black belt counties went to the Democrats. In 1896 five blacks were elected to the legislature, and George H. White was elected to Congress where he served until 1901. However, after his departure, twenty-nine years elapsed before another black person sat in the national legislature.

In 1898 four blacks were elected to the North Carolina legislature, although the Democrats recaptured control of that body partially by waging a white supremacy campaign. Altogether from 1895 to 1899, as a result of the cooperation of black Republicans with the white Populists, ten blacks served in the North Carolina legislature, and relatively large numbers held minor county and municipal offices. The Fusion legislature of 1895, for example, appointed 300 black magistrates.

The black-white coalition under the agrarian or Populist banner was an uneasy one in all the states, however. Aside from race, there were certain internal contradictions in the alliance. A considerable proportion of the white Populists were farm owners, while most black Populists were sharecroppers and tenants. Thus some of the purely economic interests of the two groups diverged. Moreover, the white agrarians, as economically depressed and socially insecure poor farmers, were particularly susceptible, because of status anxiety, to appeals to racism. They were much weaker in this respect than their conservative white opponents, composed largely of planters and businessmen. Like other whites in the South, white Populists were unable in the final analysis to rid themselves of their own racism and many were reluctant to see black enfranchisement in terms other than subordination to white supremacy. Moreover, the Populists often suffered defeat at the hands of Conservative Democrats who used their control over black voters to run up electoral majorities. Thus, when in order to counteract the Populist threat to their political dominance the Democrats raised the race issue and called for white unity against the specter of black domination, the white agrarians eventually succumbed and joined with the Conservatives in making white supremacy secure in the South.

While it is clear that the white agrarians were soft on black political equality and that their cooperation with blacks was based mainly on political expediency, it should be remembered, as J. Morgan Kousser cogently argues, that the movement in the 1890s and early 1900s to disfranchise black Southerners was led in most states by "affluent and well-educated" Democrats in the black belt counties, and frequently against white Populist resistance. The Democrats' principal objective was the elimination of blacks as a political factor. Some of them, however, wished to disfranchise poor whites as well and, to some extent, they succeeded.[21]

It should also be remembered that not all white Populists capitulated to racism. B. W. Bailey, the only Populist member of the Louisiana constitutional convention of 1898, refused to sign the resulting constitution which deprived blacks of the suffrage. Joseph C. Manning and William Skaggs, Populist leaders in Alabama, continued to denounce black disfranchisement well into the twentieth century. And Garrett Scott, wounded and bleeding as a result of a shootout with the White Man's Union that left his brother and two other men dead, left Grimes County, Texas, on November 12, 1900, with his commitment to equal rights for blacks unblemished. Some seventy years later, Scott's niece, in recounting the events of that November when she was only ten years old, recalled that "they said that Uncle Garrett was a nigger-lover. . . . He wasn't a nigger-lover, or a white lover, he just believed in being fair to all, in justice."[22]

BLACK DISFRANCHISEMENT

The first stage in making white supremacy secure involved the establishment of a white monopoly of political power by depriving blacks of the right to vote. To effect this desired result several states—Mississippi in 1890, South Carolina in 1895, North Carolina in 1900, Alabama in 1901, Virginia in 1901-1902, Georgia in 1908, and Oklahoma in 1910—amended their constitutions. Other Southern states with proportionately smaller black populations, such as Florida in 1889, Tennessee in 1890, Arkansas in 1893, and Texas in 1902, achieved black disfranchisement through legislative enactment of the poll tax and other measures.

As in 1875 Mississippi took the lead in devising measures to nullify the Fifteenth Amendment. The devices used by Mississippi and other states included literacy and property tests, secret ballot laws, character tests, poll taxes, complex registration procedures, long residency requirements, and the white primary. Most of these devices remained in effect until the mid-1960s. Under the literacy tests those who could not read or write—and, in Mississippi, South Carolina, Virginia, and Georgia, those who could not also understand portions of the state or national constitution—were disqualified to vote. Because of the high illiteracy rate among blacks at the turn of the century, but primarily because of the discriminatory administration of such tests by white voting registrars, few blacks were qualified to vote. In many cases highly educated blacks were disfranchised in this manner. As late as 1958, for example, the U.S. Supreme Court heard a case in which a white registrar had disqualified a black schoolteacher for misspelling a word on the registration application form. Ironically the registrar had indicated the misspelled word by writing "mispelled" beside it.

Several states provided constitutional loopholes by which illiterate whites could escape the literacy tests. In South Carolina those who had sufficient property need not take the test. The most infamous device, however, was the grandfather clause by which Louisiana, North Carolina, Alabama, and Georgia successively exempted from the tests those persons who were qualified or whose fathers and grandfathers were qualified to vote on January 1, 1867, or earlier. Since virtually no black person could make such a claim, none could qualify under the clause. Fortunately, in 1915, the Supreme Court declared the grandfather clause unconstitutional.

The secret ballot also acted as a literacy test. Although political reformers normally regarded it as a device to eliminate political corruption and to make voters more independent, J. Morgan Kousser has shown that the disfranchisement of illiterates, especially blacks, was the primary motive behind its enactment in the South. Under the secret ballot political parties no longer printed and distributed ballots to voters, but provided a publicly printed ballot containing the candidates' names, often without clear party identification. Unable to read the names and party affiliation of candidates and the offices for which they were running, illiterates and near illiterates found it difficult and often impossible to mark their ballots properly. The secret ballot served to disfranchise whites as well as blacks. It bore more heavily upon blacks, however, because of their higher illiteracy rate and because of escape clauses in some state laws which made it possible for more illiterate whites than blacks to get assistance in marking their ballots. In Louisiana, for example, the black voter turnout in the presidential election in November 1896 declined by 45 percent from the level of the gubernatorial election seven months earlier. White voter turnout declined by 28 percent. Between the two elections Louisiana Democrats pushed through a secret ballot law with the avowed purpose of restricting the electorate so as to assure a Democratic victory in the November election.[23]

Few blacks could qualify to vote under the good character test, which required that the prospective voter present testimony as to his character from several prominent white citizens in his community. Moreover, the disfranchisement of persons who had been convicted of minor crimes hit blacks more heavily since they were not only more frequently accused of offenses, but also more often convicted.

The poll tax of $1 or $2, which in most states was cumulative and for which a receipt for payment had to be displayed at time of registration, discouraged many potential black voters. The necessity for a long period of residency in the state, county or voting district added to the obstacles. Finally, the white primary, which barred blacks from participating in the Democratic party's selection of candidates to run for office, effectively nullified any black vote which remained, since by 1900 the Democratic party was the only real political party in the South. Whoever was chosen as the party's nominee was assured of election to the office for which he was a candidate.

The foregoing measures, combined with violence and intimidation, caused a sharp decline in the number of black voters in the South. In Louisiana, black registrants declined from 130,344 in 1896 with black majorities in 26 parishes to 5,320 in 1900 with black majorities in no parish. In Alabama in 1900 only 3,000 blacks were registered as voters in a black male voting age population of 181,471. Two years after Mississippi amended its constitution only 8,615 blacks were registered in a black male voting age population of 147,205 persons. As the twentieth century wore on, a black face at a polling booth was a curiosity in many states.

JIM CROW'S NOT SO STRANGE CAREER

Rooted in Southern custom, and finding parallels in pre-Civil War Northern practices, the separation of the races by law in the 1890s and the first decade of the twentieth century merely codified existing practices in many cases. In education, segregation was the practice in most Southern states even during the heyday of Radical rule. Only the Reconstruction constitutions of

Louisiana and South Carolina provided expressly or implicitly for integrated schools and, except for the city of New Orleans and the University of South Carolina, these provisions were generally disregarded. South Carolina amended its constitution in 1895 so as to specifically prohibit integrated schools, and Louisiana followed in 1898.

Meanwhile other Southern states had already provided for segregated schools, either by statute or by constitutional provision. As early as 1867 the legislatures of Arkansas and North Carolina, in formulating administrative regulations for the public school system, provided for the establishment of separate schools. Georgia and Virginia legislated separate schools in 1870. Texas began segregating the schools by law in 1873 and established the principle fully in 1876. Mississippi enacted a Jim Crow school law in 1876 and Virginia strengthened its Jim Crow statute in 1882. Several states, not content with the mere legislative enactment of Jim Crow laws, wrote the Jim Crow principle into their constitutions. North Carolina and Alabama led the way in 1876 and Mississippi followed in 1890. During the next two decades the other Southern states took similar action.

In other areas, however, the code of custom, although generally observed, was frequently challenged and violated during the Reconstruction period and into the 1890s. Blacks rode streetcars in Virginia, North Carolina, and South Carolina without discrimination. They also rode in integrated cars on trains in these and other states, sometimes evoking incidents, but often not. During the Radical era they were served in many white restaurants and bars in Mississippi.

Southern states began to pass legislation in the 1880s providing for segregation in railroad transportation. As early as 1881 Tennessee required railroad companies to provide separate cars or sections of cars for blacks holding first-class tickets as an alternative to forcing them to use integrated second-class accommodations. Florida passed a law in 1887 requiring the separation of the races on trains. Mississippi in 1888, Texas in 1887, Louisiana in 1890, and Alabama, Mississippi, Arkansas, Kentucky, and Georgia in 1891 followed with similar legislation. South Carolina did not enact such legislation until 1898, followed by North Carolina in 1899 and Virginia in 1900. Mississippi led the way in 1888 in specifying separate waiting rooms in railway stations for the races. Only two other states copied Mississippi in this regard before 1899. Between 1899 and 1910, however, most other Southern states adopted similar legislation. Georgia initiated the policy of requiring segregation on streetcars in 1891. Ten years later Virginia and North Carolina enacted statutes to the same effect, followed by Louisiana in 1902; Arkansas, South Carolina, and Tennessee in 1903; Mississippi and Maryland in 1904; Florida in 1905; and Oklahoma in 1907.

The segregation policy in transportation was rapidly extended to other areas in the first two decades of the twentieth century, and loopholes continued to be closed in the system of apartheid throughout the 1920s and 1930s. In virtually every area of life where blacks and whites might come together state law and local ordinances required racial separation or black subordination. Racial separation became the rule of the day with respect to hospitals, asylums, and orphanages; parks, playgrounds, restaurants, theaters, hotels and other places of public accommodation and amusement, including in some cities red-light districts and houses of prostitution; and textile mills and other places of employment. Baltimore, Atlanta, Richmond, St. Louis, New Orleans, and other cities required separate residential districts for the two races, and although these requirements were voided by the Supreme Court in 1917 they were replaced by restrictive covenants and gentlemen's agreements.

The segregation measures went to ridiculous extremes. Separate textbooks for the two races were required by North Carolina and Florida, the latter stipulating that the books be kept separate even while in storage. Oklahoma required separate telephone booths. Birmingham, Alabama, forbade the two races to play checkers together. As late as 1965, New Orleans restricted black and white taxicab drivers to clientele of their own race.

Laws and ordinances were supplemented by private acts and local customs. In Atlanta courts, black and white witnesses swore on separate Bibles, and in Atlanta buildings blacks and whites used separate elevators. Many public and private buildings in several states had black and white entrances. Blacks went to the back doors of white homes, and if served at all, were served from back and side apertures of white eating places. With the advent of the motor car and service stations blacks were provided with separate restroom facilities or none at all. Many hospitals were closed completely to blacks, and few emergencies were sufficient to effect a change in policy. From the cradle to the grave, then, separation became the rule in the Southern social order.

VIOLENCE: AN INSTRUMENT OF SOCIAL CONTROL

Where law and custom were not regarded as sufficient to sustain the Southern racial code, white Southerners resorted to violence. Violence was more of an extralegal than illegal method of keeping blacks in subordination, for rarely was any white person arrested for inflicting violence on blacks, and even more rarely convicted. Exceptions to this pattern merely served to reinforce the principle. In 1893, for example, a white mob brutally lynched an innocent black man in Roanoke, Virginia. Twenty persons were indicted for the crime and three were convicted. In the wake of community revulsion against the atrocity one man was fined $100 and sentenced to thirty days in jail. The other two men received a penalty of a $1 fine and one hour in jail.[24]

Violence took many forms, but from the end of the Reconstruction period down to World War II lynching was the more spectacular of the violent instruments of social control in the South. From 1889 to 1899 about 187 persons were lynched yearly in the United States. Over two-thirds of the victims were black people in the South. In the first two years of the twentieth century over 200 black Southerners were lynched. Between 1899 and 1918 an average of eighty-one black persons per year were lynched in the South, and from 1919 to 1937 some 516 additional black persons were lynched, the overwhelming majority in the South. In the period from 1882 to 1927 Mississippi led in black lynch victims with 517, followed by Georgia with 510, Texas with 370, Louisiana with 347, Alabama with 304, Florida with 247, Arkansas with 244, Tennessee with 213, South Carolina with 165, Virginia with 85, North Carolina with 80, Missouri with 66, West Virginia with 33, and Maryland with 25. Other lynchings undoubtedly occurred which were not reported as such.

Many of the lynchings were marked by unspeakable atrocities. The New York *Tribune* reported a lynching in Georgia in 1899 as follows:

> In the presence of nearly 2,000 people, who sent aloft yells of defiance and shouts of joy, Sam Hose (a Negro who committed two of the basest acts known to crime) was burned at the stake in a public road, one and a half miles from here. Before the torch was applied to the pyre, the Negro was deprived of his ears, fingers and other portions of his body with surprising fortitude. Before the body was cool, it was cut to pieces, the bones were crushed into small bits and even the tree upon which the wretch met his fate was torn up and disposed of as souvenirs.
>
> The Negro's heart was cut in several pieces, as was also his liver. Those unable to obtain the ghastly relics directly, paid more fortunate possessors extravagant sums for them. Small pieces of bone went for 25 cents and a bit of the liver, crisply cooked, for 10 cents.
>
> No indictments were ever found against any of the lynchers.[25]

The barbarities practiced were not limited to male victims. In Georgia in 1918, a black woman who denounced the lynching of her innocent husband and expressed the wish to see the perpetrators arrested and tried was herself lynched for her audacity. Walter White, an official of the National Association for the Advancement of Colored People, gave this description of the crime:

> At the time she was lynched, Mary Turner was in her eighth month of pregnancy. The delicate state of her health, one month or less previous to delivery, may be imagined, but this fact had no effect on the tender feelings of the mob. Her ankles were tied together and she was hung to the tree, head downward. Gasoline and oil from the automobiles were

thrown on her clothing and while she writhed in agony and the mob howled in glee, a match was applied and her clothes burned from her person. When this had been done and while she was yet alive, a knife, evidently one such as is used in splitting hogs, was taken and the woman's abdomen was cut open, the unborn babe falling from her womb to the ground. The infant, prematurely born, gave two feeble cries and then its head was crushed by a member of the mob with his heel. Hundreds of bullets were then fired into the body of the woman, now mercifully dead, and the work was over.[26]

Through such means the white South sought to save its vaunted civilization from the specter of black barbarism.

Despite the public condemnation of lynching by several Southern white political leaders and the persistent campaign waged against it (and the social values which inspired the practice) by such prominent white Southerners as John Spencer Bassett, a professor at Trinity College in Durham, North Carolina; the Reverend Quincy Ewing, an Episcopal clergyman in Louisiana; and the Gonzales brothers, editors of the Columbia *State* in South Carolina, during at least the first two decades of the twentieth century most white Southerners apparently approved of lynching as a means of keeping blacks under control. In many cases lynchings were viewed as forms of public entertainment, and white women and children wre often the most enraptured spectators. Moreover, lynchings often received the general endorsement of leading elements of the white community. Newspapers frequently fanned the flames of mob violence, and in a few cases white ministers dismissed their congregations in order that they might witness the spectacle. Other ministers and clergymen appeared to sanction lynching by their silence.

The myth that most lynchings were for the crime of rape contributed to community approval of the act. Even Theodore Roosevelt as president was seduced by the myth. In 1898, Mrs. Rebecca Felton, the widow of Congressman William H. Felton, the leader of the Georgia Independents in the 1880s, declared that if necessary to protect Southern white womanhood 1,000 black Southerners should be lynched weekly. In 1906 John Temple Graves, editor of the Atlanta *Times,* offered a reward of $1,000 for the lynching of a black man accused of rape. And while serving in the U.S. Senate, Pitchfork Ben Tillman recalled for the benefit of his colleagues that "As Governor of South Carolina I proclaimed that, although I had taken the oath of office to support the law and enforce it, I would lead a mob to lynch any man, black or white, who ravished a woman, black or white."[27]

The myth still endures. The fact of the matter, however, is that only in one case in five was rape or attempted rape even alleged, and many of the allegations were patently false. The Southern Commission on the Study of Lynching, composed mainly of white Southerners, reported in 1931 that

Only one-sixth of the mob victims between 1889 and 1929 were accused of rape. The accusations of rape and attempted rape combined
accounted for less than one-fourth of the lynchings, and investigations
after the lynchings often proved these accusations to have been un-
founded. In some cases the charges were fabrications of white persons
attempting to mask their own faults. In others, these accusations were
advanced by lynchers to absolve themselves from community blame.

Many Negroes accused of rape or attempted rape, and saved from
mobs by courageous peace-officers or other means, have been acquitted
by the courts. In some cases, girls and women who had posed as victims
acknowledged that they made these charges to cover their own derelic-
tions, to divert suspicion from some white man, to reconcile their
parents, to attract attention, or "just to have a little excitement." Later
in this report are some suggestions why Southern white men are so affected by any rumor of Negro-man-white-woman relations. The very
fact that this type of rumor enrages the mass of whites is the reason
why unscrupulous white men and women can use it so effectively in
efforts to conceal their own misdeeds.[28]

Lynching, in short, was simply a means of maintaining the system of white
supremacy. Any challenge, real or imagined, to that system by a black person
could evoke a violent reaction from whites. Thus the causes of lynching
ranged from allegations of murder on one extreme to failure to show proper
respect to whites on the other. A man might be lynched for insisting on receipts from the sale of his crops by a landlord, or refusing to say "Sir" to a
white man, or even for looking in the direction of a white woman. The real
and ultimate cause of lynching, of course, was a social order which put a
premium on the degradation of one race by another.

Race riots were another form of mob violence designed to punish blacks
for infractions of the Southern racial code. While lynchings generally occurred in rural areas, race riots were largely urban phenomena. Between the
end of Reconstruction and America's entrance into World War I major
race riots occurred in Wilmington, North Carolina, 1898; Statesboro, Georgia,
1904; Atlanta, Georgia, 1906; and Brownsville, Texas, 1906. Riots also
occurred during and after the Civil War in both the North and the South. In
virtually all cases, whites were the aggressors, invading the black community
and destroying lives and property. In Atlanta, for instance, whites who were
aroused by an irresponsible white press began attacking on September 22,
1906, every black person whom they encountered. The following day they
went on a rampage through the black community of Brownsville, a suburb
of Atlanta which contained much of Atlanta's middle- and upper-class population of businessmen and professionals as well as several black colleges.
Law enforcement officers, rather than stopping the white mob, began to

arrest blacks, many of whom had armed themselves in self-defense. When blacks resisted an attack on them by the police the mob joined in with the police in a frenzy of violence. And although blacks fought back heroically, the black community suffered heavy damages in homes and businesses looted and burned by the white mob, in the deaths of four of its substantial citizens, and in injury to many others. The failure to punish any of the white rioters and hoodlums was a typical expression of Southern justice.

So far as blacks were concerned, the Southern system of justice was also a form of violence designed to enforce Southern apartheid. Southern law, Southern policemen and sheriffs, Southern judges, and the whole Southern legal apparatus were correctly perceived by black Southerners as designed not to protect them but to keep them in a subordinate status. The black community came to regard as severely deluded any black man who expected to receive justice in a Southern court when accused of an offense against a white person or when involved in a civil contest with a white person. The litany of the injustices in the Southern system of law and order as applied to blacks—false and frequent arrests, severe punishment for alleged offenses against white persons, summary conviction by white juries, lenient penalties for alleged offenses against black persons, and police brutality—is too well known to discuss further here. It suffices to point out that Southern justice and lynching and mob violence were integral parts of an apparatus of fear designed to preserve the South's racial code.

A constituent element in the Southern system of justice in several Southern states was the convict lease system. Convicted offenders were farmed out by state and county judicial authorities to planters and industrialists for a small fee. The principal victims of the system were blacks who had been convicted summarily for minor offenses. Before serving out their terms they often were again falsely accused of some offense and thus returned to, or retained in, the system. The labor of the convicts was exploited under brutal conditions in railroad construction, in mines and turpentine camps, and on plantations. Much of the South's industrial and agricultural wealth rested upon it. Thus the system was an institution less concerned with punishing or rehabilitating criminals than with providing a cover of legitimacy for the gross exploitation of men under conditions of forced labor.

APARTHEID APPROVED

The South had a relatively free hand in erecting its white supremacy system. For the most part people in the North either approved or were indifferent to the developments in the South. Indeed, in many Northern communities a milder version of the South's racial ethic prevailed, without, however, the support of legislative enactments. Southern propaganda to the effect that blacks were inherently and hopelessly inferior and thus needed to be controlled by the white community won increasing acceptance among Northern whites. America's embarkation on an imperialist policy around the turn of the century in the Pacific and in Latin America, where many of the subject people were dark of skin, further reinforced the North's susceptibility to Southern racial propaganda.

The national government played a major role in the creation of Southern apartheid. In a series of decisions the Supreme Court either cleared the way for or endorsed Southern racial policies. In 1883, as previously mentioned, the Court struck down a federal law against discrimination in public accommodations and conveyances. In the landmark *Plessy v. Ferguson* decision in 1896 the Court explicitly endorsed Jim Crow legislation as a valid exercise of a state's police power to promote peace and harmony in society. Two years later the Court sanctioned the poll tax and literacy tests as qualifications for voting. In 1903 it refused to look behind the subterfuges devised by states to disfranchise black citizens so long as the language of the disfranchising legislation made no reference to race, color, or previous conditions of servitude. Through such decisions the Supreme Court became a party to Southern strategems that had the effect of reducing the Fourteenth and Fifteenth Amendments to "pious goodwill resolutions." The executive branch also acquiesced in New South racial policy. And under Woodrow Wilson, a Southern-born president, Jim Crow practices became officially entrenched within the federal bureaucracy. Blacks no longer could appeal, therefore, to the federal government for protection with any hope of having their grievances rectified. They hardly dared seek or expect any relief from their state government. Defined as members of an inferior group, and politically powerless, they had very few rights that white men were bound to respect.

At the turn of the century, Pitchfork Ben Tillman, a leading architect of black disfranchisement as governor and political boss of South Carolina and as U.S. Senator, surveyed his handiwork and pronounced it good. "We have done our best," he said, in speaking of black disfranchisement. "We have scratched our heads to find out how we could eliminate the last one of them. We stuffed ballot boxes. We shot them. We are not ashamed of it."[29]

THREE

The Black Response: Protest and Accommodation, 1890-1954

Black Southerners sought to meet, and even turn back, the inexorable march toward white supremacy in a variety of ways. Some made temporary political alliances with strange bedfellows in an attempt to preserve a semblance of political power and influence. Many actively opposed the new developments through public demonstrations, speeches, and boycotts. Some, feeling that resistance was futile but not willing to surrender their rights and dignity as free men, tried to escape by returning to Africa or by migrating to other areas of the United States. In the end, most blacks—disillusioned, hurt, resentful—temporarily gave up the struggle and acquiesced in the new order. But the spirit of resistance did not die out. Apathy did set in for many, but almost invariably these persons were periodically shaken out of their apathy as the indignities, atrocities, and oppressiveness inherent in the system touched them personally at vulnerable times. And so under the facade of accommodation, virtually every black person harbored feelings of bitter resentment. These feelings were carefully kept under control but were liable to flare into open revolt under the provocation of a specific event or a long train of abuses.

POLITICAL ALTERNATIVES

In order to retard the movement toward disfranchisement, black leaders cast about for viable political alliances. Many, of course, remained with the Republican party and continued to support that party on all political levels, even after the national party had abandoned them to the white South. As previously described, many of these black Republicans joined political forces with Southern white agrarians and won some assistance in some states in battling disfranchisement and other acts of white supremacists. These coalitions were fragile arrangements, however, and seldom lasted beyond 1898. Meanwhile, a number of black voters, coerced by economic pressure from their landlords and employers and intimidated by the violence of terrorist organizations, cast their ballots for the Democrats.

Black support of the white Conservatives was not always involuntary, however, nor without rewards for the black community. In 1880, for example, Lewis Adams of Tuskegee, Alabama, encouraged the black voters of his town to cast their ballots for two Democratic candidates for the state legislature. The candidates had promised Adams that they would introduce and secure passage of a bill for the establishment of a normal school for blacks in Tuskegee. The law of 1881 creating the school designated Adams as one of the three commissioners. When Booker T. Washington came to Tuskegee, Adams not only helped him select the site for the campus but in subsequent years served on the faculty as head of the tin and harness shop and helped to construct a number of the campus buildings.[1]

A few black leaders, disillusioned by the increasingly lily-white policy of the Republican party or seduced by Democratic promises of respect and protection of their rights, joined the Democratic conservatives in an alliance of paternalism. As disfranchisement advanced during the 1890s some of these leaders sought to retard its progress by acceding to new voting restrictions and demanding in return that there be no discrimination between black and white in their applications. Isaiah T. Montgomery, a wealthy Mississippi planter and businessman and founder of the all-black town of Mound Bayou, supported in the Mississippi constitutional convention of 1890 the disfranchising provisions that were finally incorporated in the state constitution. Montgomery believed that the creation of a substantial white voting majority that would result from the fair administration of the voting requirements would bring about improved race relations. In time, as they acquired education and property, most blacks would also become voters. Similarly, in Virginia in 1900 and 1901, John Mitchell, Jr., the crusading black editor of the Richmond *Planet,* maintained that if the franchise were to be restricted then it should be denied to the ignorant of both races. Color should not enter into the matter. Even W. E. B. Du Bois was not totally averse in the 1890s to the disfranchisement of black illiterates so long as their white counterparts were similarly disabled. Such too was Booker T. Washington's position. These concessions to white conservatism were of no avail, however, for the disfranchisement movement was aimed at all blacks, literate and illiterate, propertied and unpropertied. James K. Vardaman, governor of Mississippi, put the matter succinctly: "I am just as opposed to Booker T. Washington as a voter with all his Anglo-Saxon reinforcements," he asserted, "as I am to the coconut-headed, chocolate-colored typical little coon, Andy Dotson, who blacks my shoes every morning. Neither is fit to perform the supreme function of citizenship."[2]

Black Southerners also appealed to the federal government to halt such developments in the South. Most of the presidents from 1877 to 1901 acquiesced in the developing new order in the region, however. President Benjamin Harrison did respond in the early 1890s with demands for fair elections in the South but failed to push the matter. Congress considered a Federal Fair Election Bill (the Lodge Bill) in 1890 and 1891 but in the end failed to pass it. In a succession of decisions, as previously indicated, the Supreme Court rendered the Fifteenth Amendment a virtual nullity by limiting positive federal action to protect black voting rights. In the end, the blacks who sat in the constitutional conventions and state legislatures which devised the disfranchising measures could merely protest the coming order of things. They did so passionately and with irrefutable logic, but to no avail.

DEMONSTRATIONS AND BOYCOTTS

The black protest against segregation was much more forceful than that against disfranchisement, mainly because the former lent itself to greater direct pressures from the black community. Opposition to segregation had developed early in the post-Civil War period in several areas of the South. In New Orleans, in the spring of 1867, long-standing black resentment against the existence of separate streetcars for blacks and whites came to a head. From April 28 to May 7 blacks individually and in groups boarded cars designated for whites or otherwise hampered their operation. These tactics forced the temporary abandonment of the Jim Crow system. Not until 1902 were segregated streetcars reintroduced. Similar demonstrations and boycotts forced streetcar companies to abandon segregation in Richmond and Charleston in 1867, in Louisville in 1870-1871, in Savannah in 1872, in Atlanta in 1892-1893, in Augusta in 1898, and again in Savannah in 1899.

The new onslaught of Jim Crow statutes in the early 1900s met similar resistance in at least thirty cities. The Richmond *Dispatch* of January 20, 1900, reported that the black people of Chesterfield County were "a good deal excited over the passage of the separate-car bill. . . ."

They are very indignant that they will not be able to ride in the same coaches with white people. . . . They declare that they will organize and band themselves together against the whites of their neighborhood. The men say they will have their own stores and shops. They will not hire themselves out to the white people anymore, but will live of and by themselves altogether and let the whites do the same. The colored women are even more violent than the men. They say they will not cook and do the washing for the white people any more, nor will they allow of their own color to do so.[3]

Streetcar boycotts of varying duration occurred between 1900 and 1907 in Montgomery and Mobile, Alabama; Little Rock, Arkansas; Jacksonville and Pensacola, Florida; Atlanta, Augusta, Rome and Savannah, Georgia; New Orleans and Shreveport, Louisiana; Vicksburg and Natchez, Mississippi; Columbia, South Carolina; Memphis, Chattanooga, Knoxville, and Nashville, Tennessee; Houston and San Antonio, Texas; and Richmond, Portsmouth, Danville, Lynchburg, Norfolk, and Newport News, Virginia.
Prominent in the leadership of the boycott movement were ministers, newspaper editors, college professors, businessmen, and politicians. John Mitchell, Jr., editor of the Richmond *Planet,* after waging a futile battle against black disfranchisement, turned his attention to the streetcar issue. Assisted by an ex-politician, some professors from Virginia Union University, officials of fraternal orders and mutual-benefit societies, and businessmen, Mitchell led an almost year-long boycott in 1904-1905 against the streetcar company. Because of the boycott and the settlement of a costly strike, the streetcar company was forced into bankuptcy. In Nashville, Tennessee, the Reverend E.W.D. Isaac, editor of the Nashville *Clarion* and the *National Baptist Union,* and the Reverend Richard Henry Boyd, general secretary of the National Baptist Publishing Board, joined with an elite group of businessmen, clergymen, and professors at Fisk University and Meharry Medical College in leading the streetcar boycott there in 1905-1906. This group also formed the Union Transprotation Company, which consisted first of horsedrawn wagons and later of five motor buses to provide transportation for the black community. Blacks also formed transit companies in Savannah, Portsmouth, Norfolk, and Chattanooga. All of the companies, however, either because of harassment from the municipal officials, insufficient capitalization, or inability to provide regular service, soon went out of business.
The boycott movement and other forms of protest against streetcar segregation ultimately failed. White intransigence and harassment, opposition to the boycotts in the black community, especially on the part of clergymen in some cities, and the severe difficulty experienced by the black masses in finding alternate modes of transportation over a long period all contributed to the failure. Not until fifty years later was a concerted attack on the system again to be launched.

BACK TO AFRICA

By 1890 many black Southerners had already lost all hope that they could find a place of dignity and promise in Southern society. As the century faded, this feeling of hopelessness grew. Thus many sought to escape. One of the important avenues of escape offered was a Back-to-Africa movement. Unlike the streetcar boycott movement, the Back-to-Africa movement found its most enthusiastic supporters among lower-class blacks. The first major post-Reconstruction movement was organized in South Carolina in 1877 under the inspiration of Congressman Richard H. Cain and Martin R. Delany. Delany's interest in emigration projects antedated the Civil War. Other leaders in the movement were B.F. Porter, minister of the Morris Brown A.M.E. Church in Charleston, and H.N. Boney and George Curtis, jurors in the federal district court at Charleston. In explaining the interest of black South Carolinians in the movement Congressman Cain reported that "the colored people are tired of the constant struggle for life and liberty with such results as the 'Missippi [sic] Plan' and prefer going where no such obstacles are in their way of enjoying their Liberty."[4]

In the summer of 1877 the Liberian Exodus Joint Stock Company was organized with Porter as president and Boney as secretary. By the beginning of 1878 the company had raised $6,000. So great was the desire of blacks to leave South Carolina for Africa that in January 1878, a large number arrived in Charleston for the voyage to Liberia before the company had purchased a ship. The ship soon was acquired and named the *Azor*; it was christened in March 1878 at a ceremony attended by 5,000 blacks. On April 21, 1878 the *Azor* embarked from Charleston for Liberia with 209 emigrants. Because of lack of space 175 would-be emigrants were left behind. After considerable hardship 186 emigrants arrived in Liberia on June 3, twenty-three having died during the voyage. Some of the emigrants found life too difficult in Liberia and eventually returned to the United States. Others prospered, however. Because of financial difficulties, legal problems, and betrayal by a wealthy white merchant, the company was unable to carry through a planned second voyage to Liberia for 1879, and the Liberian Exodus Joint Stock Company eventually became defunct.

In the 1890s, black Southerners renewed their interest in emigration to Africa. Bishop Henry McNeal Turner of Georgia, who had been interested in African emigration since before the Civil War, was the chief sparkplug in the movement. Bishop Turner envisioned Africa not only as a haven from the oppression blacks underwent in the United States, but also as the future home of a great civilization which the black U.S. emigrants would play a major role in building. Turner was stridently uncompromising in his denunciation of racism in the United States; and disappointed at the federal government's failure to protect the constitutional rights of blacks, he declared that the Constitution was "a bloody rag, a cheat, a libel and ought to be spit upon by every Negro in the land." As for the United States as a whole Turner declared that "I wish it nothing but ill and endless misfortune, wish I would only live to see it go down to ruin and its memory blotted from the pages of history." An ardent black nationalist, Turner denounced black Americans for their worship of whiteness, "of doing nothing day and night but cry: Glory, dominion, and greatness to White." He taught that God was black, that black was beautiful, and that Africa was the tabula rasa where black Americans and black Africans could join together to build a great nation where black people would enjoy freedom and dignity and would elicit respect from the entire world. Not all blacks should go back to Africa, however. Many blacks, especially those caught up in the whiteness syndrome, were "no more fit to go to Africa," said the bishop, "than we are fit to go to Paradise."[5]

From 1890 to 1910 Bishop Turner waged a vigorous campaign throughout the South in behalf of emigration to Liberia. Although he demanded that the U.S. government should pay $40 million in reparations to blacks—in payment for two centuries of servitude—he took the lead in organizing several fund-raising drives to finance emigration and encouraged others which he thought were legitimate. Many emigration efforts capitalized on the interest he aroused. Between 1890 and 1913 such organizations as the American Colonization Society in 1890-1891, the Congo National Emigration Company in 1894, the International Migration Society in 1894, 1895, and 1896, the Liberian Colonization Society in the early 1900s, and Chief Alfred Sam's Akim Trading Company in 1913, sent perhaps some 1,500 black Southerners to Africa—the overwhelming majority to Liberia. Other blacks went to Africa on their own.

The small number who emigrated to Africa, compared to the total Southern black population, hardly reflected the extent of emigration sentiment. Many thousands wanted to go to Liberia but were prevented from doing so by inadequate finances, the incredible blundering of virtually all of the emigration organizations, and the fraud and deception practiced by charlatans. Some who could not go to Africa attempted to settle elsewhere outside of the United States. In 1895 some 800 black people under the leadership of W.H. Ellis attempted to establish a settlement in Mexico, but various misfortunes caused them to return to the United States. All of the Southern states were represented in the exodus to Africa and among those who wanted to go. Emigration sentiment appeared to be strongest in Mississippi, Arkansas, Oklahoma, Texas, Alabama, Tennessee, Georgia, Louisiana, and South Carolina. Many who left or wanted to leave Arkansas and Oklahoma for Africa had previously migrated to those states in search of greater freedom and opportunity, but had found their dreams thwarted. Had there been a well-organized, amply financed emigration project, the South would undoubtedly have lost much of its black population to Africa during this period.

INTERNAL MIGRATION

Blacks also tried to escape Southern racial conditions by migrating to western and northern regions of the United States. Black Southerners had evinced an interest in migrating to the West as early as the Reconstruction period. In the early 1870s about 500 Louisianians formed a committee under the leadership of Henry Adams for the purpose of investigating conditions throughout the South in order to determine "if it was possible we could stay under the people who held us under bondage." Convinced by 1874 that the future for blacks in the South was bleak, they organized a "colonization council," and appealed to the president and Congress for relief from oppression while considering such alternatives as requesting the government to set aside territory within the United States to which they could migrate or to appropriate money to finance their emigration to Liberia. They even considered approaching foreign governments for assistance in migrating to other countries. Distrusting politicians, avoided by preachers, and composed almost exclusively of "laboring men," the colonization council had "lost all hopes" by 1877 that conditions for blacks in the South would improve. Therefore, against the advice of most middle- and upper-class black leaders, they decided to leave Louisiana.[6]

In 1879 Henry Adams and Benjamin "Pap" Singleton of Tennessee led about 40,000 blacks from Louisiana, Mississippi, Alabama, and Georgia to the Midwest. Most of the migrants settled in Kansas while several thousand went into Nebraska and Iowa. About ten years later, Edwin B. McCabe, formerly state auditor of Kansas, inspired 7,000 Southern blacks to enter the Oklahoma territory as the vanguard of a movement which McCabe hoped would develop Oklahoma into an all-black state. Although McCabe's dream of an all-black state did not materialize, by 1910 some twenty-five black towns, including the towns of Langston and Boley, had been established. As means of escape from white oppression, other all-black towns were established between 1877 and 1914. Most of these were located in the South, but a few were established elsewhere. Among the better known were Mound Bayou, Mississippi, founded by Isaiah Montgomery in 1883; Whitesboro, New Jersey, founded by ex-Congressman George H. White; and Allensworth, California, founded by Lieutenant Colonel Allen Allensworth, a former army chaplain, in 1908.

To argue, as some scholars do, the primacy of economic motives behind black migration to the West on the grounds that most of the migrants were of the lower class is to give too little weight to the fact that lower-class blacks were the people most frequently victimized by mob violence, injustice in the courts, the convict lease system, peonage, and scores of lesser outrages. Henry Adams's complaints about blacks being killed, politically oppressed, and treated "so bad in many respects that it is impossible for them to stand it"[7] comprise persuasive testimony concerning the principal motives behind the black migration. Moreover, for lower-class black Southerners, economic exploitation and political and physical oppression, rather than being distinct elements, fitted together as a seamless web in the pattern of black subjugation.

The evidence that the desire for physical security and freedom from op-pression was as strong a motive as economic considerations is compelling. One morning in 1891, Joe McCormick, a black Alabamian, saw a procession of people coming down the road near his home. As the procession drew nearer, he saw that a black boy, tied to a buggy, was being led and followed by a gang of white people. The boy's father had been accused of raping a white woman. The driver of the buggy was McCormick's family physician, a white man whom McCormick had greatly respected for a long time. The spectacle so shocked and offended McCormick that he immediately resolved to leave the state with his family as soon as he had harvested his crops. In the same year the McCormicks moved to Oklahoma territory, finally settling in 1906 in Boley where a son and several other descendants still reside.[8]

Similarly, in 1892, after the lynching of two young owners of a grocery store, several hundred black people left the city of Memphis, Tennessee, for the Oklahoma territory. Two black ministers took their entire congre-gations with them. When one group was temporarily stalled in Arkansas by flood waters, black churches in Memphis collected over $400 on one Sunday to assist them.[9]

Before 1900 black Southerners also moved in a slow trickle to Northern cities. During the first decade of the twentieth century the number increased, culminating in large waves during the World War I period when nearly half a million left the South in search of better economic and educational oppor-tunities and relief from Southern proscriptions.

THE RATIONALE OF ACCOMMODATION

Most blacks continued to live in the South, and whether residing in all-black towns or in biracial communities, they ultimately found it necessary to make some form of accommodation to the white supremacy system. Bar-ring a violent uprising, it could hardly have been otherwise, for behind South-ern apartheid stood all the instruments of force, including the machinery of government, available to the white population. For most, perhaps, accom-modation to the proscriptive biracial system took the form of resignation rather than acceptance. Some, however, by accepting much of the social philosophy on which white supremacy was based, gave an aura of legitimacy to the system. Others were confident that segregation would pose no insur-mountable barrier to black advancement, that within the biracial system two healthy parallel societies could develop. They envisioned the building of a thriving, self-sufficient black community of farmers, artisans, business-men, and professionals that would eventually win the respect of all Americans.

Booker T. Washington articulated the accommodationist position in his famous 1895 "Atlanta Compromise" address. Washington was born a slave in 1856. His life in many ways paralleled the Horatio Alger story. Entering Hampton Institute in 1872 without funds, he worked his way through the school, graduating three years later. After teaching for several years, he helped to found Tuskegee Institute in 1881. Both Hampton and Tuskegee emphasized training in the mechanical, industrial, and agricultural arts, the type of education that Washington advocated for the mass of black people.

Washington was a very complex man. In expressing his accommodationist philosophy, he urged blacks to give up the quest for social equality and political rights and to concentrate on lifting themselves economically and morally. By developing their agricultural, business, and mechanical skills, and by practicing honesty, frugality, and Christian morality blacks would find a place for themselves in Southern society as independent farmers, businessmen, and artisans and as agricultural and industrial workers. Through such action they would gain the respect of Southern whites, who, out of economic self-interest and a sense of justice, would eventually accord blacks their political rights. Washington urged blacks to be proud of their race and to unify in behalf of the race's advancement.

Washington's views, as described above, and his general espousal of a conservative economic and social philosophy, commended him to many wealthy and powerful people in the North. Among his supporters and associates were some of the leading captains of industry. For the same reasons, Washington appealed to conservative whites in the South, who particularly liked his opposition to black protest and political activity. Because they liked his views, Washington was given recognition by these powerful whites as the spokesman for the black community in America. President Theodore Roosevelt made him his chief advisor on racial matters, and consulted him frequently in making patronage appointments of blacks and whites in the South. Because of his high standing among prominent whites, many blacks also came to accept him as their leader. Moreover, his emphasis on racial solidarity and self-help appealed to a rising class of black business and professional men in the South whose clientele was almost exclusively confined to the black community. The black masses, too, primarily concerned with economic and physical survival, found much to cheer in his program.

Yet, as August Meier and Louis Harlan have pointed out, there was another side to Booker T. Washington.[10] While "overtly" advising blacks to eschew politics and protest, Washington himself "covertly" engaged in and supported many protest efforts. On several occasions he lent financial aid and his influence to political movements and court cases opposing black disfranchisement. As Roosevelt's patronage dispenser in the South, he fought against the lily-white Republicans. He worked against the system of peonage in the South and helped to institute legal cases against railroad segregation, and supported others. These behind-the-scenes activities of Washington, to the extent that black Southerners knew of them, also commended him to the black population as their leader.

Washington's accommodationism, however, was the chief facet of his program and character which fixed him in the minds of both the black and white people of the South. To some extent, by providing a philosophical and programmatic rationale for white supremacy, he contributed to its establishment. White supremacists could find justification for their actions in his words. Black accommodationists could similarly find justification in his views for their inaction in the face of the rigid restrictions imposed on the black community. Moreover, by relegating protest and politics to a tertiary position in black life, he contributed to the political and social apathy that became characteristic of so many black people during the first half of the twentieth century, and which has not been fully remedied to this day. And although he recognized that economic power provided a necessary foundation for the exercise and enjoyment of political rights, his prescriptions were already being made irrelevant by the increasing reliance of the economic order upon labor in factories and by a political and social system in the South which, rather than providing opportunities for economic advancement and self-sufficiency, restricted most black economic activity to a matter of economic survival. Thus Washington's program provided no solution to the problem of how a subjugated people in a democratic, capitalistic society, lacking the requisite political resources to influence the economic order in their behalf and to assure their physical security, could acquire sufficient economic power to secure political and civil rights.

THE PERSISTENCE OF PROTEST

Despite general acquiescence in the South's biracial system, the protest spirit, impulse, and habit did not die. Individually and collectively, blacks challenged the sytem at every turn. Bishop Turner of Georgia continued to thunder against America's racial perfidy. In Virginia, Attorney James H. Hayes and the National Suffrage League waged a futile battle from 1902 to 1913 in the courts against black disfranchisement. In Atlanta, John Hope, president of Atlanta Baptist College, succored the spirit of protest as did Virginia Union University in Richmond. Through the *Voice of the Negro,* an Atlanta publication, J. Max Barber gave voice to black protest from 1905 to 1909. An Equal Rights Association formed in 1906 similarly carried on the tradition of protest in Macon, Georgia. Doubtless similar organizations existed in other black communities in the South. Several black Southerners, three from Atlanta and one from Richmond, were among the organizers of the Niagara Movement, a militant protest organization. Throughout its existence prominent Southerners, such as John Hope, J. Max Barber, J.R.L. Diggs (former Virginia Union University professor and then president of Kentucky State College), Reverend J. Milton Walden (of Jacksonville, Florida, and Washington, D.C.), and Reverend Sutton E. Griggs (of Nashville) were active members.

W.E.B. Du Bois, one of the founders of the Niagara Movement, was the principal spokesman of black protest in the South in the early twentieth century. A native of Great Barrington, Massachusetts, Du Bois went South in 1885 to Fisk University where he studied for three years. He then studied at Harvard and at the University of Berlin. The first black person to earn a Harvard doctoral degree, he taught at Wilberforce University and conducted social research at the University of Pennsylvania before returning South in 1897 as a professor of sociology at Atlanta University. By remaining in Atlanta until 1910, Du Bois established his credentials as a black Southerner.

By 1903 Du Bois had emerged as the leading spokesman of a group of black Northerners and Southerners opposed to the accommodationist philosophy and program of Booker T. Washington. Du Bois argued for full equality of rights and status for blacks in American society. He openly demanded the ballot, denounced segregation, condemned lynching, and called for the removal of all political, economic, and social restrictions imposed upon blacks. At the same time he called for racial solidarity in the economic sphere, recognition and respect for black cultural expression in both America and Africa, and black pride. He insisted that the "Talented Tenth" must be educated in the arts and the humanities to provide leadership for the race. In 1905 Du Bois organized the Niagara Movement to fight for the "abolition of all caste distinctions based simply on race and color." He was a leading figure in the formation in 1909-1910 of the National Association for the Advancement of Colored People (NAACP), and was the founder in 1910 of *Crisis,* the official journal of the NAACP, and its editor to 1934. Perhaps Du Bois's chief contribution lay in his rejection of a unidimensional approach to the problem of black powerlessness. However, when in the 1930s he sought to unite protest with the idea of a separate group economy as the way to the liberation of the black community, he found himself out of step with the leadership of the NAACP.[11]

From its founding in 1909 to the mid-1950s the NAACP constituted the chief organizational expression of the protest movement in the South. During its first six years, however, it remained primarily a Northern organization. With the appointment of James Weldon Johnson as field secretary and organizer in 1916, the NAACP began to expand into the South. In 1917 thirteen Southern branches were formed. By the end of 1918 there were branches in every Southern state with a combined membership of 18,701 persons. A year later there were more Southern than Northern members— 42,588 in the South, 38,420 in the North. In recognition of the predominant number of Southerners in the organization, the association held its 1920 annual conference in Atlanta, Georgia, its first such meeting south of Baltimore.

So far as Southern issues were concerned the NAACP addressed itself to lynching and other forms of mob violence, the suffrage, justice in the courts, residential segregation, and equality of educational opportunities and facilities. It sought to achieve its objectives mainly through "litigation, legislation, and education."

The NAACP waged a wide-ranging propaganda campaign against lynching. It sent investigators into the South to marshal the facts surrounding specific incidents of mob violence. One of its most intrepid investigators was Walter White who, because he looked like a white man, was able to collect some of the most intimate details about this form of Southern barbarism. In 1919, the Association published *Thirty Years of Lynching in the United States, 1889-1918*. This was followed in 1929 by Walter White's *Rope and Faggot, A Biography of Judge Lynch*. W. E. B. Du Bois also published continuing reports of lynchings in the *Crisis*. The NAACP held numerous protest meetings and conferences in all regions of the country to expose the evil. The NAACP exposures, combined with the reports on lynchings prepared by Tuskegee Institute and Fisk University, did much to develop antilynching sentiment not only in the North but also in the South. The result was the creation of a public opinion that was receptive to the need for federal antilynching legislation. In 1919 the NAACP launched its campaign for a federal antilynching law, and between 1921 and 1950 a number of antilynching bills were introduced in Congress. A few bills passed the House of Representatives but, meeting a Southern filibuster in the Senate, failed to become law. Meanwhile, largely because of developing public opinion in the South against it, lynching became a declining phenomenon.

The NAACP also worked to assure that blacks received a fair trial in the courts. In 1923, it secured from the Supreme Court an order for a new trial for an Arkansas man who had been convicted of murder in Arkansas courts. The Supreme Court held that in excluding blacks from the jury as well as engaging in other procedural irregularities the Arkansas courts had denied the defendant a fair trial. The NAACP also intervened in the infamous Scottsboro case of the 1930s in which nine black youths were falsely accused of assaulting two white prostitutes. They were quickly tried, eight of them were convicted and sentenced to death. After having spent from six and a half to nineteen years in jail they were released.

It was largely through NAACP efforts that some of the most glaring obstacles to black suffrage were struck down by the Supreme Court. In 1915 the grandfather clause was declared unconstitutional. In a succession of decisions from 1927 to 1950 the Supreme Court outlawed the white primary. And in 1949 the court refused to overturn a lower court decision outlawing the understanding test as a prerequisite for voting. The NAACP was also successful in getting the Supreme Court in 1917 to strike down residential segregation laws.

In 1936 the NAACP began to provide legal assistance to black school-teachers seeking the equalization of their salaries with those of white public school teachers. The campaign was carried on in fifteen of the seventeen states in which racially separate schools were maintained. By 1948, the principle of equal salaries for black and white teachers had been won in most Southern states. The campaign for equal teachers' salaries was a part of the overall movement to secure equal educational facilities for blacks. Between 1885 and 1915 black Southerners, as individuals or in small groups, brought suit after suit in Southern courts to secure schools for their children in areas where only white schools existed. They were successful in a number of cases.

Beginning in the 1930s, black Southerners, through the aegis of the NAACP, began to insist that the facilities provided for them be equal in fact to those provided whites, or that blacks be admitted to white institutions. Charles H. Houston, vice dean of the law school of Howard University, conducted the NAACP's campaign. As a result of a case instituted by the NAACP in 1935, Donald G. Murray won admission to the University of Maryland law school. In 1938 the Supreme Court held that Lloyd Gaines could not be denied admission to the law school of the University of Missouri simply because of his race or color and that the device of providing out-of-state tuition scholarships for blacks to attend institutions in other states did not meet the requirement of separate but equal facilities. In 1949 Ada Lois Sipuel entered the law school of the University of Oklahoma after the Supreme Court had held in 1948 that she had the same right of access to legal education supplied by the state as white persons. And in 1950 the court ordered the university to cease the practice of assigning G. W. McLaurin, a black graduate student, to a special section in his class marked "reserved for colored," to a special desk in the library, and to a special table in the dining hall. In a precursor of things to come Heman Sweatt won admission to the law school of the University of Texas in 1950 because the Supreme Court maintained that the three-room law school recently established for blacks at the Houston branch of Prairie View Normal and Industrial College was unequal in both tangible and intangible facilities to the law school at the University of Texas.

The Sweatt decision opened the way for an attack on segregation per se, and in 1951 the NAACP began to prepare several cases for the long road to the Supreme Court in which the court would be asked to declare that segregated schools were inherently unequal. The cases, from Delaware, Virginia, South Carolina, Kansas, and the District of Columbia, came before the court in the fall of 1952. A year and a half later, on May 17, 1954, the Supreme Court handed down its landmark decision. As the five black children and their parents had asked, the Supreme Court declared that school segregation was unconstitutional. A new era in Southern race relations had dawned.

INTERRACIAL COOPERATION

Although the South reacted angrily to the Supreme Court's school decision, and political leaders of the South cried "Never!" many forces had been at work in the region looking toward the moderation of Southern racial policies. Predominantly white organizations like the Commission on Interracial Cooperation, the Southern Regional Council, and the Southern Conference for Human Welfare sought to promote interracial cooperation, end racial abuses, and eliminate discrimination, if not segregation. The Commission on Interracial Cooperation, founded in 1919, was lead by such white Southerners as Will W. Alexander, Howard Odum, Jessie Ames Daniels, Emily H. Clay, and Arthur F. Raper. In addition to working for improvements in race relations within the context of the segregationist system, the organization also sponsored research on the problems in Southern society. It inspired the subsequent creation of such organizations as the Southern Commission on the Study of Lynching and the Association of Southern Women for the Prevention of Lynching. The commission pursued a gradualistic policy, relying on education and moral suasion to achieve its objectives. The Southern Conference for Human Welfare, organized in 1938, was more aggressive in seeking its ends. Composed primarily of liberal white Southerners, but having many black members, the conference attempted to aid the underprivileged and the oppressed not only by education and moral suasion but by political action where feasible.

The Southern Regional Council owes its establishment in 1944 more directly to black initiative. In 1941, Gordon Blaine Hancock, a professor at Virginia Union University and minister of Moore Street Baptist Church in Richmond, published an article entitled "Interracial Hypertension." Hancock deplored the increasing racial tension throughout the nation as reflected in riots, racial rhetoric, and other forms of interracial conflict. "If serious trouble is to be avoided" he warned, "both whites and Negroes must face the ugly fact that race relations are in a state of hypertension and rupture; that unless matters are speedily taken in hand and shaped according to some constructive plan, we shall probably lose many important gains that have been won through many years, through sweat and tears." The challenge of averting the catastrophe, said Hancock, rested with the "better-class whites and Negroes" of the South.[12]

Hancock's gloomy forecast earned him the sobriquet "the Gloomy Dean." But it so impressed Jessie Ames Daniels, a white official of the somewhat moribund Commission on Interracial Cooperation, that she went to Richmond to confer with Hancock about what should be done. They decided that black Southerners should draft a public statement challenging white Southerners to join in a cooperative endeavor to improve race relations in the areas and ways defined by the black group. With the assistance of P. B. Young, editor and publisher of the Norfolk *Journal and Guide,* and Luther P. Jackson, professor of history at Virginia State College, Hancock arranged for a meeting of black leaders. On October 20, 1942, fifty-nine prominent black Southerners—college presidents and professors, public schoolteachers, newspaper editors, clergymen, businessmen, labor leaders, social workers, and civil rights activists—met on the campus of the North Carolina College for Negroes at Durham. No white Southerners were invited. And to prevent the white South from dismissing the forthcoming proposals of the group as the work of outside agitators, Hancock also decided not to invite black Northerners. The conference was exclusively a black Southern affair.

In his opening address to the conference Hancock defined the purpose of the gathering as making the wishes of Southern blacks a matter of record and as challenging "the constructive cooperation of that element of the white South who express themselves as desirous of 'a new deal for the Negroes of the South.'" To draft the statement of challenge to the white South, a committee headed by Charles S. Johnson of Fisk University and consisting of Benjamin Mays, Rufus Clement, Horace Mann Bond, Frederick D. Patterson (presidents of Morehouse College, Atlanta University, Fort Valley State College, and Tuskegee Institute, respectively), James E. Jackson, secretary of the Southern Youth Congress, and William M. Cooper of Hampton Institute was formed.

Meeting subsequently in Atlanta the committee formulated what became known as the "Durham Manifesto," which was released to the public on December 14, 1942. Fearing to alienate the white South, the committee soft-pedaled the issue of segregation. While declaring that "We are fundamentally opposed to the principle and practice of compulsory segregation in our American society, whether of races or classes or creeds," the committee, contrary to the wishes of Dr. Mays, stopped short of demanding its abolition.[13] Instead they called for the elimination of discrimination within the biracial system. The committee demanded that the poll tax, the white primary, physical and economic intimidation, and all other barriers to black suffrage be abolished. They asked for equal salaries for black and white teachers, federal financial aid to make educational facilities for blacks equal to those for whites and to bring Southern facilities up to the national norm, elimination of discrimination in employment and in labor unions, improvements in the conditions of tenant farmers and in the wages of farm workers, access of blacks to the facilities of public hospitals, and an end to discrimination against black soldiers in travel, recreation, and rest areas and to their mistreatment by the police.

In response to the "Durham Manifesto" a group of white Southerners met in Atlanta in April 1943 and issued a statement, signed by 292 persons, that essentially endorsed the Durham proposals. They annexed a cavil to their statement, however, to the effect that the goals sought must be pursued through evolutionary rather than revolutionary means. Machinery for collaboration between the two groups was subsequently fashioned, and in 1944 the two groups were brought together as the Southern Regional Council. Under the initial direction of Guy B. Johnson, a white Southerner, and Ira

DeA Reid, a black scholar, the council launched a program to bring about equality of political rights and economic opportunities for blacks in the South and for social and educational improvements. Like earlier interracial organizations in the South, it did not go so far as to advocate social equality and the end of segregation. It began, as Dr. Mays has written, timidly and cautiously, "stepping lightly so as not to disturb the status quo of a segregated society."[14] An enlightening commentary on the state of race relations in the South at the time is that the council, although basically a conservative organization, was considered liberal, and even radical, in the South. Nevertheless, like its predecessors, it helped to lay the groundwork for the more extensive and fundamental contact between the races that the Supreme Court's 1954 decision envisioned.

VIOLENCE AS PROTEST

As previously observed, the Southern biracial order rested ultimately upon the commitment of Southern whites to the use of force, legal and illegal, to maintain the subjugation of the black population. Contributing to this commitment was the fact that violence was an endemic feature of Southern life. Despite the prevalence of interracial violence, more whites and blacks lost their lives in personal conflicts with members of their own race than were killed in interracial encounters. Violence, then, was a part of the culture of the black community as well as the white. Although usually expressed in intraracial confrontations, it is not surprising that it would occasionally be directed against whites as well. Thus, behind the facade of passivity which the black masses usually displayed to the white community during the era of Jim Crow lay the same impulse to employ violence in self-defense or in defense of a member of the community that had inspired blacks to resist white atrocities during the Reconstruction period.

Between the end of Reconstruction and the establishment of apartheid, blacks continued to intermittently resist or retaliate against white violence. In 1880 blacks were suspected of setting fire to the business area of Clarksville, Tennessee. The Chicago *Conservator,* a black newspaper, reported that "When the city was burning, they gathered in little knots and crowds; discussed the situation, witnessed with a good deal of manifest satisfaction the strenuous effort to suppress the fire, but would not lend a helping hand for love or money."[15]

Democratic fraud at the polls also occasionally evoked a violent black reaction. In St. John the Baptist Parish in Louisana black farmers became greatly angry at the stuffing of ballot boxes which gave the gubernatorial election of 1896 to the Democrats. They seized one of the ballot boxes, killed two white men, and organized themselves in preparation for an attack on a unit of the state militia that was sent to restore order.

As could be expected, physical atrocities against blacks, such as lynchings and beatings, were more likely to provoke black resistance and retaliation than fraud at the polls and other forms of white chicanery. Even relatively conservative black leaders occasionally hinted at the desirability of violent black response to such crimes. In 1885, in reaction to the murder of a respected member of the black community by a white physician, black ministers in Charleston, South Carolina, at the behest of a mass meeting of black citizens, declared: "We must warn the white people in time. They may go on depriving us of our rights until forbearance ceases to be a virtue. It may not be long before the revolutions of St. Domingo in the times of Toussaint L'Ouverture will be repeated in the South. . . ."[16]

During the twentieth century a number of black leaders endorsed the principle of individual and collective use of violence in self-defense. On several occasions between 1905 and 1935 Du Bois endorsed not only the use of violence in self-defense but prophesied a war between the races. The more moderate James Weldon Johnson, while rejecting the use of violence as a weapon to overthrow the racial order, nevertheless declared in 1934 that when faced with mob violence blacks should sell their lives "at the dearest price we are able to put on it."[17] The NAACP argued and won the same principle in 1925 in the Ossian Sweet case.

In advocating physical resistance to attack, black leaders were endorsing a principle that the black masses were already practicing. In August 1888 a group of armed black men in Fayetteville, North Carolina, kept guard around a jail to prevent an anticipated attempt to lynch two black youths charged with raping a white girl. In 1899 about a thousand armed blacks in Liberty County, Georgia, after freeing a black farmer who had been jailed for dating a white woman, took refuge in the Okefenoke swamp and rebuffed the attempts of the state militia to recapture him. Similarly, in Georgetown, South Carolina, in 1900 nearly a thousand black people, "armed with everything from rice reap hooks to rifles," surrounded a jail to prevent an expected attempt by whites to lynch John Brownfield, a respected black barber, who had killed a white deputy sheriff in an argument over taxes. One of their number admonished them: "Don't go home mens like the buckra men tell you. Stay here and save John. Bun[burn] de dam town down to ashes. Yunner kill all de buckra men and we will tend to de buckra omman and chillun. De buckra want to run over us, but we will show dem."[18] Inspired by such utterances, the blacks refused to disperse in the face of several units of the state militia until they were convinced by town officials that Brownfield would not be harmed.

As during the Reconstruction period, in clashes between blacks and whites during the Jim Crow era the whites were more likely to emerge victorious. In early July 1903, armed whites and blacks converged on the town of Norway, South Carolina. The whites hoped to thwart an anticipated attempt by blacks to liberate from jail a black man accused of killing a white man. The blacks came to prevent a prospective lynching. Unfortunately, the blacks allowed themselves to be disarmed by the whites, who then proceeded to take the man from jail and lynch him.

Despite the efforts of the black community to protect its members from lynch mobs, most lynch victims had to face the mobs alone. Some, like Robert Charles, sold their lives dearly. In New Orleans in 1900, Charles, who had shot a policeman who had shot him first, took refuge in a house and held off a mob in excess of a thousand people for several hours. Forced from the house when the police set fire to it, Charles met his death while still shooting. The mob paid a heavy price for its victory, however; seven of them, including two policemen, were killed, and nine were wounded.

The prevalence of race riots in the twentieth century was indicative of the increasing tendency of blacks to fight back when attacked or to defend a black person from the likelihood of being lynched. Such was the case in the Atlanta riot of 1906 and in the riots in 1919 in Houston and Longview, Texas; Elaine, Arkansas; Tulsa, Oklahoma; and Washington, D.C. In Longview, for example, about seventy-five well-armed black men routed a group of whites who had gone into their community in search of a black schoolteacher who reportedly informed the *Chicago Defender* of the lynching of a black man several weeks earlier. The whites had boasted that they were going to rid the community of "uppity niggers." When the whites returned, now augmented by policemen and firemen, they found that the blacks had dispersed and that the men they were especially looking for had left town. They retaliated by burning a number of homes and seizing several blacks for interrogation.

Several of the black-white confrontations, like the Elaine, Arkansas, riot of 1919, arose out of the increasing militancy of black tenants, sharecroppers, and farm laborers. During the 1930s black farmers repeatedly resisted efforts by white landlords and their police agents to crush their organizations. In 1931 members of a sharecroppers union in Camp Hill, Alabama, in an unsuccessful effort to prevent the lynching of a young black man who had wounded several deputy sheriffs in a gun battle several hours earlier, fought off a group of whites until their ammunition ran out. In December 1932, members of a sharecroppers union in Reeltown, Alabama, battled landlords and deputy sheriffs who were attempting to confiscate the livestock of a black tenant farmer. Similar clashes occurred in other communities in the South.

In taking up arms in a number of instances, black Southerners were as interested in asserting their dignity as in defending their lives. In Milledgeville, Georgia, in May 1919, a dispute over school colors between students of the black high school and the white high school threatened to erupt into a serious conflict. In a letter to W. E. B. Du Bois the commencement speaker reported that:

Upon my arrival I found the town stirred up. The blacks had sent their young men to Macon, a distance of 35 miles, for arms and cartridges. They had sworn to protect the school closing exercises to which I had to speak. Not less than 100 men were armed with rifles, pistols and shot guns while the exercises were going on inside the First Baptist Church. . . . The beauty about it is, they were not at all nervous. The mothers and sons, sweethearts, husbands and wives all walked home together. The males carrying their guns with as much calmness as if they were going to shoot a rabbit in a hunt, or getting ready to shoot the Kaiser's soldiers.[19]

The readiness of the black community to defend itself against white violence received the virtually unanimous endorsement of those black newspapers, Southern as well as Northern, which commented on the incidents. The moderate Norfolk *Journal and Guide* pointed out that "White folks don't like cold steel any more than black folks. The outcome of the rioting at Washington, and at Longview . . . is that the black masses, driven to desperation by white mobs had reached the conclusion that the only way left to them is to meet white mob lawlessness with black mob lawlessness."[20] In subsequent years even ministers increasingly expressed the same view. While cautioning blacks to avoid precipitating violence, they pointed out that inasmuch as even docile black people were victimized by mob violence, blacks should become more assertive and be prepared to defend themselves if attacked.

The precise effect of such comments on the black masses cannot be determined, for even in the absence of a doctrine of self-defense, long-simmering resentment against white repression occasionally led to individual acts of violence. When, in 1945, a white police chief in Henry County, Georgia, began slapping and cursing a black woman who had refused to surrender her seat on a bus to whites, a fifty-five-year-old black farmer came to her rescue. According to the Savannah *Tribune,* the farmer "walked up, whipped out a switchblade knife and stabbed the police officer three times." The officer was taken to a hospital in critical condition.[21]

By the 1950s, then, militant self-defense was as much a part of the black protest tradition as demonstrations, boycotts, litigation, petitioning, and appeals to the sense of justice of the American people. Whether they knew it or not, the willingness of Robert Williams of Monroe, North Carolina, in the late 1950s and the Deacons for Defense in Louisiana in the 1960s to take up arms in defense of the black community reflected an impulse that was deeply rooted in the black Southern experience.

PART TWO

THE BLACK ECONOMY

FOUR

Farmers and Tenants

THE HUNGER FOR LAND

When the Civil War ended Betty Powers's father and mother and their twelve children remained on their former master's plantation and worked on shares. Four years later her father bought some uncleared land about five miles away. The whole family then set about clearing the land and building a cabin. Nearly seventy years later Mrs. Powers recalled how they felt when the cabin was completed: "Was we'uns proud? There t'was, our place to do as we pleases, after bein slaves. Dat sho' am de good feelin'. We work like beavers puttin' de crop in, and my folks stays dere till dey dies."[1]

As an economic institution slavery was mainly an instrument for the gross exploitation of labor. To the ex-slave, therefore, the right to control the utilization and disposition of his own labor was the very essence of his freedom. As the exhilaration at being free was transformed into the desire to earn a living for themselves, the majority of the freedmen naturally turned to the land upon which they had been forced to labor without remuneration. They demanded land, for ownership of land meant ownership of one's own labor. Land ownership meant freedom and status even more than the possession of political rights.

For a while, it appeared that the freedmen's hunger for land would be gratified. When the Sea Islands and other coastal regions of South Carolina and Georgia came under Union control in late 1861, the slaves in the area flocked to the Union lines. Some 15,000 were freed. They were subsequently organized and put to work as wage laborers on the plantations vacated by the fleeing Southern planters. They worked efficiently and cheerfuly under the new arrangement, but they were not satisfied. They wanted land of their own. And when in 1863 and 1864 the government put up for sale the plantations it had confiscated, the freedmen rushed to buy the land. Lacking sufficient money, they were outbid by Northern speculators, however, and only a few acquired property. In 1865 a new opportunity to obtain land was provided by General Sherman's Field Order No. 15. According to the order cotton and rice plantations in the Sea Islands and coastal regions were to be divided into 40-acre plots and distributed to the freedmen. As a result 40,000 freedmen came into temporary possession of 485,000 acres of land.

Meanwhile, on March 3, 1865, the Freedmen's Bureau was created. One of the bureau's statutory mandates was to divide abandoned lands into 40-acre plots and to rent them to the freedmen. Bureau officials in the various Southern states were instructed on July 28, 1865, to advertise such land and to instruct the freedmen on how to obtain it. In September 1865 Thaddeus Stevens, leader of the Radicals in the House of Representatives, made a speech advocating the confiscation of large plantations and the redistribution of the land in 40-acre parcels to each adult freedman. In March 1867 Stevens introduced a bill in Congress to the same effect. Out of these developments arose the freedmen's belief that each would receive a 40-acre plot and a mule.

The Freedmen's Bureau program of land distribution hardly got off the ground, however, and the distribution of land in the Sea Islands and in the coastal areas of South Carolina and Georgia was soon countermanded. In August 1865, President Andrew Johnson, as part of his policy of pardoning and granting amnesty to ex-Confederates, began the process of restoring the abandoned or confiscated lands to the former rebel owners. In September, Johnson sent General Oliver Howard, head of the Freedmen's Bureau, throughout the South to urge the freedmen who had received land from the government to give it up and to inform others that the expected plot of land would not be forthcoming. He urged the freedmen to go to work for wages, under contract, for their former masters.

The freedmen on the Sea Islands were stunned. At a meeting on Edisto Island, some 2,000 freedmen shouted "no" to Howard's message. They could not understand, they said, why the government was taking away the land of those who had been loyal to the Union in order to give it to those who had been its enemies. They could not understand why they were being so grossly betrayed. Most refused initially to give up their land. They sent petitions to President Johnson, but to no avail. They adamantly refused to contract for work with the white planters. Some threatened violent resistance. On a Georgia plantation in January 1867, blacks armed with rifles, pistols, stones, and clubs, confronted a force of federal troops sent to evict them. Eventually these freedmen, as had others before them, faced with the threat of federal military power, gave up their land. Most, however, continued to refuse to sign wage contracts with the planters to whom the land was restored, for working in gangs under supervision even for wages smacked too much of slavery. Many abandoned their crops in the fields which they had cultivated as their own and went elsewhere. Others turned to share-cropping, hoping that by renting land they would have some control over their lives and labor and over that of their families.

FARM OWNERSHIP

The vision of 40 acres and a mule died hard, however. Some black farmers on St. Helena Island and in the South Carolina coastal region did manage to retain their land. Much of the acreage that had been confiscated under court degree during the Civil War and sold to them remained in their hands. Some took advantage of a provision of the Freedman's Bureau Act of 1866 which provided for the leasing of 20 acres of government-owned land on the Sea Islands to each freedman who was dispossessed by President Johnson's policy. The freedmen were to be allowed up to six years in which to purchase the land at $1.50 per acre. Some of the former slaves founded cooperatives whereby they pooled their resources and bought whole plantations. As late as 1924 a cooperative formed in the 1860s was still in existence on St. Helena Island and virtually every black farmer on the island owned the land on which he lived and worked. In 1950 about 88 percent of the black farmers in Beaufort County, South Carolina, were owners or part owners of the land they cultivated.

In other areas of the South, a few black farmers were able to acquire land under programs formulated by the states. In a few states agencies were established or taxing policies devised to facilitate the sale of confiscated, abandoned, or unutilized land to those desiring it. Some black families also obtained land under the Southern Homestead Act enacted by the federal government in 1866. Under the act heads of families could acquire 80 acres of public land on relatively easy credit terms provided that they lived on the land for a specified period of time and improved it. The states principally affected by the act were Alabama, Arkansas, Florida, Louisiana, and Mississippi. By 1867, freedmen in Florida had acquired 160,960 acres of land under the act while those in Arkansas had settled on 116 of the available 243 homesteads. Not enough land of good quality was available under the act to meet the needs of more than a very few people, however.

Other black farmers acquired land through private purchase. A few were able to amass sizable acreage. In 1881, when the average size of farms in South Carolina was 143 acres, Lewis Duckett owned a 796-acre farm near Newberry, South Carolina; John Thorne owned 250 acres of land and other property worth $20,000 on Edisto Island; and on four of the Sea Islands blacks owned more than 10,000 acres of land valued at $300,000. Of the 18,874 black farm owners in South Carolina in 1900, only about 4,000 had acquired their land through government programs, and nearly 79 percent of the farms owned were mortgage free. Black farm owners constituted over one-fifth of the black farm operators in the state.

By 1900 black farmers in other Deep South states had not fared as well as those in South Carolina in fulfilling their desire for land. Only 14 percent of black farmers in Georgia owned their farms. In Mississippi just a little over 11 percent of the black farmers had been successful in acquiring land of their own. In the states of the upper South, where the plantation economy was less pervasive, black farm ownership was more extensive. In 1900, nearly three-fifths of Virginia's 44,600 black farm operators owned their farms which together with their livestock were valued at $13,000,000. By 1920 the proportion of black farmers who owned their land had increased to 65 percent despite a decline of 1,279 farm owners since 1910. In North Carolina's tobacco economy less than one-third of the black farmers owned their farms in 1900. For the entire South roughly one-fourth of the black farmers were owners.

The year 1910 marked the high point of black farm ownership in the South, when some 220,000 blacks owned their farms. It ended a decade in which blacks acquired land at a greater rate than whites (16.3 percent to 11.8 percent). The number remained relatively stable until 1920 when a gradual decline began. By 1930 the number of black farm owners had declined to about 176,000. By the end of the 1930s there were 2,000 fewer black farm owners than when the decade began. White farm ownership, on the other hand, had increased by about 150,000 to 1,384,000. During World War II, for obvious reasons, the number of black farmers increased rather than declined. But between the end of the war and 1959 the number of blacks owning farms declined by one-third. In that year the number of full owners was 89,749 as compared to 141,482 nine years earlier. In 1964 only 70,799 black farmers were full owners of their land. By 1970 the number had declined to 52,593,[*] of whom 23 percent were in Mississippi.[2]

The decline in ownership, except for the World War II period, when wartime demand for farm products stimulated agricultural production, was the result of several forces. Between 1910 and 1930 many cotton farmers, black and white, abandoned their farms because of soil erosion, the depletion of fertility, and the destruction wrought by the boll weevil. This was particularly the case in South Carolina and Georgia. At the same time, and later, the expansion of cotton culture into the Southwest, even to California, placed cotton farmers in the Old South at a competitive disadvantage, and many left the farms. In recent years competition from cotton growers abroad and the production of synthetic fabrics have had a similar effect.

---

[*]The total figures for 1969 are for sixteen states— the eleven states of the former Confederacy, plus Delaware, Kentucky, Maryland, Oklahoma, and West Virginia. The number of full owners in the former Confederate states was 50, 101.

Racial factors also contributed to the decline in black farm ownership. White financial institutions were generally reluctant to grant black farmers adequate credit to purchase land and equipment necessary for efficient farm operations. Moreover, black farmers were unable to diversify their crops because of the refusal of whites to allow them to utilize community marketing facilities for new crops which whites monopolized. Discriminatory administration of federal agricultural programs by state and local agencies, which continues to exist in the 1970s, handicapped black farmers. These racial factors, as well as the Southern racial environment in general, exacerbated the unattractiveness of farm life to black youth, who migrated in increasing numbers to the cities, and thus contributed to the decline in farm ownership among blacks. Today, many of the black-owned farms in the South are not in full production because their owners are too old to do the necessary work.

Although some black farmers owned several hundred to several thousand acres of land, most farms owned fully by blacks in the South have been relatively small, averaging 66.9 acres in 1920, 64.1 acres in 1930, 59.3 acres in 1950, and 62.1 acres in 1959. By 1969, however, as a result of smaller farmers abandoning the land, and those remaining consolidating their holdings, the average black-owned farm consisted of seventy-three acres. Interestingly enough, the land holdings of part owners consistently increased over the years from 54.5 acres in 1920 to 71.8 acres in 1950 to 82.7 acres in 1959, while the number of part owners declined from 51,864 in 1950 to 31,263 in 1964. In 1969 there were about 15,500 part owners holding an average of 112 acres of land.* Contrary to common belief, many of the part owners were more prosperous than full owners. By renting land to enlarge their holdings they were often able to make more efficient use of their equipment. Morever, much of the rented land was more fertile than that possessed by full owners. During the 1930s, for example, of the 730 acres cultivated by a black farmer, his 31 mules, and his sharecroppers, near Indianola, Mississippi, 650 acres were rented.[3]

The small size and inferior quality of black-owned farms reflected both racial and economic influences. In the upper South, where the greater portion of black farmers were owners, farms generally tended to be smaller than those in the plantation area because of the kinds of crops grown. In the cotton and tobacco belts farms owned by blacks were seldom located on the most desirable land. White planters kept their holdings intact to be worked by sharecroppers and wageworkers. Generally the land available to black purchasers, if available at all, was the least desirable and often located off the main highways in isolated backwoods areas. Land in white neighbor-

---

*These figures for 1969 are for Delaware, Maryland, Kentucky, Oklahoma, West Virginia, and the eleven former Confederate states. For the states of the former Confederacy only the number is 14,728.

hoods was not available to blacks. In addition, the opportunity to purchase and retain land often exacted a social price. The black purchaser and owner had to be acceptable to the white community; he had to appear to be fully obedient to the community's social mores. If he became too prosperous he might evoke the jealousy of white neighbors. Often the most economically and socially vulnerable person in the plantation South was the black planter, who had to be very circumspect in his conduct in order to avoid attracting hostile white attention and being driven out of the community or killed.

Whitecapping, the practice of "driving Negroes off the land they owned or rented," was not an uncommon phenomenon in the South. It reached its peak in Mississippi, however, during the 1890s and the first decade of the twentieth century. White farmers, seeking to drive black tenants from merchant-owned land, which they thought was about to monopolize black labor, waged a reign of terror against the tenants until Governor Vardaman and the white elite of the state, fearing a "labor famine," put a stop to it. Although whitecapping was initially directed against black sharecroppers and tenants, it soon spread to farm owners as well, whom small white farmers were inclined especially to resent. Thus many black farmers had to live with the realization that, because the white South was not prepared to permit its black population to rise above a dependent colonial status, the reward for practicing the Christian virtues of hard work, honesty, and frugality might not be an improvement in their economic and social status but, on the contrary, the destruction of their property (or perhaps their lives) and expulsion from the community.

Despite their difficulties, farm owners usually led the most economically and socially rewarding life among the black people of the rural South. Their families were stable, their housing adequate, and their educational goals and attainments comparatively high. Along with respected ministers, they provided much of the leadership for the black community. Hortense Powdermaker discovered that the 181 black farm owners in Sunflower County, Mississippi, in the early 1930s were generally regarded with respect and even a measure of pride by other black people in the county. Along with the thirteen part owners of land they comprised 39 percent of the landowning class in the area. Those who were landlords reputedly treated their tenants better than their white counterparts. One family which had been able to clear money only three times in fourteen years of sharecropping and renting cleared twice as much in the year it 'cropped for a black farmer than during either of the years it cleared money while working for whites. Another family sharecropping on a black plantation cleared $1,000 in 1917. The largest amount it was ever able to clear on a white plantation was the $860 it made in 1918.[4] Race thus appeared to modify class differences. Considerations of race made black owners less disposed to take advantage of black tenants. Conversely, black tenants were less inclined to accept unfair treatment from black landlords. Both classes knew that the biracial system, designed to assure white domination, offered neither of them protection.

There were, of course, exceptions to this attitude. In 1959, fourteen years after he was released from prison, Ned Cobb moved onto the 200-acre farm of a black man, from whom he rented nine acres of land for $6 an acre and a dilapidated house for $6 a month. Ned remained on the farm for ten years. During that time he repaired the house, built a small barn, and had a well dug. His landlord refused to reimburse him for any of these expenditures. Ned therefore concluded that "Some of these *Negroes* here in this country lets their money speak for them, not their color. Warren Jencks, he was just as hungry as the white man was." Yet Ned knew that there was a difference. Ned's black landlord always addressed him as "Mr. Cobb," and Ned called him "Brother Jencks." While economic exploitation was implicit in their relationship, the affront to the tenant's self-respect and sense of dignity, inherent in the interracial tenant-landlord arrangement, was notably absent. Another sharecropper, interviewed in the late 1930s, was more explicit: "I'd rather work with my own color," he declared. "They talk to you like you was a man. The white man talks to you like you was a boy."[5]

SHARECROPPERS AND RENTERS

Most black farmers in the South never enjoyed the experience of owning the land they cultivated. They were tenants and farm laborers. In seventeen counties in Mississippi in 1880 black sharecroppers and farm laborers outnumbered black farm owners 100 to one. By 1900 nearly 89 percent of the farms operated by blacks in the state were operated by tenants. In South Carolina well over three-quarters of the black farmers were tenants.

During the Reconstruction period, the freedmen had objected to working under wage labor contracts. Such work often involved laboring in gangs under close supervision, an arrangement reminiscent of slavery. Unable to acquire land of their own, the freedmen sought an arrangement that would allow them to cultivate a plot of land in relative freedom. Planters, often lacking a ready supply of cash, welcomed a system that would enable them to acquire the necessary labor to cultivate their plantations. The result was the emergence of a tenancy system with many variations. From the viewpoint of the tenant the arrangement which allowed him the most independence was the cash tenancy system whereby he rented land for a fixed sum of money which could be paid in cash or a part of the crop. In 1900 about half the black tenants in the United States were cash tenants. The overwhelming majority of these, of course, were in the South. Sharecropping was the other principal form of tenancy in the South. The crop produced on the land assigned the tenant was divided between the tenant and the landlord. Where the landlord furnished "land, shelter, rations, seed, tools, stock and stock feed" his share was usually from one-half to two-thirds of the crop. When he furnished less, he usually took one-third of the crop.

If the tenant had nothing to offer but his labor, he was essentially in the same category as the wage laborer, and frequently more dependent. In some cases the arrangement between landlord and tenant resembled features of the European manorial system of the Middle Ages. Planters supplied the tenant with a house, land, and the use of a mule to work the land. The tenant, in return, not only cultivated the land leased to him but also worked a certain number of days during the week for the landlord.

Whatever form the sharecropping arrangement took, it often degenerated into a system in which both black and white tenants were grossly exploited by the planter class. Much of the abuse in the system arose out of its close association with the crop lien system under which the tenant mortgaged his crop to his landlord or a merchant in return for an advance from the landlord or merchant of food, clothing, and other supplies during the year. Frequently the tenant's share of the crop, unilaterally computed by the landlord, was insufficient to pay off his debt at the end of the year, for the tenant's debt was usually padded with high mark-up prices and high interest charges (about 37 percent in the 1930s). The process was repeated year after year with the sharecropper going ever deeper into debt. His only chance for relief from the regimen would be to leave the plantation and forfeit the debt. On a new plantation the process would begin over again, and the tenant would remain trapped in the system.

Before the practice was outlawed in the early twentieth century, some states prohibited a tenant from leaving a plantation without having paid his debt. If he ignored his debt and left the plantation he would be subject to arrest for breach of contract, and if convicted, he might then be leased by the public authorities to the landlord whom he left or to some other planter. Even when the breach of contract legislation regarding tenants was struck down by the Supreme Court, the landlord could still get his tenant back by the simple expedient of accusing him of theft or some other crime. The result was that, standing alone, the sharecropping system had the effect of transforming a large segment of the rural black population into an economically servile class. When combined with the crop lien and convict lease systems, it resulted in a form of debt slavery or forced labor.

Blacks were not the only victims of these systems, but because they were politically powerless and socially proscribed, these forms of exploitation bore most heavily upon them. Those black sharecroppers who had nothing to offer but their labor found that they had little to say about its utilization. The landlord made all the basic decisions. He decided what crops were to be grown and how they were to be cultivated and marketed. He fixed the terms of credit, kept the records of credit extended, and made the final settlement. Prevailing racial etiquette forbade the black sharecroppers to question any of these arrangements. They took what was offered them in the way of housing, furnishings, equipment, and supplies.

Occasionally, however, a sharecropper would challenge the system and win. In the late 1880s, in a rare case, an illiterate black farmer convinced an Alabama jury that his record of transactions with his landlord, consisting "of a stick, one yard long, trimmed in hexagon fashion and filled with notches, each notch representing some purchase and in some ingenious way the time of purchase," was more accurate than the books which the landlord kept.[6] Nevertheless, in the overwhelming majority of cases, tenants who dared to take their complaints to the authorities merely wasted their time and often ran the additional risk of being whipped or even killed for their audacity. The only recourse left to them, then, if their landlord did not object, was to move to another plantation where the cycle of tenure and debt would be repeated. Thus the life of most sharecroppers was not a happy one. Their incomes were meager, their houses were often shacks unfit for human habitation, and "poverty, disease, and illiteracy" characterized their general condition.

Under these circumstances, it was extremely difficult for black farmers to progress from sharecropping to farm ownership in the Deep South. While some tried and succeeded, many more tried and failed. Those who succeeded often had assistance from relatives or friendly whites or, at the least, they were not exploited by their white landlords. Beginning in 1905 one black sharecropper in the vicinity of Indianola, Mississippi, took the month of June or July off every year for seven years to go on a fishing expedition. When his landlord finally tired of his absences and dismissed him, the farmer informed his landlord that his dismissal didn't matter because he would now be going to his own 240-acre farm which he had been clearing during his absences from the plantation. To his credit, the landlord, rather than becoming angry at his former tenant's deception, offered to lend him money to purchase mules and a plow.[7]

All too often, however, the sharecropper ran into formidable obstacles in his quest for land ownership. In 1880 the father of William H. Holtzclaw decided to give up sharecropping and to rent land on a cash basis preparatory to buying a farm. He was able to rent a 40-acre farm in Randolph County, Alabama, for an annual rental of three bales of cotton or $150. Unfortunately, during the next four years he suffered a series of setbacks. During the first year a mule and a horse died. During the second year Holtzclaw's father injured his foot and was incapacitated for several months. The next year several members of the family became ill from a fever, and one child died. During the same year another child was born. At the end of the fourth year, unable to pay all of the accumulated debts, the family lost its entire cotton crop and most of its corn to creditors. If the creditors had not heeded the mother's strong remonstrations, the family would have lost their vegetables, pigs, and chickens as well. The next year the family went back to share-cropping.[8] Thus overt racial oppression was not the only hazard with which striving farmers had to contend.

During the first three decades of the twentieth century farm tenancy among blacks in the South increased. In 1900 there were about 550,000 black tenants in the South, of whom about 51 percent were sharecroppers. A high point was reached in 1920 when some 703,000 black farmers were listed as tenants. There was a decline to 636,000 in 1925, followed by a rise to 699,000 in 1930. At the end of the 1930s, however, there were 192,000 fewer black tenants than when the decade began.

The decline in the 1930s occurred mostly during the latter half of the decade and reflected the effects of the depression and increasing mechanization. Both black and white tenants were similarly affected. Government policy under the Agricultural Adjustment Act and other farm programs encouraged a reduction in acreage so as to rid the country of surplus agricultural products and thereby raise prices to the farmers. Government subsidies were paid to farmers who restricted acreage and engaged in conservation practices. Rather than allow tenants to share in these payments, landlords dismissed many of them or kept the tenants' share of the federal benefits in payment for the tenants' debts. Under the latter circumstance many sharecroppers abandoned farming altogether.

Typical of such tenants was a man identified by Arthur Raper and Ira De A. Reid simply as A.D. In 1939, after raising seven bales of cotton which sold for $338.74, A.D. ended up owing his landlord $14.75. Had the landlord given him a share of the money that he received for participating in the soil conservation program, A.D. doubtless would have ended the year free and clear with a little money left over. Disheartened by the ever recurring debt, A.D. later gave the following description of his reaction: "I looked at my cotton receipts and my debt and I said 'A.D., you's goin' to town; you had a good year, but you ain't got nothin' and you never will have nothin' as long as you stay here.' So me and my old lady and the chillun jes' lef. . . . I's through with farmin'. Through. Yes sir, through." So A.D. moved his family into town, thus joining thousands of other black farmers who had preceded him.[9]

After World War II the decline in farm tenancy reached drastic proportions. Again, government agricultural policy and mechanization were the principal causes. In 1950 there were 365,500 black tenants in the South, 80 percent of them sharecroppers. By 1964 the number had declined to a mere 82,371 of whom about 69 percent were sharecroppers. Five years later there were only 17,252* black tenant farmers in the South, the majority of whom were cash tenants.[10]

---

*For the 11 former Confederate states the figure for 1969 is 17,129.

Where did all the tenants go? Many, of course, left their rural communities and migrated to Southern and Northern cities. Some remained in rural areas, performing nonfarm work. A considerable number, however, continued in agriculture as farm laborers working for wages. Indicative of what occurred was the situation in the Mississippi Delta where from 1954 to 1964 the number of black and white tenants declined by 60 percent while the number of hired farm workers rose by 62 percent. For the South as a whole there were 311,000 nonwhite farm workers in the spring of 1960, an increase of some 13,000 since 1950. For whites however, the number of hired farm workers declined from 392,000 in 1950 to 308,000 in 1960. These figures indicate the greater employment options available to whites. Some became farm owners while others found jobs in industry.

FARM LABORERS

The change from sharecropper to hired laborer did not, in recent years, necessarily mean a decline in the economic status of the worker. By receiving steady pay during the work season, avoiding the debt usually associated with the sharecropping system, finding work outside of agriculture during the slack season, and being covered by social security as a wage laborer, many black farm workers felt that they were economically better off than when they were sharecroppers. These new circumstances marked a sharp break with historical tradition. As mentioned previously, the freedmen rebelled against the wage labor system during the early Reconstruction period, because it was too reminiscent of slavery. They turned instead to sharecropping, which appeared to be a stepping stone to farm ownership. In the rice plantations of South Carolina and Georgia and the sugar plantations of Louisiana, the wage labor system persisted, however. Nevertheless, in Louisiana, the black workers became well organized and pressured the sugar planters through strikes and other means for higher wages and better working conditions throughout the late nineteenth century.

Generally, however, the lot of wage workers in the cotton and tobacco regions of the South was precarious. They suffered from low wages and insecure employment. During the 1870s and 1880s farm workers received an average wage of from $9 to $15 per month for men and from $5 to $10 for women. In cotton production, according to C. Vann Woodward,

Prevalent monthly wages for a man's work "from sun to sun" were $8.00 to $14.00 in Alabama; $8.00 to $15.00 in Arkansas; $6.00 to $10.00 in Florida; $5.00 to $10.00 in Georgia; $6.00 to $15.00 in Louisiana; $8.00 to $12.00 in Mississippi, South Carolina and Tennessee; $8.00 to $15.00 in Texas. Daily wages were usually 50 cents with board, or 75 cents without.[11]

During the 1890s, when cotton prices declined precipitously, wages were undoubtedly lower. Although the sharecropper might receive no money income at the end of a year's work because his share of the crop had to go to pay his debts, he probably came out ahead of the wage laborer, for he was furnished housing, furnishings, food, and equipment by the landlord and the merchant. Landlords who supplied these items to laborers usually reduced their wages accordingly. In 1923, for example, when farm wages were around $30, Hosea Hudson received $10 a month "plus one bushel of white corn meal and ten pounds of white slab salt pork" for working on a farm in the Georgia Black Belt. On such an income Hudson found it necessary to buy food on credit from his employer's store. At the end of every month he found himself in debt. He was able to break this cycle only when he secured additional income by selling roasted peanuts on weekends in front of the plantation store and the local church.[12]

During the first three decades of the twentieth century farm wages fluctuated in the South from $19.71 per month in 1909 to $45.46 in 1920. In 1930 wages were down to $30.75 per month. The low point reached during the depression years came in 1933 when wages dropped to $16.58 per month. Wages did not rise again to near the 1920 level until 1943 when they were $43.97 per month. Thereafter wages rose more rapidly reaching $63.46 in 1946 and $73.55 in 1948. As late as 1963 the average hourly wage for Southern farm workers was only $.63. Blacks, of course, earned less. In 1962 the average daily wage for black farm workers in the South was $4.20, some $2.55 less than the average daily wage of white farm workers. In farm labor as in other spheres, the issue of race was omnipresent in the South.

Farm workers, like sharecroppers, were also victimized by the system of peonage. The practice was particularly widespread in the late nineteenth and early twentieth centuries in the cotton belt and turpentine regions of the South. Many workers became peons as a result of obtaining an advance on their wages in the form of money, furnishings, or housing when they entered an employment contract or when they bought food and other commodities on credit from the plantation commissary. Others fell into peonage when they were released from local jails to planters who paid their fines. Those who were unable to accumulate enough money to pay off their obligations, or who were not permitted to leave the plantation even if they did, found themselves in a system of virtual slavery. Those who tried to escape the system were often beaten and sometimes killed. Even after the illegality of the practice was repeatedly affirmed by the U.S. Supreme Court in a succession of cases, local law enforcement authorities, jurors, justices of the peace, and occasionally state judges conspired with landlords to keep the system in effect. The practice was so deeply rooted in the mores of the people of the Black Belt that the efforts of the Justice Department to suppress it were generally unsuccessful. Although peonage presumably declined before the

Great Depression, the Justice Department was still receiving complaints from victims as late as 1973. Ironically, among those recently convicted for the practice were two black men, who received sentences of three years imprisonment for holding whites in servitude.[13]

THE AGRARIAN IDEAL

Despite the problems that beset those who remained on the land, some black Southerners regarded farming as more than a means of simply making a living but as a preferred way of life. During the 1930s several former slaves spoke of their attachment to farming. Eighty-eight-year-old Eileen Payne, who lived on a farm in Texas with her husband for fifty-two years and continued to operate it after he died, declared that "We loved farm life." Similarly, another ex-slave, despite the fact that her father was a sharecropper, told her interviewer that "I is allus been crazy bout farmin, helped my paw every day when I was young with everything." During the same decade, a young woman, who as a child had cried when her parents moved the family into a dilapidated log cabin on a rental farm, testified that her years on the farm "were the happiest in her childhood. . . . She enjoyed the freedom of the country and liked working in the fields." And Ned Cobb, whose life in the rural South had been filled with trials and tribulations, nevertheless at the age of eighty-five still expressed a preference for country living. "I'm a country-raised fellow, all of my born days, and I love the country," he declared, even after he had noted with approval the greater freedom for blacks in Northern cities. "If I lived in the city I wouldn't have no trees to look on, no trees in my yard and maybe no yard; no garden and no small crops," he explained.[14]

Whether they knew it or not, these black Southerners were expositors of the agrarian ideal, articulated by Jefferson in the early years of the nation's existence and revived with renewed fervor by a number of Southerners during the half century after Reconstruction. Its most prominent apostle among blacks was, of course, Booker T. Washington.

Washington believed that contact with nature was both stimulating and ennobling. "There is something about the smell of soil—a contact with a reality that gives one strength and development that can be gained in no other way," he declared in 1903. "Life out in the sweet, pure, bracing air," he continued, "is better from both a physical and moral point of view than long days spent in the close atmosphere of a factory or store." As was his habit, Washington not only preached the gospel of agrarianism, but also attempted to practice it. "Just as often as I can when I am at home," he asserted, "I like to get my hoe and dig in my garden, to come into contact with real earth, or to touch my pigs and fowl." He liked to watch the flowers and the vegetables in his garden grow, to experience "a feeling of kinship between the man and his plants," to observe in the mornings the changes that had occurred during the night. He confessed that "This sense of newness, of expectancy, brings to me a daily inspiration whose significance is impossible to convey in words."

Like Jefferson, Washington had an aversion for the city. The black man was at his worst, he felt, "when in contact with city life." Therefore for the forseeable future black people should remain in the country where they were at their best. Moreover, he believed that in simple tillers of the soil reposed not only virtue but wisdom. "When talking to a farmer," he noted, "I feel that I am talking with a real man and not an artificial one—one who can keep me in close touch with real things. From a simple, honest cultivator of the soil, I am sure of getting first-hand, original information. I have secured more useful illustrations for addresses in a half-hour's talk with some white or coloured farmer than from hours of reading books." Washington therefore advised ministers to constantly keep in touch with the masses. "A vacation employed in visiting farmers . . . ," he declared, "would often prepare one as thoroughly for his winter's work as a vacation spent in visiting the cities of Europe."[15]

As the comments of the former slaves and Ned Cobb suggest the advocates of agrarianism were limited neither to Washington's ideological disciples nor to his era. In the midst of the Great Depression of the 1930s, when black farmers as well as city dwellers were struggling to survive, black intellectuals and community leaders continued to preach the agrarian creed. The Reverend Vernon Johns, president of Virginia Theological Seminary and College, waxed lyrical in describing the advantages of country living over city life. Unlike the city, "where the sun is viewed only before he tumbles headlong down the straight edges of a skyscraper," the country, exclaimed Johns, "is where the tomato blushes red in green and perfumed vestments. . . . This is where the forest grows night and day to feed the poor man's fire and build the shelter for his children." Johns asked his readers to contrast "Unfinished rows of dingy brick walls, stretched in one solid, sordid piece of masonry from Avenue to Avenue . . . [with] a rural sunrise, green fields and brown furrows, flocks to which the firstlings have come; dogwoods in blossom over endless acres, fields of grass golden in the harvest." "The city's reigning scent is the smell of exhaust pipes and the breath of abbatoirs," he declared, while "The odor of the country is the fragrance of new mown hay."

With such a vision before him Johns urged his readers to build a black civilization in America with "A Negro Agrarian Culture" as its foundation. Because all other groups in American society rejected blacks, "We must found our own culture," he proclaimed. "We must find the way to sustain our bodies and enrich our society. We will find these in honest and enlightened cooperation on the soil." To carry out his proposals, Johns recommended the formation of a corporation for the purpose of building and administering a group economy that would involve an exchange of goods, services, and ideas between rural and urban blacks.[16]

Even W. E. B. Du Bois was captivated by some of the tenets of agrarianism. In 1947, in a speech before the Southern Negro Youth Congress, Du Bois reiterated his vision, suggested as early as 1906, of a South in which blacks would take the lead in building a new society in which neither they nor their poor white counterparts would continue to suffer exploitation. Unlike Washington, however, Du Bois did not envisage a society of individual entrepeneurs, but advocated instead a society resting in part upon "a new co-operative agriculture on renewed land owned by the state with capital furnished by the state, mechanized and co-ordinated with city life." Du Bois exhorted black youth to remain in the South, for "Here is the magnificent climate; here is the fruitful earth; and here . . . is the need of the thinker, the worker, and the dreamer."[17]

THE AGRARIAN REALITY

Although Washington and Du Bois held opposing conceptions of the agrarian ideal, they knew as well as anyone that the life of the Southern black farmer, especially that of the sharecropper and farm laborer in the Black Belt, was anything but idyllic. In exploring the plantation districts around Tuskegee shortly after his arrival in 1881, Washington found most tenants living in one-room cabins where the entire family, sometimes including distant relatives, necessarily slept in the same room. Their basic diet consisted of fat pork, corn bread, and occasionally black-eyed peas. Lacking dishes, silverware, and other utensils, many families seldom sat down to eat a meal together. All those big enough to work spent the day from sunup to sundown in the cotton field. In the one crop economy, few grew vegetables. "In many cases," he observed, "cotton was planted up to the very door of the cabin." On Saturdays the people went into town where, with little money to shop, they milled around for several hours. Some wasted the little money they had on whiskey and other useless and detrimental products. Sunday, he observed, "was usually spent in going to some big meeting."

Washington also observed that school sessions, varying in length from three to five months, were held in unheated, dilapidated log cabins or in churches. The teachers were poorly trained and "poor in moral character." The churches and their ministers were similarly deficient.[18]

Conditions in Macon County, Alabama, were characteristic of most of the Deep South rural communities. Twenty-two years later W. E. B. Du Bois gave practically the same eyewitness description of the lives of black farm workers and sharecroppers in Dougherty County, Georgia:

All over the face of the land is the one-room cabin—now standing in the shadow of the Big House, now staring at the dusty road, now rising dark and sombre amid the green of the cotton-fields. It is nearly always old and bare, built of rough boards, and neither plastered nor ceiled. Light and ventilation are supplied by the single door and by the square hole in the wall with its wooden shutter. There is no glass, porch, or ornamentation without. Within is a fireplace, black and smoky, and usually unsteady with age. A bed or two, a table, a wooden chest, and a few chairs compose the furniture; while a stray show-bill or a newspaper makes up the decoration for the walls. Now and then one may find such a cabin kept scrupulously neat, with merry steaming fireplace and hospitable door; but the majority are dirty and dilapidated, smelling of eating and sleeping, poorly ventilated, and anything but homes.[19]

In Dougherty County, too, Saturday was a day for going to town to shop, to gossip, and with some men, to imbibe strong drink. Sunday was meeting day when the people gathered at the crossroads church to worship and socialize. During the late summer or early fall they held their revival meetings, usually of a week's duration, in which sinners "got religion" and were recruited into the church. Friends and relatives would come from the towns and cities to renew contacts with those they had left behind. Weddings, funerals, and in some communities school closing exercises were occasions for further socializing. Between these events there would be an occasional party at a cabin where the people would play games, eat, drink, and perhaps dance. Christmas week, as in slavery days, was the most celebrated holiday, but Emancipation Day and Easter were also observed.[20]

The living conditions of the poorer renters and the poorest farm owners approximated those of the sharecroppers and laborers. Most farm owners, however, lived better. Depending on the family's prosperity and prospensity toward display, houses ranged in size from three to ten rooms. Many of the families were large, and the larger number of rooms prevented overcrowding. For farm owners as well as tenants large families were often an economic asset, for children could be put to work at an early age. The diets of the owners were richer and more varied than that of most tenants. In addition to the standard fare of pork and corn bread, farm-owning families consumed wheat bread, chicken, eggs, vegetables, fruit, milk, and sometimes fish, beef, and wild game.[21] While their social activities were similar to those of the tenants, with the exception of church attendance there was not likely to be a great deal of socializing between the more prosperous owners and sharecroppers. Farm owners tended to be more highly educated than tenants. A few were graduates of normal schools and colleges. Among the latter there might be some reading material in the home. The farm owners, of course, most closely approximated Booker T. Washington's image of the agrarian man.

IMAGE INTO REALITY

Washington and a number of other black Southerners devoted their mature years to efforts to make the agrarian ideal a living reality for the black South. Rather than protest, they chose to pursue their objectives through a program of conservative reform. Although similar in many of its features and much of its rhetoric to the country life movement of the white rural progressives, it derived its impulse from the unique historical experience and contemporary condition of the black community. If black Southerners were not to remain in a position approximating slavery, change was imperative. Washington's program, then, merely represented a continuation of the post-Civil War struggle of the freedmen to carve out a place of personal dignity, economic independence, and social progress within the Southern social order. It was simply another sequence in the continuing process of reconstructing the black community.

Tuskegee Institute under Washington and his successors, therefore, trained black boys and girls in character building and in the industrial, agricultural, and homemaking arts and sent them out into the community. It also sought to reach the community directly through farmers conferences and extension programs. It drew upon the services of its faculty and staff, which included the eminent agricultural scientist, George Washington Carver.

But simply teaching better methods of crop production, animal husbandry, chicken raising, and marketing procedures was not enough. The whole life of the people needed to be transformed. Therefore, the agenda at the farmers' conferences which Tuskegee sponsored annually from 1892 included topics that went far beyond farming methods. "I wanted these coloured farmers and their wives to consult about methods and means of securing homes, of freeing themselves from debt, of encouraging intelligent production, of paying taxes, of cultivating habits of thrift, honesty, and virtue, of building school-houses and securing education and higher Christian character, of cementing the friendship between the races," declared Washington. At these conferences the women discussed not only homemaking habits, but personal grooming, sexual purity, marital obligations, and child rearing.[22]

To reach those farmers who did not attend the conferences Washington in 1906 established the "Movable School," a wagon loaded with farm implements, supplies, animals and poultry, and other agricultural items, and staffed by members of the school's agriculture department headed by George Washington Carver. Financed by Morris K. Jesup, a New York philanthopist, the wagon visited communities throughout Macon County to demonstrate improved methods of farming. This first extension service to black farmers was soon incorporated into the demonstration and extension service of the United States government. In 1918 the wagon was replaced with a truck, and the service was extended throughout the state. In keeping with Washington's emphasis on the total life of the community, the Movable

School program eventually included a nurse, a home economist, and recreational equipment for the purpose of enriching the lives of men, women, and children through sports and other games.[23]

In 1896 Tuskegee also began a rural social settlement house program on a 2,000-acre Macon County plantation cultivated by seventy-five sharecropping families. Many of the tenants were bound to the plantation because the white landlord had secured their release from jail by paying their fines. The settlement was initially under the general supervision of Mrs. Washington. Its central feature was a school to provide education for children during the day and for adults at night. Associated with the school was a "Mothers Union," which provided training in homemaking, gardening, and character building.[24]

Meanwhile Tuskegee alumni were attempting to replicate the Tuskegee model on a smaller scale throughout the South. By 1904 they had succeeded in establishing sixteen "industrial schools" in a number of Southern communities. William J. Edwards founded the Snow Hill Normal and Industrial Institute in Wilcox County, Alabama, in 1893. Soon he was sponsoring farmers and workers conferences modeled on those at Tuskegee and even organized the Black Belt Improvement Association, which sought to promote the economic, social, and moral uplift of the local community in the same way Tuskegee's Southern Improvement Company was doing in selected Southern communities. In 1903 William H. Holtzclaw, who had taught at the Snow Hill school, established the Utica Normal and Industrial Institute in Hinds County, Mississippi. Employing the same techniques as those in effect at Snow Hill, he sought to promote the progress of the black community in an area which he regarded as "the darkest section of the South for a colored man." Voorhees Industrial School at Denmark, South Carolina, is notable in that it was founded in 1896 by a female graduate of Tuskegee, Elizabeth E. Wright. It, too, attempted to uplift the black community through the same pattern of activities as the other schools.[25]

What Tuskegee and its graduates were doing for the lower South and other selected communities, Hampton Institute and its alumni were doing for the upper South, particularly Virginia. Because of the more diversified, small farm character of the economy and the somewhat less oppressive character of the racial order the task was somewhat easier in the upper South. In Virginia, for example, the sharecropping system was less prevalent, for in 1910 about 67 percent of its black farmers owned their farms. Contributing in a small way to this development were the activities and influence of Thomas Calhoun Walker.

Today, most people over forty-five years old in Gloucester and adjacent counties probably remember T. C. Walker, who died in 1953 at the age of ninety-one. Born a slave in 1862 and reared in a two-room cabin after the war, Walker enrolled at Hampton while Booker T. Washington was still teaching there. On graduating from Hampton in 1883, Walker returned to his home in Gloucester and, defying the community's notion of what an educated man should do, rented 10 acres of land and began farming. He soon became a schoolteacher and thereafter studied law and participated in politics as a Republican, holding such local offices as justice of the peace and county commissioner. From 1896 to 1902 he served as collector of customs for the port of Rappahannock.

Walker is chiefly remembered in eastern Virginia for his social betterment and uplift activities. Believing that "You can't put over a home building and reclamation project without first reclaiming the men who are to do the job," Walker in 1889 launched a temperance crusade aimed at ridding Gloucester County of its thirty-five barrooms, which he felt were largely responsible for the fact that 95 percent of the black men in the county drank. Failing to get the cooperation of the churches, Walker organized temperance societies in the schools. With the assistance of his wife, he also organized home and social clubs for the women of the community. Concerned with the well-being of youth, he took delinquent boys from the city jail in Richmond and placed them in foster homes in the county. He also took several boys into his own home from time to time.

In 1889, in order to encourage home ownership, Walker founded the Gloucester Land and Brick Company, which purchased land for resale on credit to residents in the community. For very modest monthly payments farmers could buy 10 or more acres of land, provided they promised not to build houses of less than three rooms on their plots. Walker's emphasis on home ownership earned him the sobriquet "Buy-land Walker." Against considerable white opposition, Walker also worked for expanded educational facilities for the black people of Gloucester, and was a leader among those blacks who established the Gloucester County Training School.

Walker, too, preached the ideology of agrarianism. "For me," he declared, "there has always been . . . a glorious sense of romance connected with the acquisition of land with trees and grass and flowers on it and yes, even weeds." "When the truly emancipated Negro is trained intelligently for country life and owns a little home of his own there, he will harvest joy and thanksgiving along with bumper crops."[26]

The Negro Organization Society of Virginia supplemented Walker's activities on the statewide level. Founded by Robert R. Moton of Hampton Institute in 1913, the society was a federation of various religious, educational, and secular organizations devoted to social betterment. Its motto was "Better Schools, Better Health, Better Homes, Better Farms." While it did not ignore urban problems, the society devoted its major attention to improving rural life. It inspired and helped to finance the construction of a number of rural schools and a state tuberculosis sanitorium for blacks in addition to engaging in home and farm demonstration work.[27]

Very similar to Walker's activities, but on a more extensive scale, was the work of Robert Lloyd Smith of Texas. A native of Charleston, South Carolina, Smith graduated from Atlanta University in 1880 and shortly thereafter settled in Texas. An active Republican, he served in the Texas legislature from 1895 to 1899 and as a deputy U.S. marshal from 1902 to 1909. He founded and headed from 1885 to 1902 a normal school in Oakland, Texas. An apostle of Booker T. Washington's program of self-help he formed in 1890 the Negro Farmers Improvement Society of Texas, which he headed until his death in 1943. In due course, subsidiary organizations such as the Women's Barnyard Auxiliary and the Village Improvement Society appeared. Smith also sponsored annual fairs and farmers' conferences. During the first decade of the twentieth century, the Farmers Improvement Society established an industrial school at Ladonia and a bank at Waco. By 1911 the organization had 12,000 members in 800 locals throughout the state. While land ownership, freedom from debt, and farm prosperity were Smith's principal economic goals, his organizations also stressed character building, moral uplift, reduction in crime, the strengthening of home life, and better race relations. As a concrete expression of its ideals, the Farmers Society transformed Oakland into a model community of well-kept homes and farms.[28]

After the first decade of the twentieth century, the work of Smith, Walker, Washington, and their disciples was increasingly supplemented by the activities of black county agents and home demonstration workers employed by the federal and state governments and by the programs of the state agricultural and mechanical colleges. Although it is impossible to isolate and measure the combined impact of all these forces, there is no doubt that some black farmers benefited. At the annual conferences sponsored by Tuskegee, Hampton, and the various industrial schools farmers gave testimony to the beneficial influence of the economic self-help and social uplift program upon their lives. A typical but modest success story was that of an Alabama farmer who testified that:

> I own sixty-seven acres of land. I got it by working hard and living close. I did not eat at any big tables. I often lived on bread and milk. I have five rooms to my house. I started with one, and that was made of logs. I add a room every year. I was lucky in marrying a woman whose father gave her a cow. I ain't got no fine clock or organ. I did once own a buggy, but it was a shabby one, and now we ride in a wagon, or I go horse-back on a horse I raised that is worth two hundred and fifty dollars. I have seven children in school.[29]

During the Washington era farm ownership among blacks did increase as a result of a complex of forces. In Glouster County, Virginia, the number of black farm owners rose from 195 in 1880 to 1,895 by 1913. For the entire state, black farm ownership increased by nearly 8 percent between 1900 and 1910. For the South as a whole Du Bois estimated in 1911 that blacks increased their ownership of land from about 8,000,000 acres in 1890 to 12,000,000 acres in 1910.[30] Indeed the percentage increase in black-owned farms from 1900 to 1910 was greater than that for whites (16.3 percent to 11.4 percent). Detracting from this picture, however, was the fact that tenancy among blacks rose during the same period by 37 percent, 7.1 percent more than the rise among whites. Moreover, when looked at over a longer period, from 1910 to 1930 for example, it is clear that as a group black farmers actually declined rather than progressed. The tenancy rate rose substantially, despite the migration of many tenants to the cities in both the North and the South, and the number of black-owned farms declined by 44,000.

By 1930 the relative conditions of the bulk of black farmers in the Deep South were no better than they were in 1881 or in 1900. The sharecroppers who comprised the bulk of the black tenants still lived in ramschackle one- and two-room cabins; subsisted on a basic diet of fat pork, corn bread, molasses, or sweet potatoes; worked from sunup to sundown during the week and ended the year in debt to the landlord; congregated in town or at the plantation store on Saturdays; and worshipped and socialized at the crossroads church on Sundays. The Depression exacerbated their condition, and during the next decade a million and a half blacks left the South. In the 1950s and 1960s those who remained were little better off.

As early as 1936, Thomas M. Campbell, director of Booker T. Washington's Movable School and the first black farm demonstration agent in the United States, was forced to confess that the quest for an agrarian Eden was unrealistic under prevailing conditions in the South. He complained that:

> There are to be found professional promoters who have drifted into the vicious practice of advising all Negroes to remain in the country at any cost. In their frenzied zeal, they are wont to picture to them the beauties of nature, the golden sunset, the babbling brooks, and the singing birds. But all of these have little of beauty and grandeur to the Negro farmer, who is constantly in debt, hungry, sick and cold, and without civil protection. The fact might just as well be acknowledged that unless Negroes who are urged to return to the farm from the cities, and those who are now living in the rural districts, are accorded fuller protection of the law and are given more freedom to improve without intimidation, such exhortations will not prove very effective.[31]

Although Campbell did not elaborate, his comments implied that the economic self-help and social uplift philosophy and program rested on at least two faulty assumptions: (1) that the status of the black farmer was due primarily to his own shortcomings, such as indolence, prodigality, and ignorance of proper farming methods and social relations, and (2) that an oppressive racial order would yield to a realization by whites that black progress was in their own enlightened self-interest. In short, except for Du Bois, the proponents of agrarianism underestimated the intractability of the relationship between white prejudice and the economic order. How could men and women kept in constant subjugation at subsistence levels be expected to develop those habits of thrift and industry deemed necessary for upward economic mobility, especially when they repeatedly saw the fruits of their labor expropriated by their landlords and employers? And how could they force a change in the system if they lacked political rights?

But there were other reasons why the quest for the agrarian ideal would not be successful. Natural calamities like the boll weevil and economic catastrophes like the Great Depression drove both black and white farmers off the land. The mechanization of agriculture further accelerated the process, not only replacing tenants and farm laborers, but making farming a gainful enterprise only for those with large acreage and with easy access to credit.

The sharecroppers, the renters, and the farm laborers realized the hopelessness of their position long before the leaders and the intellectuals. For the majority the most realistic solution to their dilemma was not the practice of scientific agriculture and the Protestant ethic, but escape—the abandonment of farming both as a way of making a living and as a way of life. So during the twentieth century they left the farms and the South in increasing numbers in search of the elusive goals of personal freedom and dignity, physical security, fruitful employment, and educational opportunities for their children. Several hundred thousand left the South during the decade of World War I. They continued to leave in the 1920s. The damming of the migratory flow by the depression of the 1930s merely contributed to the flood during the three succeeding decades. From 1940 to 1970 about four and a half million blacks from Southern farms and cities left the region. Of those who remained at the end of the period only 33 percent continued to live in the rural areas and small towns, and of these only one out of nine continued to make their living by farming.

AGRARIAN PROTEST

Before abandoning their quest for a fruitful existence on the farm, and fleeing to the cities, black tenants and hired farm workers in the South periodically protested the handicaps under which they labored. The formation of the Colored Farmers Alliance in the late 1880s, which eventually claimed a membership of 1,250,000, and the support which black farmers gave the Populist party in 1890, constituted an effort by black farmers to improve their lot through self-help, collective bargaining, and political action. Black farmers in Houston County, Texas, founded the Colored Alliance in 1886. They later chose R. M. Humphrey, a white man, as their general superintendent. After securing a national charter in 1888, the Colored Alliance soon established chapters in nearly every Southern state. As a self-help and racial uplift organization it established cooperatives to enable farmers to purchase goods more cheaply. It encouraged farm ownership and frugality and helped farmers obtain loans to pay off their mortgages. It also sought to improve educational opportunities for blacks by establishing schools in some communities and by raising money to finance a longer school term.

The Alliance's demise followed shortly after its unsuccessful attempt in 1891 to launch a cotton pickers' strike throughout the Cotton Belt. Humphrey demanded that wages for picking cotton be raised from $.50 to $1 per 100 pounds. Many black farm owners who depended upon hired labor to pick their cotton opposed the proposed strike. Many of the farm laborers were apathetic. And some Alliance men, like Andrew J. Carothers, feared that the strike "will engender a race feeling, bitter and deep and lasting, and one which may result in riot and bloodshed." These internal divisions and the opposition of the Southern Alliance prevented the strike from getting off the ground in all but one state. Only in Lee County, Arkansas, as a result of the tireless and courageous efforts of a young black farmer named Lee Patterson, did the strike materialize. It was quickly and violently suppressed, however, by the white planters against whom it was directed. Several of the strike leaders, including Patterson, were killed.

A similar fate had befallen the Colored Alliance in Leflore County, Mississippi, two years earlier. White merchants and planters were alarmed at the success of Oliver Cromwell, an Alliance organizer, in persuading black farmers to shop at a cooperative store of the white Southern Alliance rather than with local merchants. They were also frightened, when in response to white threats, seventy-five black men marched into the town of Shell Mound in September 1889 and delivered a note, signed "Three Thousand Armed Men," pledging to protect Cromwell from violence. In response to rumors of an impending race war, the governor sent national guard units into the area who, along with a sheriff's posse, arrested some forty blacks. When the troops were withdrawn the posse continued its work, arresting and killing a number of people. Cromwell, however, escaped.

During the first half of the twentieth century black farmers made several attempts to improve their economic and social status through organized protest. In 1919 black sharecroppers and tenants in Phipps County, Arkansas, formed the Progressive Farmers and Household Union of America in order to demand accountability from landlords so as to enable tenants to calculate their earnings for themselves. This display of independence by black tenants alarmed the white community, which in turn organized to suppress the incipient "rebellion." The result was the Elaine, Arkansas, riot of 1919. The black farmers were attacked by whites from Arkansas and by others who "poured" in from nearby areas in Mississippi and Tennessee. With the aid of federal troops many blacks were arrested by Arkansas officials. They were tried and convicted; twelve were sentenced to death and fifty-four received sentences of one to twenty years. Fortunately, by appeals to higher courts, including the U.S. Supreme Court, and by action of the governor, the twelve who were sentenced to death were eventually released.

The depression in the 1930s inspired several protest movements by black tenants and sharecroppers. In Alabama, the Sharecroppers' Union, composed primarily of black farmers organized in 1931 with the assistance of the Communist party, worked to improve the conditions of 'croppers and tenants. Their specific demands included the right to raise gardens for their own use, to seed and sell their own crops, to enjoy a three-hour rest period during the middle of the day, to receive wages for picking cotton in cash, and to receive advances of food until settlement time. In addition to these economic demands the union also insisted that the school year be extended to nine months and that a free school bus be provided for black children. Despite harassment by local law enforcement officials and landlords, who murdered several tenants during the Camp Hill and Reeltown shootouts in 1931 and 1932, the farmers persisted in their organized efforts. By the fall of 1933 the union claimed 5,500 members. It sponsored a cotton pickers' strike in 1934 and a cotton choppers' strike in 1935. It continued to exist until 1939 but won little from the planters other than the right to raise gardens and to receive food from the landlords during the nonproductive seasons of the year.

One of the local black tenants who played a conspicuous role in the union was the recently celebrated Ned Cobb. Cobb recalled in 1971 that he had become aware of the oppressive and exploitative nature of the plantation system when he was only ten or twelve years old. "It was just like slavery," he recalled, "God knows it weren't a bit of difference. In place of ever changin and getting better, it was gettin worser and worser as I come up in this world." Cobb joined the Sharecroppers Union in 1932 and worked to recruit his friends and neighbors into the organization. He was one of the leaders of the black farmers who participated in the 1932 shootout at Reeltown, Alabama. Wounded in the affray, he was arrested, convicted, and served twelve years in prison. Throughout his imprisonment he remained loyal to the union. In 1971, eighty-five-year-old Cobb expressed scorn for those blacks who were too frightened or too apathetic to join the union or who later repudiated it. In explaining his own decision to join he recalled that "My head and heart had been well loaded about the condition and the welfare of the poor—I couldn't stand it no more. I jumped in that organization and my name rings in it today. I haven't apologized to my Savior for joinin; it was workin for right. A man had to do it."[32]

Black farmers also participated in the activities of the Southern Tenant Farmers Union (STFU), formed in Arkansas in 1934 as an interracial organization of tenants and farm laborers. Its main objectives were to obtain a fair share of the federal payments to farmers and to prevent tenants from being evicted as a result of government agricultural policies. The union spread through several states and in 1937 claimed 30,827 members. It waged several strikes of cotton choppers and cotton pickers but with no durable success. Its chief contribution was to expose to the public the abuses in the sharecropping system such as peonage, forced labor, and lack of civil liberties, and to call public attention to the sharecroppers' social ills such as poverty, illiteracy, and disease. These exposures inspired a number of New Deal efforts to improve the lot of the tenants and farm workers. By 1942, however, the membership of the STFU had declined to 15,000 of whom only 2,000 were regular dues-paying members. Its decline was attributable to black-white conflict in the South, the poverty and ignorance of many of the farmers the frequent movement by tenants from one locality to another, the paternalism and dependence characterizing the landlord-tenant relationship, and the violence and threats of violence from landlord elements and their agents.

Although the national leaders of the STFU were white, blacks were conspicuously active on the local level. When the first two locals were organized in July 1954, black and white farmers debated whether they should have two racially separate unions or one interracial union. The decision to form one union came after a speech by a seventy-year-old black veteran of the Progressive Farmers and Household Union, who had seen his organization destroyed in the Elaine, Arkansas, riot of 1919. As the Populists had done in the 1890s, the farmer pointed out that both black and white sharecroppers enjoyed a common humanity and suffered a common oppression. He told the assembled whites that:

> We don't have nothing against each other but we got plenty against the landlord. The same chain that holds my people holds your people too. If we're chained together on the outside we ought to stay chained together in the union. It won't do no good for us to divide because there's where the trouble has been all the time. The landlord is always betwixt us, beatin' us and starvin' us and makin' us fight each other. There ain't but one way for us to get him where he can't help himself and that's for us to get together and stay together.[33]

The first vice-president of the STFU was Britt McKinney, a Baptist minister who had pastored some thirty-six black churches in eastern Arkansas during his ministerial career. Black tenants in the region trusted him, and he was largely responsible for the organizing success of the union in its early years. By 1938, however, McKinney, who always had resisted white paternalism, had become disillusioned with the white leadership of the union. He accused them of advancing the interest of the poor whites at the expense of the black sharecroppers who, after all, comprised over 80 percent of the union's membership and who were the chief victims of the violence directed against the organization. McKinney was irked also by the concession of the white leadership to Southern social mores, including the maintenance of segregated toilet facilities in the union's Memphis office. In assessing the role of the black farmers in the union he complained that:

> They have stood mutely and alowed what they have paid into the union to be spent to see to it that the poor whites would not be brutalized, they have spent time in the work houses and on the counties' work farms and then come out and alowed to be formed into a circus and paraded the country for difence, but the difence was to difend the white man and his family from the hard ships we are taking and will continue to take until we learn that we are the bigest fools in the world.[34]

Calling upon blacks to form their own organization and take risks only for their own benefit, McKinney left the STFU in the summer of 1938 and set about attempting to form an all-black union.

McKinney was succeeded as vice-president by Owen H. Whitfield, one of the most exciting officials of the STFU. A black Mississippian, Whitfield began farming as a sharecropper in 1923 in Missouri. He also became a preacher and while sharecropping he pastored several churches in southeast Missouri. Frustrated by the futility of his existence as a sharecropper, Whitfield joined the STFU in 1937. After his election as vice-president, and aided by his position as a minister, he was successful in organizing twenty SFTU locals with about 5,000 members in southeast Missouri by the end of 1938.

Whitfield, too, became disenchanted with the white leaders of the SFTU. In January 1939 he led a roadside demonstration of about 1,200 sharecroppers (most of them black) who were protesting against their eviction by landlords who had turned to wage labor in order to collect government parity payments that would ordinarily have gone to the sharecroppers. By camping in family groups along the roadsides of two Missouri highways for several days in cold, rainy, and snowy weather, the sharecroppers successfully dramatized their plight to the nation. The Farm Security Administration responded to the demonstration by providing financial assistance to the farmers, by building a model labor home project in the area, and by establishing other programs that were designed to improve the lives of farm families and enable them to become landowners. Despite these gains, however, no lasting changes in the lives of the sharecroppers resulted. Nevertheless, Whitfield stands forth as an important figure in the long procession of black leaders who used the nonviolent protest demonstration as an instrument for seeking improvement in the lives of the downtrodden in the black community.

FIVE

Workers and Capitalists

CRAFTSMEN AND INDUSTRIAL LABORERS

Many black Southerners who lived in rural areas, as well as those who lived in cities, made their living in nonagricultural occupations. Indeed, as Robert Starobin has shown, a considerable number, slave and free, had been employed in nonfarm work during the slavery era. Industrial enterprises, located mainly in rural, small town, or plantation areas, were using between 160,000 to 200,000 slaves (about 5 percent of the slave population) in the 1850s. Slaves were used extensively in Southern textile mills, and in hemp manufacturing, sugar refining, rice milling, and gristmilling. They were used almost exclusively as the labor force in Southern tobacco factories and as the principal workers in iron manufacturing establishments in the upper South. They were engaged in crafts such as carpentry, brick manufacturing, blacksmithing, and brickmasonry, and were also employed as machinists. Coal-, gold-, lead-, and iron-mining establishments were heavily dependent on slaves, and slaves were the principal labor force in salt production and in the extraction and production of turpentine. Slaves built Southern railroads, canals, turnpikes, and ships. They manned ferryboats, tugboats, drays, and steamboats. The South Atlantic fisheries heavily depended on them. Even municipalities, states, and the federal government extensively used slaves— as firemen, road builders and repairmen, sanitary workers, construction workers, and as builders of arsenals, naval installations, and fortifications. During the Civil War slave craftsmen and military laborers played a crucial role in enabling the Confederacy to sustain its war effort.[1]

After 1865 black Southerners continued in many of the traditional occupations in which they had been employed before the Civil War. And after Reconstruction, they played a major role in the economic and industrial growth of the New South. Professors Paul B. Worthman and James R. Green point out that:

> By 1900 almost one-third of the railroad firemen and brakemen and well over half the trackmen in the South were black. In Alabama 55 per cent of the coal miners and 80 per cent of the iron ore miners were Afro-Americans. They also held a majority of the unskilled jobs in the Gulf Coast lumber industry and in the iron and steel industry of Alabama. Two-thirds of the Virginia shipbuilders, the New Orleans dock workers, and the North Carolina tobacco workers were Afro-Americans. Even the ranching and cattle industry of the Southwest, especially along the Texas Gulf Coast, depended on black labor; more than one-fourth of the 35,000 cowboys who drove cattle north from Texas between 1866 and 1895 were black. Black drivers predominated as teamsters and draymen in Southern cities. In Atlanta, Memphis, and Birmingham, for example, they held over 80 per cent of those jobs. And black craftsmen played a significant role in the construction of Southern cities. By 1900, 15 per cent of the carpenters, 35 per cent of the brickmasons, and 38 per cent of the plasterers were blacks.[2]

Clearly then black workers were at the core of Southern economic development in the late nineteenth and early twentieth centuries. Moreover, considerably more blacks were in the South's work force than whites. Worthman and Green further point out that

> by 1900, 71 per cent of the black population over ten years of age was employed, compared to 60 per cent of the foreign-born whites and 48 per cent of the native whites. Many more black women were employed than white women (54 per cent as compared with 17 per cent), and they worked in a wide variety of jobs—as domestics, seamstresses, cotton pickers, and laborers in laundries and tobacco factories.[3]

It is obvious from the foregoing that if work alone were the key to progress and success, Southern blacks would have risen rapidly in the Southern social order and would probably have come to dominate the region economically.

What prevented blacks from rising in the economic and social order was not the failure to work, but the existence of a social system that was specifically designed to keep them in a state of economic dependence and subordination. Unskilled black workers—men, women, and children—were assigned the hardest, most dangerous, and most menial tasks, confined to the most degraded living quarters in company towns and Southern cities, and paid the lowest wages. Even skilled black craftsmen were paid considerably less than their white counterparts. In 1902, in Atlanta and Memphis, for example, black carpenters, painters, electricians, and sanitary engineers received from one-third to one-half less for the same work than white craftsmen. As late as 1928 the same pattern of wage discrimination existed in the building trades in Virginia (as indicated in Table 3) and in other industries as well.

Table 3.
DAILY RATES OF PAY FOR WHITE AND COLORED EMPLOYEES
IN VIRGINIA BUILDING TRADES, 1928

Occupation	White	Colored
Apprentices	$3.37	$2.45
Bricklayers	10.57	8.11
Carpenters	6.02	5.09
Cement Workers	6.99	4.53
Engineers	7.50	6.00
Helpers	3.62	3.29
Hod Carriers	4.70	4.18
Laborers	3.49	3.07
Lathers	4.03	4.66
Painters, etc.	5.73	4.00
Plasterers	9.22	8.11
Plumbers and Gas Fitters	8.24	4.30
Sheet Metal Workers	7.07	6.00

SOURCE: Spero, Denhard S. and Abram Harris, *The Black Worker:*
The Negro and the Labor Movement
(New York: Columbia University Press, 1931), p. 172.

Even today, despite federal law to the contrary, various devices are employed to maintain a differential in the wage rates of black and white employees in Southern industries.

Moreover, by 1910 black employment had declined in a number of occupations. Unlike the situation before the Civil War, the textile industry became the exclusive preserve of white workers. The few blacks employed were in menial capacities that ordinarily had nothing to do with the industrial process. Between 1865 and 1900 the proportion of skilled black workers—artisans and craftsmen—in the South's labor force declined well below that of the pre-Civil War level although the number of such workmen increased slightly. A government study in 1865 indicated that blacks then comprised about 83 percent of the 120,000 skilled artisans in the South. By 1890, however, in the fields of carpentry, brickmasonry, painting, plastering, and blacksmithing combined, only about 22 percent of the artisans were black. While black plasterers comprised one-third of the artisans in their field, black painters were outnumbered almost ten to one by their white counterparts. The primary decline in the proportion of black skilled workers occured before 1900, however. During the first three decades of the twentieth century the proportion of blacks in the South's skilled labor force remained relatively constant. In 1920 there were 54,059 black artisans in the fields listed above as well as 2,444 plumbers, 4,458 machinists, and 401 printers. Altogether they comprised 72 percent of the blacks in these trades in the United States.

Several developments contributed to the proportional decrease in black artisans in the South during the latter quarter of the nineteenth century. Many black artisans succumbed to mechanization and technological innovations in their trades. Others were pushed out of their trades by immigrants from Europe and from the North who came to the South after 1880 to take advantage of the new opportunities provided by Southern industrial expansion. Many black artisans and would-be artisans migrated, in turn, to Northern and Western cities in search of better job opportunities. Still other black craftsmen, in order to avoid confrontation with white skilled workers, accepted unskilled and semiskilled jobs in industry which at least offered the advantage of paying higher wages than agricultural jobs. And finally, blacks were excluded from skilled jobs by the white supremacy policy of white workers and their unions.

BLACK WORKERS AND LABOR UNIONS

The lukewarm attitude of labor unions at their best to black workers, and their outright hostility at their worst, placed black workers in a cruel dilemma. Most black workers, if they had had the choice, would probably have joined labor unions, but the exclusionary practices of the unions made many blacks receptive to Booker T. Washington's views. From the beginning, Washington seemed to have believed that black workers and white capitalists shared a greater community of interests than the workers of the two races. The racism of white workers served to reinforce his views. Committed to black uplift through educating the masses in agricultural and industrial skills, Washington was not willing to see his program sabotaged by the discriminatory practices of organized labor.[4]

Therefore, in exchange for job opportunities for black workers, Washington proposed to offer white industrialists a trained, docile and strike-free labor force. Many employers found Washington's program congenial to their social philosophy and their interests, and some made substantial financial contributions to Tuskegee, Hampton, and other industrial schools. The United States Steel Corporation even employed Tuskegee graduates to supervise educational and welfare programs that it instituted in 1908 for black workers in its Alabama steel mills and coal mines.

Excluded from labor unions some black workers in the South became strikebreakers, less because of the influence of Washington, however, than because of the need for a job or because they did not know a strike was in progress. Their actions thus served to intensify the hostility of white workers. An insight into their predicament is provided by the fact that by 1902, according to W. E. B. Du Bois, there were only 40,000 black workers in a membership of 1,200,000 in the major U.S. labor unions. And the locals of many unions that admitted blacks to membership refused to accord them recognition.[5]

Some craft unions in the South did organize black workers into segregated locals but assigned them to employment on inferior jobs in black communities. Around the turn of the century the American Federation of Labor accepted some black workers into locals of the Federal Labor Union, comprising workers in the steel and coal industries in the South. These unions failed to adequately protect and support black workers, however, and either became inactive or went out of existence. During the 1880s blacks found a more congenial home in the Knights of Labor, and they supported the union in strikes in various industries in the South during that decade. With the demise of the Knights in the South in the 1890s, many black workers, especially those in coal mining, joined the United Mine Workers Union. In 1910 many black lumbermen became members of the Brotherhood of Timber Workers. Unfortunately, most of these early efforts at interracial unionism in the South, in the face of employer opposition, the racism of white workers, and the political disfranchisement and civil subordination of the black population, did not last beyond the Progressive era.

Unable to join white unions, or relegated to inferior positions in the interracial labor movement, many black workers formed their own unions. Black longshoremen formed the Longshoremen's Protective Association in Charleston, South Carolina, in 1867; the Protective Mutual Aid Association in New Orleans in 1872; and other unions in Galveston, Texas, in 1870; in Baltimore in 1871; and in Newport News, Virginia, in the 1890s. These unions waged aggressive warfare against racist white unions as well as against employers. They succeeded in winning higher wages in a number of instances from employers and also extracted from white longshoremen a greater proportion of the work in Southern ports. Under the auspices of the International Longshoremen's Association, white and black unions in the South in the early twentieth century sufficiently overcame racial hostility to form work-sharing agreements and to present a united front in demands on employers. Black longshoremen remain today the best organized and most powerful segment of the black labor force in the South.

Black railway workers failed to enjoy the success of the longshoremen in organizing and gaining recognition from employers and white workers. The

Colored Locomotive Firemen's Association, organized in Georgia in the early 1900s, and similar all-black unions of railwaymen formed in Alabama, Tennessee, Kentucky, and other Southern states between 1900 and 1915, failed to withstand the opposition of employers and white workers, and most soon became moribund.

The case of the Brotherhood of Timber Workers is instructive. By the spring of 1912 blacks comprised about one-half of the union's membership of about 25,000 workers. Its greatest strength was in Arkansas, Louisiana, and Texas. That same year the Brotherhood, spurned by the American Federation of Labor, became affiliated with the radical Internatonal Workers of the World. In 1913 it struck the American Lumber Company in Merryville, Louisiana. With the connivance and cooperation of local authorities, the company waged a veritable reign of terror against the strikers. Their leaders were kidnapped, beaten, and even shot, and the strikers themselves were deported from the town and subsequently blacklisted throughout the South. Because of its interracial character, the union was accused by the governor of Louisiana of "seeking to destroy the Southern way of life." Similar tactics were employed in other areas of the South until "By the spring of 1914," according to Philip Foner, "the Brotherhood of Timber Workers had been effectively destroyed."[6]

Adding to the difficulties of black workers in the South before the 1930s was the convict-lease system. Convict labor was extensively used in the mining, lumbering, turpentine, and railroad industries as well as in agriculture. An investigating committee of the Alabama legislature declared that through the use of convict laborers, the Tennessee Coal, Iron, and Railroad Company in Alabama had saved $200,000 in wages by 1889. The workers under the system were horribly treated, and the mortality rate in their camps was high. Yet several industries in the South in the late nineteenth and early twentieth century owed much of their growth to this cruel form of slavery.

During the Great Depression the American Communist party attempted to revive earlier efforts at interracial unionism in the South. Through the Trade Union Unity League, formed in 1929, it organized black and white textile workers in the South into the same locals, which it subsequently united as the National Textiles Workers' Union. In the 1931 textile strike in Gastonia, North Carolina, the interracial integrity of the union was preserved in the face of efforts by the employers to create racial dissension among the workers.

Several blacks played key roles as organizers of black and white workers under Communist party auspices. At the age of seventeen Angelo Herndon became an organizer of the National Miners' Union in Birmingham, Alabama, in 1930. In 1932, Herndon, while involved in leading a demonstration in Atlanta for increased relief payments to unemployed workers, was arrested, indicted for attempting to incite an insurrection, and sentenced to eighteen to twenty years on the chain gang. In 1937, however, the U.S. Supreme Court overturned his conviction.[7]

Similarly active in Alabama as a union organizer was Hosea Hudson, a Birmingham, Alabama, steel mill worker. Hudson joined a Communist-sponsored union in 1931 and was an active worker in the Southern Negro Youth Congress from shortly after its formation in 1937 to its demise in 1948. Throughout the late 1930s and most of the 1940s Hudson also headed a Birmingham local of the Steel Workers of America, a Congress of Industrial Organizations (CIO) union. During these years he not only fought against employers but also against white supremacist elements within the union.[8]

During World War II, some progress in interracial unionism in the South was made under the auspices of the CIO. Blacks secured representation on several of the state CIO Industrial Union Councils, and in Winston-Salem, North Carolina, black tobacco workers formed a CIO union in 1943 and, with the cooperation of white workers, waged a successful strike against the R. J. Reynolds Tobacco Company. In 1947 the union (Local 22) again successfully struck the company. Paradoxically, the CIO, under the influence of Cold War attitudes, expelled the local for its supposedly left-wing stance and sought, unsuccessfully, to replace it with another, more conservative union. The struggle had the unfortunate result of leaving the workers at the R. J. Reynolds Company in Winston-Salem without a bargaining agent.

During the 1950s neither the CIO nor the American Federation of Labor (AFL) made much progress in bringing black and white workers together into an effective labor movement in the South—nor did they seriously try. The merger of the two organizations in late 1955 into the AFL-CIO changed little. Except for pronouncements in support of civil rights for blacks, the AFL-CIO remained cautious in its organizing efforts in the South, despite the pressure exerted by the Negro Labor Council, an organization formed in 1960 by A. Philip Randolph and other black trade union officials for the purpose of combatting racism within the labor movement. In 1961 Randolph accused the AFL, the CIO, and the AFL-CIO of having failed to "ever come to grips with the racial policies of the South" and of having adopted "a policy of appeasement, compromise and defeatism" in face of the need to promote true interracial unionism in the region.[9] Not until the late 1960s did black union workers in the South, inspired in part and supported by leaders of the freedom movement, make substantial progress in winning some of their principal economic objectives, as indicated by their victories in the strikes of sanitation workers in Memphis in 1968 and of hospital workers in Charleston in 1969.

EMPLOYMENT TRENDS SINCE 1930

Black employment in nonagricultural jobs became increasingly significant with the growing urbanization of the black population in the South during the twentieth century. In 1890 only 15 percent of the black population in the South lived in urban areas. By 1910 an additional 6 percent had made the trek to the cities. Ten years later black urbanites comprised one-fourth of the Southern black population, and during the next two decades their proportion in the black population increased by 12 percent. The urban trend continued during the 1940s and by 1950 almost half of the black people of the South lived in urban communities. A decade later black urban dwellers outnumbered their rural counterparts, who now constituted only 42 percent of the black population of the South. By 1970 only one black Southerner in three resided in nonmetropolitan areas.

The movement of blacks to Southern cities around the turn of the century occurred at about the same time that urban blacks were being forced out of traditionally black jobs. Barbers serving a white clientele, hotel and restaurant waiters, bellboys and elevator operators, and firemen were increasingly losing their jobs to whites. Moreover, between 1910 and 1930 black workers failed to share proportionally in the expansion of industries in which they had held a traditional foothold, while certain industries which had traditionally employed large numbers of black workers failed to expand. Whereas there was a two-thirds increase between 1890 and 1910 in the number of black male workers in nonagricultural jobs in the South, an increase due chiefly to expansion in such industries as saw and planning mills, coal mining and railroad work, the number of blacks in non-agricultural work increased by only one-third during the next two decades. During the 1930s these trends persisted and were exacerbated by the depression and the increasing migration of blacks forced out of agricultural jobs to the cities. The result was that by 1940 about 40 percent of black workers not engaged in agricultrue were employed in the extremely low-paying domestic and personal service jobs.

Between 1940 and 1965 the same forces that affected black employment in the three previous decades continued to prevail, and blacks remained concentrated in the unskilled and semiskilled jobs. Blacks failed to get a proportional share of the jobs in new or expanding industries. They continued to be replaced in jobs that traditionally belonged to them, especially when these jobs were upgraded in terms of higher wages. They lost their jobs to machines and automated processes. Labor unions continued their discriminatory practices, barring blacks altogether or assigning them to segregated locals. In integrated unions they were assigned to inferior positions within the locals and to inferior jobs in the industries. Thus, in 1960, about 83 percent of black male workers in nonagricultural jobs in the South were laborers, operatives, and service workers. About 87 percent of the black female workers were similarly employed, the overwhelming majority being utilized as domestics and service workers. By 1970, however, the position of female workers had improved considerably. The number in personal service jobs decreased from 762,000 in 1960 to 556,000 in 1970, while the number in professional and related services rose from 232,500 to 495,500 during the same period. This development largely reflected the better employment climate for blacks resulting from the efforts of the federal government to promote equal employment opportunities. Male workers also benefited, but to a lesser extent.[10]

A look at certain specific industries in the South will bring these developments into sharper focus. In the pulp and paper industry, for example, the number of black employees declined from nearly one-half the work force in 1945 to only one-sixth of the work force in 1968. Yet as one-sixth of the work force in the latter year blacks comprised four-fifths of the service workers and laborers in the industry. In the bituminous coal mining industry, similar but more drastic changes occurred. At the beginning of the century blacks comprised over one-third of the coal miners in the South. In every succeeding decade after 1910 their proportionate place in the industry declined. Between 1930 and 1950 the number of black coal miners in the South declined from 44,000 to 26,000 while the number of white coal miners rose during the same period from 153,000 to 217,000. During the 1950s, because of mechanization and certain economic factors, the number of black and white miners declined, the blacks by some 73 percent, however, as compared to a 54 percent decline for whites. Thus, in 1960, blacks constituted only 6.3 percent of the work force in Southern bituminous coal mining. Since 1960, the pattern of black-white employment in the coal mines of the South during the period from 1930 to 1950 has been repeated: the number of black miners has declined while the number of white miners has increased. By 1968, black miners were almost completely barred from strip mining, and they comprised only 8 percent of the work force in the deep mines of southern Appalachia. As in other industries in the South, they were concentrated in the most dangerous, low-paying, and low-status jobs and discriminated against by both their employers and their white union brothers. As a result more black miners have withdrawn from coal mining, few younger black men go into it, and blacks are leaving the coal mining regions in increasing numbers. If the trend continues, the black coal miner soon will become a rarity in the South.

Similar but slightly less drastic trends in black employment are observable in the tobacco industry. Between 1910 and 1930 blacks comprised between 65 and 68 percent of the combined work force in the tobacco industries in Kentucky, North Carolina, and Virginia. With mechanization and a rise in wages from 1930 to 1960, more white workers entered the industry, and the proportion of blacks decreased to about 46 percent in 1940, 37 percent in 1950, 27 percent in 1960, and 25 percent in 1966. The decline in the market for tobacco products as a result of the cigarette health scare may further reduce black employment in the tobacco industry.

Since 1930, black employment in the steel industry has fluctuated somewhat. In 1935, the 2,666 black workers in the industry, mostly in Alabama, constituted a little less than one-third of the industry's employees in the South. By 1938 they were almost 45 percent of the industry's work force in the region, although in absolute numbers fewer black and white workers were employed. During the 1940s blacks maintained a relatively high level of employment in the industry, comprising between 36 and 38 percent of the employees in Alabama. During the 1950s, however, the proportion of blacks in the industry declined, dropping to about 31 percent in 1960. The decline has continued, dropping to a little over one-fifth of the industry's employees in the South in 1968. The shift of the steel industry to the Midwest and the West Coast has been partially responsible for the decreasing number of black steel workers in the South.

The forces that contributed to declining black employment in the foregoing industries have had a remarkably different impact on the textile industry. Long considered the almost exclusive preserve of white workers— as the leading apostle of the New South, Henry Grady, had intended it to be—the industry had employed only a minimal number of black workers. In South Carolina, for example, the proportion of blacks in the textile industry remained around 4 percent betwen 1921 and 1961. White women traditionally comprised a large proportion of the employees; black women were excluded almost entirely, except for the few employed as scrubwomen or maids. In a short period of seven years, however, black employment in the industry increased dramatically, from 4.5 percent in 1961 to 16.6 percent in 1968. Two developments were primarily responsible for the change. First, with the growth and expansion of old and new industries in the South after 1950, whites left the low-wage textile industry in increasing numbers to take better paying jobs in the other industries, thus leaving a vacuum in the textile industry which blacks began to fill. Second, in its push against job discrimination, the federal government pressured the industry to hire more black workers. As a result of these concurrent developments, blacks moved into all phases of the industry although most, like their white predecessors, were concentrated in the blue-collar jobs. The most novel change in this virtual revolution in the employment pattern of the industry was the hiring of large numbers of black women.

The lumber industry in the South is probably the only other major Southern industry that has not experienced a substantial decline in the proportion of its black employees. From 1890 to 1960 there was a steady increase in the proportion of black employees in the saw mill, planing mill and logging operations. By 1964 about 42 percent of the workers in the industry in the South were black. In 1968 the proportion was essentially the same. The main reason for the high level of black employment in the industry is that it has been largely a low-wage and low-skill industry involving much hazardous work. Thus the great majority of black workers are in the operative and laborer categories. Black owners and managers, who were present in the industry in years past because they owned and cut the timber on their own land or bought it from others, have largely disappeared from the field.

Other industries in the South in which blacks have found varying degrees of employment in recent years include industries that have moved South for the most part since World War II. They are the rubber, automobile, petroleum, chemical, and aerospace industries. By 1968 blacks comprised the following percentages of the work forces of these industries: petroleum, 10.7; automobile, 10.3; rubber tires, 11.5; chemical, 7.3; and aerospace, 4.4 percent. In all of these industries blacks were concentrated in the blue-collar jobs as operatives, laborers, and service workers. These relatively new industries were thus unable to avoid reflecting community mores and the results of past discriminatory practices and patterns in the South.

The economic effects of the South's discriminatory labor patterns as well as of the region's whole biracial system can be seen in the relative income status of black and white families. Despite a narrowing of the gap between black and white family incomes in the South by 8 percent from 1965 to 1970, black family income in the latter year was still only 57 percent of that of whites. The median family income for Southern blacks was $5,222 compared to $9,240 for Southern whites. The discrepancy in incomes between black and white families would be substantially greater if the black families did not contain a much greater proportion of working wives. The untenable economic position of black Southerners was further indicated by the fact that in 1970 36 percent of the black families in the South had incomes below the poverty level, and only 28 percent had incomes of $10,000 or more as compared to 60 percent of the white families.[11] By 1974 the relative economic status of black families to whites had even slightly declined with black family income in the South constituting only 56 percent of that of whites. Thus black Southerners continue to bear the burdens of the South's long history of racial injustice.

THE CAPITALISTIC IMPULSE

Black Southerners were not immune to the entrepreneurial fever that the economic revolution and the concomitant rise to wealth and prominence of a new business elite created among Americans in the latter decades of the nineteenth century. Like other Americans they too imbibed much of the social and economic philosophy that underlay the economic behavior of the era. Many disciples of the Puritan ethic, the gospel of wealth, laissez-faire economics, and even Social Darwinism could be found in the black community. Black Southerners also shared in a modified vision of the New South, in which men of capital and business acumen could play a part in developing and enjoying the benefits of a diversified economy.

Adding to the entrepreneurial impulse in the black community was the spirit and philosophy of racial solidarity and self-help which constituted one of the forms of black response to the developing biracial system in the South. Both black militants and black accommodationists could be found in the self-help and solidarity camp. To some blacks, racial cooperation and self-help offered a viable means of eventually overthrowing the hated racial caste system in the South. To others the biracial system was on balance a positive asset, for it offered blacks the opportunity to develop community institutions and resources that would parallel those in the white world. To still others, the existence of a segregated black community provided them with a captive market and clientele for their business enterprises. The entrepreneurial urge among blacks thus contained elements of both humanitarianism and selfishness.

After Reconstruction, black leaders increasingly stressed business enterprise as a key to race advancement and as a means of securing economic independence for the masses. At a meeting of the Fourth Atlanta University Conference in 1898 on "The Negro in Business," John Hope, president of Atlanta University, articulated many of the views that had been circulating in the black community for over two decades. Hope, a proponent of black protest and a believer in a liberal arts education for blacks, nevertheless felt that in a society where "business seems to be not only simply the raw material of Anglo-Saxon civilization, but almost the civilization itself," blacks must enter the world of business or else face suicide as a race. He insisted that the traditional pattern, in which whites as employers monopolized the wealth and resources which black labor created and developed, must be altered so that the fruits of black labor could remain in black hands. Moreover, as whites were increasingly moving into jobs traditionally held by blacks, he maintained that in the very near future "employment will have to come to Negroes from Negro sources. . . . Negro capital will have to give an opportunity to Negro workmen who will be crowded out by white competition. . . ." However, unlike Booker T. Washington, who was inclined to share the view of many Americans that business enterprise and material progress were the essence of civilization, Hope hastened to add that "I do not believe that the ultimate contribution of the Negro to the world will be his development of natural forces. It is to be more than that. There is in him emotional, spiritual elements that presage gifts from the Negro more ennobling and enduring than factories and railroads and banks. But without factories, railroads and banks, he cannot achieve his highest aim."[12]

While Hope, the militant, articulated the rationale for the black business movement, Booker T. Washington, the conciliator, provided the organizational thrust, as well as a philosophy, for the movement. In 1900 Washington, with the financial assistance of Andrew Carnegie, organized the Negro Business League. Under his leadership the league waged an aggressive promotional campaign in behalf of black business enterprise. Numerous local leagues were organized in both the North and South. By 1915, the year of Washington's death, 600 such leagues had been formed.

BLACK ENTERPRISES

The first three decades of the twentieth century witnessed a substantial increase in business activity within the black community. Some of this activity was probably the result of the Negro Business League's influence, although there is no way to determine this with exactitude. In 1898, W. E. B. Du Bois identified 1,906 black business enterprises in the nation. Nearly one-half of these ventures were located in Alabama, Georgia, South Carolina, Tennessee, Texas, and Virginia. In order of numerical importance the principal businesses included grocery stores and general merchandise stores, barbershops, publishing and printing establishments, and funeral homes.[13] By 1930 there were 70,000 black business establishments in the nation, most of them in the South. The numerically predominant enterprises of 1898 were still preeminent, but banks, insurance companies, and real estate agencies were much in evidence.

Black-owned enterprises were by no means a new phenomenon in the South. Free blacks had engaged in numerous ventures before the Civil War, which they continued into the postwar period. Before the upsurge of business activity among blacks in the early twentieth century black Southerners owned barbershops, hotels, catering services, and hauling concerns. Many carried on a variety of occupations as independent craftsmen. Blacks were among the leading building contractors in Charleston, South Carolina, until after World War I. They were also prominent in the barbering, butchering, and shoemaking trades in that city. As merchants, real estate dealers, and owners of various other enterprises, a few black Southerners were able to amass respectable fortunes.

There were significant differences between these earlier entrepreneurs and those who came later, however. The earlier businessmen and artisans catered to a predominantly white clientele. Moreover, they generally came from the class of pre-Civil War free blacks or were the mixed-blood descendants of favored house slaves. Robert R. Church, Sr., of Memphis, for example, who by the time of his death in 1912 had amassed a fortune in excess of a $1 million through dealings in white real estate, was the mulatto son of a wealthy white man. The later ventures were established by a new rising class of black men, composed to a large extent of ex-slaves and their descendants. Many were darker in color than the earlier group, and they catered almost exclusively to the black clientele within the segregated black community. Even the older class of entrepreneurs, in the face of technological changes and as a result of the hardening of the racial caste system in the South which cost them their white patronage, found it necessary to fall back upon the black economy if they hoped to survive. Thus, most of the black business ventures begun in the South after 1890 were specifically directed at the black market. Madame C. J. Walker of St. Louis, for example, became a millionaire through the establishment of a uniquely black enterprise resulting from her invention of a hair-straightening process for black women.

BANKS AND INSURANCE COMPANIES

Although blacks did not become owners of railroads, as John Hope had envisioned, they did establish banks and factories. Despite their unhappy experience with the Freedmen's Saving Bank established by Congress in 1865 to accept and safeguard the savings of the freedmen, blacks' interest in banks did not subside with the bank's failure in 1874. Beginning with the establishment of the True Reformers' Bank in Richmond, Virginia, and the Capital Savings Bank in Washington, D.C., in 1888, blacks had organized banks in every Southern state by 1930, and in several Northern states as well. In addition to the two banks organized in 1888, three others were founded by 1900. The Mutual Trust Company in Chattanooga, Tennessee, was founded in 1889; the Alabama Penny Savings and Loan Company in Birmingham in 1890; and the Nickel Savings Bank in Richmond, Virginia, in 1896. From 1900 to 1905 twenty-eight additional banks were organized, and available records indicate that at least 134 banks were established by blacks by 1934, the overwhelming majority in the South. Twenty-five had been organized in Virginia alone. Fourteen had been founded in Georgia, twelve in Mississippi, and eleven in North Carolina. Most of these institutions were short-lived, however. Many failed during the early years of the depression, but most collapsed before that time. By 1934 only twelve banks were still in existence.

Many of the black banks had been established as subsidiaries of insurance companies, while others shared with insurance companies a common origin in the host of fraternal orders and mutual-benefit and burial societies which expanded and proliferated among blacks after the Civil War. Notable as the parent of both insurance companies and banks as well as a variety of commercial ventures was the Grand Fountain of the United Order of True Reformers, founded in Richmond, Virginia, in 1881 as a fraternal insurance order by William Washington Browne. Before the Civil War Browne was a slave in Georgia and Alabama. During the war he escaped to the North and joined the Union Army. He returned to the South after the war and engaged in politics as well as in the work of fraternal orders in Alabama. Under Browne's leadership the True Reformers expanded rapidly in both members and business enterprises. In addition to establishing the first black bank in 1888 the True Reformers went on to found a newspaper and printing business, department stores in five cities, a hotel, a real estate agency, a funeral business, a nursing home, and a 650-acre cooperative farm designed to become the nucleus of an all-black community. By the time of its collapse in 1911 as a result of overexpansion, it had become a mutual-benefit stock company with a membership of 100,000 and with operations in eighteen states.

Existing concurrently with the True Reformers in Virginia was the Independent Order of St. Luke, the noted fraternal order for women founded in Richmond in 1865. After Maggie L. Walker became head of the order in 1900, it too grew rapidly, increasing its membership to 20,000 by 1907. It also organized a bank, a retail store, and published a newspaper. It still survives to this day.

NORTH CAROLINA MUTUAL

The example set by the True Reformers was soon followed by other fraternal orders and mutual-benefit societies. Indeed, many of the insurance companies founded in the late nineteenth and early twentieth centuries were established by former agents of the True Reformers. Such is the case in the founding of the North Carolina Mutual Insurance Company, one of the largest and most successful business enterprises among blacks in the nation.

In 1883, John Merrick, a former slave, and several other black men in Durham, North Carolina, acquired control of the Royal Knights of King David, a fraternal insurance company. Fifteen years later, Merrick, now a somewhat prosperous petit businessman with six barbershops (three for blacks and three for whites) and a real estate business, joined with six prominent black North Carolinians in forming the North Carolina Mutual and Provident Association. Merrick's associates were Dr. Aaron M. Moore, Durham's first black physician; William Gaston Pearson, a school principal and teacher and president of the Royal Knights of King David; Edward A. Johnson, dean of the law school at Shaw University; James E. Shepard, a clergyman active in North Carolina fusion politics and later the founder and president of North Carolina College for Negroes; Pinckney William Dawkins, a school teacher; and Dock Watson, a tinsmith. In 1900 the association was reorganized when four of the original founders withdrew, leaving the venture in the hands of Merrick and Moore. Merrick and Moore brought in C. C. Spaulding who served initially as janitor, agent, and general manager of the enterprise.

Under Spaulding's direction, and with the assistance of Merrick and Moore, the company, after a slow start, began to make sound progress. By 1904 it had 40,000 policyholders. By the spring of 1906 the number of policyholders had doubled. A year later the Association had 100,000 policyholders and assets of $28,413. In 1913 the Association dropped its assessment feature and became a legal reserve company, and in 1919 it changed its name to the North Carolina Mutual Insurance Company. By that time it had $1 million in assets, a premium income of $1,224,541, and $26 million of insurance in force. It had also sprouted a number of other enterprises, including the Mechanics and Farmers Bank (1907), the Merrick, Moore, Spaulding Real Estate Company (1910), the Durham Textile Company (1910), and two drug stores, a lumber mill, and an iron works. Satellite enterprises acquired or established subsequently included the Bankers Fire Insurance Company (1920), the Mutual Building and Loan Association (1921) and the Mortgage Company of Durham (1929). All of these enterprises were independent legal entities, but their interlocking directorates made them all members of the Mutual family. Except for the manufacturing establishments and the real estate company, all have survived in some form to this day.

The North Carolina Mutual Insurance Company was preeminently a child of the New South. Durham was a New South city, with a relatively new and developing economy. Its character had much to do with the success of the company. When the Mutual was developing, the black community in Durham lacked the rigid social distinctions between ex-slaves and their descendants on the one hand and the descendants of the old free and house servant class on the other that existed in such cities as Charleston and New Orleans. To a considerable extent the rise of the Mutual contributed to social stratification within the Durham black community as the leaders in the Mutual family of enterprises came to constitute the black upper class. Moreover, the domination of the Durham economy by the Dukes, the owners of the American Tobacco Company, provided the Mutual with the protective covering of a relatively benign and paternalistic racial climate in which to develop. In addition, the blacks who came to Durham to work in the tobacco factories, cut off from their associational moorings in their former rural communities, provided the company with much of its insurance market. The Mutual, of course, also fed on its own success. White financiers in Durham found it easy to "help" the company with money and financial assistance, for such help meant profits for them. In addition, having established a reputation as the premier black business enterprise in the nation, the Mutual became a magnet attracting able and talented blacks to Durham, either as employees of the company or to work in the community in some other capacity. The Mutual "myth" even infected the black masses of Durham, who while lacking any financial stake in the company, nevertheless shared vicariously in the company's image. In 1933 a woman told C. C. Spaulding that "Your company is what keeps our heads up when we don't do enough to help ourselves."[14]

North Carolina Mutual and its satellite enterprises earned for Durham the title "The Capital of the Black Middle Class." Today, despite the fact that Durham's black population numbers only about 30,000 people, the company is still among the largest black business enterprises in the United States. By the end of 1974 it had about $138.6 million in assets. The Mechanics and Farmers Bank with $37 million in assets in 1973 was among the top six black banks in the United States in this regard. With the Mutual Savings and Loan Association having about $13 million in assets, as of 1973 the three companies combined accounted for $288.6 million in assets alone. This was about 20 percent of the combined assets of all similar black institutions in the United States.

FAILURES AND SUCCESSES

A number of other insurance companies were formed in the South in the early twentieth century. Due to overexpansion, poor management, and lack of mortality data on which to establish sound actuarial practices, most of these ventures were ephemeral. Many began as promising enterprises. Standard Life Insurance of Atlanta, founded by Herman Perry in 1913, began with a capitalization of $100,000. Within a short time the company had written $250,000 worth of insurance, acquired a well-trained and influential core of directors, officers, and staff, and soon became the largest black-owned legal reserve company. By 1922 the company claimed assets of $2 million and was receiving an annual premium income of some $1,200,000. Perry, however, engaged in reckless expansion, forming numerous subsidiary enterprises. In order to meet pressing obligations, the Standard also absorbed the Mississippi Life Insurance Company—founded in 1909 as the first black legal reserve company by W. A. Attaway, a young physician—and then sold it to a white company. This did not save Standard Life, however, for in 1924 its other subsidiaries went into the hands of white mortgagees. Pride of race then entered the picture. In order to bring Standard Life back under black control, the National Benefit Life Insurance Company, which had been organized in 1898 in Washington, D.C., by Samuel Rutherford, a former agent of the True Reformers, reinsured Standard Life in 1925. Shortly thereafter National Benefit abandoned its conservative investment policy and cautious premium writing practices and began to engage in some of the same practices that had gotten Standard Life into difficulties. Among other ill-advised actions, it rapidly expanded into twenty-eight states. As a result, it collapsed in 1931.

Many black insurance companies, in addition to North Carolina Mutual, did survive, however. In 1972, of the ten leading black-owned legal reserve insurance companies in the nation, seven were in the South. The Atlanta Life Insurance Company, founded in 1905 by Alonzo Herndon, a former Georgia slave and the successful owner of a barbering business serving white clients, stood second behind North Carolina Mutual in the hierarchy of black insurance companies in the United States. The current president of the company, Norris B. Herndon, the founder's son, is reputed to have a personal fortune of $18 million. In addition to the legal reserve companies there were fifteen mutual-benefit societies in the nation in 1963 with assets of $17 million, ten limited assessment companies with $9 million in assets, and five burial societies with $71,697 in assets. As of 1972, thirty-two of the forty black insurance companies were located in the South, as were twenty-five of the forty-one savings and loan associations and nineteen of the thirty-seven banks. All of these enterprises in the South had combined assets in 1972 in excess of a billion dollars.[15]

Standing alone the assets of black financial institutions may appear impressive. When compared with the assets of similar white institutions, the black resources are puny indeed. The assets of black insurance companies amount to less than half of 1 percent of the total assets of American Insurance companies. In addition, they no longer operate today behind the protective wall of the biracial system. They must compete with major white companies not only for policyholders, but also for personnel. Prudential Insurance Company, for example, which refused to insure blacks in 1881, now aggressively seeks black policyholders and actively recruits black insurance agents and other personnel. The fact that insurance companies stand at the apex of black business enterprises is symbolic of the inability of black capitalism to do what John Hope felt that it must do; that is, provide employment for the black working class. Insurance companies are not major employers of labor. The service enterprises are generally single proprietorships or partnerships employing few workers. Aside from cosmetics firms, blacks have no factories of any significance. Thus the black community is limited in its business capacity to small nonproducing financial and service type enterprises which yield very little power in behalf of the economic needs of the members of that community. Therefore, most black people today in the South, as in the nation, constitute a dependent working class whose economic fate is dictated by white society. Consequently, as Andrew Brimmer of the Federal Reserve Board has observed, they live and work "in the backwaters and eddies of the national economy in the United States."[16]

PART THREE

SOCIAL AND INSTITUTIONAL LIFE

SIX

The Search for Knowledge

"Grown men studied their alphabets in the fields, holding the 'blueback speller' with one hand while they guided the plow with the other. Mothers tramped scores of miles to towns where they could place their children in school. Pine torches illumined the dirt-floored cabins where men, women and children studied far into the night."[1]

The freedmen's intense interest in learning, as reconstructed by Horace Mann Bond in the above passage from reminiscences by Booker T. Washington,[2] represented an attempt to overcome one of the more burdensome vestiges of the institution of slavery. The master class, in one of the many strange ironies which the slave system engendered, forbade anyone to teach slaves to read and write. Yet, at the same, it justified the institution of slavery partly on the grounds that the slaves were inherently incapable of mental development and were therefore uneducable. If white Southerners were disturbed by this glaring contradiction in their views, they obviously felt it to be more important to yield the latter point in order to keep the slaves under control.

For the slaves then, the inability to read and write was a badge of servitude. Booker T. Washington undoubtedly reflected the feelings of many bondsmen when he recalled that as a slave

> The idea that books contained something which was forbidden aroused my curiosity and excited in me a desire to find out for myself what was in these books that made them forbidden fruit for me and my race.
> From the moment that it was made clear to me that I was not to go

to school, that it was dangerous for me to learn to read, from that moment I resolved that I should never be satisfied until I learned what this dangerous practice was like.[3]

Thus for the ex-slave freedom meant more than physical emancipation. It also meant the removal of the shackles of ignorance—the ability to reproduce and decipher the written word—as a means of achieving full status in the social order.

ANTEBELLUM EDUCATION

Although most freedmen had emerged from slavery unable to read and write, many had successfully breached some cracks in the walls of the system. Despite laws to the contrary, some masters had given their slaves rudimentary instruction in reading and writing in order to make the most profitable use of them as artisans, skilled craftsmen, and household workers. A few masters had provided extensive education for favored house servants. Still others, curious to see if slaves really had the capacity to learn, had "experimented" with particular slaves. Indeed, even free blacks were objects of skepticism as to their mental abilities. John Chavis, for example, a free-born native of North Carolina, was sent by Presbyterians to Princeton in the late eighteenth century for the purpose of determining if a black person was capable of absorbing higher learning. After studying at Princeton and Washington Academy, Chavis became a Presbyterian minister and served in that capacity in Virginia and North Carolina. He later established a school in North Carolina and taught the children of many of the great planters in the state. Not infrequently, white children on the plantations taught their slave playmates to read and write. In addition, some enterprising slaves learned to read and write surreptitiously by spying on the instruction given to white children. Moreover, before the tightening up of the slave system following Nat Turner's rebellion in 1831, some religious and philanthropic organizations had endeavored to teach slaves, and a few black children had attended classes with whites.

Free blacks, who in 1860 comprised a little over 6 percent of the black population in the South, also made some strides toward becoming educated. As indicated in Chapter 1, they maintained schools in several Southern cities, despite the generally hostile attitude of whites toward such institutions. They often instructed their children through their churches and mutual-aid societies. Some children were taught at home by their parents, other family members, or by some person specifically employed for that purpose. By 1860, then, probably about 5 percent of the black people in the South were literate.

EDUCATION AND THE UNION ARMY

The Civil War gave a great impetus to black education in the South. The Union Army itself, as black enlistees entered its ranks and as refugees crowded within its lines, took some steps to educate its charges. In order to enhance the efficiency of the black soldiers, many brigade and regimental commanders instituted programs of instruction, especially for black noncommissioned officers. Black soldiers were taught by their officers, by white and black civilian volunteers, and by Northern teachers paid by the soldiers themselves. Most were eager to learn, and those who were initially recalcitrant were offered various kinds of rewards as incentives.

Union Army commanders also instituted programs to provide education for black civilians in the areas under their command. As early as February 1862, General Thomas W. Sherman appealed to Northern philanthropists to provide teachers for the freedmen in the Sea Islands of South Carolina. Between 1862 and 1865, in response to Union Army initiative and appeals, schools for blacks were established in various areas of the South. In the Department of Tennessee (Tennessee and parts of Kentucky and Mississippi) there were seventy-four schools by 1865 in which 6,267 students were receiving instruction from 102 teachers. In North Carolina in July 1864 some 3,000 black students were being taught by sixty-six teachers. And by December 1864, in the well-organized program established by General Nathaniel Banks in the Department of the Gulf (Louisiana, Mississippi, Alabama and Texas) 162 teachers were instructing 9,571 children and 2,000 adults in ninety-five schools.

BLACK SELF-HELP

Preceding, assisting, and complementing the educational efforts of the Union Army were the various educational activities of private individuals and organizations. A number of blacks were in the vanguard of these activities. In September 1861, Mary Chase, a free black woman, opened a school in Alexandria, Virginia, for black refugees from the war. In the same month, Mrs. Mary Peake, working for the American Missionary Association, opened a school for refugees near Fortress Monroe, Virginia. A Miss Deaveaux, who had clandestinely maintained a private school for blacks in Savannah, Georgia, since 1838, offered her services openly when the Union Army moved into the city. Similarly, Mrs. Mary D. Price, who had moved from Ohio to New Orleans in 1858 in order to provide education for black students, put her school at the disposal of the freedmen when the Union Army assumed control over that city in April 1862. A Miss L. Humphrey opened two schools for freedmen in the vicinity of Nashville, Tennessee, in the fall of 1862. And among the first group of teachers to minister to the educational needs of the freedmen in the Sea Islands of South Carolina and Georgia was the cultivated Charlotte Forten, a black teacher from Philadelphia.

In a letter to the American Missionary Association in 1863 Mrs. E. Garrison Jackson provided a simple explanation of these women's motives when she wrote:

> I have a great desire to go and labor among the Freedmen of the South. I think it is our duty as a people to spend our lives in trying to elevate our own race. Who can feel for us if we do not feel for ourselves? And who can feel the sympathy that we can who are identified with them? I should like to go as soon as possible: for I feel as though there is much work to be done, and I would like to do my share.[4]

In April 1865 Mrs. Jackson began to do her share as a teacher of freedmen at Port Deposit, Maryland. As the Civil War drew to a close others like her were to move deeper into the South to participate in the effort to bring to the former slaves the benefits of the advantages they had already enjoyed as free people in the North.

Near the end of the war and throughout the Reconstruction period, black religious denominations and secular societies also established schools for the freedmen or made financial contributions to schools established by others. The African Methodist Episcopal Church, the African Methodist Episcopal Zion Church, and the various black Baptist churches were all active in the educational field. The African Civilization Society, a secular organization, established schools for blacks in Washingotn, D.C. The freedmen themselves, despite their meager resources, made substantial financial contributions toward their own education. By 1870 they had expended through the Freedmen's Bureau about $673,000 in tuition and taxes, and they had donated about $500,000 through their churches. In Louisiana, Tennessee, and Virginia freedmen by 1867 had maintained entirely through their own resources forty-six schools, bought thirty-three buildings, and had partially supported forty-two other schools.

WHITE ASSISTANCE

Individually and collectively, Northern whites made the greatest contribution to black education during the Civil War and Reconstruction era. Religious and secular organizations and private individuals both cooperated and vied with each other in providing educational opportunities for the freedmen. In the forefront of the educational endeavors was the American Missionary Association, an arm of the Congregational Church. Beginning with the establishment of a school at Fortress Monroe in Virginia in 1861, the association had by 1863 also organized schools in Washington, D.C., and in Newport News, Portsmouth, Suffolk, and Yorktown, Virginia. During the Reconstruction period at least 467 black men and women, over half of whom were residents of the South, served the organization as teachers, assistant teachers, and religious workers. It was soon joined by other religious and secular bodies such as the American Baptist Home Mission Society, the Freedmen's Aid society of the Methodist Episcopal Church (North), the Friends Association for Aid to the Freedmen, the Board of Freedmen's Missions of the United Presbyterian Church, the American Church Institute of the Episcopal Church, and the various secular societies to aid the freedmen. Between 1861 and 1870 schools offering elementary, secondary, and college instruction were founded.

The Freedmen's Bureau, set up in early 1865, cooperated with the religious organizations and benevolent societies in establishing, staffing, and maintaining the schools. Generally the bureau appropriated money for school buildings while the societies provided teachers. During its five-year existence the Bureau expended $5,145,124 on education for the freedmen. Benevolent societies and religious bodies probably contributed an equivalent amount between 1861 and 1870. The black community, as previously indicated, contributed over $1 million in taxes, tuition, and gifts. By 1870, 4,239 schools were maintained under the auspices of the Freedmen's Bureau. They employed 9,307 teachers in the instruction of 247,333 pupils.

PUBLIC SCHOOLS

The educational activities of individuals, religious and benevolent societies, the Union Army, and the Freedmen's Bureau established the foundation for the creation of a system of public education in the South. A nascent public school system had been established for white children in several Southern states before the Civil War, but these schools suffered from woefully inadequate financial support, an inadequacy compounded in some states by having to share state funds with private schools. In addition, these schools suffered from being characterized as pauper schools. Blacks, of course, were barred from the schools. Between 1863 and 1867, however, several border states—West Virginia, Missouri, and Kentucky—and the District of Columbia did make limited and tentative provisions for the education of blacks. Financial support was generally limited to funds that blacks paid in poll and property taxes, however. Before Radical Reconstruction only two Deep South states made any provisions for educating their black population. Through the efforts of General Banks, Louisiana provided tax-supported schools for blacks in 1864. Florida, under the control of the Union Army, made similar provisions in 1866. These schools were established under duress, however, and did not represent the will of the white people of these respective states.

The Southern state governments under Southern white control from 1865 to 1867 refused to establish schools for blacks, although provisions were made for the education of whites. Most Southern whites opposed education for blacks. Some simply believed that blacks were uneducable. The majority, however, feared that educated blacks would be inclined to reject a subordinate status for themselves in Southern society. Many whites, therefore, attacked the schools that were already in existence. They burned some schools, pressured black parents who were their employees to withdraw their children from the schools, harassed Northern white teachers through social ostracism, physical assaults, and even murder in some cases, and waged relentless propaganda against any education provided for the freedmen except that maintained under Southern white auspices. Thus the establishment of statewide public schools for blacks had to await the coming of Congressional and Radical Reconstruction.

One of the major achievements of the carpetbag-scalawag-black governments in the Southern states was the establishment of a public school system for black and white pupils that did not carry the stigma of pauperism. Under these regimes, state-supported education on the lower levels was established as the democratic right of all citizens. Black delegates to the state constitutional conventions in 1867-1868 and black members of the state legislatures were among the chief proponents of public schools. Their allies in the public school movement were whites from the North who regarded public education (for black and white) as an essential attribute of a democratic society, and Southern whites who viewed public education as essential to the progress of their children and to the advancement of the South generally.

The question of whether the schools should be integrated was an important issue in the constitutional conventions and state legislatures. Black leaders and legislators prophetically feared that specific constitutional or legislative stipulations providing for separate schools for the two races would result in gross inequality in the dispensation of funds for the education of black children. Therefore, while primarily interested in guaranteeing that there would be equal educational opportunities and facilities, they pushed for integrated schools, being willing to accept separate schools only if equality could be assured. Only the constitutions of Louisiana and South Carolina, however, provided for integrated schools. And only in New Orleans were the public schools actually integrated for any length of time. Despite some initial difficulties, black and white students studied together in New Orleans from 1870 to 1877 in relative peace and equanimity. In South Carolina, black leaders, unlike those in New Orleans, did not push the issue, and only the University of South Carolina was integrated. Richard T. Greener, the first black graduate of Harvard, served as professor of philosophy at the University of South Carolina from 1874 to 1877. During his tenure the majority of the students were black, most white students having withdrawn. In 1875, of the 233 students enrolled in the university, 90 percent were black.

The constitutions of most of the other ex-Confederate states were silent on the issue of mixed schools, and the schools that were established were segregated. Although resenting the social stigma involved, blacks acquiesced in the separate schools so long as there was no inequality in the educational opportunities and facilities made available to the two races. In five states—Arkansas, Louisiana, Mississippi, Florida, and South Carolina—blacks served as superintendents of education at some time during the Reconstruction period. Some notably able men who served in this capacity were Jonathan C. Gibbs of Florida, an alumnus of Dartmouth College and the Princeton Theological Seminary; J. C. Corbin of Arkansas, a graduate of Oberlin College; and W. G. Brown of Louisiana. In North Carolina, the only significant state office outside the legislature held by a black person was that of assistant superintendent of public instruction, a post filled for several years by James Walker Hood.

As long as the Southern states were under Republican regimes, there was little or no discrimination in the dispensation of state funds for black and white education. Because of the weakness of the Southern economy, taxpayer resistance to financing education for blacks, the misuse of public funds, and the diversion of monies designed for education to other uses, the funding was usually inadequate for both races. Nevertheless, considerable progress was made. Black illiteracy, estimated at 90 percent in 1860, declined to 81 percent in 1870 and to 70 percent in 1880.

With the return of Southern Democrats to power in the 1870s, the already inadequate public school system began to suffer more. Several state governments refused to provide more than token financial support for the schools. Because of this, schools were closed in Georgia in 1872 and in Arkansas in 1874 for lack of funds. Similarly, fund cuts resulted in the closing of many schools in Mississippi and North Carolina when the governments of these states were captured by the Democrats. Under these financial stringencies, black schools, of course, suffered the most. With a rising demand from whites for public education for their children, the Southern states began to give ever larger proportions of their limited funds for education to white schools, a process which became more formalized as blacks were increasingly disfranchised, Jim Crowed, and otherwise confined by legal, illegal, and extralegal means to a subordinate caste status.

BLACK TEACHERS FOR BLACK SCHOOLS

While the vision of equal although separate schools was proving to be illusory, blacks hoped to ameliorate some of the deleterious effects of the developing Jim Crow system through the employment of black teachers in black schools. On returning to power, however, the Democrats were not only disinclined to provide the black community with equal educational facilities, but they also sought to assure that the black schools that did exist or were subsequently established would be under the control of Southern whites. Therefore, they proceeded to replace the Northern white teachers in these schools with whites from the local communities. Under the tutelage of Southern white teachers black students, rather than being prepared to assume the role of free people, would be taught to observe the interracial etiquette of slavery days, including the practice of addressing whites as "Massa" and "Missus."[5]

The policy of the Democrats naturally evoked black protest. During the 1870s and 1880s blacks in Atlanta, Montgomery, Nashville, Raleigh, Richmond, and numerous other communities petitioned their city councils and local school boards to appoint black teachers to black schools. They frequently coupled their demands with requests for additional schools or better facilities. "Give us a High and Normal School where our young people may be instructed by those who have our interests at heart," demanded the *Virginia Star* in 1882. Proclaiming that "We are tired of having the treadles of all the machines run by whites," the *Star* urged the "Noble descendents of Ham [to] stand up for pride of race."[6]

The term "pride of race" embraced both ideological and pragmatic considerations. Those black Southerners who wanted their schools staffed by members of their own race wanted black children to be informed of the great heroes and contributions of the race as an antidote to the degrading image of blacks that whites were inclined to perpetuate. They also wanted teachers with whom black students could identify and who could serve as models of achievement for their students to emulate. Manifestly, Southern white teachers could perform neither of these functions, as their mission was to train blacks to accommodate to white supremacy. Moreover, inasmuch as the white teachers usually came from the ranks of those who could not find employment in white schools, blacks thought, correctly, that many of them were simply incompetent. Finally, blacks argued that since black teachers would not be hired to teach in white schools, the black schools should be reserved as places of employment for the increasing number of black college graduates.

By 1890 most black communities had won their campaigns for black teachers in black schools. Under the Readjusters, black teachers replaced whites in the black public schools in Virginia in the early 1880s. The one notable exception was the Colored High and Normal School in Richmond which continued to be administered by whites until 1924. In other communities as well, the Conservatives, desiring to save money by paying black teachers lower salaries and finding that competent white teachers could be absorbed by the new schools being established for whites, gradually acceded to black demands. As a result the black community was able to salvage a small measure of autonomy over one of its most important institutions. In the hands of creative and daring teachers and principals such schools, despite inferior facilities, could instill in their students a sense of group pride and personal dignity and thereby subvert some of the basic tenets on which the system of white supremacy rested.

SEPARATE AND UNEQUAL

The increasing discrimination in the Southern social order following Reconstruction was clearly reflected in the public school system. Between 1876 and 1895 white enrollment in public schools increased by 106 percent while the black enrollment increased by only 59 percent. More clearly expressive of racial injustice, however, was the greater amount of money expended for educating white children than was spent for blacks. In 1880, the Democrats in South Carolina, after having provided equal funding for black and white education for three years, began to severely discriminate in the allocation of funds for the education of the two groups. Between 1880 and 1895 per capita expenditures for white pupils rose from $2.75 to $3.11 while such expenditures for black pupils declined from $2.51 to $1.05. Thus, in 1895 South Carolina was spending three times more on the education of a white child than on a black child.

During the first half of the twentieth century the trend not only continued but worsened. By 1915, the white pupil in South Carolina was receiving more than ten times the amount of public money that the black child received. Even by 1930 the situation had not changed as the per capita expenditures for the education of white children were $52.89 as compared to $5.20 for black children. At the same time South Carolina was paying its black teachers only one-third as much as it paid their white counterparts. In addition, the average school term for black children was fifty-nine days less than the term for white children.

By 1940 the financial picture for black pupils had improved somewhat, as they then received an amount equal to about 30 percent of the expenditures for white pupils. By 1952, largely as a result of pressure from the NAACP and other civil rights forces, South Carolina, beginning to be apprehensive that integration of the schools would be ordered if the gross discrepancies in expenditures for black and white education were not corrected, had upped per pupil expenditures for black education to within 60 percent of that for whites.

In many cases the local situation was much worse. In Adams County, Mississippi, for example, the per pupil expenditures for blacks in 1900 were $2 while white students were receiving $22.25.

The wide discrepancies in money spent on white and black education in Mississippi and South Carolina were characteristic, to varying degrees, of all the states of the Old Confederacy. In 1915 for the South as a whole, white pupils received more than two and a half times the amount of public monies that their black counterparts received. By 1930 they were receiving almost three times as much as each black student. The gap had narrowed somewhat by 1940 when whites received a little less than twice the amount spent on black students. By 1952, two years before the Supreme Court's desegregation decision, per pupil expenditures for blacks had risen to 70 percent of the expenditures for whites. Throughout the early 1900s black teachers were also paid considerably less than their white counterparts. White teachers were paid almost twice as much in 1910 than black teachers. Moreover, while the average annual salary for white teachers rose from a little less than $200 in 1900 to $900 in 1930, the salary for black teachers rose from $100 to only $400 in the same period. Even as late as 1950 black teachers were earning only 85 percent of what their white associates received.

By 1900, then, the biracial system of public education in the South was fully established and rationalized, and through the principle of separate but equal expounded in the case of *Plessy v. Ferguson* (1896), had received the endorsement of the U.S. Supreme Court. For nearly fifty years, neither the Supreme Court nor other branches of the federal government cared to look behind the principle to determine whether public school facilities for blacks were in fact equal to those for whites. When it did address itself to the question in the late 1940s and early 1950s, it is not surprising that the court, in reviewing past and still existing gross inequalities in public support for separate black and white schools, would ultimately conclude that separate schools were inherently unequal.

White Southerners rationalized their neglect of black education on several grounds. Some felt that blacks should not be educated at all. Others felt that blacks were incapable of learning beyond a certain level, and that consequently only primary schools should be maintained for them. A variation on the latter view was the belief that whether they were capable or not, blacks should not be educated beyond their status in Southern society; otherwise they would become discontented and pose a threat to the Southern social order. Still others maintained that black education should be supported only to the extent that blacks financed their own education through taxation. Thus it was both legitimate and moral that the bulk of public funds for education should go to white schools inasmuch as whites paid the greater bulk of taxes. These Southerners either chose to ignore or were unaware of a report made at the Sixth Atlanta Conference for the Study of Negro Problems in 1901 that from 1870 to 1899 blacks contributed to education some $25,000,000 in direct school taxes, $45,000,000 in indirect taxes and over $15,000,000 in tuition and fees to private schools.[7]

POST-RECONSTRUCTION
SELF-HELP AND PHILANTHROPY

The South's gross neglect of black education was somewhat ameliorated by the self-help activities of the black community and by aid from Northern philanthropy. In order to supplement the meager public funds, black communities staged fund-raising drives through school leagues and through their churches, and many black people contributed out of their pockets to support their schools. Often blacks supplied the buildings (frequently their churches) in which school was held. They sometimes assessed themselves with fees to help finance the building and operation of schools in their communities. Between 1913 and 1932 blacks contributed in the form of direct donations 19 percent of the $28 million expended by white donors, the Rosenwald fund, and the Southern states for the construction of about 5,000 school buildings in fifteen Southern states. Some blacks, finding the public schools inadequate, sent their children to private schools, some of which had been established and were being operated by blacks.

After the Civil War and Reconstruction periods, private philanthropy continued to play a major role in black education in the South. Church organzations continued their support, concentrating more and more, however, on assisting black colleges. The George Peabody Education Fund contributed over $3,500,000 to Southern education between 1867 and 1914, much of it going toward the education of black students. The John F. Slater Fund, established in 1882 with an initial gift of $1,000,000, provided funds for teacher-training programs in church and private schools, for assistance to public schools, and for the establishment and promotion of county training schools where blacks could be trained in vocational and industrial skills. Black education also shared in the largesse of John D. Rockefeller, who between 1902 and 1909 gave about $53,000,000 to the General Education Board for the purpose of aiding education at various levels for all races throughout the United States. In 1905, Anna T. Jeanes, with a gift of $200,000 to the General Education Board, supplemented in 1907 by an additional gift of $1 million, established a fund specifically designed to improve the education of blacks in rural areas. Special teachers were appointed to carry on industrial and extension work in the rural schools. A pioneer Jeanes teacher was Miss Virginia Randolph, who established in Henrico County, Virginia, the pattern of visiting rural schools in order to help teachers to train their students in those industrial arts and home skills needed to improve living in rural communities.

Through the impetus provided by the Julius Rosenwald Fund over 500 school buildings were constructed for blacks in the South between 1913 and 1932. The Rosenwald Fund and the Slater Fund gave an important and necessary boost to black high school education. When Rosenwald first began to evince an interest in black education about 1910, no public schools for blacks in rural Southern areas offered a curriculum beyond the seventh grade, and none in urban areas offered as much as two years of approved high school work. The high school education available was either provided by the black colleges or by normal schools established and operated under private auspices.

With the assistance of private philanthropy, state funds, and their own self-help efforts, the black population made substantial progress in education following the end of Reconstruction, despite the very grave social, economic, political, and financial handicaps imposed on them. Between 1870 and 1900 black school attendance increased from 10 percent of the black school age population to about one-third. By 1910 over 45 percent of the 3,403,237 black children were attending school; by 1950, 75 percent were attending. Increasing school attendance signified increasing literacy. In 1860, between 5 and 10 percent of the black people in the South could read and write. By 1900 well over 50 percent were literate. By 1930 over 80 percent were in the literate category. Between 1890 and 1930 the black literacy rate in the South increased by about 93.8 percent, while the rate for the South as a whole increased by only 32 percent.

Increasing school attendance also signified that, despite intermittent periods of apathy, discouragement, and disillusionment, most blacks maintained an interest in education. Twelve years after the Civil War Laura Towne still marveled at the continuing desire of the children on the Sea Islands of South Carolina to learn to read, write, and count. She reported that even on rainy days nearly every child came to school. "Some of them walk six miles and back, besides doing their task of cotton picking. Their steady eagerness to learn is just something amazing," she exulted. "To be deprived of a lesson is a severe punishment. 'I got no reading to-day,' or no writing, or no sums, is cause for bitter tears." Towne prophesied that "This race is going to rise. It is biding its time."[8]

PHILOSOPHIES AND OBJECTIVES

The type of education which black students received in the Southern schools reflected the educational philosophies and practices of the schools' sponsors. The schools established during the Civil War and Reconstruction periods by Northern religious and secular societies were generally based on the New England model. Their curriculums were designed to instruct the freedmen not only in the fundamentals of reading, writing, arithmetic, grammar, and geography, but also to instill moral values, mental discipline, and an appreciation for what were considered the finer things of life. Occasionally some instruction in certain of the manual arts was also provided in order to supply the students with basic skills to maintain their homes and to improve their physical environment. A few schools even included industrial arts as vocational subjects. In general, the instruction provided was designed to fit the students for life in Southern society as full and useful citizens.

As white Democrats assumed control of the state and local education programs after Reconstruction, education for blacks was perceived by its new sponsors in an entirely different light. To the extent that blacks were to be educated, they were to be trained to fit into the South's biracial system. They were to be taught to assume, accept, and hopefully like an inferior role and subordinate status in Southern society. Most philanthropic foundations found it feasible to acquiesce in the white South's design. A few, like the Peabody fund, provided aid for only racially separate schools.

White Southerners who favored education for blacks believed with Booker T. Washington that the best education for them was training in agricultural and industrial skills. Unlike Washington, however, who viewed industrial education as the means by which the black masses would establish an economically viable position in Southern society as a stepping stone to the achievement of political rights and social status, white Southerners regarded industrial education as an instrument for keeping the black population in a permanent state of economic, political, and social subservience. Education was simply to be another means—along with disfranchisement, Jim Crow laws, economic control, and violence—for keeping the black community in its place.

The post-Reconstruction philanthropists, mostly businessmen or industrialists, felt a special affinity for the idea of providing industrial skills for black Southerners. Industrial education would be mutually beneficial to both the black and white South. It would promote a degree of economic prosperity among blacks while providing the South with a trained labor force. This could be accomplished without disturbing the South's biracial caste arrangement. Thus the Northern philanthropists made their financial contributions to both white and black education in the South on the basis of an understanding with white Southerners that assistance to black education would not tend to subvert the Southern way of life. A large proportion of the funds contributed were specifically directed toward the training of blacks in the industrial arts, and most of the funds expended were channeled through organizations and personnel approved by the white South.

HIGHER EDUCATION

The black colleges were not immune to the industrial education vogue. Indeed they were the focal point of the great debate within the black community on the issue of whether training in the liberal arts or in the industrial arts was the more practical and desirable form of education for black Southerners. Booker T. Washington of Tuskegee and W. E. B. Du Bois of Atlanta University were the principal spokesmen for the opposing positions.

Black colleges came into existence through many of the same agencies that introduced primary and secondary schools for blacks. Between 1865 and 1900 the religious and secular organizations, seeing the need for trained ministers, teachers, professionals, and leaders to serve the black population, established a number of institutions of higher learning. Among colleges still in existence the American Missionary Association was instrumental in establishing what became Atlanta Unversity in Georgia in 1865, Fisk University in Tennessee in 1866, Talladega College in Alabama in 1867, Hampton Institute in Virginia in 1868, Tougaloo College in Mississippi in 1869, and Le Moyne College in Tennessee, in 1870. To the extent that the American Missionary Association was related to the Congregationalist Church, it also may be regarded as a founder of Howard University in Washington, D.C., in 1867.

The American Baptist Home Mission Society helped to found Virginia Union University in Richmond, Virginia, and Shaw University in Raleigh, North Carolina, in 1865; Morehouse College (Atlanta Baptist College) in Atlanta, Georgia, in 1867; Benedict College in Columbia, South Carolina, in 1870; and Spelman College in Atlanta, Georgia, in 1881. Several institutions established by the society, including Shaw University, eventually came under the control of black Baptist conventions.

Colleges still in existence that were founded by the Northern Methodists include Meharry Medical College in Nashville, Tennessee, in 1865; Morgan State College in Baltimore, Maryland, in 1866; Rust College in Holley Springs, Mississippi, in 1867; Claflin College in Orangeburg, South Carolina, in 1869; Clark College in Atlanta, Georgia, in 1870; and Bennett College in Greensboro, North Carolina, and Wiley College in Marshall, Texas, in 1873. Southern Methodists founded Paine College in Augusta, Georgia, in 1884.

The Episcopalians and Presbyterians also joined the parade of founders of black colleges after the Civil War. St. Augustine College, founded in Raleigh, North Carolina, in 1867 and St. Paul Polytechnic Institute in Lawrenceville, Virginia, in 1883 are the best known of the Episcopalian schools. Colleges established under Presbyterian auspices include Johnson C. Smith University in Charlotte, North Carolina, in 1867; Barber-Scotia College in Concord, North Carolina, in 1867; and Fort Valley State College in Fort Valley in Georgia, in 1895. Knoxville College in Knoxville, Tennessee, was established by the United Presbyterians in 1875.

The black Methodists were also very active in the college field. The African Methodist Episcopal Church assumed control of Wilberforce University in Ohio during the Civil War. After the war it founded in the South such institutions as Shorter College in Rome, Georgia, in 1873; Allen University in Columbia, South Carolina, and Paul Quinn College in Waco, Texas, in

1881; and Morris Brown College in Atlanta, Georgia, in 1885. Later it also established Kitrell College in North Carolina and Edward Waters College in Jacksonville, Florida. Livingstone College, founded in 1879 in Salisbury, North Carolina, was the only institution of note established by the African Methodist Episcopal Zion Church. Similarly, Lane College in Jackson, Tennessee, established in 1870 by the Colored Methodist Episcopal Church, was the principal contribution of that denomination to black higher education. The Colored Methodist Episcopal Church and the white Methodist denomination in the South cooperated in operating Lane, Paine, and Miles Memorial College (now called Miles College) in Alabama.

Often the establishment of a college was the result of the efforts of mainly a single individual. Livingstone College (Salisbury, North Carolina), for example, came into being primarily through the efforts of Joseph C. Price, a dynamic black educator and leader, who might well have rivaled Booker T. Washington in influence had he not died at the young age of thirty-nine. As the founder of Tuskegee in 1881, Booker T. Washington, of course, is the best known of those who established colleges for blacks during the Reconstruction and post-Reconstruction eras. The tradition set by Price and Washington was followed in the twentieth century by James E. Shepard, founder in 1910 of what is now North Carolina Central University, one of the best black liberal arts colleges in the country. In 1924 a merger of Cookman Institute for Boys at Jacksonville, Florida, with a normal school for girls established by Mary McLeod Bethune at Daytona Beach in 1904 led to the creation of Bethune-Cookman College. Mrs. Bethune was typical of several black women who established normal schools in the South in the late nineteenth and early twentieth centuries. The best known of these were Lucy Laney, who founded Haines Normal and Industrial Institute in Augusta, Georgia, in 1886 and Charlotte Hawkins Brown, founder of Palmer Memorial Institute in Sedalia, North Carolina, in 1904.

State-financed institutions for blacks were also established between the end of the Civil War and 1900. Most of these colleges were established as land-grant institutions under the provisions of the Morrill Acts of 1862 and 1890. Because the Morrill Act of 1862, which provided for agricultural and mechanical colleges in the states, did not specifically provide for a division of funds along racial lines, the institutions established or aided under the act in the Southern states did not enroll black students. Before the passage of the Morrill Act of 1890 only Mississippi founded a land-grant college for blacks. This was Alcorn College, established in 1871. Virginia designated Hampton Institute as its land-grant institution for blacks in 1872, and South Carolina similarly designated Claflin as a recipient of land-grant funds in the same year. As a result of the Morrill Act of 1890 seventeen states had designated black institutions as land-grant colleges by the end of 1892. As a result Hampton was succeeded by Virginia State College as Virginia's land-grant college and Claflin gave way to the State Colored Normal, Industrial, Agricultural, and Mechanical College of South Carolina as South Carolina's black land-grant institution.

During the nineteenth century and well into the twentieth century, a considerable number of the black institutions of higher learning had elementary and high school departments, thus helping to fill the gap in the provisions for black education in the public schools. Thus many early students who finally received college degrees had spent most of their student careers at the institution from which they graduated. As the public schools assumed more of the responsibility for educating the black population, particularly through high school, the black colleges gave up their lower departments. For those who did not go on to college, these institutions, by providing them with training on the lower levels, rendered a great service to the black community.

LIBERAL ARTS VERSUS INDUSTRIAL EDUCATION

Most of the colleges established under religious auspices offered primarily a liberal arts program, although a few courses in the industrial arts and homemaking often were taught. The land-grant colleges, of course, and Hampton and Tuskegee emphasized industrial and agricultural education. Near the close of the nineteenth century and continuing well into the twentieth century, the different programs of the two types of schools became a matter of intense philosophical debate. At issue was the question of which type of education most realistically met the needs of the black population. Booker T. Washington became known as the chief black spokesman for industrial education while W. E. B. Du Bois advocated a liberal arts education for the "Talented Tenth." At the heart of the issue was the place the black man could and should expect to occupy in American society.

The debate over industrial versus liberal arts educaiton did not occur in a vacuum. The white community was also considering the issue with respect to education for whites. During the latter half of the nineteenth century an industrial education vogue developed throughout the nation. During the 1880s numerous white high schools placed industrial education courses in their curriculums. The Morrill Acts merely reflected the temper of the times.

The black community, too, had long considered the matter of industrial education. The desirability of establishing manual labor schools for blacks had been discussed frequently in black conventions before the Civil War. Frederick Douglass had advocated industrial arts training as a laudable educational program for black youth and had hoped to see a school for that purpose established in Rochester, New York. After the war Douglass continued to support the idea of industrial education for blacks.

Many of the freedmen's schools established during the Reconstruction period claimed to offer industrial training along with their regular programs and, under the impact of the Slater Fund, many black institutions, in order to tap the fund's largesse, incorporated industrial and agricultural education into their secondary-level curriculums. Courses in one or more such fields as home economics, carpentry, shoemaking, bricklaying, blacksmithing, printing, painting, and tailoring and sewing were taught. The salaries of the teachers of such courses were often paid by the Slater Fund or by similar foundations.

Samuel Chapman Armstrong, the white president of Hampton Institute from its founding to his death in 1893, preceded Booker T. Washington as the chief spokesman for industrial training as the proper form of education for blacks. Armstrong spent the first twenty-one years of his life in Hawaii, where he was impressed with the educational program for Hawaiian youth at the Hilo Boarding and Manual Labor School. At Hampton, Armstrong devised an educational curriculum that was modeled on that of the Hilo school. In a speech before the National Education Association in 1872, Armstrong revealed the racial philosophy behind his program. The black student, he asserted, was "capable of acquiring knowledge to any degree, and to a certain age, at least, with about the same facility as white children; but lacks the power to assimilate and digest it. The Negro matures sooner than the white, but does not have his steady development of mental strength up to advanced years. He is a child of the tropics, and the differentiation of races goes deeper than the skin."[9]

Armstrong regarded manual labor and training in the trades, along with academic training, as a means of building character as well as preparing for a career. Hampton graduates were expected to impart to the black community not only occupational skills but also the moral virtues and mental discipline which were instilled in them at Hampton. Armstrong's successor, Hollis Burke Frissell, who had served as chaplain at Hampton for thirteen years before becoming president in 1893, was even more enamored with industrial education than Armstrong. While preaching the value of manual labor, Armstrong awarded credits toward graduation only for academic work. Frissell sought to elevate the trades to first place in Hampton's curriculum. Beginning in 1895, trade certificates were awarded. In 1904 Frissell claimed that a curriculum in which academic work was subsidiary to the trades was superior to the reverse arrangement in building "character, initiative, and intellectual force."[10]

As an alumnus of Hampton and a disciple of Armstrong, Booker T. Washington carried the Hampton philosophy to Tuskegee. Catapulted by his white admirers to the position of chief spokesman for the black community as a result of his Atlanta Exposition Address in 1895, Washington became a dominant force in influencing educational policy for blacks in the South. As a firm believer in the Protestant ethic and Social Darwinism in its paternalistic aspects, the dominant social philosophies of the late nineteenth century,

Washington was preeminently a man of his age. In terms of the New South philosophy being articulated by a coterie of white Southern newspaper editors, Washington, by advising accommodation in the political and social realms, and by urging blacks to accept much of the economic role assigned to them, was the New South's principal black spokesman.

Washington firmly believed that training in the agricultural and industrial arts was the most fitting education for the black masses. Such training not only built character but contributed to the development of the students' minds. It would result in the creation of a valued population of self-sufficient farmers, entrepreneurs, and skilled laborers. He did not deprecate a liberal arts education for the few, but maintained that for the many "the opportunity to earn a dollar in the factory just now is worth infinitely more than the opportunity to spend a dollar in an opera house."[11] As previously indicated, under Washington's leadership, Tuskegee sponsored conferences for black farmers in which the raising of one's own food, the buying of homes, and the intensive and scientific cultivation of small farms rather than inefficient cultivation of large acreage of poor quality were emphasized.

As an acceptable black leader, and as chairman of the executive committee of the Anna T. Jeanes Fund and a close associate of the administrators of the Julius Rosenwald Fund and other philanthropic foundations, Washington exerted tremendous influence on black education at all levels. Largely through his influence Northern philanthropy was directed into industrial education. To attract funds, colleges and secondary schools incorporated the term "industrial" in their titles, and even overwhelmingly liberal arts colleges found it expedient to add a course or two in the trades or in home-making. In the minds of the administrators of philanthropic funds and white public education officials in the South, the industrial school and black education became virtually synonymous.

W. E. B. Du Bois, a graduate of Fisk University and professor at Atlanta University from 1897 to 1910, led the opposition to the industrial education vogue. Du Bois was not unalterably opposed to industrial education, for he thought that many blacks would benefit from it and learn to appreciate the dignity of labor; but he disliked the accommodationist context in which it was being offered. Feeling strongly that the race needed a class of broadly educated leaders, men of "intelligence, broad sympathy, knowledge of the world that was and is, and of the relation of men to it,"[12] in order for the race to throw off the shackles of the caste system, Du Bois stressed the necessity for higher education in the liberal arts. Building manhood, he insisted, must be the object of education, and not the mere making of money-makers. Du Bois denounced Washington's role in promoting the dispensation of funds from philanthropic agencies to industrial schools rather than to liberal arts colleges. He maintained that it was from the ranks of graduates of liberal arts colleges that teachers for the black public schools would be found.

The debate over industrial or vocational education versus liberal arts education was centered largely on a false issue. Obviously, as many predecessors and contemporaries of Washington and Du Bois realized, the proper kind of each type of education was needed. During the 1880s William J. Simmons, president of the liberal arts State University of Kentucky at Louisville, advised against promoting one form of education at the expense of another. "If the industrial craze be not watched," he warned, "our literary institutions will be turned into workshops and our scholars into servants and journeymen." Simmons urged the black community to "Keep the literary and industrial apart . . . and attempt not the task of grinding scholars out of the industrial nor finished workmen from the literary schools. Each has a legitimate sphere and let us stick to it." In keeping with his dual educational perspective Simmons not only administered the school at Louisville but, shortly before his death in 1890, he founded a school for industrial training at Cane Spring, Kentucky.[13]

Joseph Charles Price, president of Livingstone College, shared Simmon's views. He would, however, be prepared to combine liberal arts and industrial training in the same institution. "The necessity of a connectional school not only for normal and academic culture, but also for theological training and industrial development admits of no argument," he declared in 1892.[14]

During the early decades of the twentieth century, other black leaders expressed similar views. "The question of higher education or industrial training is one that depends entirely upon the individual; and there should be no limit placed upon the individual's right of development," asserted James Weldon Johnson in 1901. "It is as absurd to say that every Negro should be made to receive an industrial training as it is to say that every Negro should be given a college education," he concluded. Johnson did not believe, however, that the curriculum for blacks should be in all respects the same as that for white students. Black students should be made aware of the contributions of the race and of its great men, for "the knowing of one Crispus Attucks is worth more to the race than the knowing of one George Washington; and the knowing of one Dunbar is worth more than the knowing of all the Longfellows that America will ever produce."[15]

Kelly Miller of Howard University, a monitor of the Washington-Du Bois controversy, echoed the sentiments of many black people in 1908 when he described the debate over industrial versus liberal arts education as a futile attempt to determine "which is of greater importance to man, air or water." Criticizing the partisans in the debate as "one-eyed enthusiasts [who] lack binocular vision," Miller maintained that "the two forms of training should be considered on their relative, not rival claims." Miller saw the two types of education as mutually beneficial to the black community and pointed to the fact that the most prominent proponents of industrial education, including Booker T. Washington, had received academic training. The issue to Miller, therefore, was "merely one of ratio and proportion, and not one of fundamental controversy."[16]

Nevertheless, the debate continued, with the leading partisans of industrial education becoming locked in their position by their desire to attract state and philanthropic funding and to placate the white South. It was the central issue in the controversy in the 1920s over the transformation of Hampton Institute from a normal school into a college. And in the 1950s, when Hampton officially threw off the mantle of industrial education and declared itself a liberal arts institution, many alumni and supporters bemoaned the passing of an age.

Hampton's transformation reflected realities that were becoming evident even in the last years of Booker T. Washington's era. The debate over industrial education was therefore resolved less by rhetoric than by the economic and social imperatives that the black community had to face. Despite the fact that much public and private money was funneled into industrial education programs, little actually came of such training. Some of the types of skills (for example, broom and mattress making, blacksmithing, and hand laundering) which were taught under the guise of industrial arts were already being made obsolete by technological developments and the growth of factory production. Furthermore, whites were increasingly taking over such skilled crafts as carpentry, brickmasonry, tailoring, and painting, and no amount of skill could recapture these occupations for blacks. Moreover, blacks were excluded from the skilled jobs in manufacturing by the prejudice of employers and white workers and by the inadequate training they received in the industrial schools. The Southern racial caste system prescribed that the bulk of black farmers should be tenants and laborers, not owners. In addition, because of economic developments and technological changes, the number of blacks and whites in agriculture was to decline over the years. In short, the program of agricultural and industrial education that Armstrong, Washington, and the white philanthropists were advocating was geared to an era that had already passed or was on its way out. Where it still had some relationship to existing economic conditions, its promise was negated by the proscriptions on blacks in the South's social system.

Thus, the great majority of the students trained in the black land-grant colleges and the industrial training institutes had to find other outlets for their talents. Like the graduates of the liberal arts colleges, most turned to public school teaching. They in turn trained students in scientific farming and vocational skills, as well as in liberal arts subjects. Those who went on to college returned to their communities as teachers, not as farmers and craftsmen. Thus, as Henry Allen Bullock has observed, "As time passed, the occupational pattern of the Southern Negro's labor force became neatly structured to accommodate the region's caste system rather than the product of its Negro colleges."[17]

Indeed, the industrial arts never penetrated very deeply into the curricula of most black schools on any level. In the colleges, teacher training, heavily based on liberal arts courses, became the chief academic activity. This was the case even in such institutions as Arkansas Agricultural and Mechanical College, Prairie View Normal and Industrial College, Alabama Agricultural and Mechanical College, Florida Agricultural and Mechanical College and, even to an extent, at Hampton Institute. At Florida A and M, for example, the first two presidents, Thomas de Saille Tucker (1887-1901) and Nathan B. Young (1901-1921) gave lip service to vocational education but actively promoted the academic curriculum, to the consternation of white state officials and trustees who feared that "To be educated like a white man begets a desire to be like a white man."[18] As a result of such policies, these institutions, established primarily as industrial schools, have also served along with their frankly liberal arts counterparts as the training ground for much of the black professional class.

PROBLEMS AND FAILURES OF BLACK COLLEGES

The black colleges faced formidable obstacles in attempting to meet the educational needs of the black population in the South. Most did not begin to offer truly college level work until well into the twentieth century. An educational foundation had first to be established on the elementary and secondary levels. Insufficient funding was and is a perennial problem. Consequently, problems of inadequate curricula, facilities, and teaching staff have haunted most of the institutions throughout their existence. Many failed to survive. Because of the cultural and social backgrounds of many of their students, some colleges have found it extremely difficult to create a serious academic and intellectual atmosphere on their campuses.

Black colleges have also been severely circumscribed in their internal operations and in their social role in the black community by the restrictions of the racial caste system. State-supported institutions prior to recent times have not dared to take a public stand against the Southern racial order. A college would be penalized by the political forces within the state for harboring dissident faculty members and students. Even the best college administrators had to recognize the limited sphere in which they were free to operate. Great skill was required to maintain the intellectual integrity of an institution while at the same time securing necessary funding from a racially reactionary state legislature and governor.

Even private colleges found it expedient not to pose too great a challenge to the South's racial mores for fear that the holders of political power in the states would give them trouble. Two black colleges in Columbia, South Carolina—Benedict College, a Baptist institution, and Allen University, a college of the African Methodists Episcopal Church—felt the power of a hostile state political establishment as late as 1957. Both institutions were forced by Governor George Bell Timmerman to dismiss several faculty members who had been outspoken against the state's oppressive racial practices. Since the names of five of the six faculty members involved were in the files of the Un- American Activities Committee of the U.S. House of Representatives, the governor maintained that they were Communists whose presence in South Carolina besmirched the fair name of the state. That Benedict and Allen should be allowed to give them sanctuary was unthinkable. To force the colleges to dismiss the professors, the governor and the state board of education withdrew state certification of Allen's teacher-training program and threatened the same action against Benedict. As 90 percent of the students of these institutions would seek certification as teachers upon graduation, the colleges eventually capitulated to Governor Timmerman's demands.

A generally unperceived problem of the black colleges was their uncritical acceptance of the programs of white institutions as their models. This situation reflected both the history of the origins of the black institutions and the nature of their administration. Except for the schools founded by the black Methodists, most of the colleges had been established by Northern whites who naturally attempted to copy the Northern models. Moreover, for a long time many of the institutions were controlled by predominantly white boards of trustees, administered by white presidents, and staffed by many white faculty members. The American Missionary Association colleges were particularly slow in appointing blacks as presidents and faculty members. Howard University, for example, did not appoint its first black president until 1926, and Fisk University did not get a black president until 1947. The Baptist colleges, which depended heavily upon black churches for financial support, and the Methodist institutions, whose church bodies contained many black members, had appointed many blacks to their teaching staffs by 1900. Many of them were still late, however, in choosing black presidents. This state of affairs was partially responsible for the student protests in the 1920s at such institutions as Hampton, Fisk, and Howard.

Although the issue became explosive in the 1920s, the black community had long been divided over the appropriateness of the continued presence of white teachers and administrators in the black colleges. As early as the 1870s, contemporaneous with the campaign to replace white teachers with blacks in the public schools, black leaders and educators in several states also demanded that the private black colleges sponsored by white religious organizations employ more blacks as faculty members. Some even insisted that "Negro teachers exclusively be employed to teach Negro schools."[19] Other blacks disagreed, and the debate continued into the twentieth century.

By 1900, however, the arguments on both sides of the issue had been clearly formulated. Those who opposed placing black colleges exclusively or predominantly in black hands emphasized the shortage of qualified black teachers and administrators, the racism and ingratitude such a step would represent, the continuing need of the black community for white intellectual and cultural guidance and moral support, and the inability of blacks to finance their own institutions and to solicit white contributions. "It takes a white man to get a white man's money," declared one black educator in 1901, "and since it is necessary to get a white man's money to support these institutions, it is also necessary to put their management into his hands."[20]

Those who favored placing black colleges in black hands stressed racial pride, the function of the black teacher as a role model, and the need to provide job opportunities for black teachers. "How many young students of history in the white-taught schools remember being drilled to revere the glorious memory of Lincoln, and Sumner and Garrison and Wendell Phillips, and how few remember being drilled to remember Crispus Attucks and the fifty-fourth and fifty-fifth Massachusetts?" asked Alice Ruth Dunbar, wife of the celebrated Paul Laurence Dunbar. "How many students of literature are taught of the first woman writer in America to earn distinction, Margaret Hutchinson, but how few are reminded of her contemporary, Phyllis Wheatley?" she continued. And "What is the use of training teachers, of spending time and money acquiring college training if there is no place to use such training?" she further inquired.[21]

Black college students during the 1920s asked similar questions. They also complained about the rigid discipline that white administrators imposed upon them, which they correctly interpreted as being indicative of white beliefs that blacks were less civilized and less emotionally and sexually responsible than whites. They demanded changes in their curriculums that would bring them into the mainstream of American academic and intellectual life while at the same time, in a few cases, paradoxically insisting upon more attention to courses that would today be called black studies. They protested what they regarded as the degrading practice of being required to sing "darkey songs" for visiting white luminaries and philanthropists. And they agreed with W. E. B. Du Bois that too many black institutions, in order to accommodate the white South and Northern philanthropists, were following an educational policy that was "sapping the manhood of the race . . . , breeding cowards and sycophants . . . , [and] lifting fools and flatterers to place and power and crucifying honest men."[22] They also charged white administrators with being racist, thereby lending credence to Carter G. Woodson's charge in the early 1930s that one white president of a black college "never entertains a Negro in his home," while another "does not allow students to enter his home through the front door."[23]

The protests of the students and their adult supporters did bring about some changes in the black colleges, including the appointment of more black teachers and administrators. However, assumption of administrative and teaching posts in these institutions by blacks did not essentially change the orientation of most of the colleges. Many of the black teachers and administrators had received their graduate training at white Northern universities. Thus the thrust of the educational programs of the colleges was toward preparing students to eventually enter the mainstream of American society. Consequently, most members of the college communities, including the students, felt that the proper avenue for entering the mainstream was assimilation into white culture. So pronounced was this attitude from the 1930s to the early 1950s that at some institutions teachers, students, and administrators continued to object to the inclusion of the spirituals in the repertoires of their college choirs, and a few college presidents forbade the singing of James Weldon Johnson's "Lift Every Voice and Sing," long regarded as the Negro National Anthem.

The consequence of the too heavy reliance on white educational and social models was the failure of these institutions to devote sufficient effort to searching for creative solutions to the academic problems and deficiencies of their students. Instead, the colleges looked to such prominent white institutions as Columbia, Harvard, Yale, and Chicago for assistance in how to teach their culturally different students, the kinds of students with whom these institutions had no experience or interest. Moreover, while uncritically accepting the white models as desirable, the black colleges contributed to their own image as inferior institutions, for measured against the more prominent white colleges and universities on the basis of the models accepted, they could be regarded at best as only adequate. An even more damaging consequence of the fixation on mainstream standards was the lending of academic respectability to the idea that what was different from mainstream norms was undesirable or even pathological.

Perhaps the greatest handicap that black colleges have suffered is their sharing in the low-status image of the black community in the American social order. A number of black institutions which have been far superior to many similar white colleges have not had that superiority recognized. They have thus suffered from sweeping generalizations made about them by prominent but woefully uninformed white commentators. As a result their ability to attract funds and staff has been adversely affected as have the occupational opportunities of their graduates.

CONTRIBUTIONS OF BLACK COLLEGES

Despite their handicaps the black colleges have made lasting contributions to the black community and to American society. Before the Southern states made substantial provisions for educating their black citizens, these colleges helped to fill the gap by providing primary and secondary education for black youth. In 1900, two-thirds of the 9,068 students enrolled in the black colleges were studying at the primary and secondary levels. These colleges have also supplied the teachers, physicians, lawyers, clergymen, and many of the businessmen and leaders of the black community. By 1900 they had graduated 2,000 students. Of these, 37.2 percent were teaching in the black schools at the time, 11.2 percent were ministers of churches, 4 percent were physicians, 3.3 percent were lawyers, and 1.4 percent were farmers. Others were working as merchants, store clerks, and civil service employees. Thirty years later teaching, the ministry, medicine, business, and the postal service were the principal fields in which the graduates of the black colleges were employed. Even today 74 percent of the black Ph.D.'s and 83 percent of the black physicians are alumni of these colleges. In the meantime the number of graduates from black colleges has steadily increased. Between 1939 and 1952 the black colleges graduated 69,433 students. From 1953 to 1963, there were 71,372 students receiving degrees from these institutions.

In spite of heavy teaching loads, inadequate or total lack of research funds, and difficulty of access to publishers, scholars at black colleges produced much of the early literature in the area of black studies. W. E. B. Du Bois, as a faculty member at Atlanta University, supervised a wide-ranging study on black life in America covering such topics as the family, the church, education, business, work, crime, and morbidity and mortality. While at Atlanta he also published his celebrated *Souls of Black*. Du Bois, already known for his *The Suppression of the African Slave Trade to the United States* (the first publication in the Harvard Historical Series) and *The Philadelphia Negro*, published numerous other historical and sociological works, including his classic *Black Reconstruction*, as well as novels, poems, and essays after leaving Atlanta. He also encouraged creative literary activity by other blacks by opening the pages of the NAACP's *Crisis* to young writers. After returning to Atlanta University in 1934, Du Bois in 1940 founded *Phylon: A Journal of Race and Culture*, which has published a wide range of articles not only on black subjects but on topics dealing with other racial and ethnic groups in the United States and throughout the world. Also published during his second tour at Atlanta was his *Black Reconstruction*.

Monroe Work taught at Georgia State College in Atlanta from 1903 to 1907. In 1908 he went to Tuskegee where he established and headed the department of records and research. Work collected information and published numerous articles on the life of black people in America and Africa. Between 1912 and 1938 he published nine editions of *The Negro Yearbook*, which became a standard reference in libraries throughout the nation. His *A Bibliography of the Negro in Africa and America*, when published in 1928, was the most complete bibliography of its kind. It has remained the foundation of other bibliographical works on black topics which have been published subsequently. Tuskegee's annual reports on lynchings also constituted a major source of information on race relations in the American South.

At Fisk University, Charles S. Johnson, chairman of the department of social science from 1928 to 1947, and president of the institution from 1947 to his death in 1956, led his students and colleagues in research projects that made Fisk "the leading research center in race relations in the world." By 1947 Johnson was the author or coauthor of seventeen books, the contributor of articles or chapters in fourteen books, and the author of over sixty articles. He continued to write and publish after becoming president of Fisk. His major works included *The Negro in American Civilization* (1930), the result of research conducted from 1926 through 1928 under the auspices of the National Interracial Conference, an organ of sixteen national organizations devoted to improving race relations; *Shadow of the Plantation* (1934); *The Negro College Graduate* (1938); *Statistical Atlas of Southern Counties* (1941); *Patterns of Segregation* (1943); *To Stem the Tide: A Survey of Racial Tension Areas in the United States* (1943); *Into the Mainstream; A Survey of Best Practices in Race Relations in the South* (1947); *Education and the Cultural Crisis* (1951); and with Edwin R. Embree and Will W. Alexander, *The Collapse of Cotton Tenancy* (1935).

At Howard University in Washington, D.C., black scholars in a variety of disciplines have produced numerous works dealing with the black experience in America and throughout the world. Historians such as Kelly Miller, Rayford Logan, Merze Tate, John Hope Franklin, Williston Lofton, Benjamin Brawley, Charles H. Wesley; the great sociologist E. Franklin Frazier; librarian Dorothy Porter; literary scholars such as Sterling Brown, Alain Locke, Mercer Cook; economists and political scientists such as Abram Harris and Ralph Bunche; educationists and psychologists such as Dwight O. W. Holmes, Kenneth Clark, Doxey Wilkerson; and a host of other scholars have produced notable works in the area of black studies. For many years, for example, William Leo Hansberry was one of a few scholars in America who were conversant with the history of Africa.

Carter G. Woodson, the founder of the Association for the Study of Negro Life and History, was also briefly associated with Howard. In 1916 Woodson began publication of the *Journal of Negro History* and some years later of the *Negro History Bulletin.* His efforts to stimulate scholarly research and study of the black experience and his own historical works qualify him for the title of "father of black history." Articles in the *Journal of Negro History* and the writings of Woodson himself provide considerable material for courses in black history.

Numerous other scholars at various black institutions have contributed to the literature on the black experience as well as on other subjects and in other fields. The list is entirely too long to mention here. It should be pointed out, however, that the recent upsurge of interest in black history and related subjects did not find the scholarly community without resources. The pioneering work in the field had already been done by black scholars, most of whom were on the faculties of black colleges in the South at some time, and by a small number of whites, many of whom were Southerners. Therefore, the assertion by white scholars in the 1960s that there was insufficient scholarly material available to sustain courses in black history, literature, and the social sciences reflected not only the profound ignorance and arrogance within the academic community, but a large degree of intellectual racism as well.

Although the black colleges have harbored their share of accomodationists, they have also succored the spirit of protest. The private colleges, especially, with greater freedom of inquiry and action, have frequently challenged the racist assumptions that undergird the American social order. At a time when it was not feasible for a college president to do so, John Hope of Atlanta vigorously protested against the racial caste system in the South. Benjamin Mays, president of Morehouse College, was an outspoken critic of racial discrimination and segregation in the United States. On every college campus there were black and white professors who taught their students that the subordination of black people was neither ordained by God nor by the Constitution. Many were active in organizations devoted to the elimination of racist practices in the United States.

Moreover, as the students participated in the intellectual ferment of college life, they became less willing to accept the status quo in race relations. It is not surprising, then, that graduates of these institutions would challenge the system, first in the courts and then in the streets. Certainly Benjamin Mays and Morehouse College must have planted the seeds of resistance in Martin Luther King. Most of King's close associates were graduates of black colleges. Virginia Union University alone is the alma mater of a number of leading protest and political leaders. Wyatt T. Walker, one of King's chief lieutenants; Virgil Wood, active in the protest movement in Lynchburg, Virginia, during the King era; Channing Phillips, nominated for president at the Democratic National Convention in 1968 and once an active figure in politics in the District of Columbia; and Walter Fauntroy, a District of Columbia delegate in the U.S. House of Representatives and a civil rights activist, all attended Virginia Union in the late 1940s and the early 1950s. The sit-in movement, which eventuated in the dismantling of the most glaring symbols of Southern apartheid, was begun and sustained mainly by students from black colleges.

In these and other ways, then, the black colleges have been vital forces in the life of the black community and the nation. Although most of the 105 in existence today have serious problems, only a few can validly be classified as an "academic disaster land." Some black universities, in fact, in an effort to counteract their image as inferior, have traditionally had a more rigid academic program than many of their better regarded white counterparts. For this reason they have occasionally been avoided by academically weak black students who, seeking graduate training, have preferred to attend more lenient white institutions for this purpose. In the final analysis, those who have doubts about their historical usefulness need only ask: what would be the condition of the black community today had they not existed?

SEVEN

Black Religion and the Church

ORIGINS OF THE BLACK CHURCH

On July 7, 1867, the thirty-eight black members of the predominantly white Fairfield Baptist Church in Northumberland County, Virginia, addressed the following petition to the church:

> Without alluding to the Providence that so mysteriously changed our social and political relation, we conceive that under the new order of things we are not only advanced in our religious privilege, but that solemn and weighty responsibilities impose upon us a new class of duties in which we should be wanting in fidelity if we did not seek to place ourselves in that position in which we could best promote our mutual good, both in reference to ourselves and our posterity. In this new relation the subject of a separate church organization presses itself upon us as the best possible way in which we can best promote those indispensable interests, such as an ordained ministry, a separate congregation with all the privileges of church organization, stated church meetings, regular religious service, Sabbath schools, etc.[1]

On August 10, 1867, the white members of the church in their regular meeting unanimously and cordially acceded to the petitioners' request for separation. Shortly thereafter, the black secessionists formed the Shiloh Baptist Church and began worship services under the leadership of Hiram Kenner and James Robinson, two illiterate former slave exhorters. Soon, however, the members, with an eye to their practical as well as spiritual needs, chose the Reverend Pyramus Nutt, a carpenter as well as a preacher, as their minister. Under Reverend Nutt's direction, the congregation built its first sanctuary. Again, with remarkable foresight, the congregation designated a young member of the church, Levi Reese Ball, to become its future pastor. To prepare himself for his future role, Ball, at the urging of the church and with the assistance of some white citizens of the community, entered Howard University in the early 1870s. In 1880, upon completing his college training, Ball assumed the pastorship and served Shiloh in that capacity for the next thirty-seven years. Upon his death, the Reverend John Malcus Ellison, who had been selected as assistant pastor some five years earlier when he was a student at Virginia Union University, succeeded to the pastorship. Ellison served the church from 1917 to 1926, when he resigned to assume the post of director of religious activities at Virginia State College. In 1941 he became the fourth president of Virginia Union University, serving in that capacity until 1955.[2]

The early history of Shiloh is representative of developments that occurred throughout the South following the Civil War. Fulfilling a long standing desire for a status of freedom and dignity, a status denied them in the churches of their former masters, the freedmen quickly severed their connections with the white churches after the war and established or joined independent black congregations. Some took this step sooner than the Shiloh group; others made the break much later. But by the end of the Reconstruction period virtually all black Southerners of all denominations were organized into separate black congregations.

An understanding of the freedmen's haste in seceding from white religious bodies requires a brief examination of their religious status as slaves during the antebellum period. During the early colonial period whites debated the question of whether slaves should be allowed to convert to Christianity. Many whites believed that Christian doctrine permitted only the enslavement of heathen, and that conversion to Christianity automatically conferred freedom on the slave. Soon, however, responding to their economic interest in slavery, white Christians either modified their earlier beliefs or reversed them altogether. Christianity conferred only spiritual, not physical, freedom on the slave, maintained Cotton Mather, the Puritan divine. Others insisted that slavery was divinely ordained by God as revealed in the Bible.

Whatever the position taken, the result was that Christianity became a means by which slaveholders both justified the institution of slavery and sought to keep slaves under control. Thus slaves in the South were often required to attend church with their masters, where they were assigned to separate sections in the rear of the church or in the gallery. They were frequently the object of the minister's special attention, as he quoted appropriate scriptural references to support his admonition that they be joyfully obedient to their masters and content with their servitude. They had no voice in church affairs, however, and were essentially spectators rather than full members of the congregation.

That the slaves resented this state of affairs is indicated by the freedmen's suggestion in many cases that as an alternative to separation from the white churches they be allowed a fuller role in church affairs. In considering their obligations to "promote those indispensable interests" arising out of their changed social and political status, the freedmen of the Fairfield Baptist Church asked: "Can we not do this and preserve the unity of the faith and continue in church fellowship with our white brethren; and thereby perpetuate our church identity, so that in all the general interest of the church we may be mutually interested and to some extent co-laborers?"[3] Since the answer was obviously "no," the freedmen chose to depart rather than remain in the subordinate position in the white church.

In some instances, blacks in the South did have separate churches or separate church meetings before the Civil War. The first known black Baptist church in the United States was founded at Silver Bluff, South Carolina, between 1773 and 1775. The second black church was founded on a plantation near Savannah, Georgia, in the late 1770s through the efforts of George Liele and his successor, Anthony Bryan (both slave preachers, although Liele was later freed). The difficulties they underwent, and the persecution they suffered (particularly Bryan) were reminiscent of the sufferings of the early Christians in the era of the Roman empire. Under Morris Brown, an African Methodist Episcopal Church flourished in Charleston, South Carolina, from 1817 to 1822 until white pressure forced Brown to leave the state. In many instances white Baptists, Methodists, Presbyterians, and Episcopalians established separate churches for blacks, slave and free. Moreover, black slaves frequently met as a group in "praise meetings" where they conducted their own services and listened to their own preachers.

In virtually all cases, however, these churches and meetings were under white supervision or surveillance. In some cases a white minister served the church. In other cases a few whites were always in attendance at the meetings to watch the slaves or free blacks. This surveillance and supervision was designed, of course, to prevent the plotting of slave insurrections, a very real possibility as the Denmark Vesey and Nat Turner conspiracies, both fomented by black preachers, had demonstrated. The whites of the South were determined that religion was to be a means of social control rather than an instrument of black liberation.

The whites' desire to maintain control over the black population did not disappear with emancipation. Many white church leaders were initially opposed to the withdrawal of the black members from their churches, feeling that it was in the self-interest of blacks to remain and hoping to continue to keep blacks under surveillance and supervision. The specter of blacks in groups plotting rebellion died hard, if at all. Yet, although they wanted to retain their black members, white churches were unwilling to abolish segregated seating arrangements and permit blacks a role in administering the institutions. Consequently, the black members withdrew. In many cases, out of a sincere desire to help or a conscious or unconscious desire to still have some influence over black affairs, white churchmen assisted their former black brethren in setting up the new black churches, often donating money, land, buildings, and organizational assistance. Shiloh Baptist Church, for example, was built on land donated by a white member of the Fairfield Baptist Church.

As H. Shelton Smith has shown, however, most white churches did not agonize over the withdrawal of black membership. Indeed, after some initial misgivings, they either welcomed or encouraged it. This was especially true for the Southern Baptists and Methodists as early as 1866, and for other denominations by the end of Reconstruction. Thus for different and opposite reasons, both black and white Southerners early agreed on the desirability of racially separate churches.[4]

GROWTH OF THE BLACK CHURCH

Because of its decentralized and democratic structure and the fervor of its religious worship services, the Baptist denomination attracted the greatest number of freedmen and spawned the greatest number of churches. By the end of the nineteenth century the Baptists claimed more black members than all the other denominations combined. The black Baptist churches arose either as a result of the withdrawal of black members from white churches or the assumption by former praise groups of a more formal structure. Once established, the churches proliferated rapidly. Because of their loose structure Baptist congregations frequently divided into smaller congregations as factions developed and seceded from the parent church. By 1898, for example, seven black churches in a region of Mississippi could trace their origin to the parent Pine Grove Baptist Church in Aberdeen. Other churches arose through the missionary activities of ambitious ministers. The Reverend Monroe Boykin, the first pastor of the Mount Moriah Baptist Church, founded in 1866 in Camden, South Carolina, eventually organized five additional churches which he served as minister. Another minister in South Carolina, the Reverend Alexander Bettis, who like Boykin was a former slave, organized over forty Baptist churches between 1865 and his death in 1895. Throughout most of this period he served as pastor of four churches, and for a brief period he pastored ten concurrently.

Although each Baptist church existed as an independent entity in the social and spiritual firmament, the black Baptists early evinced an interest in cooperation. Churches in a given community or county or region of a state came together in conventions or associations. These local and regional associations then eventually combined into state conventions, and as time passed the state bodies merged into national conventions. Black Baptists in

North Carolina came together in a state convention as early as 1866, followed by Baptists in Virginia and Alabama in 1867. By 1870 such conventions existed in all the Southern states. In 1867 the Consolidated American Baptist Convention, the first national black convention, was organized. It was superseded in 1880 by the National Baptist Convention formed in that year at Montgomery, Alabama. This organization united with other groups in Atlanta, Georgia, in 1895 as the National Baptist Convention of the United States, claiming at that time some 3 million members, most of whom were in the South.

The second strongest religious denomination among blacks was the Methodist. Making the greatest appeal to blacks in the lower South was the African Methodist Episcopal Church (AME), organized in 1816 as a result of the secession of a group of blacks led by Richard Allen from a white Methodist church in Philadelphia in 1787. After the Civil War it made its greatest strides in South Carolina, resuming the work it had abandoned when Morris Brown was forced from the state in 1822. After it was reorganized in the state by Bishop Daniel Payne in 1865, it expanded rapidly under his leadership and that of Richard Harvey Cain and other energetic ministers, claiming a membership of 44,000 by 1877. Reverend T. W. Stringer came to Mississippi in 1865 as the AME's chief emissary. Within five years the denomination had thirty-five churches with about 5,000 members in the state. In 1880 the denomination claimed a national membership of 400,000, then concentrated mostly in the South.

The African Methodist Episcopal Zion Church, also a result of the black withdrawal from the white Methodist church in Philadelphia in 1787, grew rapidly after the Civil War as a result of its proselytizing work among the freedmen. It increased its membership from 26,746 in 1860 to 200,000 in 1870.

Other black Methodist congregations grew out of white churches after the Civil War. At the close of the war the predominantly white Methodist Episcopal Church, South, claimed over 250,000 black members. Like the white Baptists, the white Methodists initially wanted to retain their black members; but like their Baptist counterparts, the black Methodists were unwilling to tolerate their inferior status in the church any longer. Many, therefore, withdrew, joining other Methodist bodies in the South (particularly the African Methodist churches) or the Baptists. In 1866 less than 78,000 blacks remained as members; and these appealed to the General Conference for separate status. Separate status was granted in 1870 when the Colored Methodist Episcopal Church was organized in a general conference held at Jackson, Tennessee. Henry Miles of Kentucky and Richard H. Vanderhorst of Georgia were ordained as bishops. The Colored Methodist Episcopal Church, because of its close ties with the white Southern Methodists, was initially suspect among many blacks who referred to it variously as "the Old Slavery Church" or the "Rebel Church." By 1890, however, much of the suspicion had dissipated, and the denomination grew steadily thereafter. But it still remained the smallest of the black Methodist churches in membership.

The Northern Methodist Episcopal Church also proselytized heavily among the freedmen after the Civil War, and most of its members in the South were black. In South Carolina in 1881, for example, it had 36,000 black members and only sixty-nine white. Though generally desiring to be an integrated church, and attempting to assure blacks equality of status, the Northern Methodists also succumbed to the temper of the times, and with the succession of black bishops and lower clergy to church offices, it became essentially a black denomination in the South.

Other denominations to which blacks belonged in the South were the Presbyterians and the Episcopalians. At the close of the Civil War black members of these churches either withdrew entirely and joined other denominations or established separate churches for themselves. By the beginning of the twentieth century, the white and black members of these denominations in the South were in separate church bodies.

RELIGIOUS EXPRESSION

Most observers agree that the black church has been the most important institution, except for the family, in the life of the black community. It has been a principal carrier of the religious and cultural tradition of black people in America. Its religious services, especially in the traditional Baptist and Methodist churches, represent a synthesis of the African, European, and the Afro-American religious and cultural experience.

The main characteristic of religious service in the traditional (lower- and lower-middle-class) black church in the South was the congregation's participation in virtually every facet of the service. In a typical Baptist church service it was someone from the congregation (often an officer of the church but frequently an ordinary member) who led the congregation in prayer. These prayers were often long, eloquent, and moving. In many cases they had been partially memorized, but they were seldom merely recited, for the deliverer of the prayer would often improvise where his memory failed or in order to make the prayer relevant to his own experiences or to the experiences of the congregation. Expressed or implied in most prayers were the ideas of an omnipotent, omniscient, and sometimes capricious but merciful God; the difficulties and sorrows of earthly life; and the desire for security and salvation. Although it is impossible to capture the eloquence and spirit of these prayers through the written word, the following example may illustrate some of the ideas expressed:

Father, we are thankful for our blessings and we do thank Thee and give praise to Thy name. We know You know the secrets of our hearts

and that You know sometimes what we need better than we know ourselves. You know sometimes the way gets dark and troubles get heavy
upon us and we have heavy burdens to bear. Sometimes we are called
everything but a child of God; but in the midst of all our trouble, we
pray and expect to fight until the war is ended. Have mercy upon me,
oh Lord, and hear my cries. You promised You would be with me in
the midst of my affliction and that You would not forsake me. . . . Talk
with us, walk with us, help us to come closer together and to find more
grace, and in the end, prepare for Thy servants a place in Thy Kingdom
where we can live and praise Thee world without end. Amen.[5]

As already indicated, many of the prayers would be delivered eloquently,
often surpassing the minister's sermon in this respect. One suspects that
some of the men giving the prayers may have harbored a secret passion to
become ministers themselves. The overall effect of the prayers was enhanced
by the response of the congregation through the intonation of such expressions as "yes Lord," "have mercy Lord," and "Amen." Often shortly
before the prayer ended someone would softly strike up a hymn or spiritual,
and the congregation would join in, further enhancing the impressive atmosphere of the service.

The traditional black church also made it possible for members of the
congregation to express themselves musically. Where a formal choir existed,
it often provided music for only part of the service. During other parts of
the service where music was appropriate, any individual was free to lead the
congregation in song. Occasionally, the person who led the song would improvise by introducing new phrases and verses or by interjecting a verse from
one song into another. In this way new songs would come into being almost
spontaneously, and would be taken up by other singers and perpetuated.
Muted stamping of the foot, rather than a musical instrument, would often
accompany the congregational singing. Some musicologists maintain that
such foot stamping constituted a vestigial representation of the African drum,
whose use had been banned during slavery times because masters feared that
it would be used to foment insurrection. As time passed the formal church
choir gradually replaced the free singing of the congregation. Even here,
however, certain vestiges of African culture may have been evident in the
lining-off of the hymns by the minister followed by the singing of the lines
by the choir and congregation. Another explanation for this practice may be
that there were too few hymnbooks or that many in the congregation may
have been illiterate, and by reading the lines of the song to the congregation,
the minister gave everyone an opportunity to participate in the singing. Moreover, the lining-off of hymns was also in accord with the leader and chorus
pattern of singing which was found not only in African singing but in Anglo-
Saxon vocal music as well.

If is important to note that before the choir became a formal part of the church services, the most traditional Baptist churches discouraged the use of musical instruments in religious worship. Such instruments were regarded as proper only for secular music, for, contrary to the opinion of some scholars, before the emergence of gospel music, most black religionists made a sharp distinction between the music of God and the music of the world. Even after the choir became a fixture in the black church, only the piano and the organ were regarded as acceptable instruments for religious worship. For a long time the conservative black Baptist church looked askance at the gospel music that became increasingly popular in the 1920s. Even after gospel music won the sanction of the National Baptist Convention in 1930, many traditional black churches refused to accept it. Finally, however, gospel music did win a place in the Southern black religious service, compromised by the fact, however, that often a separate choir or chorus was established to accommodate it, while the regular choir continued to sing the Euro-American hymns and the spirituals. To a large extent, the music rendered by the gospel chorus was regarded more as a form of entertainment than as an integral part of the worship service of the church, the congregation preferring to listen to it rather than join in the singing.

The congregation also participated in the minister's sermon. The sermon itself was designed to serve a variety of functions: to enlighten, to arouse emotionally, or to entertain. In the ideal sermon, there was a virtual "dialogue" between the minister and the congregation—with the people listening, absorbing, feeling, understanding, and evaluating what was being said and occasionally responding with an expression of approval such as "amen." The minister, in turn, feeling a sense of communion with his audience, would be stimulated by the congregation's response. Thus the whole congregation would be brought into spiritual communion with God and with each other; they would experience a sense of oneness. Not all preachers were capable of inducing this kind of response. Many tried by employing various kinds of emotion-producing techniques in which the sermon and its delivery became essentially an empty, stylized form of behavior. In such cases the congregation often responded in kind with a feigned emotionalism devoid of any meaningful content.

The best minister prepared his sermons with care, making certain to use Biblical and other references that the people could relate to their own lives. He often delivered the sermon in dramatic, even poetic fashion, making wide use of imagery. Some scholars maintain that the dialogue (call and response pattern) between the minister and the congregation and the tendency of ministers to employ animal and bird symbolisms (as in the popular sermon theme "The Eagle Stirreth Her Nest") reflect the influence of the African heritage.[6] While rarely seeking to evoke emotion for emotion's sake, few people remained unmoved by the minister's message, and many went away from the church with sufficient "spiritual food" to mull over during the weeks and months ahead.

Perhaps the most famous of the old-time Southern black preachers was John Jasper of Richmond, Virginia. Before the Civil War Jasper was a slave preacher, confined to preaching under white supervision and surveillance to black congregations in the Petersburg and Richmond areas. After learning to read, Jasper read the Bible avidly to the extent that he could almost recite it from memory. Still as a slave he became famous for the eloquence of his funeral sermons. After the war, he organized a church in the Jackson Ward area of Richmond with an initial congregation of eight persons. The congregation soon swelled to 2,000 members. His fame as a preacher spread throughout the nation as a result of his sermon entitled "The Sun Do Move," in which Jasper, using vivid word pictures and an impeccable logic based on scriptural references, "disproved" the heliocentric theory that had the unanimous endorsement of astronomers. Jasper was not only a great orator, but he was also an able pastor, attempting to minister to the educational and social needs of his congregation.

Many of the sermons preached by men like Jasper became classics, and were used frequently by other black ministers throughout the nation. James Weldon Johnson captured much of the wording and spirit of these sermons in his *God's Trombones*, a collection of sermons which he put in verse form. "The Creation" is perhaps the best known of the sermons in Johnson's collection. Many black schoolchildren, including the author, memorized and recited it at church and school programs. Another well-known sermon that contains the imagery, drama, relevant illustrations, and poetic rhythm of the old-time, best black sermons is Johnson's "Go Down Death—A Funeral Sermon," which follows:

Weep not, weep not,
She is not dead;
She's resting in the bosom of Jesus.
Heart-broken husband—weep no more;
Grief-stricken son—weep no more;
Left-lonesome daughter—weep no more;
She's only just gone home.

Day before yesterday morning,
God was looking down from his great, high heaven,
Looking down on all his children,
And his eye fell on Sister Caroline,
Tossing on her bed of pain.
And God's big heart was touched with pity,
With the everlasting pity.

And God sat back on this throne,
And he commanded that tall, bright angel standing
    at his right hand:

Call me Death!
And that tall, bright angel cried in a voice
That broke like a clap of thunder:
Call Death!—Call Death!
And the echo sounded down the streets of heaven
Till it reached away back to that shadowy place,
Where Death waits with his pale, white horses.

And Death heard the summons,
And he leaped on his fastest horse,
Pale as a sheet in the moonlight.
Up the golden street Death galloped,
And the hoofs of his horse struck fire from the gold,
But they didn't make no sound.
Up Death rode to the Great White Throne,
And waited for God's command.

And God said: Go down, Death, go down,
Go down to Savannah, Georgia,
Down in Yamacraw,
And find Sister Caroline.
She's borne the burden and heat of the day,
She's laboured long in my vineyard,
and she's tired—
She's weary—
Go down, Death, and bring her to me.

And Death didn't say a word,
But he loosed the reins on his pale, white horse,
And he clamped the spurs to his bloodless sides,
And out and down he rode,
Through heaven's pearly gates,

Past suns and moons and stars;
On Death rode,
And the foam from his horse was like a comet in
    the sky;
On Death rode.
Leaving the lightning's flash behind;
Straight on down he came.

While we were watching round her bed,
She turned her eyes and looked away,
She saw what we couldn't see;
She saw Old Death. She saw Old Death,
Coming like a falling star.
But Death didn't frighten Sister Caroline;

He looked to her like a welcome friend.
And she whispered to us: I'm going home,
And she smiled and closed her eyes.

And Death took her up like a baby,
And she lay in his icy arms,
But she didn't feel no chill.
And Death began to ride again—
Up beyond the morning star,
Into the glittering light of glory,
On to the Great White Throne.
And there he laid Sister Caroline
On the loving breast of Jesus.

And Jesus took his own hand and wiped away her tears,
And he smoothed the furrows from her face,
And the angels sang a little song,
And Jesus rocked her in his arms,
    and kept a-saying: Take your rest,
Take your rest, take your rest.

Weep not—weep not,
She is not dead;
She's resting in the bosom of Jesus.[7]

Much has been made of the emotional nature of traditional black worship services. Some have seen in such emotionalism an expression of the African heritage. Others have maintained that it is simply a replica (with a black patina, of course) of the religious behavior of lower-class Southern whites. Still others have simply regarded it as the natural response of a people to the experience of being slaves and social pariahs in the South. Perhaps the truth lies in a synthesis of the three explanations. Undoubtedly the emotionalism in the black church has served a cathartic function, as a vehicle for the release of pent-up feelings generated by the social, economic, and personal repression to which black people have been subjected by white society in the South. Within the confines of the church blacks have been able to find respite from the inhibitions on expression imposed by the white community. They could feel free for a brief period of time. Moreover, emotionalism, when not carried to the extreme, created within the congregation a feeling of warmth and a sense of unity. When carried to extremes, however, it became a spectacle in which most members of the congregation often refused to participate.

The extent of emotionalism in a church often varied with the social status of a majority of the members. In most upper-middle and upper-class congregations, shouting and other forms of spontaneous expression were frowned upon and seldom occurred. Lower-class members of such congregations usually took their cue from the other classes. In the predominantly middle- and lower-middle-class congregations, restrained emotionalism was permissible. Even in the lower-class congregations, however, except for the holiness churches, there was seldom an orgy of emotionalism as some commentators have contended. A few people might shout and otherwise vividly vent their emotions, but the rest of the congregation, though moved by the spiritual experiences of their brothers or sisters, would sit as quasi-passive observers of the more active members.

As the black population became increasingly better educated, overt emotional expression declined, but did not totally cease. Many educated clergymen discouraged such behavior as did the better educated laymen. Iconoclastic youth have further served to dampen the old religious enthusiasm of the traditional church. Today, shouting has largely disappeared from the mainstream black church in the South. It still can be observed, however, in some of the so-called cult churches such as the House of Prayer for All People and the various holiness churches. And even in some of the more restrained churches occasionally an elderly women who has survived the trials and tribulations of several scores of years cannot hold back a cry of remembered pain or a shout of exultation.

THE DEBATE OVER EMOTIONALISM

While the educated black clergy has usually disapproved of extreme forms of emotionalism they have been divided over the efficacy of general religious fervor as a characteristic of black worship services. At the Negro Young People's Christian and Educational Congress of 1902 in Atlanta, attended by over 7,000 religious and lay people from throughout the nation, several well-educated ministers condemned the emotionalism, "animalism," "excitements," and "great physical agitation," that marked the services of many black churches. Other equally well-educated clergymen demurred, however. "Emotionalism? This is a peculiar characteristic of the race. Cultivate it; it is a precious inheritance," advised one minister. "I hope the day will never come when the Negro will cease to be emotional," declared another. And still another minister, Rev. Will Jackson of Sedalia, Missouri, confessed that while he, too, once condemned emotionalism and "thought that all that was needed to overcome it was education," he had come "to consider it in a different light."[8]

For thirty-five years I have watched its obstinate persistence through the stages of social and intellectual progress which the Negro has . . . made in that period of time. I discover that it survives the encroach-

ments of education and culture. It can not, therefore, be a mere resultant of temporary conditions as I had thought. It seems to me to be
an indestructible element of Negro character.

The clergyman went on to praise the "intense emotional enthusiasm" of
the black race, attributing to it the ability of black people to keep "alive the
principles and aspirations of true manhood" in the face of "demoralizing
pressure of powerful adverse influences." Rev. Jackson concluded that:

> Had it not been for this irrepressible and ever-assertive element of
> his character, the Negro would have degenerated into the depths of a
> hopeless and irretrievable infidelity. It has kept him in touch with his
> God, and that means also in touch with the possibilities of his moral,
> religious and intellectual resurrection.[9]

Later generations of highly educated ministers have also applauded the
religious fervor of the masses. They have seen in it not only a useful instrument through which to impart theological doctrine and social and moral
values but also a means of stimulating support for social programs. No
minister was more skillful in this respect than Miles Mark Fisher, whom one
scholar has characterized as "a remarkable combination of intellect and
emotion, old-time religion and the social gospel, lower-class sympathies and
upper-class training and station. . . ."[10] Fisher, a University of Chicago
Ph.D. in church history and author of the acclaimed *Negro Slave Songs in
the United States* and several lesser known works, served as pastor of White
Rock Baptist Church in Durham, North Carolina, from 1933 to 1967. White
Rock was the church of the Durham black elite of businessmen, college
professors, public school teachers, and other professionals as well as of tobacco workers and other lower-middle- and lower-class black residents of the
city and surrounding communities.

Although highly educated and of upper-class parentage, Fisher encouraged
respect for the folk culture and traditions. He devoted at least one sermon
and worship service a year to a special commemoration of the spirituals. He
supported the establishment of a gospel choir, and invited black evangelists
to conduct revival services. At the same time, however, he delivered sermons
on scholarly topics, taking care to make his message clear with appropriate
examples from black life. Believing that the emotionalism of the masses
could as easily be employed in behalf of a social gospel as in an otherworldly
religion, he declared on the occasion of the tenth anniversary of his ministry
at White Rock that "A chief duty was to cultivate this native gift of enthusiasm of a people not as an end in itself but as a means of promoting the old
time religion. Before any objective is submitted to the church, sermons as
enthusiastic as I can make them review reasons for the enterprises." Fisher,

therefore, did not attempt to impose restraints on his congregation. Believing that the people should be allowed to "reserve the churches for their holy fun," he maintained that "The expression of religion . . . presupposes that people can demonstrate enthusiasm without embarrassment, if they feel like it, and that their outlook shall be earth-centered, expecting the goods of life to reach them."

Fisher's earth-centeredness was the social gospel. During the first ten years of his leadership White Rock established a recreation center and a touring ping-pong team, housed a day nursery and a health clinic, sponsored a regular series of musical recitals by visiting artists, and hosted an organizing meeting of the AFL Tobacco Workers union.[11]

THE CHURCH IN ITS SECULAR ROLE

In its institutional capacity the church occupied a central position in the life of the black community. In the rural South the physical boundaries of a given community often accorded with the outer residential limits of the communicants of a particular church. This was particularly true in the early days, as limited modes of transportation necessitated the location of a church within walking distance of the majority of the members. Since it was usually the only community institution whose internal administration was under the complete control of the black population, it performed a variety of functions and services.

As E. Franklin Frazier has pointed out, one of the first functions of the black church after the Civil War was to provide a moral and social code for the black community and to institute sanctions for its violation.[12] It encouraged monogamous family life and condemned irregular social relationships. Expulsion from the church often awaited those who violated the prescribed sexual mores. In small communities, where the lives of the people were closely tied up with church activity, expulsion could be a severe penalty. In other matters, too, the church adopted a rigid puritanical stance. Swearing, gambling, and drinking were, of course, condemned; but so were dancing and card playing. To a considerable degree, one's social standing in the community was determined by the extent to which he adhered to the moral standards prescribed by the church. On this basis the black community, particularly in rural areas, was stratified into the respectable and the not so respectable.

In the social sense, the church also provided respite from the monotony and drabness of everyday life. Church services offered people an opportunity to socialize. Frequently, the entire Sabbath was spent in attending various services and programs at the church. In many communities there were also church functions during some nights of the week. The Wednesday night prayer service was common to both the rural and urban church in many areas. In addition, the church building frequently served as the community's theater and concert hall, where religious (and secular) plays and singing programs would be held.

Through the church people also were able to satisfy their urge for a modicum of prestige and power. Shut out from the larger society by the racial caste system, they found in the church a means of participating and exercising influence in the life of the community. Every member could feel a sense of worth through service in some church organization—the choir, the usher board, the missionary society, the men's and women's clubs, the trustee board, the deacon board, the Sunday school, and similar bodies. In a sense the church was a political arena, a center of black politics, as individuals and groups contested for positions of power, influence, and leadership. Much of the proliferation of churches, particularly among the Baptists, arose out of factional quarrels within a congregation with one of the contending groups seceding and forming another church.

Since religious leadership offered black people one of the few avenues of power and prestige in the community, ministers also competed with each other for status. Church conventions were often marked by the bickering, bargaining, and strife characteristic of a political party convention. In many ways the experience gained by the members and leaders in running church affairs constituted preparation for political participation in a wider arena. Because of the influence that ministers wielded in the black community as church leaders, and because of their experience in the political arena of the church, it is not surprising that some of the most effective and able black politicians during the Reconstruction period were clergymen. Moreover, many of the ordinary voters during that period had already had some experience with the political process through their participation in church affairs.

The black church also gave birth to many of the mutual benefit and burial societies that arose in the black community after the Civil War. As previously indicated, many of these societies were forerunners of banks, insurance companies, and other business enterprises in the black community. As expected, the founders of many of these businesses were clergymen. The mutual-aid societies expressed the church's concern with social welfare. Even where such societies did not exist, virtually every church sought to provide some assistance to the needy in the community—the sick, disabled, and the victims of some disaster. Where provisions were not made for such services in the regular budget, special collections were taken up at the Sunday meetings. As early as 1898 Du Bois reported that several of the more prosperous churches also maintained orphanages and homes for the elderly.[13]

As already mentioned, the church played a major role in the development of educational programs for the black community. Religious denominations founded and maintained colleges and secondary schools. Individual ministers and churches organized or inspired the establishment of elementary and secondary schools in their respective communities. In many communities in the late nineteenth and early twentieth centuries the church building doubled as the school house. As late as 1920, the church in a few communities helped to pay the salary of the teacher in the one-room school. Even as late as the 1940s churches helped to raise funds to support the public schools in some areas of the South. The church's influence in education was also evident in the cases where ministers served as public school teachers or principals. Frequently the churches in the community helped to finance the college educations of young church members. Such assistance ranged from regular scholarship programs in the large and well-organized churches to the taking of special collections in the regular church service on the eve of the student's departure for college.

The church as also been a major carrier of the black cultural tradition. To some people, the forms and spirit of religious worship reflect the African cultural heritage. Certainly the memory of the slave experience has been transmitted through sermons and music. Through the church the spirituals have remained alive, and new musical forms, notably gospel music, have emerged. The vitality of the church as the preserver of the black social and cultural heritage was clearly evident in the black protest movement in the South in the late 1950s and the early 1960s as the black participants relied heavily upon black religious patterns to build up and sustain their morale.

WEAKNESSES OF THE CHURCH

Even though the church was the most independent of black community institutions, it could not escape the external and internal restrictions on the social environment in which it existed. It could cushion the impact of racial oppression and provide some psychological relief for those burdened with the day-to-day problems of survival, but until the late 1950s it was not in the forefront of those actively working to overthrow the Southern biracial system. Indeed, many critics of the black church have viewed it as essentially an instrument of accommodation, dissipating the black community's potential for social activism and social protest into a socially negative emotional and otherworldly oriented religion. Rarely indeed, critics maintain, were there such religious leaders as the Reverend Henry M. Mitchell, president of Virginia Baptists in the 1890s who, according to his grandson, "is remembered as the preacher who put a gun out of every window in his church to protect a black man and his wife from lynching."[14]

To the extent that the critics of the black church are correct in their assessment of its negative historical role in social activism and black protest, there are several explanations. Most of these explanations are merely a catalog of the weaknesses within the black community which in turn were reflected in the community's major institution.

During the nineteenth century and for several decades of the twentieth century, the black church was predominantly a rural institution, since most of the black population in the South resided in rural areas. To the extent that the church members were dependent on white people—landlords, creditors, and employers—for their livelihoods, then to that degree the church as an institution was limited in its social activist role. If the pastor of a church attempted to challenge the racial caste system, white people in the community could call him to account through their economic control over the church members. Furthermore, as was often the case in the plantation South, the minister himself might be a sharecropper, a tenant, a schoolteacher, or hold some other position which made him economically dependent on whites.

Contributing to the black church's powerlessness within the larger social environment of the South was its often deficient leadership. Booker T. Washington complained about the ignorance and low moral character of many rural ministers in the late nineteenth and early twentieth centuries. Others complained that sometimes even the most moral ministers, jealous of their status in the community, stood as barriers to social progress. For example, when Ellen Cotton and her husband went to Miller's Ferry, Alabama, in the early twentieth century to operate a Presbyterian school for black children, they found their efforts initially resisted by the local Baptist minister who feared both their education and their Presbyterianism.[15]

As Booker T. Washington acknowledged long before his death, the quality of the black clergy steadily improved as education and theological training became more widely available. Nevertheless, seventy-five years after the Civil War, the majority of the black ministers were still undereducated, and many were overworked and poorly paid. In 1940 about 40 percent of the experienced black clergy throughout the United States had no high school education, while only 21 percent were college graduates. By 1960 these figures were 22.5 percent and 33.3 percent, respectively. Ministers in rural areas were even less educated. In a study of 141 Virginia ministers who had attended the summer school for ministers at Virginia State College from 1943 through 1946, Harry W. Roberts discovered that only about 8 percent of the rural ministers had both a college and a seminary degree, although over two-thirds did have education beyond the elementary school level.[16] In terms of education this group may have been somewhat atypical in that their attendance at the summer school indicated that they were a highly-motivated group. There were exceptions to this pattern of a poorly educated rural ministry, however. As early as the mid-1930s, four of the eight ministers interviewed in Northumberland County, Virginia, held both college and seminary degrees, while three others had completed or nearly completed high school, and two had taken seminary courses.[17]

The low educational standing of rural black ministers as late as the 1940s was a reflection of the historical inequality of educational opportunities for blacks throughout the South, the tendency of some rural people to maintain that a call from God rather than education was sufficient qualification for one to become a preacher, and the dependence of ministers on secular occupations to earn a living. Lack of education was a serious defect in the rural minister, for he was often the community's chief leader as well as personal and social adviser. Without a reasonable education he was ill equipped to understand the many forces that determined the conditions and status of his people; and even if he understood, he lacked sufficient personal flexibility to provide the necessary leadership to effect social change. It is significant to note that most of the religious leaders of the black protest movement of the past decade and a half have been college-trained ministers.

Because ministers were poorly paid they often had to pastor several churches or hold other jobs. Of the ninety rural ministers who attended the Virginia State College summer school for ministers from 1943 through 1946, Roberts reported that seventy pastored more than one church, thirty-six pastored more than two churches, and twelve pastored more than three churches. Two ministers served five churches, and one pastored six churches. Furthermore, over three-fourths of these ministers were engaged in other occupations.[18] It is obvious, then, that most of these ministers were unable to exercise any significant leadership in either their churches or the communities where the churches were located. They generally resided outside of the communities which they served and did little more for their churches than preach one or two Sundays during a month. Such "transient" or "absentee" leadership was hardly any leadership at all.

Contributing to the poor quality of the rural ministry was the existence of too many churches in relatively close proximity to each other. In the late nineteenth and early twentieth centuries numerous churches were desirable since long-distance transportation facilities were not available. Also, the church with a small membership enabled each member to actively participate in the affairs of the church and maintain intimate social relations with the other members. The urban storefront church in the North came into existence through the efforts of rural migrants from the South to recapture the intimacy of the small Southern rural church. But democratic participation in church affairs and social intimacy exacted a rather high social cost. Overchurching meant that few churches could afford a well-trained resident minister. It also meant that few churches could marshall sufficient resources to bring about the necessary fundamental changes in society. Thus, for too many churches, the minister was merely an occasional functionary on some Sunday morning and at funerals and weddings. In too many communities, the church was essentially a status quo organization in that it lacked the leadership and material resources to be anything else.

Although the black church has always been an important element in the lives of black Southerners, it has never commanded the active participation of all members of the black community. Women have generally been more active in church affairs than men, except in the higher church offices. The extreme upper class and the extreme lower class have not found the church very appealing. For the most part the church's greatest support has come from the middle group of hardworking people to whom most black Southerners belong. Black youth have always been a challenge to the church, as they have tended to look with a jaundiced eye at some of the church's personnel, services, and programs. As the youth became better educated, many found it difficult to accept the leadership of the less well-educated ministers. A result was the alienation of many young people from the church. It is a mistake then to regard the church as virtually synonymous with the black community. Although it touched most people either directly or indirectly, there were many people who were beyond its purview.

During the past two decades the church in the South has been somewhat revitalized. There are fewer churches, and the ministers are better trained. Moreover, the reactivation of the church's protest role in recent years—in the tradition of Denmark Vesey, Nat Turner, Bishop Henry M. Turner, and others—has also served to bring new life to the church in the South. It may well be that the black church today, like its forebears during the Reconstruction period, may be in a new era of service to the black community and to the South.

EIGHT

The Family

THE RECONSTRUCTION OF THE FAMILY

Shortly before the Civil War ended Smart and Mary Washington of Beaufort, South Carolina, had already lived together as man and wife for more than forty years during which time they had become the parents of nineteen children. Nevertheless, in January 1865 the couple took their first formal wedding vows and received a certificate of marriage. At the conclusion of the ceremony Smart happily acknowledged the congratulations of friends and well-wishers with the comment: "Him's [she's] my wife for sartin, now. Ef the ole hen run away, I shall cotch him [her] for sure."[1]

Although spoken in jest, Smart's observation reflected a tragic reality of black life in the antebellum South. An intrinsic attribute of slave status in America was the absence of the right to a secure family life. While numerous slave families (perhaps a majority) remained intact, all lived under the omnipresent threat of forced separation and many families were broken up through the sale of parents or offspring. It is not surprising, then, that at the close of the Civil War freedmen like the Washingtons included a stable and independent family life among their highest aspirations.

For several months after the war freedmen throughout the South sought to reestablish family ties that had been severed during slavery. Many wandered about from place to place searching for their wives, husbands, parents, and children. As time passed some who could not travel advertised in newspapers, while others secured the services of schoolteachers and literate friends in writing letters to distant places, where they thought their relatives had been taken. Others, discouraged by the unlikely prospect of finding former spouses, or failing in the attempt, established new relationships. Those who had never been married, but who had formed affectional unions during slavery, or had wished to do so, consummated and legitimized their relationships. Most were anxious to receive legal sanction for the marriages and unions they entered during slavery or contracted shortly afterwards. Indeed, during the first year of the Civil War, and before the Emancipation Proclamation was issued, slave couples in the contraband camps of the Union army insisted on the formality of a marriage ceremony in order to legalize and sanctify the unions they had established when they were under the authority of their former masters.

For young people, freedom made it possible to consummate contemplated marriages with persons of their choice without the alien intrusion of members of the master class. Not all restraints were removed, however. During the post-Civil War period many parents continued to keep a watchful eye over the courting practices, romantic attachments, and marital choices of their children, especially their daughters. A former Arkansas slave, who married in 1870, recalled that in order to win the hand of his future wife he promised her father that he would "go to the mourners bench," a pledge which he kept "just a month after I got her."[2] Similarly, Lucy Dunn, a former North Carolina slave, recalled that during the whole year of her courtship with her future husband, they were seldom alone. Her mother not only accompanied them when they walked home from church, but she also forbade Lucy to walk her suitor to the gate at the end of his Sunday visits to her home. However, after he proposed, Lucy finally won permission to walk him to the gate provided her mother "was settin' dere on de porch lookin'." Thereafter, the romance progressed to its inexorable but still chaperoned climax:

> Dat Sunday night I did walk with Jim to de gate and stood under de honeysuckles dat was a-smellin' so sweet. I heard de big ole bullfrog a-croakin' by de river and de whipporwills a-hollerin' in de woods. Dere was a big yellow moon, and I reckon Jim did love me. Anyhow he said so and asked me to marry him and he squeezed my hand. I told him I'd think it over and I did and de next Sunday I told him dat I'd have him.
>
> He ain't kissed me yet but de next Sunday he asked my mammy for me. She says dat she'll have to have a talk to me and let him know. Well all dat week she talks to me, tellin' me how serious gettin' married is and dat it last a powerful long time. I tells her dat I knows it but I am ready to try it and dat I intends to make a go of it, anyhow.
>
> On Sunday night Mammy tells Jim dat he can have me and you ought to seed dat black boy grin. He comes to me without a word and

he picks me up out dat chair and dere in de moonlight he kisses me
right before my mammy who am a-cryin'. De next Sunday we was
married in de Baptist church at Neuse. I had a new white dress, though
times was hard.[3]

While the marriage rites of most freedmen were relatively simple, usually
involving no more than the taking of an oath before a justice of the peace, a
Freedmen's Bureau official, or a clergyman, they often evoked complex
emotions. A Northern white teacher on Port Royal Island, South Carolina,
recalled that when one unmarried couple and their daughter and her fiance
spoke the marriage vows in a double ceremony before the same minister, "It
was touching to see the eager, expectant look on the faces of the old couples.
They were aiming for something higher and better of which they had as yet
but a dawning conception. . . ."[4]

Yet behind many of the marriage ceremonies lay much confusion and pain.
Slaves who had taken new partners after being forcibly separated from
former mates through sale, sometimes faced difficult choices when freedom
came. Four years after his wife and his two children were sold, James McCullum of North Carolina married again. He and his second wife also had two
children. When the war ended McCullum's first wife and children returned
to him. To resolve his dilemma, McCullum sought a ruling form the Freedmen's Bureau court in Lumberton, although he personally believed that
only his first marriage was legal.[5]

Many ex-slaves facing a similar dilemma chose to return to their first
spouses, indicating that many of their initial marriages were based on genuine
affection or a strong respect for family obligations. Jane Ferguson of Port
Royal, South Carolina, whose first husband, Martin Barnwell, had been
sold away from her and her infant son, had no doubts about where her first
loyalty lay. Before marrying Ferguson, her second husband, she had extracted from him a promise that if Martin ever returned, Ferguson would
give her up. After the fall of Charleston in February 1865, Jane received
word that Martin was still alive and wanted to rejoin her. Despite the protests of Ferguson, who was now a Union soldier, and the intercession of his
chaplain, Jane unhesitatingly decided to return to her first husband, emphatically declaring: "Martin Barnwell is my husband. . . . I am got no husband
but he."[6]

Other ex-slaves, faced with the problem (or opportunity) of choosing between spouses, were less decisive. After Tina's first husband, Sam, was sold
away from her, she married Kit. When Sam returned to Port Royal early in
1865 Tina attempted to solve her dilemma by spending alternate months with
each of them. Kit was sorely distraught over this state of affairs for, as he
confessed to Elizabeth Botume, a Yankee schoolteacher, "I married her for
love, an' I lub her now more an' better than I lub myself." Kit's love finally

prevailed, for Tina, concerned that "poor brother Kit is all alone . . . [and] ain't got nobody but me," decided to give up Sam and to reside permanently with Kit. When she died many years later, Kit refused to allow any other woman to live with him, explaining that " 'I don't want Tina to think I would bring shame upon she.' " [7]

Kit's devotion to Tina was not uncommon, especially among ex-slave couples who had shared the slavery experience together. Concern for the welfare of her surviving husband inspired one woman to attempt in a death-bed ceremony to marry her husband to her friend and neighbor. She explained that " 'I is going shortly, an I can't lef' poor Billy all alone. So I axes sister Hagar to come here and tuck my place, an' min' Billy, an' the house, an' the dumb creetures for me.' " Unfortunately, after she died, the elders of Billy's church refused to recognize the marriage because Hagar did not have a di-vorce from her first husband, from whom she had been separated for several years. Nevertheless, Billy and Hagar lived together as man and wife, but Billy always regretted that their marriage did not have the sanction of the church. [8]

For many years after the Civil War there were numerous men like Billy who believed that having a family based on the model of the respectable white family was a symbol of their free status. An ex-slave who married in 1885 recalled that his wedding was "a sure enough affair with the preacher saying the words just like the white folks' marriage." [9] Black men also re-garded the possession of a wife and children as a testament to their mascu-linity, the recognition that they, too, were capable of performing the social role of men in American society. Elizabeth Botume observed that as early as 1865 freedmen on Port Royal Island acted as if they owned their wives. [10] But most importantly, former slaves of both sexes undoubtedly saw in the family the only institution that could assure the kinds of emotional satis-factions that the continuous presence of a spouse and children can provide.

The respect for marriage and a stable family life was by no means univer-sal among the freedmen. Some who married during the early months of free-dom soon came to regret their action. Two days after receiving his certificate of marriage a Port Royal man who discovered that " 'he didn't like that woman nohow' " attempted to return the document for the dollar he paid for it. Another man whose wife absconded with all of his property—two ducks, three chickens, and a hominy pot—sought an immediate divorce so that he might marry someone else. [11]

If the reports of both hostile and friendly witnesses are to be accepted, there were also many freedmen who associated freedom with enhanced op-portunities to engage in free love. During the early postwar years former slaves seemed to move from mate to mate with or without benefit of clergy, and some men apparently lived with several mates at the same time. Contrary to the belief of white observers, however, not all of these arrangements repre-sented promiscuous behavior. Much of the sequential mating arose out of the ex-slaves' attempts to rid themselves of spouses forced on them during slavery and to establish more congenial relationships with entirely new partners or to renew ties with their first husbands and wives. Apparently polygamous arrangements often represented the initial effort of freedmen whose families had been broken up during slavery to care for two or more wives and families with whom they had been reunited after the war.

As time passed several forces converged to strengthen the freedmen's own inclinations toward stable unions with one spouse. As a result of pressure to formally marry from military authorities in the contraband camps, from agents of the Freedmen's Bureau, and from Yankee missionaries and teachers, ex-slave couples came to regard the marriage certificate as one of the symbols of their free status. Also black churches and the black press kept up a steady barrage of propaganda in behalf of formal marriage and the legitimation of children, and several freedmen's conventions passed resolutions in the same vein. Moreover, implicit in the various state laws which gave legal recognition to the unions formed during slavery was the assumption that under the new condition of freedom informal arrangements were neither legally valid nor morally justified.

From five to fifteen years after the end of the Civil War blacks throughout the South had made considerable progress toward creating the type of family life to which they were inclined or encouraged to aspire. In the Whitestone district of Lancaster County, Virginia, for example, the overwhelming majority of black families identified in the census data for 1870 and 1880 consisted of married couples, a situation which probably reflected the relative integrity of the antebellum slave family as well as the freedmen's postwar aspirations for a legitimate family status. Similarly, as Peter Kolchin has pointed out, in several rural and urban communities in Alabama in 1870 there was no significant difference in the family structures of blacks and whites. The typical family in each case consisted of a husband, wife, and two or three children—the so-called nuclear model. Additional evidence of the structure of the black family lies in John Blassingame's well-documented observation that in New Orleans by 1880, "the Negro family had evolved into a patriarchal institution almost as stable as the white family." Blassingame also concludes that although family instability was rather pronounced among blacks in Savannah by 1870, twenty years later the situation had considerably improved with most families conforming to the nuclear model. Herbert Gutman's findings that in such diverse communities as York and Princess Anne counties in Virginia in 1865; Montgomery County, Virginia in 1866; and Natchez and rural Adams County, Mississippi; Richmond, Mobile, and Beaufort, South Carolina, and St. Helen's Township and St. Helena Island, South Carolina, in 1880; the proportion of black households containing "a husband and wife or just a father" ranged from 70 percent in Natchez and Beaufort to 87 percent in St. Helena Township, while the range of strictly two-parent households "spreads from 50 percent in Natchez to 80 percent in St. Helena's Township" with the other communities falling in between, reinforces the view that throughout the South the typical black family by the late nineteenth century consisted of married couples and their minor children.[12]

THE PERSISTENCE OF THE TWO-PARENT FAMILY

The freedmen's desire for a stable family life and their aspirations for land and other economic opportunities were interrelated. For the majority of black Southerners, however, the anticipated economic opportunities, including the acquisition of land, did not materialize. Nevertheless, despite economic and social strains, the two-parent family has continued to exist down to the present as the representative black family in the South. In 1900, when the bulk of the black population throughout the nation resided in the rural South, there was little structural difference between black and white families. Studies by W. E. B. Du Bois in the early twentieth century and by a number of sociologists in the 1930s of specific black communities in the South, while tending to emphasize the minority of unstable families, paradoxically confirmed that the majority of black families continued to conform to the two-parent pattern.[13] And as late as 1950, nearly four out of five black families throughout the nation consisted of a husband and a wife as compared to about nine out of ten white families. By 1970, despite growing instability brought on by a host of factors, 68 percent of the black families in the United States still adhered to the nuclear model. By 1975, however, for reasons that are not yet clear, the proportion of two-parent families among blacks had declined to 61 percent. Until recently, however, blacks in the rural South diverged less from the two-parent pattern than those in other regions of the country.[14]

While the available evidence supports the conclusion that the great majority of black Southerners have subscribed to the ideal of the nuclear family since the end of the Reconstruction era and that until recently at least three out of four who have been married have conformed to the model in practice, the stability of such families as measured by the duration of marriage and the number of times a given partner has been separated, divorced, or widowed is less easily established. A number of studies have indicated that many black marriages have been of short duration, and that among lower-class blacks desertion has been fairly common. In addition, it is seldom possible to determine from the census data whether couples who stated that they were formally married actually lived under common-law arrangements.

Nevertheless, without claiming representativeness, a casual examination of the WPA slave narrative collection compiled in the mid-1930s leads to the impression that a majority of the first marriages of the ex-slaves interviewed lasted until one of the partners died. Of the Texas ex-slaves who gave information about the duration of their marraiges, over 85 percent indicated that their first, and frequently only, marriage ended with their spouse's death. Many of these marriages had lasted more than thirty years.[15] Among former slaves who were still married to their first spouses, a few had been married for sixty years or more.

Several of those whose partners had died as well as those whose spouses were still living spoke appreciatively of their mates and their family life. An eighty-seven-year-old resident of Oklahoma who had spent his early manhood in Texas testified that his deceased spouse "was sure a good wife and for no reason did I take the second look at no woman. That was love, which don't live no more in our hearts." The same sentiment was expressed by a ninety-eight-year-old former Georgia slave, who, in recalling that he and his deceased wife had fallen in love at first sight, declared that there "Ain't been no other woman but her and she's waiting for me wherever the dead waits for the living." And eighty-five-year-old Bert Luster, a former slave in Tennessee, whose wife was still alive, proudly proclaimed that "I married my woman . . . 58 years ago. Dat was after slavery, and I love her, honest to God I does."[16]

Appreciation of good marriages was by no means confined to former slaves. In 1971, Ned Cobb, an Alabama tenant farmer, paid high tribute to his first wife, to whom he was married for forty-four years. He recalled that when she died in 1950:

> I just felt like my very heart was gone. I'd stayed with her forty-odd years, and that was short, short—except bein pulled off and put in prison. I picked her out amongst the girls in this country and it was the easiest thing in the world to do. I loved that gal and she dearly proved she loved me. She stuck right to me every day of her life and done a woman's duty. Weren't a lazy bone in her body and she was strict to herself and truthful to me. Every step she took, to my knowledge, was in my favor.[17]

These tributes which men paid their wives should not be taken to imply that most couples enjoyed an ideal relationship. The short duration of many marriages and the relative frequency of multiple sequential marriages indicate that for black Southerners the historical experience of enslavement and of economic and social subordination and exploitation in the post-Civil War South often exacerbated the normal tendencies toward conflict that characterize most intimate human relationships. These tributes do suggest, however, that in addition to loving and valuing their wives, black men often found in an enduring marriage a psychological refuge from the emasculating climate of the Southern biracial order.

THE PATERNAL FAMILY

In attempting to establish families consonant with their free status black men during the Reconstruction period strove to assert their primacy within their respective households. In 1867 Laura Towne noted with some displeasure that while black men on St. Helena Island appeared to be somewhat timid in seeking political freedom, they regarded "domestic freedom—the right, just found, to have their own way in their families and rule their wives . . . [as] an inestimable privilege." She suggested that this transformation in the role of the sexes was due to the fact that "Several speakers have been here who have advised the people to get the women into their proper place. . . ." As a consequence "the notion of being bigger than women generally, is just now inflating the conceit of the males to an amazing degree."[18]

The attitude that men should play the dominant role in family life, particularly as providers and as decision makers on fundamental issues, permeated all levels of black society. In New Orleans, according to John Blassingame, the black press and certain members of the black literati, while conceding to women the management of the household, contended that ultimate authority on family matters should reside in the men. By the turn of the century, however, these attitudes were being increasingly challenged by educated black women. While believing that women had a special role to play in maintaining the home, in rearing children, and in lifting the moral and social standards of the race, middle- and upper-class black women saw no reason why women should not have an equal voice in family affairs, provided, of course, they *and* their husbands possessed the standards of decency and fairness and the knowledge requisite to making intelligent and selfless decisions. Lower-class black women probably held similar views.[19]

Following the model maintained by their former masters, freedmen also encouraged their wives to give up working in the fields and to confine their activities to taking care of the home. As a result, for a brief period white planters in some areas found it difficult to employ black women as laborers. The bias against wives (and daughters) working for whites continued well into the twentieth century, and many men and women assessed their status and that of others by the degree to which they could maintain this independence. Frustrated in their aspiration for economic self-sufficiency, however, most black men had to surrender their vision of their mates as exclusively housewives, although many continued to hold out. Throughout their life together from 1906 to 1955, tenant Ned Cobb discouraged his wife from even working in the fields with him on his own allotted acreage, despite her desire to do so. Moreover, he forbade her to "go about washin for white folks." "I didn't want any money comin' into my house from that," he declared. "My wife didn't wait on white folks for their dirty laundry. There was plenty of 'em would ask her and there'd be a answer ready for 'em." Ned Cobb's strictures against his wife working for whites was so severe that when she tried to take in washing while he was in prison, his eldest son, out of respect for his father's wishes, refused to permit her to do so.[20]

Many black women, however, returned to the fields, and others became servants or day workers in white households. They thus came to play a strong economic role in the black family. Du Bois observed that by 1900 four out of every ten black females over ten years of age worked outside the home, compared to one out of every six white females. "They furnisht a half million farm laborers, 70,000 farmers, 15,000 teachers and professional folk, 700,000 servants and washerwomen, and 40,000 in trades and merchandising."[21] By 1910 about 55 percent of black females over ten years of age were employed as compared to 19 percent of the white females in the same category. In 1930 the proportion of black females employed was back to the level of 1900 while the percentage for whites was about the same as in 1910. Of more significance for the family, however, was the fact that about one-third of the married black women in 1930 were in the work force. In the former Confederate states the proportion of married black women employed ranged from 20 percent in Arkansas to over 43 percent in Florida. Only 9 percent of married white women, however, were in the work force in 1930.[22]

The Great Depression and World War II eras were characterized by abnormal labor force conditions. However, recent trends in the employment patterns of women indicate that married women throughout the United States are playing an ever greater role as workers in the economy. In 1967 about one-half of the married black women in the United States were employed outside the home. Throughout the first half of the 1970s about 54 percent have been in the work force. The trend in the employment pattern of married white women has been even more striking. By 1967 the proportion of married white women in the labor force had quadrupled over that of 1930. In 1974 over two out of five were employed outside the home.[23]

Despite their significant role in the black family as wage earners, married women earned too little to give them a dominant voice in decision making solely on economic grounds. Those who worked outside the home generally earned much less than their husbands. In 1949 the median income of black women was only 43 percent of that of black males. In 1959 the ratio had declined to 40 percent. During the late 1960s and the early 1970s, as a result of the shift in the employment of black women from domestic and other service type jobs to industrial and professional occupations, the earnings of black wives in proportion to those of their husbands increased dramatically. In the South the mean income of married black women who worked a fifty-to-fifty-two-week year was 71 percent of the mean income of married black men. However, for all Southern black wives in the work force, including those who worked less than a full year, the average income was only 53 percent of that of their husbands. Thus the Southern wives who worked in 1973 contributed less than one-third of their families' income, although those who worked for a full year provided 42 percent of the black family's income.

Earnings were higher in the North and West, but the percentage distribution between husbands and wives was not significantly different from that in the South.[24]

In the lower-class black family the role of the man as the principal provider conformed to the national and regional patterns for all black families. In her study of thirty-eight lower-class black couples with young children in a Georgia community of about 10,000 people, conducted in the early and middle 1960s, Virginia Heyer Young discovered that in twenty-three of the households the husband was the sole source of income, in two households the husbands provided the bulk of the income, and in thirteen households the spouses contributed equally. In none of the families did the wife earn more than her husband. On the basis of an analysis of the 1959 census returns, Heyer concluded that the pattern which prevailed in the community she studied was probably typical of the entire state.[25]

More importantly, Heyer found that in the Georgia community "men are usually accorded or assume authority in the home. Women act as though their husbands had authority, and children are respectful of them."[26] Studies of a number of scholars over the past twenty years that have been free of the preconception of the black family as pathological tend to support Heyer's conclusions as typical of most Southern black families. Some scholars have even suggested that those husbands whose wives worked were frequently forced to participate more fully in decisions regarding the routine functions of the household than those men whose wives remained at home. These scholars' principal finding, however, is that authority within the family was often shared by both spouses with the unspoken assumption that in the final analysis the decision of the husband on fundamental matters would prevail.[27] Whatever the findings, it seems reasonable to conclude that the personality and the social and ethical values of the respective spouses would often have as much bearing on the locus of authority in the family as who supplied the bulk of the family's income.

THE MATERNAL FAMILY

Paradoxically, despite the historical predominance of married couples among black families since Reconstruction, it has been the single-parent or broken family that has received the most attention in popular and scholarly literature on the black family. Consequently, the subject deserves some consideration here.

The overwhelming majority of single-parent families among blacks have traditionally been headed by women as a consequence of widowhood, desertion or divorce, and unmarried motherhood. Between 1910 and 1950 widowhood accounted for most of the single-parent families among black Southerners. It was a reflection of the low socioeconomic status of black men as expressed in the difficult and dangerous jobs which they held, the frustrations involved in many of their interpersonal relationships, and the unavailability of adequate medical and sanitary facilities to the black community. In 1910, for example, one in four black women in the South who had ever been married had also been widowed, as compared to only one in seventeen who had been divorced or deserted. By 1960, however, as a result of a number of developments, including the migration of many black males to Northern and Western cities, the situation had changed. Then one in seven married or previously married black women had been widowed while one in five had lost their husbands through desertion or divorce. Throughout these years, however, as Reynolds Farley has pointed out, the view that a majority of black men and women throughout the United States lived apart from their spouses is contradicted by census data that "indicates that at each [census] date about four-fifths of the married men and three-fifths of the women lived with their mates. . . ."[28]

Throughout the United States the proportion of black families headed by women has progressively increased. In 1900 there was little distinction between black and white families in this respect. By 1940, however, 19 percent of the black families in the United States were headed by women. By 1960 the proportion of black families headed by women had increased to 22 percent. During the past fifteen years, the number of maternal families has grown much faster than in any earlier period. There was a 7 percent increase in the proportion of such families from 1960 to 1971 and an additional 6 percent increase over the next four years. By 1975, then, over one out of every three black families in the United States was headed by a woman.[29] The situation in the South was much like that throughout the nation, with the notable exception of the rural South where female-headed families were less in evidence.

Accompanying the increase in the number and proportion of maternal black families has also been a shift in the relative prominence of the overt reasons for the existence of such families. In 1974, nearly half (46 percent) of the heads of these families were separated or divorced, 29 percent were widowed, 21 percent were never married, and 3 percent had husbands in the armed forces or in correctional institutions.[30] Behind these reasons, of course, stand more fundamental causes, such as migration to the cities, the "culture of poverty," welfare regulations, changing sexual attitudes, and a host of other factors.

Another seldom given explanation for the prevalence of female-headed families is that traditionally there has been an excess of females over males in the black population, particularly in the cities. In New Orleans in 1870 there were 100 black females in the fifteen to forty-five age category for every sixty-five males in the same age group, and the ratio had not changed substantially by 1880. Blassingame observes that as a result "Negro women had to fight (almost literally) to obtain husbands." Many, of course, never succeeded. Similarly. Peter Kolchin notes that in the early years of Reconstruction in Alabama, black men enjoyed a "buyer's market" of women because of the numerical disparity between the sexes in the twenty to twenty-nine age group.[31]

In 1908 Kelly Miller noted that the same phenomenon existed in 1900 in all U.S. cities (except Chicago) that had a black population in excess of 20,000. In fourteen such cities, twelve of which were in the former slave states and the District of Columbia, the number of black females for each 100 males ranged from 103 in Memphis to 143 in Atlanta. "These left-over, or to-be-left-over, Negro women," Miller asserted, "falling as they do in large part in the lower stratum . . . of society . . . especially if they be comely of appearance, become the easy prey of the evil designs of both races." In his *American Negro Family,* W. E. B. Du Bois quoted some of Miller's observations. In 1940, Oliver C. Cox gave a more extended treatise on the subject. And most recently, Jacqueline Jackson has also argued persuasively that there is a causal relationship between the surplus of females in the black population and the prevalence of the female-headed family.[32] As U.S. census reports show, the sex ratio that concerned these scholars has been characteristic of most of the cities of the United States with a sizable black population for the past 100 years.[33]

Obviously the numerical discrepancy between the sexes has limited the opportunities for single black women to marry and for those who have been widowed or separated by divorce or desertion to remarry. Miller, Du Bois, and Cox were primarily concerned, however, with the impact of the unfavorable sex ratio upon the morals and social welfare of the black community as reflected in the problem of unmarried motherhood and the care of children born out of wedlock.

All classes within the black community have traditionally preferred that children be born only to married couples. Consequently, attitudes toward premarital pregnancy have ranged from severe disapproval to resigned acceptance. It was once the practice in many black Southern rural communities for unmarried pregnant girls and their paramours to be suspended or expelled from the church. Even when such censure did not occur, premarital pregnancy was rarely welcomed by the girl or her parents. This attitude ran through all social strata, but was likely to be more pronounced among the middle and upper classes and among those of the lower class who aspired to middle-class status or adhered to middle-class values. Because abortion was generally frowned upon, premarital pregnancies usually resulted in births, and those mothers who did not marry kept their offspring or allowed them to be raised by grandparents or other relatives.

Fortunately, the black community has not affixed to the children of unmarried mothers the stigma attached to premarital pregnancy. Except among some segments of the middle and upper classes little distinction has been made between the offspring of licit and so-called illicit relationships. Indeed, the child born out of wedlock has frequently been adopted informally into the home of his grandparents and accepted and treated as a full and beloved member of the household.

Families headed by women cannot be defined as necessarily pathological. Common sense dictates that many single-parent families may be healthier and happier than those with both parents in the home. Indeed, some unmarried mothers have preferred to remain single rather than enter a marriage in which the emotional and economic needs of their children would be sacrificed to the facade of "respectability." Moreover, several social scientists have recently noted that in terms of social values, aspirations for their children, and in providing masculine expressive roles for their male children, black families headed by women have not differed significantly from black and white families with both parents present. The chief weakness of such families has been economic. In 1967 the median income of black families headed by women in the United States was just $3,000 as compared to over $5,700 for black families headed by men. In 1974 the discrepancy was even greater: the median income of black female-headed families was only $4,465 as compared to $10,365 for black male-headed families. Over half of the families headed by women had incomes in the poverty category while only 14 percent of the paternal families were so disadvantaged.[34] Therefore, because black women in the South as elsewhere have not earned as much as black men, and because women heads of families cannot enjoy the benefits of income from two spouses, female-headed families have found it difficult to provide an adequate economic foundation for the multiple socioeconomic functions which the family is expected to perform.

In the rural South the family with only one parent present has not only been less evident than in urban areas but, until recently, it has probably been less disadvantaged as well. Where the family engaged in farming, children, upon reaching a certain age, could be a definite economic asset to the household. Even in urban areas, however, the head of the family might get considerable assistance from other relatives in meeting the economic, social, and emotional needs of the family, especially, as was often the case, if the family lived in the home of the children's grandparents. Also lending strength to the black family in rural areas was the tendency of the whole community to share in the responsibility of disciplining children. Family friends and acquaintances would tell parents of their children's misdeeds and would occasionally discipline the children themselves and then inform the parents of their actions. The parents, in turn, would then discipline the children further. Thus, to a significant degree, the rearing of children was a community affair.

THE EXTENDED FAMILY

A common, though neither a dominant nor unique feature of family life among black Southerners has been the tendency of married couples and their children to share living quarters with other relatives. Usually such couples either lived in the household of the wife's or husband's parents or their parents have lived in the couple's home. Thus a sizable number of blacks in the South have grown up within modified nuclear or semi-extended families. Such families often have enabled their members to cope with forces in Southern life that otherwise would bring about the family's dissolution.

As already noted, the extended family was of crucial assistance to unmarried mothers and their children. These mothers usually remained in their parents' homes until they later married and established their own household. The children, therefore, received not only their mother's care but also the doting attention of their grandparents. Since a majority of these extended families were headed by men, usually (but not always) the maternal grandfather, the children were exposed to a strong masculine influence in the home.

For the poor as well as for the well-to-do, the extended family, by the sharing of economic resources, served to prevent or lessen dependence on public charity and to give the household a sense of economic security. Economic cooperation, in turn, often created, strengthened, and reflected emotional bonds which contributed to the family's social and psychological health. In their study of black life in a Mississippi community in the 1930s, Allison Davis and Burleigh and Mary Gardner discovered how important the extended family could be to the economic well-being and social health of black farmers. They reported that:

> All of the eight colored managers who were interviewed had married sons working with them, or renting from them, on that part of the plantation which the manager himself rented. One of these extended families made from 20 to 30 bales of cotton a year between 1928 and 1932, five to eight times as many bales as the average tenant-family raised. Another tenant-manager had three married sons and their wives working with him. The communal division extended even to the wives each of whom had an established round of duties for each day in the week. A third tenant-manager had been able to buy a farm through the combined work of an extended family, including a nephew and a son-in-law, in addition to his own children. When they left him, he lost his farm.[35]

The extended family also helped blacks to cope with the pressures of living in the urban South. Allison Davis and John Dollard found that in New Orleans in the late 1930s a black lower-class family consisting of a married couple, their five children, and maternal grandparents, although on relief, composed a relatively happy and economically and socially secure household. The only girl in the family, although unattractive by white standards, had grown into a happy, well-adjusted teenager as a result of the attention and emotional support she had received from her closest relatives. In explaining

why the girl apparently turned out so well, Davis and Dollard pointed out
that:

> At least three women have been influential in her bringing up: her
> mother, grandmother, and paternal great-aunt. The latter took care of
> her a great deal when Mary was small because both the mother and the
> grandmother were working. The grandmother often took care of her
> at night so that the young mother could go out. A group of blood-
> bound relatives trained her and all regarded her in some sense as "my
> chile." She was therefore the center of competition and kindness. . . .
> Indeed, her mother felt that the grandmother was too nice to Mary and
> that the old lady made her sassy. Her father "never did take time with
> his children," but the grandfather was forever playing with her and
> picking her up.[36]

Modified versions of the extended family still exist in the South, although
probably in lesser numbers than formerly. Those that do exist continue to
serve the dual function of bringing several generations of the family together
and of providing economic and emotional support to the youngest and oldest
members alike.

NO MOTHERLESS CHILDREN

As much as they valued the freedom to marry whom they liked, the ex-
slaves valued even more the right to unrestricted control over their children.
The reunion of parents and children after the Civil War were usually joyous
occasions whether they came immediately after the war or many years later.
Tragedy, of course, attended some of the attempts at reunion. One former
Tennessee slave who had been sold along with her mother away from her
father and two brothers when she was only seven years old did not hear from
her father again until thirty years had passed. Somehow her father had heard
that she was still alive and residing in Missouri and began to correspond with
her. She never did see him again, however, for while journeying to visit her
he drowned in the Missouri River.[37]
Other freedmen sometimes experienced difficulty in obtaining possession
of their children from their former master. A Mississippi woman who had
fled the plantation to escape the unwanted attentions of the black overseers,
and left her husband and children behind, returned to the plantation after
the war to reclaim her children. The former master gave her all her children
but one. According to her daughter, the woman persisted in getting all her
children, however, emphatically informing the planter that "she want me,
too, dat I was her'n an' she was gwine a-git me." When the woman returned

to the plantation with appropriate papers from the provost marshall, the ex-master gave up the child.[38]

Although most planters did not attempt to keep children formally en-slaved many were extremely reluctant to surrender their control over them and continued to physically discipline them as in slavery days. Black parents protested. A Salisbury, North Carolina, woman complained to a Freedmen's Bureau agent in 1865 that her former master "was beating her children con-tinually and when she asked him not to do it, ordered her off his place and told her not to come back."[39]

After the war, children old enough to know the meaning of freedom sensed their new status and sought refuge from planter discipline in the embrace of their parents. In 1865 a Virginia planter bitterly complained that when his adult son slapped a servant girl for disrespectful remarks to him, "She immediately left her work, all unfinished, and betook herself to her father's house. My son sent for her, but she did not return, and we have seen nothing of her since." When the planter went to the house of the girl's father and insisted that he punish her for her disobedience, the father ada-mantly refused, and the girl's mother continued to defend her conduct even in the face of threats that the family would be evicted from the plantation.[40]

Planters also met resistance when they attempted to use the apprentice-ship laws applying to minors and orphans to practically re-enslave black children. Because planters could charge that they were not being properly cared for, children who had only their mothers or grandparents to take care of them were especially vulnerable to being bound out without their mothers' or guardians' consent. In Alabama, black opposition to such practices led to their abandonment when the state came under Radical rule in 1868.[41]

The concern of ex-slave parents for children was not limited to their own offspring. During the Reconstruction and post-Reconstruction periods several observers marveled at the tendency of blacks to care for orphaned and abandoned children. In 1890, a white New England schoolteacher, who had begun work in the Deep South in 1869, described Southern blacks as "a very sympathetic people, very kind." She went on to explain that "Possibly one reason why there is so little pauperism among them is that almost every colored family has adopted orphan children. They will always open their doors to orphans."[42] During the 1920s, Rossa B. Cooley made virtually the same observation about blacks on St. Helena Island in South Carolina. "Even in the large families we can find the "'dopted,'" she reported. "No 'mud-derless,' as our orphans are called, is allowed to stay on the island."[43]

During the 1930s scholars who studied black life in Southern communities found numerous households containing children other than the parents' offspring, especially in rural areas. A majority of these children may have been relatives (some born out of wedlock)—grandchildren, stepchildren, nieces, nephews, and cousins—but many were unrelated to the parents by blood.

The willingness of blacks to care for children not their own can be attributed to several factors. The sense of community—the feeling that they were all members of one big extended family—which blacks developed on many slave plantations, continued into the postwar period and was often strengthened by the plantation experience under freedom. But as Hortense Powdermaker observed in the 1930s in Mississippi, "Children are taken for the joy of having them, the assistance they may bring, or merely because they need a home."[44] Since many adults had themselves been reared as "adopted" or by relatives who were not their biological parents, they, too, were inclined to continue the tradition.

In the cities and towns, however, there were many homeless children who could not be accommodated in existing families. Consequently, shortly after the Civil War, several black communities attempted to establish orphanages to care for such children. In New Orleans, as early as 1864 and 1865, churches, benevolent societies, and concerned individuals raised substantial amounts of money to establish and maintain orphanages. By 1883 Savannah had the Colored Orphan Asylum, established by a black fraternal society. In 1898 the Atlanta University Conference noted the existence of orphanages in such disparate cities as Americus and Atlanta, Georgia; Nashville, Tennessee; and Petersburg and Richmond, Virginia. The Carrie Steele Orphanage in Atlanta consisted of a three-story building containing not only residential quarters but also a hospital and a school. It cared not only for orphans but, in the absence of a state reformatory for blacks, for juvenile delinquents as well. Thirteen years later, the Atlanta University Conference reported the existence of considerably more orphanages in the South, listing many which it had overlooked in 1898. In New Orleans alone there were five institutions that cared for orphans. Other communities in which orphanages existed that were not mentioned in 1898 were Charleston and Columbia, South Carolina; Courtland and Hampton, Virginia; Augusta, Covington, and Macon, Georgia; Bennettsville and Oxford, North Carolina; Bellevue, Jacksonville, and Pensacola, Florida; and Austin and San Antonio, Texas. The majority of these institutions were supported almost exclusively by blacks, but a few received some assistance from white philanthropists and local governments.[45]

Like the Carrie Steele orphanage, which in 1908 had ninety-seven inmates, many orphanages served as juvenile reformatories, accepting children neglected by their parents or whose parents were involuntarily institutionalized. While parental irresponsibility lay at the root of much parental neglect of children and the resultant delinquency, the fact that so many wives had to work was probably the principal reason for the neglect. Domestic workers who spent long hours caring for white people's children found it difficult and frequently impossible to devote sufficient time and care to their own children, unless, of course, they had the assistance of other adults in the home.

The dilemma that live-in domestic workers in the South faced was reconstructed graphically by a newspaper in 1912 from an account given by a black woman in Georgia:

> I frequently work from fourteen to sixteen hours a day. I am com-
> pelled by my contract, which is oral only, to sleep in the house. I am
> allowed to go home to my own children, the oldest of whom is a girl of
> 18 years, only once in two weeks, every other Sunday afternoon—
> even then I'm not permitted to stay all night. I not only have to nurse a
> little white child, now eleven months old, but I have to act as a play-
> mate or "handy-andy," not to say governess, to three other children
> in the home. . . . I see my own children only when they happen to see
> me on the street when I am out with the children, or when my children
> come to the "yard" to see me, which isn't often, because my white
> folks don't like to see their servants' children hanging around their
> premises.[46]

To relieve such problems, black Southerners began in the first decade of the twentieth century to establish day nurseries and kindergartens.[47] The movement accelerated as time passed, but given the black community's limited resources the problem was simply too massive to be met by voluntary efforts alone. Thus working wives and, until the recent inauguration of the aid-to-dependent children program of the federal welfare system, poor black women without husbands had to rely on relatives, friends, and the general community for assistance in raising their children.

CHILDREN REARING UNDER APARTHEID

In his 1974 study of three generations of poor black parents in a Southern community, Levi Jones found that all three generations had shared the same basic goals: the survival of the family, the education of the children, and "Raising children up right"—teaching them to treat everybody good, to be honest and hard working, to save their money, and to help their brothers and sisters.[48] Studies of black life in the South by sociologists and anthropologists in the 1930s confirm Jones' findings of the aspirations of the two earlier generations for their children. And the ex-slaves' great enthusiasm for education and some of the reports in the Atlanta University Studies suggest that black parents in the late nineteenth and early twentieth centuries also held these desires for their children.

Black parents differed, however, in both the strength and level of their aspirations for their children and in their ability to achieve them. Some ex-slave parents were satisfied if their children simply learned to read and write, while others made tremendous sacrifices to see that their children received all the education that was available. Because he needed him to work on the farm, Benjamin Mays' father opposed his son's aspirations for a college education. The father of William Holtzclaw, on the other hand, who badly needed his son's assistance, released him from any obligation to the family provided he promised to educate himself.[49]

As the diversity of reports which Du Bois received from communities throughout the South and the nation on how black parents were disciplining and rearing their children as well as the efforts of Booker T. Washington and his disciples to improve the home environment and to promote family uplift clearly attest, many black parents who wanted to assure the family's survival and to raise their children up right simply lacked the requisite knowledge and skills. Some, therefore, gave up the struggle and resigned themselves merely to eking out an existence for themselves and their children or took the radical step of abandoning their spouses and children altogether. The great majority, however, continued to strive and hope. In attempting to bring their children up right some parents, like the father of Ned Cobb, overworked or beat their children severely while others, remembering the chastisements of slavery days, were inclined to be lenient, thereby arousing criticism from both blacks and whites that they were not disciplining their children properly.[50]

Because of Southern apartheid, all black families faced special problems in raising their children aside from those involved in the process of making a living. Their basic dilemma was how to instill in their children a positive self-image while equipping them at the same time with the social habits and attitudes necessary for their survival under the oppressive biracial system. In the twentieth century, the pre-1930 generation of parents, while disdaining to teach their children that they were inferior to whites, nevertheless taught them to observe the etiquette of Jim Crow. Many, in fact, emphatically taught their children that they were just as good and perhaps better than whites, yet undermined their assertions by their own deferent behavior. Their resentment of the need for this contradictory behavior, however, was not lost on their children. In virtually every black family, no matter how servile, children overheard numerous conversations about the perfidy and deficiencies of the white man, charges which the children were frequently able to confirm by their own observations and experiences.

In order to restrict the number of situations in which their chldren would have to surrender their dignity in order to survive, many black parents encouraged their children after they had reached a certain age to stay away from white people. Although in certain communities white children would come to the homes of black children to play, black parents forbade their children to go to white homes for fear that they would be required to observe the rituals of Jim Crow. In situations where contact between black and white children was unavoidable and conflict ensued, black parents differed in their advice to their children. Some taught their children to fight back when attacked or insulted by white children. Others advised their children to avoid fighting if possible and to ignore insults.

Succeeding generations of parents were inclined to be progressively less accommodating. Many children grew up in the 1930s and later with no special instructions from their parents on how to act in the presence of whites, and those parents who did advise their children to be deferential were often ignored. Parental reaction to such defiance was likely to be mixed. Former slaves who complained in the 1930s that children no longer respected old people nevertheless took pride in the fact that the younger generation was less deferential to whites as well.

Between the end of Reconstruction and the black revolution in the 1960s, all generations of black parents enjoined their young people to avoid becoming involved in romantic or sexual relations with whites. Although the injunction was not always observed, all classes in the black community knew what was at stake: for black males, their lives; for black females, their self-respect, the dignity and morale of the male members of their families, and the reputation of the race.

THE DILEMMA OF WIVES AND DAUGHTERS

Inherent in most caste systems is the vulnerability of the female of the subordinate class to sexual exploitation by the males of the dominant caste. Continuing the tradition of slavery days, white men after the Civil War felt free to attempt to seduce or force their attentions on black women and girls. After the entrenchment of Jim Crow the practice became even more virulent. Black women of all classes were frequently propositioned by white men, on the plantation, in the streets, and in their places of employment. Domestic servants were particularly vulnerable. A black domestic told a newspaper correspondent in 1912 that as a result of her observations and her own experiences, as well as information gathered from conversations with fellow workers, that she believed that "nearly all white men take, and expect to take, undue liberties with their female servants—not only the fathers but the sons also. Those servants who rebel against such familiarity must either leave or expect to have a mighty hard time, if they stay."[51]

This state of affairs was general knowledge throughout both the white and black communities, and witnesses from both communities were often prepared to give testimony to outsiders on the subject. Rossa B. Cooley remarked in the 1920s that "The Negro mothers try to protect their girls, but even so a Negro girl has a hard time. The poorest type of white man feels at liberty to accost her and follow her, and force her."[52] The subject was also a prevalent refrain in the interviews which black Southerners gave scholars in the 1930s.

Because black men were denied access to white women, the practice was a bitter affront to the self-respect and dignity of both black men and women and a threat to the integrity of the black family. "It would be all right," declared several black women to Hortense Powdermaker in the 1930s, "if it worked both ways, if colored men and white women could go together. . . ."[53] These women knew that the clandestine liaisons between black men and white women were too deeply hidden and too fraught with peril for black men for the black community to derive a sense of equity from them.

Blacks of all classes and political persuasions—from the lowly farm and urban laborer to the wealthy landowner, businessman, and professional; from the conservative accommodationist to the militant radical—bitterly resented the dilemma of their women, and the inability of the men to protect them. Du Bois expressed the sentiment of most blacks when he asserted in 1919 that while he could forgive the white South for slavery, for the Civil War and its continued commemoration, for its emphasis on white supremacy, and for its passion and pretentiousness, he could "never forgive, neither in this world nor the world to come; its wanton and continued and persistent insulting of the black womanhood which it sought and seeks to prostitute for its own lust." Even the conservative Robert Russa Moton, Booker T. Washington's successor as principal at Tuskegee, felt constrained to protest in the early 1930s the lack of "redress or protection" available to "Negro women of refinement and culture" who "are constantly exposed to unwelcome and uninvited attentions from a certain type of white man. . . ." And while reflecting on the eight decades of his life in the South, Ned Cobb spoke for both the high and the low in the black community when he proclaimed that "if I catch a white man havin nature-course with a colored woman, I don't like it. I'm mad as the devil. I don't want him messin with my color, he don't want me messin around with his color."[54]

Blacks did more than protest the liberties which white men attempted to take with black females. In 1863 or 1864, freedmen in Yorktown, Virginia, in repulsing the attempts of a group of Union sailors to rape a black girl, shot one of the sailors to death. In Wilkes County, Georgia, freedmen in 1865 formed a society called the Sons of Benevolence, one of whose declared purposes was "the protection of female virtue." The society apparently pressured black women to eschew social relations with white Yankees and white Southerners alike. As previously noted, in 1867 a town in Hale County, Alabama, narrowly escaped being burned to the ground by a group of infuriated blacks in retaliation against the killing of a black man who objected to the attempted seduction of a black girl by a white man.[55] And throughout the 100 years since Reconstruction there were also occasions when black men, individually and collectively, came to the defense of individual black women as well as to the symbol of black womanhood. In the 1930s, in Indianola, Mississippi, for example, two black youths severely beat two white men for making advances to black girls. A decade earlier a group of black men beat several black prostitutes for consorting with white men and were persuaded only with great difficulty from shooting one of their white clientele.[56]

Such violent reactions to white exploitation of black women carried grave risks, however, and even milder forms of protest were not without hazards. In the early twentieth century a black man in Georgia who went to a white man's home to protest the man's advances to his wife was arrested and subsequently fined $25. Sometime during the same period a Tennessee woman who shot and slightly wounded a white man who attempted to rape her almost brought about the lynching of her husband in retaliation. And in the 1930s a black minister who condemned liaisons between black women and white men from the pulpit was subsequently visited by a group of white men who warned him to refrain from utterances on the subject in the future.[57] Obviously, if black women were to be protected without black men losing their lives more subtle means were necessary.

For middle- and upper-class black women the problem was irritating but not acute. Since a majority of these women remained in the home or worked in all-black situations, simple avoidance of white men was usually sufficient. Moreover, such women usually possessed the requisite wit and social skills to repulse the advances of white men. Sometimes the husbands of these women were able to tactfully remind upper-class white offenders that the latter were violating the racial mores. When a white judge in a Mississippi town in the 1930s attempted to make a date over the telephone with the daughter of a black physician, she cursed him out. In order to prevent retaliation as well as to assure that the judge did not bother his daughter again, the physician called the judge and suggested that the judge probably had been drinking and therefore thought he was calling someone else. The judge, given an opportunity to excuse his conduct without losing face, acknowledged his error and promised to refrain from making further advances to the physician's daughter.[58]

Lower-class women had a much more difficult time of it, since the opportunities to avoid whites were more limited; and there were some who voluntarily succumbed to the enticements of white men. Some were motivated by a desire to avenge themselves against white women. If black women were so inferior, they reasoned, then why did the husbands and sons of white women prefer them. Others consorted with white men in order to retain their jobs, to secure special favors or, in case the relations were with upper-class white men, for the prestige they thought accrued to them. Here, however, the social sanctions of the black community came into force. At all levels of society, with the exception of the under-class, black women who consorted with white men were socially ostracized. Those who lived openly with white men were usually considered to be outside the community's social structure; as Allison Davis and John Dollard confirmed in the late 1930s, they lived in "a subsociety of their own."[59]

On numerous occasions black men, lacking the power to control the conduct of white men, took special steps to assure that black women observed the community's taboos against sexual liaisons with white men. Deep South ministers occasionally alluded to the subject in admonitions from the pulpit. One black man always turned on his porch light when the white paramour of his neighbor visited her.[60] And occasionally, as previously observed, black men assaulted black prostitutes who catered to white men. In conjunction with general community censure, expressed in gossip and social isolation, these activities contributed to a marked decline in interracial liaisons as the twentieth century progressed.

The Jim Crow South's interracial sex code had myriad ramifications for the integrity of the black family. In something of an overstatement, Du Bois, referring to both slavery and postslavery days, complained in 1903 that the "hereditary weight of a mass of corruption from white adulterers threaten[ed] almost the obliteration of the Negro home."[61] In both its direct effects and in the assumptions that lay behind it the code sapped the morale of husbands and fathers, placed an added strain on overburdened wives and daughters, and created tensions between black men and black women. In giving rise to an insecure, illegitimate mulatto progeny whose claim to high status on the basis of color was undermined by the black community's knowledge of its lowly origins in the illicit unions of sporting white men and declasse black women, it also exacerbated intraracial social tensions.

There were also more subtle effects. In attempting to erect protective barriers around their daughters, many black parents have struggled to provide their daughters with sufficient education to escape the necessity of working in white households and of holding other types of jobs that would expose them to white sexual exploitatin. The result has been that in many communities in the South girls have attended public school longer than boys, and women students have traditionally outnumbered male students by a wide margin in black liberal arts colleges. Several consequences for the black family have flowed from this tradition. First, educated males as potential spouses have been at a premium. Second, many college-educated women, failing in their quest for a husband of equal education, have preferred to remain single. Third, many black wives have been more highly educated than their husbands. And finally, the tendency toward egalitarianism within the nuclear family has probably been strengthened.

NINE

Class and Leadership

Early in 1891 Joseph Charles Price, president of Livingstone College in Salisbury, North Carolina, assured white Americans that while blacks were adamant in their demand for civil and political rights they were not at all anxious to consort with whites socially, for sufficient social differentiation existed in the black community to satisfy the social preferences of nearly all of its members. "There is no social equality among Negroes," Price observed, "notwithstanding the disposition of some whites to put all Negroes in one class. Culture, moral refinement, and material possessions make a difference among colored people as they do among whites." Implicit in Price's observation was the question: why would blacks feel the need to associate with whites when within their own race there were "fairly intelligent ministers and often learned ones, capable lawyers, skilled physicians, well trained teachers, versatile and energetic newspaper men, accomplished musicians, men in comfortable and frequently wealthy circumstances, and women of culture and refinement?"[1]

SOCIAL STRATIFICATION TO 1900

Born in 1854 to a free black woman and an artisan slave father who became the president of a Baltimore shipping company after the Civil War, Price well knew that blacks in America have never constituted a homogeneous group. Even before the Civil War there were distinctions among them, not only in the North but in the South as well. While most blacks in the South were slaves, there were some 240,000 free blacks in that region by 1860. Discernible among them was a propertied upper class, a middle class of skilled artisans, and a lower class of unskilled laborers. There was some social differentiation, too, among the slaves. In the plantation areas the chief social distinctions were between house servants and field hands, the skilled and the unskilled, and, on the basis of the prestige model provided by the master class, blacks and mulattoes. Frequently, however, using criteria arising independently from their own situation and culture, slaves gave high-status recognition to their preachers and to those who were devoted to, or skilled at, undermining the system—the daring and rebellious and those who were adept at the art of deceiving the master class.

Between the end of the Civil War and the end of the nineteenth century black society in the South was highly fluid. Emancipation threatened to subvert the social position of the old free elite as they now became indistinguishable in their civil and political status from the freedmen. Some suffered economic reversals, as they lost the protection and patronage of influential white friends. Others found themselves competing with an aggressive class of freedmen and poor whites for a significant economic role in the post-Civil War South. Nevertheless, with certain notable exceptions, social stratification within the black community during the Reconstruction and post-Reconstruction eras continued along pre-Civil War lines. Those who had been free before the war and their descendants, the old house-servant class and their descendants, and migrants from the North who came South during and after the war as ministers, teachers, lawyers, politicians, and entrepreneurs, provided the bulk of those in the upper and upper-middle classes. Former field hands and slave artisans and their descendants who subsisted as small farmers, tenants, and agricultural laborers in rural areas and as domestics, artisans, and unskilled service and industrial workers in urban communities made up the bulk of the lower middle and lower classes.

There obviously was much overlapping in the social status of members of these two large groups, and the indices for social differentiation remained blurred throughout much of this period, particularly in rural areas where manners and morals were frequently as important in determining social status as property ownership, family background, and occupation and income.

As time passed, however, social distinctions became somewhat sharper. In rural areas of the upper South landholding, education, occupation, and moral and social values and behavior became the principal criteria of social status. The upper class consisted of the owners of fairly large farms and such professionals as teachers, doctors, lawyers, and educated ministers. The middle class embraced the small farm owners and renters, a few skilled artisans, the uneducated ministry, as well as the "respectable" domestic servants and agricultural and service workers. One's status within each of these two classes would be enhanced if he could claim descent from the antebellum free black population or from household servants of rich planters. The lower class consisted of those landless laborers, domestic servants, and shiftless persons who could not meet the test of respectability with respect to moral behavior and church attendance.

In the lower South, where plantation agriculture and the sharecropping system predominated, the upper class consisted of the few black planters and more substantial numbers of farm owners as well as the few professionals. Relatively prosperous renters occupied the upper rungs of the middle class. Among the rest of the population, composed primarily of sharecroppers and agricultural laborers, manners and morals constituted the predominant index of status, and the community was stratified into largely the respectable and the unrespectable. Those who followed or subscribed to the values and forms of respectable behavior regarding the consumption of alcoholic beverages, sex and family relations, and church attendance fell within the middle and upper levels of society while those who made little effort to follow a conventional mode of moral behavior were relegated to the lower rungs of the lower class or, in some communities, to the status of an under class.

Urban areas provided greater scope for social differentiation than rural areas, largely because of the greater variety of occupations that were available to the black population. Prior to 1900, in terms of occupation, the upper class in such old South cities as Charleston, New Orleans, Atlanta, Mobile, Savannah, Augusta, and Richmond consisted mainly of members and descendants of the antebellum free black and household slave populations. From these segments of the black population came many of the servants of wealthy white families, pullman porters, and skilled artisans and entrepreneurs with predominantly white clientele. A few black professionals—college professors, physicians, lawyers, and educated clergymen—who served the black community were included in this class. They were often distinguished, too, by the fact that they took their manners and life-style from the old Southern planter aristocracy rather than from the less "cultured" and less sophisticated white bourgeoisie. As James Bryce, the British observer, suggested in 1894, had the racial mores permitted interracial socializing, the white Southern aristocracy would undoubtedly have found many members of the black aristocracy more socially congenial than lower-status whites. Bryce bemoaned the fact that "Wealthy and educated Negroes, such as one may now find in cities like Baltimore, Louisville, Richmond, Atlanta and New Orleans" were "as little in contact with their white neighbors as the humblest laborers, perhaps even less so."[2]

CHALLENGES TO THE OLD ARISTOCRACY

By 1900, largely as a result of the establishment of a rigid Jim Crow system and the maturation of institutions like churches and schools within the black community, a new group of blacks were rising in some Southern cities to challenge and subvert the position of the old aristocracy. The newcomers consisted largely of businessmen and professionals whose clientele was primarily or exclusively black. Some of them traced their ancestry to the field hands of the slavery era, and many were darker in color than the members of the old aristocracy. Most of them were inclined to subscribe to the self-help and racial solidarity philosophy of Booker T. Washington.

As the twentieth century wore on, the new men established themselves more firmly in the economic and social life of their respective cities and either fused with or supplanted entirely the old aristocracy. This development occurred sooner and more completely in some cities than in others. As August Meier has pointed out, the change came late in Charleston, South Carolina, where the black upper-class entrepreneurs, professionals, postal employees, and artisans of antebellum free black lineage were not superseded by the descendants of house slaves until after World War II. In New Orleans the change came in the early twentieth century. Creole migrants from other parts of Louisiana who came to New Orleans and established insurance companies and other businesses, and Protestant professionals who had been educated at the black Protestant colleges in New Orleans and who were the descendants of the house servants of wealthy planters, considerably enlarged an upper class which had formerly consisted of mulatto creole artisans and building contractors. Nashville, like New Orleans, also witnessed in the early twentieth century the displacement of its old black aristocracy of contractors, barbers, and merchants serving primarily white customers by a new class of businessmen and by physicians and professors associated with Meharry Medical College and Fisk University.

It was in Atlanta and Durham, however, where the new black elite became the most conspicuous. By the turn of the century in Atlanta an ambitious black bourgeois class of insurance and real estate men, professionals—physicians, dentists, lawyers, educators—and artisan entrepreneurs, distinguished mostly by their dependence on the black community for their livelihood, was beginning to challenge for status and to enlarge the older, upper-class elite composed of a selective number of barbers, grocers, draymen, contractors and realtors, lawyers and doctors, undertakers, postal employees, and teachers and college professors, most of whom were descended from the house-servant class and many of whom served a mainly white clientele. By 1930 the newer group had achieved upper-class status, either by supplanting the older elite or by merging with it through marriage and business unions. Contributing to their ascent was the older group's loss of its white market due to Jim Crow, the migration of some of the old elite and their children to other cities (particularly in the North), and the increasing availability of a college education to the black masses. Today, the upper class in Atlanta consists primarily of the members, descendants, and associates of the new bourgeoisie of the early twentieth century.[3]

Durham's black elite was created in the late nineteenth and early twentieth centuries. As one of the newest of the New South cities Durham had no old black aristocracy. Former slaves and their descendants from other parts of North Carolina and the South who came to Durham after the Civil War and who established small businesses, bought real estate, or earned their livelihood as artisans laid the foundations of the Durham black community. The elite arose from those who in 1898 established and subsequently developed the North Carolina Mutual Life Insurance Company and its satellite banking, real estate, and manufacturing enterprises. As the twentieth century progressed they were joined by a coterie of professionals—physicians, lawyers, and college educators—many of whom became connected with the Mutual establishment through marriage or business dealings. It has been estimated that this group comprised about 5 percent of Durham's black population in 1960. Their life-styles have been characterized by an insistence on a high standard of morality and, until recently, by a notable eschewal of the normal bourgeois pattern of conspicuous consumption.

THE EXPANDING MIDDLE CLASS

The black middle class has always been a somewhat ambiguous entity; it shades imperceptibly at its upper and lower ends into the upper and lower classes, respectively. Moreover, movement from the lower class to the middle class has usually been relatively easy, with education being the quickest vehicle of social mobility. Increasing urbanization and the growth in economic and educational opportunities, however, have contributed to the expansion of the black middle class in the South while at the same time providing more definite criteria for distinguishing it from the lower class. Thus education, occupation, and income have progressively superseded family background, manners, and morals as the primary indices of class status. Today in the South, on the basis of income alone, a significant proportion of the black population may be counted as middle class. In 1974 over one-half of the black families in the South had incomes in excess of $6,700 while nearly one-third (31 percent) had an income of $10,000 or more.[4] Those who fall within the middle class category today are mainly low-level professionals, small businessmen, white-collar workers, skilled craftsmen, and fairly well-paid blue-collar workers, farm owners, and managers.

The recent expansion of the black middle class in the South has come in the face of grave obstacles. One of the most pernicious of these has been racial discrimination in the hiring of public school teachers. With the desegretion of schools many black teachers lost their jobs, and other potential teachers were not hired. The National Education Association has estimated that between 1954 and 1970 such discrimination "had cost the black community 31,584 teaching positions and $250-million annually in salaries."[5]

CLASS PRETENSIONS AND ANTAGONISMS

In recent years upper-class blacks and those in the upper level of the middle class, referred to collectively as the black bourgeoisie, have received a great deal of criticism, articulated most persuasively by the sociologists E. Franklin Frazier and Nathan Hare.[6] Castigated for their individualism and materialism, accused of aping some of the worst characteristics of their white counterparts and of engaging in gross parodies of white middle-class social behavior, and condemned for supposedly attempting to sever their connection with the black masses in their mad rush to identify with white society, upper-status blacks have recently been on the defensive.

These strictures against the black elite, arising out of the interclass antagonisms that have long existed in the black community, are by no means a recent development. Because the black aristocracy in such old South cities as Charleston, New Orleans, Natchez, Savannah, Mobile, Nashville, and Richmond was composed largely of light-skinned mulattoes until well into the twentieth century, color differences provided a convenient symbol around which class protagonists rallied. For well over a half century after Reconstruction, the old mulatto elite in several of these cities continued to place great value on their skin color and their white ancestry, which they usually traced (sometimes falsely) to the white planter aristocracy of the antebellum and early post-bellum South. As the presumed heirs and carriers of the genteel tradition of upper-class white Southerners, they tended to look down on the lower-status blacks and to remain socially aloof from them. Those at the apex of the elite, the "blue veins," socialized only among themselves, and those of some wealth kept up a network of personal relationships with those of similar status in other cities. Dark-skinned blacks were usually excluded from their intimate social gatherings. Dark-skinned women were rarely selected as spouses, and dark-skinned men of a modicum of wealth and professional standing found it only a little less difficult to enter the "charmed circle."

Until recently, certain segments of the Creole community in New Orleans and other areas in Louisiana even refused to acknowledge kinship with the black community. Proud of their white French ancestry and Catholic culture, but denied recognition as whites, they preferred to perceive themselves as occupying the precarious position of an intermediate caste in the Southern biracial order, with an internal class structure, based on family background, education, and occupation and wealth, of their own. There were also isolated pockets ("racial islands") of "white Negroes" in other Southern states who attempted to maintain a separate identity through a posture of social aloofness and endogamous marriage, even among close relatives.

In most Southern communities, however, the mulatto elite, while keeping its social distance from the black masses, nevertheless maintained their identity as members of the black community, a tendency that was reinforced by its progressive transformation from a group of descendants of pre-Civil War free blacks and house servants into a class of professionals, business-men, and white-collar workers of varied lineage. Despite the distrust which lower-status blacks often exhibited toward them, they, paradoxically, fre-quently headed the institutions and organizations that were designed to serve the masses. A modified form of the "mulatto escape hatch," reflecting the superior educational, economic, and social advantages which they in-herited from the slavery era, often served to make them the choices of both blacks and whites for positions of preferment within the black community. Building upon their initial head start, they were able for several decades to utilize their close social ties to advance the interests of members of their class, thus remaining several steps ahead of the masses in the pursuit of the limited opportunities available to blacks.

Middle- and lower-class blacks reacted to the snobbishness and superior advantages of the mulatto aristocracy with a mixture of envy, amused con-tempt, and outright hostility. Much of the intracommunity hostility went far back into the pre-Civil War period. In Charleston, for example, the social antipathies that were responsible for the formation in the late eighteenth century of the Brown Fellowship Society and its rival, the Society of Free Dark Men, survived into the post-Civil War era and, as Thomas Holt has observed, threatened to undermine the mulatto elite's claim to leadership of the freedmen during the Reconstruction period.[7] In New Orleans during the same period, black leaders who were distrustful of their light-skinned politi-cal associates established a newspaper in 1865 called the *Black Republican,* claiming that the mulatto-owned New Orleans *Tribune* did not speak for them. Similarly, in 1866, a black newspaper in Mobile charged that mem-bers of a forty-five-year-old organization of Creoles, "inflated with pride at their presumed superiority to 'common niggers,' have assumed airs [so] that sensible people are heartily disgruntled at them." The paper concluded that "These easily become the tools of the enemies of the race." In Savannah, too, blacks and mulattoes exhibited hostility toward each other. When the mulatto members of St. Stephen's Episcopal Church sought in 1872 to ex-clude their darker coreligionists from the congregation, the Reverend Robert Love, the dark-skinned rector, resigned and joined with other black seces-sionists from St. Stephens in founding the St. Augustine Mission, another Episcopal church. Sixteen years later the declaration by a black speaker at a mass meeting in the city that he was "opposed to the mulatto clique, who for years had considered black Negroes entitled to nothing but the vote," clearly indicated that interclass animosities symbolized by differences in color had not abated.[8]

It would be a mistake to conclude however, that the black community was divided into two camps on the basis of color, for among the severest critics of the social exclusivity and pretensions of the mulatto aristocracy were some of its own members. Journalist John E. Bruce's satiric description in 1877 of the foibles and fancies of the "fust families" of Washington, D.C., many of whom were the servants and former retainers of the upper South white aristocracy or free blacks who had migrated to the city from other areas of the South before the war, was equally applicable to many of the first families of the lower South. Bruce described "Washington's Colored Society" as "this species of African humanity which is forever informing the uninitiated what a narrow escape they had from being born white. They have small hands, aristocratic insteps and wear blue veins, they have auburn hair and finely chiseled features." He accused them of being forever occupied with tracing their white ancestry. "One will carry you back to the times of William the Silent and bring you up to 18 so and so. . . . His father was ex-Chief Justice Chastity of South Carolina or some other state with a polygamous record." Bruce therefore was inclined to accept the rumor that many of black Washington's elite families "secretly hope to become absorbed by the white or caucasian race," despite the manifest indisposition of the Anglo-Saxon race to indicate "any perceptible desire to swallow the Negro 'up or down' except by ways which are dark and tricks which are not always vain." Bruce also made fun of the first families for their attachment to the material symbols of white social status such as the possession of "A servant, two dogs, a tom cat and a rifle that saw service in 1776."[9]

Fifty years later, despite the transformation in Washington's old aristocracy by the increasing number of professionals, businessmen, and government workers, many of them refugees from the severe racial proscriptions of the lower South, the poet Langston Hughes expressed a similar disenchantment with the "best people" of the race in the nation's capital and, by implication, those of similar pretensions who remained in the lower South. Hughes bemoaned the fact that in flaunting their family backgrounds, fraternal affiliations, college degrees, and homes, cars, and fur coats, and in their admiration of a light complexion, the best people of Washington were distressingly emulous of the conspicuous materialism and other social values and forms of middle-class white society. "Never before anywhere, had I seen persons of influence,—men with some money, women with some education,—quite so audibly sure of their own importance and their high places in the community," complained Hughes, already a world traveler. "So many pompous gentlemen never before did I meet. Nor so many ladies with chests swelled like pouter-pigeons whose mouths uttered formal sentences in frightfully correct English."[10]

Probably the most severe indictment of the new black aristocracy published before the appearance of E. Franklin Frazier's *Black Bourgeoisie* (1957) came from young Allison Davis in 1929. A Phi Beta Kappa graduate of Williams College, where he was class valedictorian of 1924, Davis was professor of English at Hampton Institute, a graduate student at Harvard, and about three years away from beginning the research on black life in the South which culminated in the publication in 1941 of his *Deep South: A Social Anthropological Study of Caste and Class* (coauthored with Burleigh and Mary Gardner), when he wrote his critique. Davis therefore was preeminently a member of the class that he was stirred to denounce.

Davis accused the "mulatto upper class" of "lawyers, doctors, school teachers, real estate sharpies, businessmen and society women whose contribution is limited to fur coats, packards, armchair solutions of the race problem, football classics and fraternity dances" in both the South and the North of "divided racial allegiance, typical of all half-bloods," and of setting up "more social inequalities based upon shades of color than the most ingenious Klansman could devise." "The Negro's faith in the mystic superiority of a light skin would be a delightful bit of irony," he asserted, "if we were not so farcically stupid and insane. We are color-mad, duped by a phantasm conjured up by egomaniac whites. Our complete acceptance of the white man's pathological admiration of his skin color entirely unfits us to believe in our own manhood and equality." In language as biting as that of Marcus Garvey, Davis charged that the aims of the mulatto upper class "are to exploit and drain the masses for all they are worth, to draw apart from them physically and socially, to build a light-skinned world of its own and to ape the white world in luxury and amusement." Such a class was a danger to the race, he maintained. "They are of no value to the masses and the best interests of the race demand that they be refashioned or cast off."[11]

THE DECLINE OF COLOR SNOBBISHNESS

The critique of the new black upper and upper-middle class by E. Franklin Frazier in the 1950s resembled those of Hughes and Davis in all particulars but one. As Frazier had already pointed out in several previous studies, at the very time that Hughes and Davis published their commentaries, the immoderate concern with color as a symbol of elite status was in the process of steady erosion.[12] Rising members of the middle class moved into the vacuum left by the migration of many of the old elite to other areas of the country or married the light-skinned women of the old aristocracy who, already facing the prospects of spinsterhood because of the shortage of eligible males within their own group, lost or suppressed their aversion to dark-skinned men crossing their threshold.[13] Thus a brown rather than a near-white or high-yellow generation had emerged by the 1930s as the characteristic upper class in most Southern black communities.

While some of the "blue veins" in the Deep South continued to hold out, and a light skin continued to have high esthetic value, the new upper class, because of its economic and cultural roots among the black masses, either could not afford or was disinclined to be as overtly color conscious as its predecessor. Moreover, because of the increasing black revulsion against sexual relations between black women and white men and the tendency of the upper class to value stable family relationships, a complexion which carried with it the stigma of remote or recent bastardy was often of dubious social value.

Indeed, even among the old aristocracy, a light complexion by itself was never an indication of high social status. Only when such color reflected the appropriate combination of the proper kinds of such characteristics as family background, culture, education, occupation, and income was it an index of elite standing. Thus the majority of mulattoes were found in the middle and lower classes, along with most of the darker members of the race.

For most blacks, then, color was largely incidental to other constellations of circumstances that marked class status. In his study of eight counties in Alabama, Georgia, Mississippi, North Carolina, and Tennessee in the 1930s, Charles S. Johnson observed that "there is little correlation between class and color in the Southern rural area. Differences of complexion and hair create problems of adjustment, but do not mark class lines within the rural Negro group."[14] A study of the black community in the southern Virginia community of South Boston in the 1940s served to confirm Johnson's observations. The author reported that "In the upper class color ranges from the very dark to very light," and that "In their intimate social groups no person was discriminated against because of his color."[15]

In fact, as several scholars discovered in the 1930s, there were black families who expressed pride in their presumed pure African ancestry and dark skin color and who disdained to intermarry with persons of lighter hue.[16] These families could be found in all classes within the black community. Some, lacking the necessary socioeconomic indices of high status, claimed such status on the grounds that they were descendants of African royalty. Even a number of mulattoes, seeking to escape the stigma of bastardy, denied having white blood, and attributed their light color to a mixed African-Indian ancestry. For the few who cared about such matters the color spectrum as an indication of ancestry could be highly confusing. Individuals of black-white or black-Indian ancestery spanned the entire color range within the black community while those of supposedly pure African ancestry ranged in color from black to medium brown. Even within the same family there was often a wide range in color among the children of the same parents, causing in some cases intrafamilial tensions. For most blacks, however, color alone was relatively insignificant in determining choice of friends and associates and, for the upper class, was more a symbol than the substance of social status.

Where the color factor was neutralized by a lack of color consciousness or where the classes were indistinguishable from each other in the color range among their members, social antipathies were nevertheless evident. A 1929 study of a Charlottesville, Virginia, black community, for example, revealed that the tendency of individuals in the lower and upper classes to remain aloof from each other and to denigrate each other's way of life reflected mainly cultural differences.[17] Similarly, Allison Davis noted that in Natchez and the surrounding Mississippi counties during the 1930s, much of the antagonism between social groups seemed to have an economic base. The respective parties in the relationships between landlord and tenant, business-man and customer, and professional and client all seemed to feel that each was in some way exploited or improperly treated by the other. One conse-quence of this feeling was the refusal of many lower-class blacks to support black-owned business enterprises, despite appeals to race pride and solidarity.[18]

UNITY WITHIN DIVERSITY

It would be a mistake to conclude that the antipathies among blacks were of sufficient depth and substance to constitute class conflict in any funda-mental sense. The findings and views of Allison Davis notwithstanding, the gaps among the various classes in black society were too narrow and the economic and political power of the bourgeoisie too meager to enable one class to substantially oppress and exploit the other. Whatever the nature of the disharmony among elements of the black community, the major concern of all classes was their collective subordination as a group to whites, not the internal rivalries that often marked their relations with each other.

Thus, while much in the indictment of the black bourgeoisie is true, it is not the whole story. The tragicomic foibles of upper-status blacks as well as their substantial achievements can only be understood within the context of their origins. As Samuel Proctor has pointed out, a large number of upper middle-class blacks have come up from the depths of poverty, "from homes where there were several children who could not get a college education and from communities where few adults did anything except domestic work." "Many," says Proctor, "are first generation urban dwellers, a bachelor's degree away from squalor, welfare, and the whole bit." They "have fought and cried and sweated their way through the wilderness of racial hostility and the morass of poverty." It is understandable, then, Proctor further points out, that they would wish to enjoy their hard won gains and are not prepared to give them up.[19]

At the same time, as Proctor and others acknowledge, members of the black upper and middle classes have made significant contributions to the life of the total black community. They have provided the leaders, the skilled personnel, the social technicians, and the professionals without which the black community in the South would not have been able to maintain a viable existence. They furnished the impulse and the leadership of the freedom revolution in the South in the late 1950s and early 1960s. They continue to perform many of the unspectacular, day-to-day functions that keep a community going. Today, many in this class are making a determined effort to identify emotionally, psychologically, and physically with the total black community. What Sidney Kronus has said recently about middle-class blacks on the Chicago Southside can probably also be said of the majority of middle-class blacks in the South: ". . . they appear to live within their means, to take life seriously, and to accept their responsibilities to family, work, and community."[20]

LEADERSHIP

Leadership within the Southern black community has generally come from the upper socioeconomic levels. During the Reconstruction period the most influential leaders were politicians, clergymen, and skilled craftsmen. Following Reconstruction, and particularly after the establishment of apartheid in the South, politicians exercised progressively less influence. The few who continued to exist between 1900 and 1950 were relegated largely to holding and dispensing a few minor patronage jobs and begging for a few concessions for themselves and the black community in return for maintaining their political allegiance and delivering what was left of the black vote. Not until the 1960s, as a result of federal court decisions and federal legislation removing barriers to black voting, did politicians again emerge as important members of the black leadership class.

Meanwhile, leadership devolved upon a variety of personages. Clergymen continued to remain influential, particularly in the rural communities in which they resided and carried out their ministry. Other functional leaders included educators, businessmen, lawyers, physicians, newspapers editors and publishers, heads of fraternal, social, and race advancement organizations, and officials of labor unions. These people derived their influential positions from their occupations or their service as heads of institutions and organizations. Other were regarded as leaders because of their wealth and social status. In some rural communities well-to-do farmers held the mantle of leadership. In many urban communities businessmen and artisans were important leaders. Some individuals, irrespective of their occupations or wealth, were regarded as leaders because of their personal characteristics and influence. Others were catapulted into leadership roles around a specific issue that animated the community. Still others were deliberately selected by the white establishment to serve as its agents within the black community.

Many of the black leaders, particularly those in functional roles, devoted most of their leadership efforts to developments within the black community and thus avoided substantial contact with whites. Many clergymen, for example, concerned themselves almost exclusively with church and intra-community affairs.

Most public school principals and teachers restricted their activities to the internal operation of their schools and to school-related community events. The physician was naturally the community's leader on health matters.

Another type of leader consisted of those who defined their leadership role in terms of their dealings with whites on behalf of the black community, and matters involving race relations filled a large portion of their leadership portfolio. No leader, however, including those mainly involved in intra-community activities, could escape the pervasive influence of the biracial caste system. At some point every leader had to face the baneful effects of racial segregation and discrimination on the people of his community. And the manner in which he responded could span a continuum from accommodation to protest.

ACCOMMODATIONIST LEADERSHIP

A classic example of accommodationist leadership can be seen in the career of Booker T. Washington. Washington's brand of leadership was often mirrored in the careers of many leaders on the local level. Accommodationists frequently owed their status and influence in the black community to their being recognized or designated as black leaders by prominent whites. Their role was often exceedingly complex, however. The influence which white endorsement conferred was frequently counterbalanced by the suspicions such endorsement aroused in the black community. Anyone who became stigmatized as the "white folks' nigger" could hardly hope to enjoy the full confidence of any significant segment of the black population. Most blacks realized that since these leaders derived their authority from whites, they would find it impracticable to overstep the boundaries that the white community dictated. Nevertheless, skillful accommodationists often found considerable room for maneuvering within the boundaries drawn.

At one end of the accommodationist leadership spectrum were the "Uncle Toms." They included black opportunists who simply carried out the wishes of whites with respect to the black community for their own personal gain. Uncle Toms also consisted of those who actually internalized the Southern white view of the proper place for blacks in Southern society.

More typical of accommodationist leaders, however, were those who did not internalize caste values but who nevertheless were willing to work within the Jim Crow system to secure limited benefits for the black community. Many college presidents, public school principals and teachers, post-Reconstruction politicians, and clergymen fell within this category. College presidents, for example, when faced with the dilemma of giving lip service to the racial status quo or receiving no funds to operate their institutions, opted to keep their schools open. Booker T. Washington was the archtypical ac--commodationist in this respect. There were others, however, as skillful as he in playing the game. James E. Shepard, founder of North Carolina College (now North Carolina Central University) and its president until 1947, patronized, flattered, and cajoled influential white legislators into appropriating sufficient funds to make his institution one of the best for blacks in the South.

Of course most public school educators, who depended on the white establishment for their jobs, and many businessmen and professionals as well who were personally indebted to whites, adopted an accommodationist stance. In relations with whites they were generally deferential, and they usually sought benefits for themselves and their black constituencies through requests rather than demands.

Despite the presumed independence of the black church, many ministers were also accommodationists. Some, by attempting to restrict their leadership role to religious matters and intracommunity affairs, were accommodationists by default. Among these were many rural ministers who pastored several churches and were therefore unable to devote their energies to the problems of a single community. Many ministers were also uneducated and, consequently, were limited in their capacity to perceive and pursue alternatives to existing conditions. Even those ministers active in community affairs which brought them into frequent contact with whites stopped short of directly challenging the Jim Crow system and its attendant proscriptions on the black community.

Moreover, black churches were often not as independent of the white community as appearances indicated. Whites frequently held mortgages on church property and on the property of church members. Prominent whites in the community occasionally enriched church coffers through small financial contributions. And many church members were dependent on whites for employment. In addition, clergymen (as well as other leaders) in some communities were fully aware that a challenge to the Jim Crow system could bring physical retaliation from whites—their homes could be destroyed, or they and their families could be killed or driven from the community. Thus many leaders could see no viable alternative to accommodation.

An interesting development around the turn of the century was the descent of former militant leaders into the ranks of accommodationists. Two examples may suffice. From 1899 to 1908 the Reverend Sutton Griggs of Nashville published novels and essays excoriating the racial practices of the white South, defending the race against the literary invectives of Thomas Dixon, Jr., and urging black Southerners to unite behind protest leaders in strengthening black institutional life and in pursuing the goal of equality. Unlike most of his ministerial and intellectual colleagues in the South, Griggs also joined the Niagara Movement.

After 1908, however, Griggs, disappointed at the failure of blacks to in-

dicate their endorsement of his program by buying his books, moved progressively toward accommodation with the white South. On becoming pastor of the Tabernacle Baptist Church in Memphis in 1913, he began to preach
a conservative philosophy of racial adjustment. Subscribing to Social Dar-
winist notions of the inferiority of the black race, Griggs proposed that through
a program of moral regeneration and domestic and industrial training, blacks
could prepare to become efficient employees in the homes and enterprises
of white Southerners. At the same time he became an apologist for Southern
racial practices. Publicizing his ideas in pulpit and press, Griggs won the
commendation and support of the white Memphis business community,
who urged the black community to follow his leadership. During his seven-
teen-year residence in Memphis, however, Griggs failed to persuade black
Memphians, many of whom regarded him as a "white man's nigger," of
the efficacy of his prescription for the advancement of the race. He died
early in 1933 in Denison, Texas, "a despondent man, almost unwept, and
unhonored."[21]

John B. Rayner, the foremost black Populist in Texas in the 1890s, underwent a similar metamorphosis. After leaving the dying Populist cause in 1898,
Rayner devoted his energies to promoting self-help programs along the
Booker T. Washington line. Through his promotion of a project to construct
a "Hall of Faithfulness" in honor of the black mammy of slavery days at
the industrial school where he was a financial agent, his participation in
the founding and work of the Texas Law and Order League, and in his critical comments about white Northerners, Rayner sought to curry favor with
the white South. Although he was moderately successful as a fund raiser for
educational projects, including those of R. L. Smith, Rayner failed to recover even a modicum of the influence he had enjoyed during his Populist
years.

COMPROMISE LEADERSHIP

Numerous black leaders who were forced into an accommodationist position nevertheless harbored strong "protest attitudes." Designated as "compromise" leaders by Oliver C. Cox,[22] they suppressed or muted the expression
of such sentiments because of their personal or institutional vulnerability to
the white establishment. Yet, while maintaining a facade of compromise,
they worked covertly and subtly for protest goals. After the failure of the
streetcar boycott movement in Richmond, Virginia, in 1904-1905, John
Mitchell, Jr., of the Richmond *Planet,* for example, continued for many
years to personally boycott Richmond's streetcars while at the same time
advising black Virginians to cultivate harmonious relations with the better

class of whites and to eschew the militant rhetoric of protest. As Southern society became less restrictive with the passage of time, many compromise leaders threw off the accommodationist mantle and openly sought identification as protest leaders.

Even the most militant black leaders were required at times to compromise with the Southern biracial order. An agonizing example, cited by Oliver C. Cox, was the case of John Hope, president of Atlanta Baptist College (later Morehouse College) in the early 1900s. An admirer and disciple of W. E. B. Du Bois and his protest philosophy, Hope was nevertheless forced to seek the intercession of Booker T. Washington in order to obtain funds from philanthropists to keep his institution open. Prior to this, Hope's efforts to secure funds had been a dismal failure.[23]

Another example of compromise leadership has already been described in a previous chapter. The efforts of Gordon Blaine Hancock and the signers of the Durham Manifesto to obtain improvements in the conditions of blacks in the South within the framework of a segregated society smacked of accommodationism. "The only reason any Negro ever lived in the South and departed alive was due to his ability to compromise," explained the pragmatic Hancock to a Northern critic.[24] Nevertheless, despite the group's refusal to heed Benjamin Mays' call for an explicit declaration against segregation, they recognized that the demands they were making would eventually mean an end to the Jim Crow system.

The black elite of Durham, North Carolina, has provided one of the best examples of compromise leadership over an extended period of time. The leadership cadre there has traditionally consisted of an interlocking group of businessmen, educators, clergymen, physicians, and lawyers who have generally taken their cues from the officials of the North Carolina Mutual Insurance Company and its satellite enterprises. The pattern of leadership, like that in other areas of the South, has usually been a reflection of the state of race relations within the larger community. Since the racial caste system in Durham has been somewhat less oppressive than in many other Southern communities, Durham's black leaders have had more room in which to maneuver. Moreover, since the early 1930s, Durham blacks have increasingly exercised the franchise. Consequently their leaders have had a greater range of options in dealing with the white community than leaders elsewhere in the South.

In 1935 the Durham Committee on Negro Affairs was formed and soon became the institutional forum through which the various segments of the black community channeled their requests and demands. It was largely dominated, however, by the Mutual Insurance group, most of whom apparently no longer found the 1898 advice of its founder, John Merrick, adequate to meet the needs of their own time. Merrick had urged black North Carolinians to leave politics alone and to concentrate on making a living as businessmen, workers, and farmers. "What difference does it make to us who is elected?" he asked. "We got to serve in the same different capacities of life for a living. . . . We got to haul wood, and don't care who is elected."[25] Although some Durham leaders were outright accommodationists, most followed a strategy of compromise. In the ensuing years they were successful in obtaining many benefits for the black community, such as paved and lighted streets, better school facilities, black policemen, and a strong voice in political affairs. They supported those white candidates and public officials who were sympathetic to black needs.

In 1953 Durham blacks elected one of their number to the city council. They increasingly held the balance of power in city elections, and as a result, their leaders could bargain rather than plead with the white establishment for concessions. Before the Supreme Court 1954 desegregation decision, however, most Durham leaders kept their activities within the bounds of the biracial system and confined their segregation challenges to court litigation. After the 1954 decision, these leaders, like their counterparts in other Southern communities, were increasingly challenged by events and by their followers to adopt a more militant stance.

From 1948 to 1958 a similar but more loosely structured compromise political organization existed in Richmond, Virginia. A confederation of church, civic, labor, and fraternal groups, the Richmond Civic Council was instrumental in getting Oliver Hill, a black attorney, elected to the city council in 1948. Under the leadership of conservative ministers, the Civic Council failed to accomplish much of substance. It was succeeded in the late 1950s by the more aggressive but still moderate Crusade for Voters, an organization whose leaders came largely from the ranks of physicians, lawyers, and college professors and administrators.

MILITANT LEADERSHIP

As we have seen, the spirit of protest remained alive in the South even after the system of apartheid had been fully established. In the rural South, however, opportunities to pursue protest goals, to seek openly to break down the walls of segregation and to end the concomitant discrimination were severely limited, as the fate of the various farmers' protest movements amply attests. Thus most militant black leaders between 1900 and 1955 were found in the urban South where the size and diversity of the population gave them some degree of freedom. Militant leaders were often associated with protest organizations. After 1910 they were likely to be members of the NAACP. They also frequently occupied functional leadership positions in their communities. Some, however, derived their leadership status solely from their protest activities. Intellectuals such as W. E. B. Du Bois, John Hope, and

Benjamin Mays; clergymen such as Bishop Henry M. Turner of Georgia and James Hinton of South Carolina; newspapermen such as Clifton F. Richardson, Sr., and Carter W. Wesley of Texas, and Louis E. Austin of Durham; and a host of others were representatives of functional leaders who were also protect leaders.

Sometimes militant leadership arose from unexpected quarters. In 1939, Levi Byrd, a plumber, took the lead in forming a branch of the NAACP in his hometown of Cheraw, South Carolina. He subsequently inspired the merger of all branches of the organization in the state into the South Carolina Conference of the NAACP. He served the latter body as treasurer for many years. Working with Byrd in these endeavors was a cross section of functional leaders within the state: ministers, a few newspapermen, college professors, businessmen, and physicians.

In Durham, North Carolina, in the late 1940s and early 1950s, one of the prominent leaders in the attack on the Jim Crow system in the state was Louis E. Austin, crusading editor and publisher of *The Carolina Times.* Austin helped to spearhead the efforts to integrate the University of North Carolina and other state educational institutions. He frequently employed language and tactics which the Durham black leadership establishment found to be anathema to what they considered their more moderate approach and objectives. Nevertheless, through his efforts, Austin helped to move the Durham elite into a less compromising stand. There were others like him in Durham and throughout the South who stood in the vanguard of the pre-1960 protest movement. The progressive dismantling of the Jim Crow system in the late 1940s and throughout the 1950s was a tribute to their efforts and vision. Paradoxically, however, their very successes contributed to a fundamental change in the meaning and character of the various types of leadership which have been described. Indicative of the change was the tendency by the late 1960s for many of the earlier militants to be described by their successors as moderates and, even in some cases, as accommodationists. Clearly then, leadership typology within the black community can be accurately understood only within the context of time, place, and circumstances.

"The First Vote" During Reconstruction
Source: *Harper's Weekly,* November 16, 1867
Wood engraving by A. R. Waud
(Courtesy Library of Congress)

Memphis, Tennessee, Riot of May 2, 1866
Source: *Harper's Weekly*, May 26, 1866
Wood engraving by A. R. Waud

**The Lynching by Burning of Jesse Washington
Waco, Texas, May 15, 1916**
Photo by Gildersleeve
(Courtesy Library of Congress)

A Traveling Classroom
From Booker T. Washington Collection
(Courtesy Library of Congress)

**Union of Black Bricklayers,
Jacksonville, Florida, 1900**
Photo from Paris Exposition Collection
(Courtesy Library of Congress)

Turpentine Workers—Georgia, July 1937
Photo by Dorothea Lange
(Courtesy Library of Congress)

A Business That Failed—
Coleman Manufacturing Co., A black-owned
Cotton Mill in Concord, North Carolina, 1900
Photo from U.S. Exhibit at Paris Exposition, 1900
(Courtesy Library of Congress)

A Business That Succeeded—
North Carolina Mutual Insurance Company 1976
Photo by Charles H. Cooper
(Courtesy North Carolina Mutual Insurance Company)

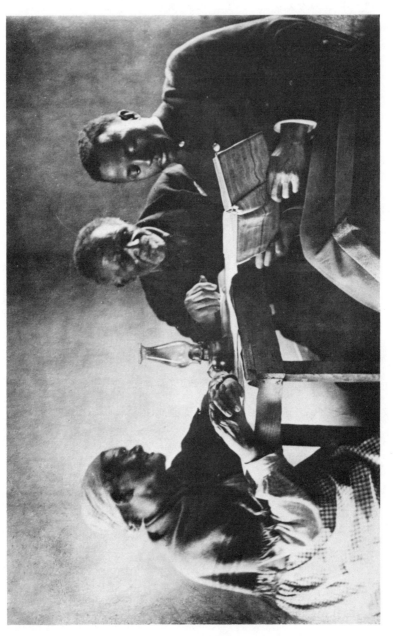

The Freedman's Search for Knowledge
(From Booker T. Washington Collection, Library of Congress)

Separate but Unequal—
A Black School Near Summerville, South Carolina, December 1938
Photo by Marion Post Wolcott
(Courtesy Library of Congress)

**Mother Teaching Children Numbers and Alphabet in
Home of Sharecropper, Translyvania, Louisiana, January 1939**

Photo by Russell Lee

Atlanta University Nursery School, March 1942
Photo by Arthur Rothstein
(Courtesy Library of Congress)

Marriage of a Black Soldier at Vicksburg by Chaplain Warran of the Freedmen's Bureau
Source: *Harper's Weekly*, June 30, 1866
(Courtesy Library of Congress)

Feggen Jones and Family, Zebulon, North Carolina, March 1942
Photo by Arthur Rothstein

Home of Black Farmer Near Beaufort, South Carolina, December 1938
Photo by Marion Post Wolcott
(Courtesy Library of Congress)

Home of Robert Richard, Memphis, Tennessee, 1900
Photo from U.S. Exhibit at Paris Exposition, 1900
(Courtesy Library of Congress)

Jitterbugging in a Juke Joint on Saturday Evening, Outside Clarksdale, Mississippi Delta, November 1939
Photo by Marion Post Wolcott
(Courtesy Library of Congress)

**Shopping and Visiting on Main Street of Pittsboro, North Carolina,
Saturday Afternoon, July 1939**
Photo by Dorothea Lange
(Courtesy Library of Congress)

PART FOUR

BLACK EXPRESSION: SOUTHERN ROOTS AND SOUTHERN THEMES

TEN

Fiction and Drama

ORAL LITERATURE

Under slavery, blacks in America developed a rich expressive culture of folk tales, folk poetry, and folk music. Resting on an African base, but also infused with Euro-American forms, traditions, and concepts, the culture of the slaves reflected not only the slavery experience but mirrored Afro-American conceptions of universal phenomena as well. As quasi-free people after slavery, black Southerners continued to draw on their antebellum folklore heritage for entertainment and inspiration and as a conceptual medium through which to comprehend, interpret, and describe their contemporary circumstances. In the process they embellished the earlier lore, adapted it to their experiences as a free people, and created, in turn, new folk tales, folk poetry, and folk music.

Many of the subjects and themes in the oral literature of the slaves continued to be a part of the postwar oral expression of the freedmen and succeeding generations. Animal tales that featured such denizens of field, forest, and jungle as the rabbit, the fox, the bear, the terrapin, the opposum, the wolf, the lion, the monkey, and the elephant and such domestic creatures as the mule, the ox, the cow, and the horse, continued to be used to symbolize aspects of the human condition. Bird tales, too, that featured the eagle, the crow, the goose, the buzzard, and barnyard fowl were similarly employed. The rabbit, of course, was the most favored of all the creatures; its prominence in black American folklore was undoubtedly derived from the pervasiveness of the hare in both West African and European folklore as well as from the ubiquitous presence of the rabbit in the American environment.

Among the human types prominent in oral literature were such black characters as slave and free laborers, and preachers and badmen. The white characters were usually people in authority such as masters and mistresses and their agents, landlords, and sheriffs and other law-enforcement officials. Ghosts, conjurers, and witches comprised the quasi-human types frequently mentioned in the folk tales while God and the Devil and their respective agents were the principal extraterrestrial characters.

A prominent theme in antebellum folk literature was the defeat of the strong by the weak through the use of wit, guile, and cunning. Brer Rabbit was usually the trickster animal, but occasionally the terrapin, the opposum, or the monkey played a similar role. In describing how these animals successfully avoided performing assigned tasks or won psychological and material advantage over stronger adversaries, the folk tales of the trickster genre symbolized the efforts of slaves to subvert or "repudiate," at least psychologically, the hegemony of the master class over them.

In addition to often containing repudiative themes, folk tales in which magic, voodoo, and conjuration were employed, and in which ghosts and other inhabitants of the terrestrial-spiritual world were the main subjects, provide evidence of the continued attachment of the slaves and their descendants to the evocative motif in African religious and cosmological thought, wherein demigods are expected and solicited to play an active part in human affairs. The fact that white Americans also inherited a belief in these supernatural forces and beings from their European background undoubtedly served to nourish the traditional African beliefs among Afro-Americans.

Changes that occurred in narrative folklore after the Civil War were basically of two kinds: there was a more explicit rendering of the repudiative theme, and there was an expansion or embellishment of the lore to include new subjects, themes, and experiences that arose under conditions of freedom. In the freer environment of the post-Civil War decades, blacks in the South felt less need to disguise their feelings of protest against white oppression under the Brer Rabbit rubric. Instead, they tended to make the trickster hero a human being. He frequently is a slave, called variously John, Jack, or Buck, who usually succeeds in deterring the master and his agents from a course of action that would be inimical to the slave. The bad man hero, such as Stackolee and Railroad Bill, also emerges, who explicitly and violently rebels against the social constraints of his environment.

Paradoxically, as Houston Baker has pointed out, the postslavery circumstances of the freedmen also led to the creation of folk tales in which the slavery experience was romanticized. With the passage of time, many former slaves, concerned with the hardships and insecurity of their contemporary existence, allowed the unpleasant aspects of their earlier life to recede from their consciousness.[1]

From the new conditions of freedom emerged a host of other subjects and

themes that were treated in narrative, poetry, and song. Economic and occupational life involving sharecropping, peonage, whitecappng, work on
the railroads, and other forms of semi-industrial labor were prominent
topics. The system of justice, featuring the chaingang and lynching, was
frequently mentioned. Thoughts of migrating to the North or actually doing
so, and of traveling from town to town in the South were expressed in both
narrative and song. And interpersonal relations within the group, particularly
between men and women, were frequently discussed.

As the institutional church developed into the major social agency within
the black community, and as the black preacher fortified his position as the
local community's principal leader, an oral literature evolved which expressed
the ambivalent attitudes that black people held toward these two influences
in their lives. Preacher tales reveal the minister as both a figure of respect
and as an object of envy, humor, and ridicule; as a strong moral force within
the community, on the one hand, and as a violator of the ethics he espoused
and as an exploiter of his people, on the other. Simultaneously, however,
classic expressions of black religious lore in the form of sermons, testimonials,
and prayers were carried over from the slavery era and refined and enlarged.

LITERARY FICTION TO WORLD WAR I

Because teaching slaves to read and write was prohibited in the South, and
because the antebellum Northern black population was relatively small as
well as limited in its access to educational opportunities, the pre-Civil War
output of written black literature was restricted. In the main essays, pamph-
let literature, a few historical works, some poetry, a play, a few works of
fiction, and several slave narratives comprise the literary production of this
period. For the most part, however, fiction in the form of novels and short
stories had to await the end of the slavery era. Not surprisingly, when fiction
written by blacks did appear, it was authored by individuals with Southern
roots or dealt with Southern themes or both. Moreover, even after the Northern urban environment increasingly claimed the attention of black writers,
the South continued to be a significant theme in black literature, attracting
the interest of Southern-born and Northern-born writers alike. For whether
born and raised in North or South, most black writers, like most black people
in America, were directly or atavistically rooted in the Southern experience.

William Wells Brown, an escaped slave whose literary career spanned
portions of both the antebellum and postbellum periods, wrote *Clotel, The
President's Daughter* (1853) which is generally regarded as the first novel by
a black American writer. Its main character was the female offspring of a
mulatto woman and a white planter. The novel helped to perpetuate the
tragic mulatto genre of fiction to which many black and white writers be-

came addicted in ensuing years. Although Brown continued to write after the Civil War, he was eventually eclipsed by Paul Laurence Dunbar and Charles Waddell Chesnutt as the most eminent Afro-American writers of fiction up to World War I.

Dunbar, a native of Dayton, Ohio, was the son of former slaves from Kentucky. While influenced by the plantation stories of white writers, he undoubtedly also derived the ideational roots for some of his literature from his parents. Some of his prose fiction as well as his dialect poems, for which he is best known, attempted to portray life among blacks in the antebellum plantation South.

Although he is chiefly known as a poet, Dunbar's published works include four novels and four volumes of collected short stories. Two of the novels include scenes of the South. In *Fanatics* (1901), which deals with the Civil War, the main characters are white, and the blacks who do appear are plantation stereotypes. In *Sport of the Gods,* (1902), Dunbar portrays Southern blacks more realistically. Most of the action in the novel, however, takes place in the North.

Of the seventy-three short stories contained in Dunbar's short story collections—*Folks from Dixie* (1898), *The Strength of Gideon, and Other Stories* (1900), *In Old Plantation Days* (1903), and *The Heart of Happy Hollow* (1904)—most of those dealing with the South, like his dialect poetry, present the lives of blacks in a romantic vein. Three notable exceptions are "The Lynching of Jube Benson" in the collection *The Heart of Happy Hollow,* "The Tragedy of Three Forks" in *The Strength of Gideon,* and the "Ordeal of Mount Hope" in *Folks from Dixie.* The first two stories deal with racial violence in the post-Civil War South. The third story follows the career of a black minister from the North who strives to awaken a Southern black community to a realization of its economic and educational possibilities.

By usually depicting slavemasters as kind and benevolent and the slaves as contented and loyal, and by describing postwar race relations in the South in the same vein, Dunbar failed to provide a realistic portrait of Southern black life. Like many of his literary contemporaries he was a romanticist. Nevertheless, he was one of the earliest black writers to attempt to incorporate the oral literature and idioms of the black folk into written prose and poetry.

Charles W. Chesnutt was more successful than Dunbar, his contemporary, in capturing the qualities of the South and the temperament of Southern black people. His roots in the South were much deeper than Dunbar's, although he, too, was born in Ohio, in Cleveland. Chesnutt's parents were natives of Fayetteville, North Carolina, the city where he spent his childhood and early manhood years. Between the ages of sixteen and twenty-five he was first a schoolteacher and then a principal of a black school. When he left North Carolina in 1889 to sojourn briefly in New York City and then to return to Cleveland, he had come to know the South well.

Chesnutt wrote, in part, to counter the image of blacks as vicious, depraved, and ignorant beasts, which Thomas Nelson Page, Thomas Dixon, and other Southern white writers were promulgating around the turn of the century. In his principal novels—*The House Behind the Cedars* (1900), *The Marrow of Tradition* (1901), which was based on the Wilmington, North Carolina race riot in 1898, and *The Colonel's Dream* (1905)—and in his collection of short stories, *Wife of His Youth, and Other Stories of the Color Line* (1899), Chesnutt excoriated the race prejudice of whites and color prejudice among blacks. In *Conjure Woman* (1899), his other major collection of short stories, Chesnutt delved deeply into the traditions and lore of the black Southern masses and, as Sylvia Render, one of the principal students of his life points out, "introduced North Carolina folk life to literature and utilized it effectively for social protest."[2]

As one would expect, social protest was also the theme in the more prosaic fiction of W. E. B. Du Bois. Known principally as a scholar, essayist, and civil rights activist, Du Bois was nevertheless the author of five novels, several short stories, and a number of poems. *Quest of the Silver Fleece* (1911), his first novel, is concerned with the development of the social consciousness of a young black farm couple who, after a sojourn in Washington, D.C., and the North, returns to the South and helps black sharecroppers form cooperative settlements as a means of escaping the oppressiveness of a cotton economy controlled by Northern capitalists and their collaborators among the planters.

In the multifariousness of his talents and career—educator, lawyer, newspaper editor, poet, song writer, novelist, U.S. consul, and field and general secretary of the NAACP—James Weldon Johnson surpassed most of his American contemporaries. His contributions in belle lettres spanned the second three decades of the twentieth century and included the period of the Harlem Renaissance. He was born and reared in Jacksonville, Florida, educated at Atlanta Unversity, and spent the early years of his career in his home city as the principal of a large public school.

It is not surprising, then, that the South is the setting for about one-fourth of the pages of Johnson's first novel, *The Autobiography of an Ex-Coloured Man,* which appeared in 1912. A prominent theme in the novel, as in so much of the literature concerning blacks of the early decades of the twentieth century, was miscegenation and passing. The Southern experiences of the main character, a light-skinned Afro-American born in Georgia but raised in Connecticut, involve an abortive attempt to enroll in Atlanta University, an extended residence in Jacksonville, Florida, observing and experiencing the Jim Crow customs of the South, and participating in the lives of the varied classes within the black community. Johnson's novel was republished in the 1920s and, along with the other works that he produced shortly before and during that decade, marked him as both a harbinger and a symbol of the Negro Renaissance.

THE HARLEM RENAISSANCE, THE GREAT DEPRESSION, AND THE WORLD WAR II YEARS

The flowering of Afro-American literature, art, and music during the 1920s, referred to as the Harlem Renaissance, was marked by an attempt on the part of black writers to discover and portray the essentials of black life and character. Since most Afro-Americans had historically lived in the South, where a substantial majority still resided despite the great migration northward during World War I, the search for roots, for the quintessence of black culture, led many black writers to delve into the Southern black experience. Accordingly several writers went South to research the customs and collect the oral traditions of black rural and small town folk.

Arthur Fauset, a Philadelphia schoolteacher, was among those to make the trek southward. Fearing that the memories and the traditions that comprised the black Southern heritage would soon be swept away by the growing urbanization of the region, Fauset went South in 1925 and collected and recorded black folk tales in their pristine form.

Similarly, Zora Neale Hurston, a native of the all-black town of Eatonville, Florida, returned to her home state from New York and utilized her anthropological training in recording, like Fauset, the stories, the traditions, and the speech idioms of the people. She published several short stories based on this material during the 1920s, and in 1935 a collection of her folk stories called *Of Mules and Men* appeared. Her novel *Their Eyes Were Watching God* (1937) was also based upon the folk motif, including the use of folk speech. Like earlier black writers as well as several of her contemporaries Hurston also dealt with miscegenation and the color line. Her novel *Jonah's Gourd Vine* (1934), partly based on the life of her father, followed the worldly career of the son of a black woman and a white tenant farmer. She did not limit herself to black themes, however. In *Seraph on the Suwanee* (1948) she explored the traditions and mores of poor Southern whites.

Literary scholars today regard Jean Toomer as one of the most percipient and artistically talented of the Harlem Renaissance writers. A native of the District of Columbia, Toomer's Southern ties went back to his grandfather, P. B. S. Pinchback, who served as lieutenant governor and acting governor of Louisiana during the Reconstruction period. In 1921 Toomer taught school for four months in Sparta, Georgia, and took advantage of his position to observe and immerse himself in the life of the black people around him. The result was the publication in 1923 of an integrated series of short stories, sketches, poems, and a playlet called *Cane*. The first and third parts of the three-part *Cane* are set in the South. The black inhabitants of the region are portrayed as resourceful people of considerable spiritual strength and physical and psychic beauty. The more memorable characters are women; they are physically vital and appealing, yet emotionally elusive and unfulfilled. Toomer's great achievement in *Cane,* according to Nathan Huggins, lies in the fact that he "chose as his focus the essentials of Negro identity rather than the circumstances of Negro life."[3]

Walter White, an official of the NAACP, wrote two novels during the Renaissance period. A native of Atlanta, Georgia, and a frequent visitor to the South on official missions, White was intimately acquainted with life in the region. His first novel, *Fire in the Flint* (1925), provides a realistic description of the life of a black Georgia family and the tragedies, including a lynching, that surround their lives. In *Flight* (1926), White explored the life of a mulatto girl among Atlanta's black bourgeoisie and her subsequent sojourn in Philadelphia and New York City. Some historical events, such as the Atlanta race riot of 1906, are related in the novel.

Arna Bontemps was among the several writers who began their literary careers during the Renaissance but did not publish major works until the next decade. He was born in Louisiana, but his father, finding the biracial order in Louisiana demeaning, moved the family to California while Arna was still a young boy. Bontemps subsequently returned to the South where he spent twenty-two years as librarian of Fisk University in Nashville, Tennessee. Throughout his adult life he maintained a broad and intense interest in black folk life and attempted to portray its various aspects in his novels, short stories, and poetry.

Bontemps' first novel, *God Sends Sunday* (1931), utilizes the life of Little Willie, a black racehorse jockey, to capture the flavor of the racetrack and gambling worlds of New Orleans and St. Louis. *Black Thunder* (1936), his second novel, is a fictionalized account of the Gabriel Prosser slave rebellion in Virginia in 1800. In the novel Bontemps skillfully employed the folk concepts and idioms of the slaves and sharply delineated the various personality types within the slave population. In the short stories recently brought together under the title *The Old South* (1973), Bontemps explored the lives and personalities of the various segments of the twentieth-century black population of the South.

A revealing exposure of race relations and black life in Mississippi during the thirties and within the blues and jazz circles along Beale Street in Memphis, Tennessee, was provided by George W. Lee in his novel *The River George* (1937). Lee, himself a Mississippian, depicted the frustration, the mental agony, and the physical danger encompassed in the lives of those Southern blacks who struggled to get ahead but who were forced finally to surrender their dreams, their spirits, and sometimes their physical existence to the dictates of white supremacy.

Ollie Miss (1935), a novel by George W. Henderson, was somewhat unique among the works of fiction dealing with the South which appeared during the 1930s. In writing about rural black life in his native Alabama, Henderson hardly mentions race relations. White characters appear only fleetingly. The main character, Ollie Miss, is a girl farmworker who simultaneously exudes an air of mystery, dignity, quiet strength, tenderness, and sensuality; and the black community in which she lives appears to be a self-sufficient social entity. In *Jule* (1946), however, the sequel to *Ollie Miss* and Henderson's second novel, the race relations theme is prominent. Jule, Ollie Miss's son, is forced to leave the South after a fight with a white man over the affections of a black girl. He goes to Harlem, the scene of more than half the novel, and returns to Alabama only to attend his mother's funeral.

Prior to 1950 the destructive impact of the South's racial mores on the lives of its black inhabitants received the most graphic treatment in the writings of Richard Wright. Born and reared in Mississippi, Wright's experiences as a youth in that state made an indelible impression on him. Although he dealt with a wide variety of themes, scenes, and characters during his extended literary career, his best works were about the lives of lower-class Afro-Americans. His autobiography, *Black Boy* (1945), according to Nick Aaron Ford, was "more than an account of one Negro born and raised in Mississippi; it is a picture of the entire gamut of Negro/white relations in the South during the twentieth century."[4]

When Wright came to prominence upon the publication of *Native Son* (1940), a novel of black life in Chicago, his earlier and "artistically superior" collection of short stories, *Uncle Tom's Children* (1938), had already identified him as an able portrayer of the oppressiveness of the racial environment of the Deep South. A central theme running through the four stories in the original edition was the physical and psychological rebellion of blacks against one or more of the concrete forms in which the oppression was expressed. The rebellion usually occurs in the form of violence against whites and often results in the rebel being killed by a white mob. However, it is in the act of rebellion that the protesters find their identity and their self-esteem as human beings. Although twenty years elapsed between the appearance of *Uncle Tom's Children* and *The Long Dream*, Wright's second major work of fiction about the South, the two works possessed similar characteristics.

Wright's works dealing with the South revealed his deep understanding of the folk ways and mores of the Southern black community, a knowledge stemming from his own early existence in the folk culture but sharpened by his familiarity with the works of other black writers in which folk material had been extensively used. Yet, because of the nature of his own personal experiences in the South, Wright painted a somewhat one-dimensional picture of Southern black life. His stress on the bleakness, bitterness, frustrations, and interpersonal conflicts which characterized the existence of many blacks caused him to give too little attention to the warmth, humor, dignity, and sense of community which often pervaded the day-to-day relations of black people.

The affairs of black residents of the upper South also received the attention of black writers during the 1930s and 1940s. Waters Turpin, whose literary career spanned several decades, followed the fortunes of a black family in his native Eastern Shore of Maryland through four generations in *These Low Grounds* (1937), his first novel. He clearly showed that the poverty and racial oppression so characteristic of the lower South was also endemic to his region. After treating the rise of a man from a farm laborer in Mississippi to a prosperous businessman in Chicago and his subsequent decline back into humble circumstances in *O Canaan* (1939), his second novel, Turpin returned to the Maryland scene in *Rootless* (1957). The latter novel deals with slavery in the region in the eighteenth century, and the main character is a slave who refuses to acquiesce in the degrading features of the system.

Another novel describing conditions in the upper South during the 1930s is William Attaway's *Blood on the Forge* (1941). The story begins with a portrayal of the lives of three brothers as tenant farmers in Kentucky and the racial environment which stifles them. It then follows the migration of the brothers to the North and their subsequent existence in a Pennsylvania steel mill town.

Even fiction of the post-World War I decades that concerned Northern locales frequently provided insights into the Southern experience. Rudolph Fisher's novels and short stories of the 1920s and 1930s usually were set in Harlem, but "Miss Cynthie," a short story, provides an excellent glimpse of the values in black Southern life as personified in an old but alert woman who has made her first trip outside the South to visit her grandson in Harlem.[5]

FICTION SINCE WORLD WAR II

Despite the increasing concentration of the black population in Northern urban centers, events in the South have made that region a continuing subject of interest to black writers, and developments involving education, family life, and civil rights have all been treated in fiction.

J. Saunders Redding, long a professor at Hampton Institute and at several other black colleges in the South, published a timely novel in 1950 called *Strangers and Alone*. Redding attempted to expose the deficiencies in the systems of public and higher education for blacks in the region. Beginning in the 1920s, his story covers some three decades. The principal character is a timid and conservative black male who first as a college student and then as a college instructor and public school administrator becomes both a victim and a perpetuator of the system.

Deficiencies in the Southern system of higher education for blacks also received attention in Ralph Ellison's widely acclaimed *Invisible Man* (1953), a novel with a predominantly Harlem locale. The novel begins with the Southern scene, however, and vividly adumbrates the social typologies and pathologies of the region. Among these are a black college president who maintains his position and the solvency of his institution by deceiving and deferring to whites and at the same time sacrificing the aspirations and self-respect of some of his students. There is a black sharecropper who by an accidental, single instance of incest embarrasses the black college community, but in relating the incident to a puritanical white Northern philanthropist and trustee of the college, affords the latter a similar experience vicariously. And there is a group of Southern white men who seek to gratify their own lust by forcing a group of black boys to engage in a boxing match and to look at a nude white woman, thereby acting out the white fantasy of black males as potent and brutal savages.

The dynamics of family life among blacks in the South are explored in Chester Himes' *Third Generation* (1953). Himes was a native of Missouri, but he spent part of his childhood in Mississippi and Arkansas. In the novel he examines the phenomena of color prejudice as the cause of tensions within a black middle-class family. The novel is partly autobiographical, based in large measure on the lives of Himes' parents and their three sons. Those portions of the novel that have a Southern locale also provide some insights into black college life in that area.

John Oliver Killens's novel *Youngblood* (1954) is another family chronicle. A native of Macon, Georgia, Killens relates the efforts of two generations of a black Georgia family to achieve an existence of dignity, material security, and personal satisfaction within their Southern environment. The South occupies only a small space, however, in Killens's second novel, *And Then We Heard the Thunder* (1962). Concerned with the experiences of black soldiers during World War II, the novel covers briefly the problems of discrimination that black soldiers training in the South suffered during that period. In *Great Gittin' Up Morning* (1972) Killens turned to the slavery era, and perhaps in an attempt to counter the image of blacks that William Styron's *Confessions of Nat Turner* evoked, produced a fictionalized account of the Denmark Vesey conspiracy in 1822 in South Carolina.

One of the best family novels written since World War II is Margaret Walker's *Jubilee* (1966). Walker, a native of Alabama and a long-time resident of the Deep South, reached back to the slavery and Reconstruction eras to produce a thoroughly researched historical novel which relates the life and times of her maternal great grandmother and the efforts of the latter and her spouses to build and maintain a viable family life in Georgia. Walker's declaration that "I always intended *Jubilee* to be a folk novel based on folk material: folk sayings, folk belief, and folkways. As early as 1948 I was conceiving the story in terms of this folklore,"[6] is evidence of the deep and pervasive influence of oral black literature on many black authors.

Ernest Gaines is perhaps the most widely acclaimed Southern black writer to emerge in the 1960s. A native of rural Louisiana, Gaines, in a series of novels and short stories in which the main characters are either a man, a woman, or a boy, has provided authentic insights into the thoughts, emotions, and life-styles of the kinds of people with whom he grew up. Family life is a theme in several of his fictional works, and such emotions as love, loyalty, and mutual respect among family members is tellingly depicted.

The first version of Gaines's story, *Long Day in November,* which appeared in 1964, describes a day in the life of a black family on a Louisiana plantation in the late 1930s or early 1940s. The plot revolves around a family crisis that has been created by the father's attachment to a car. The crisis is resolved when the father, faced with the choice of keeping his wife or keeping his car, on the advice of a voodoo queen publicly burns the car. To salvage her husband's pride and to assure that he continues to be respected by the other plantation residents, the wife, in turn, forces her husband to beat her with a switch.

In addition to his collection of short stories published in 1968 under the title *Bloodline,* Gaines has written three novels—*Catherine Carmier* (1964), *Of Love and Dust* (1967), and the critically acclaimed *The Autobiography of Miss Jane Pittman* (1971). The latter, through the agency of the activities and observations of a black woman, chronicles aspects of the lives of Louisiana blacks from the Civil War years to the civil rights demonstrations of the 1960s.

In *Many Thousands Gone* (1967) Chicago novelist Ronald Fair describes the subversive impact on a Mississippi town of the arrival of a copy of *Ebony* magazine. The magazine, containing pictures of prosperous black people in the North, including a cover photograph of a former resident of the town, awakens the black community from its lethargy. The black residents of the town appeal to the president of the United States for relief from white oppression, but when the federal officials sent to their aid prove ineffective, they proceed to burn the town down.

Although several writers in addition to Gaines and Fair have touched on aspects of the school desegregation crisis and the civil rights and black power demonstrations of the 1950s and 1960s, a first-class novel by a black writer devoted exclusively to these events has yet to appear. The human drama involved in these developments have been illumined in several short stories, however. Representative of the genre are the stories of Diane Oliver and Mike Thelwell. In "Neighbors," the late Diane Oliver of Charlotte, North Carolina, reveals the anxieties and conflicting emotions that lie behind the last minute refusal of a black family to allow their little boy to be the first black child to integrate the local elementary school.[7] In "Organizer," Mike Thelwell, a West Indian native who spent some time in civil rights work in the South during the 1960s, delineates the various character types who emerged during the events of that decade. There are the slain local civil rights leader, the black civil rights organizer from the North, the white sheriff and his deputies, the courageous black matron, the Uncle Tom preacher, and a determined group of black protesters. The story revolves around the efforts of the organizer to provide means by which the protesters can release their anger over the slaying of their leader while at the same time restraining them from acts which will get them killed by the police and the national guard.[8]

Several black writers, including a number discussed in the foregoing pages, have attempted with uneven success to move outside the black milieu for choice of theme and subject. Among novelists, Frank Yerby, a native Georgian and a former instructor in several Southern black colleges, has been the most prolific in this respect. The overwhelming majority of his twenty-five novels have whites as the central characters, and those with a Deep South locale treat the region through white lenses. Nevertheless, as Darwin Turner has observed, in dealing with racial themes, as all of his Southern novels do to some extent, and in depicting those whites who adhere to the region's old racial mores, Yerby subtly but severely censures the South, explodes its social myths, and frequently holds it up to ridicule.[9] One of Yerby's more recent novels, *The Dahomean* (1971), dealing with life in the Old West African kingdom of that name, may presage his return to Afro-American themes, which characterized his early fictional works.

DRAMA

Drama has served as a useful medium through which blacks have been able to explore their history and culture. As was true of other forms of literature, plays authored by Afro-Americans antedated the Civil War. In 1821 a play by a black American was presented in New York City; and in 1858 William Wells Brown's *The Escape, Or a Leap to Freedom* was published. In his play Brown interspersed among the melodramatic episodes involving a beautiful slave girl, her slave paramour, and a "lustful master" satiric views of the personalities and situations present in slave society.

For several decades after the Civil War, however, few black playwrights received any recognition either inside or outside the black community. And prior to World War I most drama involving blacks as subjects and actors consisted of minstrel shows in which white and black actors performed in blackface; musical comedy shows of somewhat greater sophistication than minstrels and somewhat less demeaning to the Afro-American image; and plays written by whites in which such black character stereotypes as the "Buffoon, the Tragic Mulatto, the Christian Slave, the Primitive, and the Black Beast," generally were portrayed.

A few black playwrights such as Joseph S. Cotter, Sr., in *Caleb, the Degenerate* (1903) and Angelina Weld Grimke in *Rachel* (1916) tried to counter the stereotypes; however, it was not until such white writers as Ridgely Torrence and Eugene O'Neill began in the second decade of the twentieth century to give a more realistic and dignified treatment to black life and culture that black playwrights found a congenial environment in which to present their versions of the Afro-American experience.

The Harlem Renaissance era spawned a number of playwrights, several of whom addressed themselves to the Southern experience. In *Bole, A Sketch of Negro Life* (1922), Jean Toomer explored the lives of black farmers in Georgia. John F. Matheus, of West Virginia, illustrated the tensions generated within a Georgia family over the question of whether to migrate to the North in "Cruiter," a play which won a drama prize in *Opportunity* magazine in 1926.[10] Also the winner of an Opportunity drama prize in the same year was Frank H. Wilson's "Sugar Cane," a play depicting the disruptive influence of the visit of a black Northerner to a somewhat prosperous but socially apathetic black farm family in Georgia.[11] In *Flight of the Natives* (1927) Willis Richardson of Wilmington, North Carolina, turned to the slavery period for themes. His main character was a slave man who refuses to allow anyone to whip him and runs away in order to avoid being sold into the Deep South because of his recalcitrance.

Langston Hughes, one of the most prolific of the Renaissance literati, produced several plays in the 1930s and 1940s dealing with aspects of Southern life. His *Mulatto* (1937), which depicted the contradictory emotions aroused in a black youth and his white Georgia father by the former's effort to win filial recognition, ran for over two years on Broadway. Hughes also dealt with Southern themes in *Don't You Want to Be Free?* (1938), a play which dramatized the Afro-American experience down to the Great Depression, and in *The Sun Do Move* (1942), a play about slave life on a Southern plantation.

Among the lesser-known black writers who produced plays of Southern life during the 1930s and 1940s were two native Louisianians. Augustus Smith's drama, *Louisiana,* which involved the use by blacks of voodoo and Christian rituals to rescue a young girl from immoral influences, was staged by the Negro Theater Guild in 1933. During the same decade Smith also collaborated with Peter Morrell in writing *Turpentine,* a play denunciatory of the abuse of black workers in the Southern timber industry. Theodore Ward's *Our Lan',* which dramatized the unsuccessful efforts of freedmen during the Reconstruction period to retain the land promised them by the government, was produced on Broadway in 1946, five years after it was written.

EDUCATIONAL THEATER

Contemporaneous with the appearance on Broadway of plays by Afro-Americans dealing with the South was the considerable dramatic activity occurring within the Southern black community itself. As early as the 1920s Southern black colleges were increasingly utilized as community theaters, and served, in the process, as training ground for black actors and playwrights.

Randolph Edmonds, a native of Lawrenceville, Virginia, and a teacher for over forty years at such institutions as Morgan State College, Dillard University, and Florida A. and M. University, was a central figure in these developments as a drama teacher, playwright, director, and founder of drama associations. Associated with him or involved in similar endeavors were Melvin B. Tolson of Langston Unviersity, Owen Dodson of Atlanta and Howard Universities, James Butcher of Howard University, Anne Cook of Atlanta University and Hampton Institute, John Ross of Fisk University, and Fannin Belcher of Virginia State College. Carlton Molette II and Barbara Molette of Spelman College and Clifford Lamb and Waters Turpin of Morgan State College have augmented their ranks in recent years as drama teachers and playwrights.

Theatrical activity within the black colleges was carried on principally through the medium of drama clubs, which were established in increasing numbers between the two world wars. In 1930, on the initiative of Randolph Edmonds, drama teachers from Hampton, Howard, Morgan, Virginia Union, and Virginia State met in Baltimore and formed the Negro Intercollegiate Dramatic Association. By the end of 1937 five other schools had joined the association. Again on Edmonds initiative, the Southern Association of Dramatic Speech and Arts, comprising the drama units of sixteen colleges in the lower South, was formed during the 1936-1937 academic year. In 1951 the organization changed its name to the National Association of Dramatic Speech and Arts.

Although the college drama clubs presented plays on a wide variety of subjects, the drama associations placed their emphasis on the production and staging of plays on Afro-American life; and many of the early dramas that were written and performed were based on the black folk motif. Through annual drama festivals and contests, the associations and their constituent clubs carried live theater to segments of the Southern black community. Their plays were sometimes sponsored by high schools, churches, college alumni groups, and chambers of commerce.

From the drama laboratories of the Southern colleges came a number of plays written by drama instructors and their students. Of the college playwrights, Randolph Edmonds, who wrote some fifty plays, was the most prolific. In *Six Plays for a Negro Theatre* (1934) Edmonds used dialect in an attempt to represent the language of the average black Southerner and as an expression of his commitment to black folk material. All but one of the plays in the collection dealt with Southern life. "Breeders" depicts the agony suffered by two young slaves in love with each other when the master forces the girl to marry a slave whom she does not love. "Bad Man" treats the transformation of a bad man into a constructive leader and hero of a group of black sawmill hands in Alabama who face a threatened lynching by a white mob. "Nat Turner" is a dramatization of the Southampton, Virginia, slave rebellion of 1831. "Bleeding Hearts" attempts to illumine the religious concepts and rites involved in the response of a black farm family to sickness and death. And "The New Window" deals with the violence and superstitions attending the lives of black moonshiners in southern Virginia.

While neither Edmonds nor his college associates confined their play writing to Southern themes, most of them wrote at least one play dealing with life in the region. Owen Dodson's *Bayou Legend* is a surrealistic tale, featuring a blending of folklore and myth, of the loves and adventures of a young black man in the Louisiana bayou country. Similarly, James Ross's best play, "Wonga Doll," is also set in Louisiana and features the folklore of that state. Finally, Melvin Tolson also depicted aspects of Southern life in two plays: "Moses of Beale Street" and "Southern Front," the latter dealing with efforts to unionize Arkansas tenant farmers.

DRAMA SINCE WORLD WAR II

Black playwrights have been in the forefront of the literary artists who have addressed their art to the stirring post-World War II developments in the South. William Branch, who spent part of his early life in Charlotte, North Carolina, captured the developing mood of the postwar decade in his first play, *A Medal for Willie* (1951). In accepting a medal awarded posthumously to her son by the army at a ceremony arranged by the officials of a Southern town at the local black high school, a black mother exposes and castigates the hypocrisy of the Southern biracial system. Later Branch wrote the award-winning television script dramatizing the life of Mary McLeod Bethune, which the National Broadcasting Company presented as *Light in the Southern Sky*.

The inherent drama of the civil rights struggle of the 1950s and 1960s did not escape the attention of playwrights. In *A Land Beyond the River* (1957), Loften Mitchell dramatized the civil rights activities and resultant vicissitudes of the Reverend Joseph A. Delaine, a leader in the equal rights efforts of blacks in Clarendon County, South Carolina, whose goals progressed from better school bus service to desegregation of the schools. Even James Baldwin found the events in the South to be irresistible material for drama. In *Blues for Mr. Charlie* (1963), he bitterly censured the Mississippi system of values and justice which allowed the murderers of such people as Emmett Till and Medgar Evers to go unpunished.

Two comedies produced in the 1960s were equally censurious of the Southern racial order. Ossie Davis's hilarious *Purlie Victorious* (1961), in mocking "fake Negro humility and pompous white pride," ridiculed most of the stereotypical racial images and values with which Davis, as a native of Georgia, was thoroughly familiar. Of similar comedic quality is Douglas Turner Ward's *Day of Absence* (1966) in which the author, a Louisiana native, humorously portrays the trauma and anxiety afflicting whites of a Southern town when they discover that the black population, upon whom they economically and psychologically depend, has suddenly disappeared.

The black middle class comes in for some pungent criticism in a play by Carleton W. and Barbara J. Molette, two Spelman College instructors. Their play, *Rosalee Pritchett* (1972), first presented at Spelman in 1970, ridicules the priorities to which elements of the black bourgeoisie cling in the face of civil rights demonstrations and riots in their town. While dramatic events are occurring around them, a group of women remain preoccupied with card playing and with preparing for and staging a debutante ball. They take only passing notice of the rape of one of their number by white national guardsmen.

THE FREE SOUTHERN THEATER

Conceived in 1963 by three young black civil rights activitists, two of whom were field directors of the Student Nonviolent Coordinating Committee (SNCC), the Free Southern Theater was organized in Jackson, Mississippi, in 1964 as a cultural arm of the Southern freedom movement. The organizers expressed their aims as:

> Through theater, we think to open a new area of protest. . . . One that permits the growth and self-knowledge of a Negro audience, one that supplements the present struggle for freedom.[12]

Immediately after its formation, the theater, with the assistance of drama students and instructors at Tougaloo and Jackson State Colleges, began to hold theater workshops. Later it moved its headquarters to New Orleans, where it was assisted by a Tulane drama professor and several black and white actors and actresses who came down from the North.

During the several years of its existence the Free Southern Theater brought plays by several black and white playwrights to communities in Mississippi and Louisiana, and to some audiences who had never before seen live theater. It also presented improvised performances of civil rights activities that were taking place within the communities. As the freedom movement became increasingly oriented toward black nationalism so too did the Free Southern Theater. By 1969 it had become almost exclusively black in its staff, its casting, and in the authorship of the plays it performed. Although the original organization expired, a remnant remained in existence; and the rise of other community theatre groups in the South during and since the 1960s, such as Black Image in Atlanta, Dashiki in New Orleans, Sudan and Urban Theater in Houston, and Theater of Afro-Arts and "M" Ensemble in Miami, is part of its inspirational legacy. All of these groups, except Black Image, were still in existence in the mid-1970s.

ELEVEN

Poetry and Music

POETRY TO 1950

Like other forms of literature, poetry, too, is deeply rooted in the Afro-American past. The earliest black poets in America were undoubtedly those "Black and Unknown Bards" to whom James Weldon Johnson paid tribute in his poem of that name.[1] These were the folk poets of the slavery and post-slavery eras who through song, sermon, and cant gave vent to the variety of emotions, visions, and experiences which were common not only to the black tradition in America but to universal human conditions as well.

Black literary poetry also goes well back into the slavery era, to the works of such Northern pioneers as Lucy Terry (1730-1821), Phyllis Wheatley (1753-1794), Jupiter Hammond (1720-1806), and Gustavas Vassa (1745-1801?). In the slave South only George Moses Horton attained some recognition as a literary poet. A native of North Carolina, Horton wrote numerous poems; many were commissioned for romantic purposes by students at the University of North Carolina at Chapel Hill. Usually circumspect, Horton nevertheless expressed his deep resentment of his enslavement in several poems, notably "Slavery," "The Slave's Complaint," and "On Hearing of the Intention of a Gentleman to Purchase the Poet's Freedom."[2]

Between the end of the Civil War and the beginning of the twentieth century several black poets used the South as thematic material in their poetry. Frances E. W. Harper (1825-1911), a Baltimore native, traveled throughout the South during this period as a lecturer on social reforms. Her poems first came to public notice in 1854, but her poetic output continued into the twentieth century. Among her several volumes of poetry was *Sketches of Southern*

Life, which appeared in 1872, and a larger edition of the same title published in 1896. Several of her poems such as "Slave Auction" and "Bury Me in a Free Land" excoriate slavery and its attendant evils.

Joseph Seaman Cotter and Alberry A. Whitman were two Kentuckians who by the turn of the century had surpassed most of their black contemporaries in the volume of poetry they produced. The poetry of both men covered a wide variety of subjects and themes, but in such spic poems as *Not a Man and Yet a Man* (1877), *The Rape of Florida* (1885), and *An Idyll of the South* (1901), Whitman dealt respectively with slavery, the treatment of the Seminole Indians and their black allies, and life in the antebellum South.

In an effort to represent the speech idiom of Southern blacks, several black poets tried their hand at dialect poetry during this period. Daniel Webster Davis, who for most of his life resided in Richmond, Virginia, published a volume of dialect poetry in 1897 entitled *Weh Down South.* James Edwin Campbell of Ohio, in a collection of poems probably written before 1900 but not published until 1905 as *Echoes from the Cabin,* was remarkably successful in representing the real speech patterns of plantation blacks.

Paul Laurence Dunbar was the first black poet of the post-Civil War era to win acclaim in America, however. Although he wrote over two-thirds of his poems in standard English, Dunbar's dialect poems, which constituted his effort to utilize the folk traditions and cadences of the slaves, were the most popular. Nevertheless, in giving Southern plantation life a benign and, in some cases, an even idyllic image, in portraying his black characters in a humorous vein, and in describing social relations among blacks and between blacks and whites as invariably warm and friendly, Dunbar misrepresented the reality of Southern life. Only in his nondialect poems did Dunbar reveal the deep well of bitterness that lay within him. That he realized that his dialect poems did not reflect the real conditions of his people can be seen in these lines of his poem, "We Wear the Mask":

We wear the mask that grins and lies,
It hides our cheeks and shades our eyes,—
This debt we pay to human guile;
With torn and bleeding hearts we smile
And mouth with myriad subtleties.

Why should the world be otherwise,
In counting all our tears and sighs?
Nay, let them only see us, while
   We wear the mask.

We smile, but, O great Christ, our cries
to thee from tortured souls arise.

We sing, but oh the clay is vile
Beneath our feet, and long the mile;
But let the world dream otherwise,
  We wear the mask![3]

With respect to mood, themes, and chronology, W. E. B. Du Bois and James Weldon Johnson were transitional poets, bridging the distance between the Dunbar school of poetry and the poetry of the Harlem Renaissance. Du Bois spurned dialect, but he utilized poetry as well as prose in assaying the social realism of the South. His most moving poem was "Litany at Atlanta," in which he gave vent to the emotions aroused in him by the Atlanta race riot of 1906.[4]

James Weldon Johnson was a better poet and more of a transitional figure than Du Bois. The poems in the section designated "Jingles and Croons" in *Fifty Years and Other Poems* (1917), his first volume of poetry, are dialect pieces in the tradition of Dunbar. In the same volume, however, are such poems as "Brothers," which deals with the horror and viciousness of lynching; "Black and Unknown Bards," a tribute to the poets of the oral tradition; "Go Down Death," a poem which captures the imagery and the cadence of the folk sermon; and other poems dealing with a variety of subjects, many unrelated to the black experience.

Johnson was also a poet of the Renaissance. His chief poetic creation of the period was *God's Trombones: Seven Negro Sermons in Verse* (1927). Without using dialect, Johnson expressed in these poems the imagery, the cadence, "the idioms," and the "emotions and aspirations" of the prototypical black preachers of the South as exhibited in their sermons. By this time Johnson had come to believe and asserted that dialect was too limited a vehicle for "giving expression to the varied conditions of Negro life in America, and much less capable of giving the fullest interpretation of Negro character and psychology."[5]

Of the poets who wrote during the Renaissance era, Langston Hughes eventually became the most prolific. While much of his poetry reflected his observations of Harlem and urban society, he also wrote about the South in such poems as "The South," "Mulatto," "Silhouette," "Christ in Alabama," "Ku Klux Klan," "Georgia Dusk," and "Bombings in Dixie."[6] His principal testimonial to the culture of the black South, however, was his skillful inculcation of black musical forms and themes and the thematic motifs and cadences of black sermons into his poetry.

Sterling Brown, long-time professor at Howard University, has been similarly wedded to folk material. In his volume of poetry called *Southern Road* (1932) Brown, a native of Washington, D.C., employed some of the language and many of the themes and forms of the Southern black oral tradition. Through the media of work songs, ballads, spirituals, and the blues, he revealed the innermost thoughts and emotions of the people of the region and utilized tragedy, humor, and satire to make forceful comments about conditions in the South. In "Slim in Hell," for example, Brown tells the story of a black man who, after dying and going to heaven, is sent by Saint Peter on a mission to Hell to investigate conditions there. Slim finds that Hell is very similar to Dixie. There are bawdy houses, cabarets, gambling, and hypocritical preachers; there are pitchfork wielding white devils who are throwing black devils into fiery furnaces; and the devil himself turns out to be a white Southern sheriff. In another poem, "Old Lem," Brown provides a realistic portrait of the plight of Southern blacks in the face of the overwhelmingly superior forces which the white community had arrayed against them.

As Brown's work indicates, the poetic energy unleashed during the 1920s spilled over into the 1930s. Frank Marshall Davis addressed himself specifically to social and economic conditions in the South during that decade in several poems of social protest. In "Snapshots of the Cotton South," landlords, poor whites, the Southern Tenant Farmers Union, and the Southern churches all fall prey to his biting criticism.[7]

The 1930s was also the decade in which Margaret Walker, who was eventually to gain fame as both a poet and a novelist, published her first volume of poems. In "For My People" she first described the bitter past and the current vicissitudes of both Southern and Northern blacks, and then issued a call to them to rise up, mobilize their forces, and bring about a new era in their lives. In the 1960s Walker commemorated the events and martyrs of that decade in such poems as "Street Demonstration," "Girl Held Without Bail," "For Malcolm X," "For Andy Goodman—Michael Schwerner—and James Chaney," and in "Prophets for a New Day," a poem which can be regarded as a sequel to "For My People."[8]

Anne Spencer, of Lynchburg, Virginia, began writing poetry before the Renaissance era. She wrote several poems during that period and continued to write poetry into the 1970s, when she was over ninety years old. Unlike most of her black contemporaries, however, she has eschewed racial and regional themes, preferring instead to write of private feelings, private visions, and personal relationships.[9]

POETRY SINCE 1950

In addition to Margaret Walker, many other poets have been moved by the post-World War II developments in the South. In his "Emmett Till" James A. Emanuel paid tribute to the black youth of that name who was murdered by white bigots in Mississippi in August 1955.[10] A number of poets have poured out their emotions over similar atrocities that occurred in the South during the 1960s. In "Ballad of Birmingham," for example, Dudley Randall eulogized the four young girls who were killed in 1963 when their church was bombed.[11] Several poets have similarly eulogized Martin Luther King, who was assassinated in 1968 in Memphis, Tennessee. As is well known, these events, and the developments with which they were associated, contributed to a new mood among black Americans, a mood to which poets were not immune.

A new poetry movement arose out of the black protest and black power movements of the 1960s. It was characterized by a rejection, in varying degrees, of western culture—of western poetic forms, techniques, and themes, and western social values. Instead, the new black poets, mostly twenty or thirty years old, committed themselves to writing radical and revolutionary poetry, a poetry that was directed mainly at black audiences, and that occasionally employed the speech idioms of ghetto street habitues.

In the South, the new black poets fell largely within two groupings. One group was the Blkarsouth Poets, who were an offspring of the Free Southern Theater. Through their publication, *Nkombo,* these poets attempted to carry out the new radical mandate. Few of their poems, however, dealt explicitly with the South. The other more amorphous grouping of poets consists of the college poets, mostly students in the Southern black colleges. The *Ex Umbra* poets of North Carolina Central University, who began publishing their poems in the late 1960s in their *Ex Umbra* magazine, have received the greatest recognition as a group thus far.[12] Neither grouping was exclusive, however, for undoubtedly the *Nkombo* poets welcomed contributions from their college student counterparts.

But even for the new poets, as for their older colleagues, the South conjures up mixed images and ambivalent emotions. Alabama native Julia Fields in two of her poems, "Alabama" and "Birmingham," speaks of a South of contrasts—of physical harshness and physical beauty; of cold, barren, changeless reality diffused by a sense of unreality.[13] In *Floodtime* Askia Muhammed Touré, a native of North Carolina, is concerned with the drought-stricken, flood-beseiged black tenant farmers of the South.[14] But in "Knoxville, Tennessee," Nikki Giovanni pauses in her social and revolutionary concerns to reminisce about Tennessee summers and the Southern cuisine, church picnics, gospel music, and enjoyment of family and nature that such Southern summers can afford.[15]

The ambivalence characterizing the relationship of black Southerners to their region in earlier years is partially explained by Dudley Randall, an older poet who has assiduously promoted the works of the new black poets. In "Legacy: My South," he asks:

What desperate nightmare rapts me to this land
Lit by a bloody moon, red on the hills,

Red in the valleys? Why am I compelled
to tread again where buried feet have trod,
To shed my tears where blood and tears have
flowed?

And then he answers:

Compulsion of the blood and of the moon
Transports me. I was molded from this clay.
My blood must ransom all the blood shed here,
My tears redeem the tears. Cripples and monsters
Are here. My flesh must make them whole and
hale.
I am the sacrifice.[16]

MUSIC

For several decades after slavery, the poetry and prose literature of the slaves as represented by the spirituals, jubilee songs, work songs, and field hollers continued to comprise the basic musical repertoire of black Southerners. As time passed, however, and under the pressure of the new circumstances of black life, the music of the former slaves underwent changes. New themes, new techniques, and new instruments were introduced, and in some types of music European patterns of melody and harmony became more evident. Eventually, out of the modified versions of the older music, new forms and types, such as gospel songs, ballads, blues, ragtime, and jazz evolved.

THE SPIRITUALS

The spirituals are undoubtedly the best known of the musical creations of the slaves. Arising out of the slave environment and consisting of an integration of African with European musical motifs, the spirituals contained themes that encompassed the entire range of human emotions and experiences. They expressed the contrasting moods of joy and sorrow, revolt and resignation, and earthly aspirations and heavenly longings. They revealed not only the dynamics of day-to-day earthly life but depicted the slaves' cosmological and eschatological views as well. Their purposes and characteristics varied. They were designed to inspire the individual and the community, to serve as vehicles of communication, to express reverence for God, and to evoke through the magic of poetic expression God's intercession in the slaves' daily lives. They are filled with symbolism and innuendo; but on occasion they are starkly literal in their expression of discontent with the slave status or of the joy which the contemplation or attainment of freedom brings.

After the Civil War the spirituals continued to serve many of the same purposes they had served during slavery. At the same time, they constituted one of the major agencies for keeping the memory of the slavery experience alive in the freedmen and for transmitting aspects of that experience to later generations. Black Southerners continued to sing them in their churches despite the efforts of church leaders like Bishop Henry M. Turner to discourage the practice. Many upper-middle-class and educated blacks shared Turner's view that the singing of the crude idioms of the spirituals served to perpetuate undesirable habits stemming from the slave heritage. For such blacks the Southern colleges played a more important role than the churches in making the spirituals respectable as transmitters of the memory of slavery.

The Fisk Jubilee Singers, formed by George L. White, began the tradition of formal presentation of the spirituals by trained singers. When the Fisk Singers, composed of five women and four men, all but one former slaves, added spirituals to their repertory of white Christian hymns and popular songs on their first tour to the North in 1871, they won immediate acclaim. As they continued their tours in subsequent years, not only in the North but in Europe as well, their fame increased. They received the adulation of President Ulysses S. Grant, several monarchs of Europe, and the political and social elites of both Europe and the northern United States. In the process, they raised substantial amounts of money for Fisk University.

In 1873 a singing group from Hampton Institute, inspired by the success of the Fisk Jubilee Singers, traveled to the North on a concert tour with spirituals as the mainstay of their repertory. In subsequent years, groups from other colleges followed. By the middle of the twentieth century most of the private black colleges in the South had replicated in varying degrees the Fisk and Hamptom examples. Independent singing groups and high school choirs were prompted, in turn, to include spirituals among their musical presentations. In this way these institutions played a significant role in preserving and perpetuating the musical tradition of the slavery era.

In the hands of the college choirs, however, the spirituals underwent certain stylistic transformations. In an effort to cleanse them of so-called crudities of form and language, many of the choir conductors altered or dropped the dialect and also made some changes in the melodies in order to make the songs more compatible to white ears. Despite these changes, however, the essential integrity of the form and the themes of the spirituals were maintained.

The spirituals also provided talented black composers and arrangers with a musical ethos within which to exercise their creative aptitudes. In the South these composers and arrangers were usually associated with the black colleges, and most had received extensive musical training at leading white schools of music in America and Europe. Among the better known composers, arrangers, and choir directors was Nathaniel Dett of Hampton Institute whose compositions and arrangement of spirituals included *Religious Folk-Songs of the Negro* and the *Dett Collection of Negro Spirituals.* Also at Hampton was Clarence Cameron White whose works included *Forty Negro Spirituals* and *Traditional Negro Spirituals.* At Fisk University John Wesley Work and John W. Work, III, collected a number of spirituals as well as other folksongs. Among the collections of the latter were *American Negro Songs, Ten Spirituals,* and *Jubilee.* William L. Dawson, arranger-composer-choir director at Tuskegee, was among the most celebrated of the college musicians. His *Negro Folk Symphony,* which was based upon spiritual motifs, won him widespread acclaim. Other musical directors at black colleges also explored the religious folk music of their people and sought to bring to their performances techniques and insights that came from their extensive musical training as well as from their personal backgrounds and experiences.

Despite the works of the college composers, the spirituals of the most lasting duration were those which arose out of the slavery environment and presumably were the creations of groups of slaves rather than of single individuals. A few new spirituals appeared during and after the Civil War in the same manner. During the war itself spirituals celebrating freedom or its coming, such as "O Freedom," "No More Driver's Lash for Me," "We'll Soon Be Free," and "Many a Thousand Die," were created. In later years other songs appeared such as "Death's Little Black Train Is Coming," and "Getting on Board the Gospel Train," which reflected the new experiences of the freedmen. Generally, however, later generations of black people produced few spirituals, for despite the changed circumstances of life, the old songs possessed a universality that made them functionally timeless.

GOSPEL MUSIC

Although the post-Civil War black community produced few spirituals, it did create the gospel song, a close parallel. While not popularized until the twentieth century, gospel music was known to some segments of the black community several decades earlier. Indeed the spirituals and jubilee songs of the slavery era are its antecedents. In terms of style gospel music also owes much to blues and jazz, its secular contemporaries.

Gospel music first developed in the holiness and sanctified churches of the rural South. These church services were characterized by spirited forms of worship that included an active display of emotion, rhythmic hand clapping, and rhythmic music provided on such instruments as the organ, the piano, and in many instances, percussive and horn instruments as well. This form of worship spread to cities of the South and North along with the migration of communicants of the holiness churches to these areas, and became the principal style of worship in many of the storefront Baptist churches. From these churches, and largely through the deliberate efforts of individual gospel singers, gospel music slowly infiltrated the traditional Baptist churches.

The Reverend Charles A. Tindley, a Baptist minister, and Mrs. Lucie Campbell, a choir director, were among the earliest known individual composers of gospel songs. Paradoxically Tindley, although a native of the South, did not become attached to gospel music until he moved to Philadelphia, where he sang gospel songs in his church. His "Stand by Me" and "We'll Understand It Better By and By," which he composed in 1905, are among the best known gospel songs. In the same year, Mrs. Campbell of Memphis, Tennessee, composed "Something Within Me," which along with her "He'll Understand and Say Well Done," composed thirty years later, became gospel standards. Both of these gospel music pioneers were known to Thomas A. Dorsey, and Tindley influenced him directly.

Thomas A. Dorsey, as "composer, publisher, performer, teacher, choir director and organizer," was the moving force in the popularization of gospel music. The son of a rural Georgia minister, Dorsey learned to play blues and jazz music while still a boy in his native state. In 1919, at the age of 20, he went first to Gary, Indiana, and then to Chicago, where he perfected his skills. Throughout the 1920s he alternated between playing church music, blues, and jazz. In 1932, he finally decided to devote himself to religious music. By this time he had already composed several gospel songs including "If I Don't Get There" and "Someday, Somewhere." Of the over 400 songs which he eventually composed throughout his long career, his "Precious Lord, Take My Hand" was the most famous and the most widely sung.

Unlike the spirituals, the spread of gospel music throughout the black communities of the North and South was due mainly to the efforts of individual promoters such as Dorsey and his contemporaries. During the early 1930s Dorsey himself traveled through several Southern states proselytizing his music and sent an emissary into a number of Northern states. He personally influenced several well-known gospel singers of later years such as the Ward Singers and Mahalia Jackson. The traditional Baptist churches resisted the music at first. They eventually succumbed, however, at least to the extent of having gospel songs sung by special choirs, as the blues and jazz components of the music, characterized by improvisation, a pronounced use of instruments, shifting moods, and "swinging rhythms" proved irresistible to the congregations.

THE BLUES

As a recognized musical form the blues, like the gospel music it influenced, also traces its ancestry back to the music of slavery times—to the sorrow songs and field hollers of plantation slaves and the work songs of slave stevedores and rivermen. Blues songs are also related to the work songs, prison songs, and ballads of the post-Civil War period, which celebrated the exploits of the heroic and bemoaned the misfortunes of the victimized. Ballads such as "De Grey Goose" "De Ballit of De Boll Weevil," "John Henry," and "Stackolee" all contain motifs that are found in the blues.

Long before W. C. Handy began composing blues in the early 1900s, blues music had appeared in various parts of the South. The contents of the early blues songs reveal both their Southern origins and, to a lesser degree, the times in which they were created. While most blues dealt with the capriciousness of the love relationship, they frequently included lyrics about economic and social hardships associated with Southern living and often made symbolic use of the flora, fauna, and other physical features of the Southern landscape. Thus there are blues about the boll weevil, cotton fields, floods, droughts, landlords, debt peonage, chain gangs, and a host of other subjects. Even many of the love lyrics are set within a Southern rural context as indicated by such lines as "You been a good ole wagon, daddy, but you done broke down," "Ef you don't like my peaches, don't you shake my tree," "My gal's got ways like a levee camp mule 'fore day," and "Just hitch me to your cart and drive me for your mule."

The principal moods exhibited in the blues are sorrow, disappointment, remorse, and pain. Nevertheless, there are also notes of humor, stoicism, and optimism. While the latter moods often involve "laughin jes to keep from cryin," just as frequently they represent a determination on the part of the singer to survive and maintain his dignity in the face of misfortune and tragedy. Typical of the stoicism is the line, "Been down so long that down don't bother me"; a sense of optimism is expressed in these terms: "I went to the depot, an' looked upon de boa'd. It say: dere's good times here, dey's better down de road."

William Christopher Handy, son of an Alabama Methodist minister, is chiefly credited with inspiring public recognition of the blues as a special art form of the black community. Well-trained in traditional western music, Handy was nevertheless captivated by the music of the black folk. With the publication of his "Memphis Blues" in 1912 and his "St. Louis Blues" in 1914, he was well on the way toward earning the title "Father of the Blues."

During Handy's era the blues achieved much popularity among certain segments of the black population. Blues singers such as "Ma" Rainey and Bessie Smith carried the blues message throughout the South and North. That message struck the most responsive chords in the lives of the black lower classes, particularly the churchless masses, whose experiences the blues lyrics mirrored. Educated, middle-class, and church-oriented blacks, including Handy's parents, tended to reject the blues, feeling that such music represented the life-styles and lower instincts of the disreputable elements in black society. In recent years, however, the so-called respectable classes in the black community have progressively altered their attitude toward the blues as this type of music has won increasing recognition as a special art form and as all elements within the black population have sought greater identification with each other.

JAZZ

Early jazz represented to some extent an attempt to express instrumentally the voice tones, the moods, and the lyrics of the blues singer. Some authorities have therefore contended that it shares with the blues such slavery era antecedents as field hollers. As instrumental music, however, the immediate precursor of jazz was ragtime music. Ragtime developed shortly after the Civil War as black musicians turned from the fiddle and the banjo to the organ and the piano to beat out syncopated rhythms for listening and dancing. Soon ragtime music became the mainstay in cheap entertainment and sporting places in such cities as St. Louis, Memphis, and New Orleans. By 1900 the music had spread throughout the nation, and was played by both black and white musicians, it was used prominently in the minstrel shows, and in the early decades of the twentieth century, prominent black musicians like Bob Cole, J. Rosamond Johnson, and Will Marion Cook wrote ragtime songs for their musical shows. In the South, however, the pioneer ragtime composer was Scott Joplin of Texarkana, Texas, who made his reputation between 1885 and 1900 as "King of Ragtime" by playing the music in St. Louis and other Missouri towns and by finally publishing in 1899 a ragtime composition called *Original Rags.*

Although the place of origin of jazz is clouded in doubt, there is general agreement that New Orleans was its principal Southern source. In New Orleans jazz evolved from the fusing in the 1890s of the French-influenced music of marching brass bands and dance orchestras and ensembles played by Afro-Creoles such as John Robicheaux and Henry Nickerson with the ragtime and blues style music of such black musicians as Charles "Buddy" Bolden and William Geary "Bunk" Johnson. Most prominent in its early stages of maturation , however, were Ferdinand "Jelly Roll" Morton, Joseph "King" Oliver, and Louis "Satchmo" Armstrong.

Morton began playing music as a child, and in 1900, at the age of fifteen, took his first job as a piano player in a New Orleans bawdy house. Two years later he wrote *New Orleans Blues,* his first blues composition. Soon thereafter he turned to writing jazz compositions. His *Jelly Roll Blues,* published in 1915, is regarded, according to Eileen Southern, as "the first published jazz arrangement in history."[17]

"King" Oliver and Morton were the same age and their musical development occurred about the same time. Oliver's musical career in New Orleans, first as a cornetist in a children's brass band, then in a succession of adult bands and ensembles, and finally as a band leader, lasted from 1899 to 1918. In the latter year he went to Chicago where in 1920 he formed the Creole Jazz Band. Two years later he was joined by Louis Armstrong, his New Orleans protégé.

Armstrong was fifteen years younger than Morton and Oliver, but like them, he began playing music at an early age. His first trumpet was a gift from Oliver, who also gave him lessons on the instrument. Armstrong worked in a succession of bands in New Orleans, including the famous Kid Ory's band, and perfected his skills on a variety of instruments. When he joined Oliver in Chicago, he was already an accomplished cornet and trumpet player. By the time of his death in 1971, he had become the best known personality in the history of jazz music.

Characterized by innovation, improvisation, instrumental vocalization, and the antiphonal call and response pattern, the "classic" jazz of Morton, Oliver, and Armstrong shared with both the spirituals and the blues certain common elements. Jazz also contributed to the emergence of gospel music. The organic connection among these various forms of music was merely indicative of their common roots in the culture of the black South. Over the years each form has evolved into configurations somewhat different from the original, a transformation that has enabled each to reflect the changing circumstances and changing needs of the black community. The utilization of spirituals as an arm of the freedom movement of the 1960s is striking evidence of the continued serviceability of one of the oldest forms of Afro-American music.

PART FIVE

THE FREEDOM MOVEMENT

TWELVE

The Black Community and the Freedom Movement

THE ROOTS

The victory won by Linda Carol Brown and her parents against the school board of Topeka, Kansas, in 1954, in the form of the Supreme Court's decision outlawing segregated schools, reflected the influence of both international and domestic developments on American race relations. The participation of American blacks in World War II and the Korean War; struggles interpreted in the United States as crusades for freedom; America's involvement in the cold war, in which the United States posed as the moral and political champion of the "free world"; and the decline of Western hegemony over Asia and Africa and the subsequent efforts of the United States to draw newly independent nations on those continents into its sphere of influence all served to point up more than ever before the blatant contradiction between America's professed world role and mission and its racist domestic values and practices.

On the domestic level, the court's decision was the capstone of a series of efforts by the national government, beginning early in World War II, to respond to demands by blacks and their white supporters that the nation's practices with regard to its citizens of darker hue be brought more into conformity with the nation's creed. In June 1941, President Roosevelt, yielding to A. Philip Randolph's threatened march on Washington, issued an executive order prohibiting discrimination in federal employment and in defense industries. Between 1945 and 1952, President Truman took a number of steps to advance the cause of civil rights. These included the creation of committees to study and make recommendations concerning problems of racial discrimination, the issuance of orders desegregating the armed forces and prohibiting discrimination in federal employment, and pushing, albeit unsuccessfully, for the passage of civil rights legislation by Congress.

During the same period the Supreme Court and lower federal courts, acting on cases brought before them by the NAACP, handed down decisions negating many of the state laws and practices blocking the access of black people to the ballot, housing, and institutions of higher education. The 1954 school desegregation decision thus culminated over a decade of vigorous assaults against the citadel of apartheid. It also represented a victory for the NAACP and its method of seeking justice through established processes.

More significantly, the 1954 decision deprived the system of apartheid of its principal legal and ideological foundation, the fiction of separate but equal. It therefore inspired black Southerners to broaden their visions and to raise their level of expectations. The cries of Southern politicians that the decision was unconstitutional, that the Court had overstepped its bounds, and that the South would massively resist the decision only served to enhance its psychologically liberating impact.

As a member of the Montgomery, Alabama, NAACP, Mrs. Rosa Parks had undoubtedly been stirred by the Supreme Court's decision. Its implications may have flashed through her mind as she refused to surrender her seat on a city bus to a white man on the evening of December 1, 1955. She also may have been conscious of a ruling by the Interstate Commerce Commission less than a week earlier outlawing segregation in interstate travel. In any case, these two events were certainly in the minds of the leaders of Montgomery's black community as they rallied to Mrs. Parks' support and launched the Montgomery bus boycott movement.

Yet the roots of Mrs. Parks' defiance lay deeper than court decisions, administrative rulings, and executive orders. Her act and the actions of her supporters sprouted from the profound frustration, resentment, and weariness of black Southerners with the lunacy of the Southern racial caste system. They were not alone in their weariness. Even the black men aboard the same bus as Mrs. Parks who obeyed the driver's command to surrender their seats were resentful, as indicated by the hesitancy with which they responded. Moreover, within the preceding eighteen months, at least four other black citizens of Montgomery—Claudette Colvin, Mrs. Amelia Browder, a Mrs. Smith, and the Reverend Vernon Johns (Martin Luther King's predecessor as pastor of the Dexter Avenue Baptist Church)—had indicated their displeasure with the system when they, too, on separate occasions refused to obey an order to give up their seats to white passengers. Perhaps no one in Montgomery was more impatient with the Jim Crow order than Ed D. Nixon, head of the local chapter of the NAACP, a pullman porter, and a follower of A. Philip Randolph in the March on Washington days of World War II.

It was he who called together the black leaders of Montgomery to protest Mrs. Parks' arrest and the general practice of bus segregation in the city.

Martin Luther King, Jr., a young Baptist minister selected by the leaders to direct the bus boycott movement, articulated the prevailing mood at a mass meeting four days after the Parks' incident. In the cadence of those of his profession, King pointed out that:

> There comes a time when people get tired. We are here this evening to say to those who have mistreated us for so long that we are tired— tired of being segregated and humiliated, tired of being kicked about by the brutal feet of oppression. We have no alternative but to protest.[1]

The feelings which King described were longstanding. While continuity between the streetcar boycotts around the turn of the century and similar forms of protest in the 1950s may be open to question, several unheralded incidents during the 1940s were clearly harbingers of the developments of the next two decades. In 1944, for example, fifty students at Savannah State College in Georgia boarded a streetcar near their campus, deliberately occupied all the seats from front to rear, and ignored the driver's demands that they surrender the front seats to whites. Two of the students were arrested and convicted on the charge of attempting to riot. However, the Georgia Court of Appeals overturned the convictions on the grounds of insufficient evidence.[2]

Four years later, fifty Hillside High School students in Durham, North Carolina, perhaps inspired by the challenge in 1947 to their state's Jim Crow transportation statutes by an interracial group of CORE freedom riders and the subsequent judicial proceedings against the group, staged a sit-in at an ice cream company in protest against the company's racial practices.[3] During the same decade similar direct-action forms of protest occurred in other communities in North Carolina and in other states.

The black mood of the 1950s, therefore, was not an aberrant phenomenon. What was new in 1955 was that events on the national and international levels relating to race relations served as a catalyst, intensifying the existing mood of frustration while simultaneously giving blacks a greater sense of their own ability to alter their circumstances.

The black community in Montgomery chose King as a man who embodied in his person the best of the Southern black tradition. Son of a prominent Baptist minister in Atlanta, a scion of the black upper-middle class, an alumnus of Morehouse College and Crozer Theological Seminary, and holder of a doctoral degree from Boston University, King was at home in both the religious tradition of the black folk and in the literature and thought of leading Western theologians and secular philosophers.

As a teenager, King was scornful of the tendency toward an accommodationist religion among blacks. But at Morehouse College he learned from Benjamin Mays, the president, and George Kelsey, a professor of philosophy, that a ministerial career could involve more than simply providing an emotional outlet for blacks on Sunday mornings; that such a career could be intellectually stimulating and socially useful as well. At Crozer and Boston University, through the study of the views of such men as Walter Rausenbusch, Rheinhold Neibuhr, Paul Tillich, Thoreau, and A. J. Muste, he came to appreciate more fully the potentialities for social activism within the Christian religion. During these years he also became familiar with the work and views of Mahatma Gandhi. Thus he brought to the protest movement a philosophical and strategic fusion of elements from the black tradition, Western religious and secular philosophy, and the Gandhian concept of satyagraha.[4]

The Montgomery bus boycott movement of 1955-1956, which culminated in a federal court decision requiring desegregation of the buses, established much of the pattern that was to be followed subsequently by black protesters in other Southern cities. Bus boycotts followed in Tallahassee, Atlanta, and Birmingham. The boycott technique was soon used to secure other objectives, such as removal of barriers to voting and to employment and the desegregation of other public facilities. From June 1957 to 1960, for example, blacks in Tuskegee, Alabama, boycotted white merchants in protest against a legislative gerrymander that effectively disfranchised Tuskegee black voters by placing them outside of the town's limits through the redrawing of its political boundaries. Victory came with a Supreme Court decision nullifying the gerrymander.

ELEMENTS OF POWER

The boycotts served to reveal the latent power within the black community. There was, for example, the power of ideology. Resting their case upon the best elements of the American liberal creed—the efficacy of a free and democratic society and respect for the rights and dignity of the individual—and adhering to nonviolent tactics and advocating a philosophy of nonviolence, black protesters virtually preempted the moral position on the racial question. Consequently they attracted support from people throughout the nation and the world.

Another source of power was the black purse. Although lacking individuals and business enterprises commanding huge amounts of wealth, the black community in Montgomery and in many other Southern cities provided as consumers the margin of profit for many white businesses. The bus company in Montgomery derived 70 percent of its revenue from black patronage, and it suffered visibly from the boycott. White merchants were also hurt, losing in excess of $1 million during the first two months of the boycott.

Black institutions and organizations that were relatively free of white control comprised a third element of power. Black churches and their ministers were preeminent in this category. The selection of King to lead the Montgomery bus boycott movement represented the traditional tendency of black Southerners to look to their ministers for leadership and to their churches for succor. During this period, unlike many instances in the past, the churches and their ministers rose to the challenge and mobilized and forged the resources of the black religious tradition into instruments of social activism and social uplift. The Southern Christian Leadership Conference (SCLC), formed by King and his ministerial lieutenants in 1957, represented the black church militant; and until the beginning of the student sit-ins in 1960, black Baptist ministers, mostly graduates of black colleges, provided the leadership of the protest movement. Even in small towns and rural communities in the Deep South, despite the presence of preachers who were "fearful of rocking the boat," there were always clergymen who rallied around the civil rights workers, gave them moral and material support, and continued to carry on the movement after the activists who were not indigenous to their communities had departed.[5]

Enhancing the role of the institutional church in the protest movement was the spirit of black religion. The warmth of congregational participation, the Christian hymns, spirituals, and gospel songs, and the rhetorical cadence and vivid imagery in black preaching helped to inspire and sustain the freedom movement as they had sustained the morale of black people in the South for several centuries. Also a part of the black religious tradition was the experience of suffering combined with a tendency toward nonviolence—a fusion of an otherworldly orientation with the pragmatic necessity, as well as the Biblical injunction, to turn the other cheek in order to survive. Thus the burning and bombing of numerous churches by Southern whites constituted a testimony to the stellar role the physical and spiritual church played in the freedom movement.

Along with the church were other institutions and organizations that supported the civil rights movement. Active in Montgomery, for example, were a black labor leader, the Women's Political Council (formed in 1951), and the NAACP. Similar organizations, including fraternal orders and various social clubs, existed in other communities, and many made at least a financial contribution to the movement. The national office of the NAACP, after some hesitancy, endorsed and joined in the direct action tactics of SCLC, The Congress of Racial Equality (CORE), and The Student Nonviolent Coordinating Committee (SNCC) while continuing its traditional methods of litigation and lobbying. In several Southern communities, local NAACP chapters initiated and carried the brunt of the direct action crusade. Frequently the leadership and membership of the state and local chapters of the organization overlapped with those of the more militant protest groups. Indeed, the varying approaches of the different organizations complemented each other. Many of the issues raised to public consciousness through boy-cotts, marches, sit-ins and other demonstrations were finally resolved in the courts and Congress as a result of the litigation and lobbying activities of the NAACP.

In launching the sit-in movement in Greensboro, North Carolina, on February 1, 1960, Ezell Blair, Franklin McLain, Joseph McNeil, and David Richmond revealed that black colleges were another source of underutilized power in the South. Their school, the Agricultural and Technical College for Negroes, had been established by the state, like other such institutions in the South, to train black students for and accommodate them to the Southern biracial order. In the hands of seemingly conservative administrators, ivory-tower faculty members, and students motivated primarily by individualistic and materialistic concerns, such institutions, like many of their private counterparts dependent on white philanthropy, appeared to be carrying out the stipulated mission.

Nevertheless, as Henry A. Bullock has suggested,[6] the very existence of institutions of higher learning for blacks constituted a potential Trojan horse within the camp of apartheid. Behind a facade of quietude there were always some administrators, some faculty members, and some students who managed to convey in both open and subtle ways, their strong and deep contempt for the Jim Crow system. Moreover, no black faculty member was likely to subscribe to the notion of inherent black inferiority, the rationale of the Jim Crow system. Nor were students, whose intellectual and social horizons were broadened through their studies, likely to forever tolerate a system that was offensive to their dignity and stifling to their personal ambitions. Their distaste for the system was evident long before the 1950s as indicated by the existence of chapters of the NAACP and other protest organizations on many college campuses.

On the college campuses students were also temporarily isolated from the restraining influences of protective parents, and they were thus more susceptible to the views of their peers. Consequently, a few bold and enthusiastic students with a popular cause were able to mobilize themselves and others into the kinds of protest activities common during the early 1960s.

So out of the black colleges came the "new abolitionists." In April 1960, on the campus of Shaw University in Raleigh, North Carolina, and under the aegis of the Southern Christian Leadership Conference, these new abolitionists formed the Student Nonviolent Coordinating Committee (SNCC). Impatient, enthusiastic and bold, they moved more vigorously against the bastions of segregation than SCLC, their mentor organization. Suffering beatings from policemen and white onlookers, they deliberately courted jail as a point of honor. But within a year, often singing to keep up morale, they effected the desegregation of places of public accommodation in 140 cities in the South.

Music was a mainstay of the protest movement. Old spirituals were revived and modified to serve as freedom songs. Many new songs were created, some spontaneously and some through the conscious efforts of individuals and such formal groups as the SNC Freedom Singers. Included in the musical repertoire of the freedom movement were such old, new, and modified songs as "I'll Never Turn Back," "This Little Light of Mine," "We Shall Not be Moved," "Ain't Gonna Let Nobody Turn Me 'Round," "Freedom Is a Constant Struggle," "O Freedom," "If You Miss Me from the Back of the Bus," "Cause I Want My Freedom Now," and "I Can See a New Day." In their relaxed moments and in informal settings, the freedom workers also used and modified songs from the rhythm and blues tradition.

The most famous song, of course, was "We Shall Overcome," which became known around the world, even as far away as South India. Less well known, except among certain segments of the black community, was its provenance. The melody and some of the words of the song were based upon the spiritual, "I'll Be All Right," which was sung as early as the late nineteenth century in black Baptist and Methodist churches in both the lower and upper South. During the 1940s, as Bernice Reagon records, a version of the spiritual, sung variously as "I Will Overcome" or "We Shall Overcome," was used to sustain the morale of striking black tobacco workers in Winston-Salem, North Carolina, and Charleston, South Carolina. In 1947, Zilphia Horton, in a workshop of the Highlander Folk Center in Tennessee, picked up and developed a version of the song from white participants in the Charleston strike. At Highlander the song came to the attention of folk singer Pete Seeger who subsequently made some minor changes in the lyrics and popularized it among various groups in New York. Six years later Guy Carawan heard the song in California.

As musical director of the Highlander Folk Center during the late 1950s and early 1960s, Carawan taught the song to college students and adults who participated in a series of the Center's workshops. When invited by Nashville College students in 1960 to participate in the sit-ins, Carawan included the song in his musical repertoire. Because of its roots in the black ethos, it, more than any other song, immediately caught on, and at the organizational meeting of SNCC in Raleigh, North Carolina in April 1961, which Carawan attended as a song leader, it was almost instinctively adopted as the theme song of the freedom movement.[7] Thus, having traversed from its origins and use in black folk religion through minor transformations as an inspirational vehicle in the secular struggles of black and white workers, "We Shall Overcome" was reclaimed by the black community in the 1960s to serve the greatest social movement which black Americans had yet undertaken. However, like so much of the black musical tradition, the song was too powerful a statement of universal human conditions and aspirations to remain a black monopoly, and it was soon employed in the struggles of divers people in various parts of the world.

The freedom movement posed new challenges for the Southern black press.

Its traditional role as the chief source of the news and views of the black community was jeopardized by the widespread coverage given to the civil rights crusade and related developments among blacks by the national (and international) media. Moreover, in necessarily articulating positions on the various controversial issues involved in the movement, the black press faced the prospects of either alienating its Southern white advertisers or its black subscribers or both.

Most black newspapers met these challenges rather well. In countering and correcting the distorted and biased reports and editorials in the Southern white media the black press continued to serve the important function of providing black perspectives on the events of the era. To the extent that they supported the goals or the tactics of the civil rights movement, Southern black newspapers also refuted the contention that the movement was primarily the work of outside agitators. The Birmingham *World,* for example, consistently endorsed the objectives and the nonviolent tactics of the various civil rights groups from the beginning of the Montgomery bus boycott in 1955 to the articulation of the black power slogan by Stokely Carmichael and Willie Ricks in 1966. During the Montgomery bus boycott it exulted: "Attend one of the informational meetings and you come away with a feeling that all the leaders know what they want, how to go after it, and the price they will have to pay to get it. All of the leaders speak the same language." During the Meredith march in Mississippi in 1966, the *World* used the occasion to denounce the apathy of black Alabamians and to encourage them "to make the little walk to the voter-registration places."[8]

Similarly, the moderate Norfolk *Journal and Guide,* long accustomed to supporting the gradual and legalistic tactics of the NAACP, moved from cautious endorsement of the student sit-ins of 1960 to full commitment to responsibly conducted, nonviolent, direct-action forms of protest in 1963. On the eve of the 1963 March on Washington the *Guide* declared that "nonviolent protest [was] totally consistent with the American doctrine of peaceable assembly for the redress of grievances." It went on to assert that "There can be no denying that since the first sit-in demonstration about three years ago, the Negro has won more battles for his constitutional rights and human rights than had been won in all the other ninety-seven years since the Emancipation Proclamation."[9]

Neither the *Journal and Guide* nor the Birmingham *World,* however, could make the abrupt shift from their commitment to integration to the separatist implications of the black power slogan. The *Guide,* concerned that the slogan represented a denial of the sacrifices of whites to the black cause and a retreat to black nationalism, called it "an unfortunate and unnecessary" catchword. The *World* denounced the concept as an expression of black racism. Even the militant Memphis *Tri-State Defender* was initially taken aback by "the sudden transformation of the Student Nonviolent Coordinating Committee into a black nationalist movement." After James Meredith was shot, however, the *Defender* was prepared to accept the black power concept so long as it did not exclude whites from continued participation in the movement for black rights.[10]

The protest movement inspired the founding of several new black newspapers, particularly in areas where the older newspapers seemed reluctant to support or actually opposed the direct-action campaign. In response to the expressed need of local SNCC leaders for "an aggressive community organ" to counteract the influence of the conservative Atlanta *Daily World,* a group of young black businessmen founded in 1960 the Atlanta *Inquirer.* Six years later, Edward T. Clayton, an experienced journalist who had served as a public relations consultant for SCLC, established another liberal black newspaper, the *Voice,* in the same city. Thus the black press continued to provide a forum for the expression of the many perspectives within the black community.

RADICAL TACTICS, CONSERVATIVE GOALS

The protest movement of the late 1950s and the early 1960s represented a departure from the legalistic and gradual tactics that had been employed since 1910 by the NAACP and other organizations. In the boycotts of transportation facilities it harkened back to the early years of the twentieth century. And although blacks in the North had employed the sit-in before the Civil War, and blacks in the South had employed it sporadically during the 1940s, its massive use as a protest tactic was a phenomenon of the early 1960s. More significantly, as Professor Joseph Himes has observed, the movement, drawing on resources within the black community, transformed race relations in the South into power relations.[11] Naked physical confrontation of the Jim Crow establishment became the order of the day. Blacks demanded rather than pleaded, bargained rather than cajoled. Thus within the Southern environment the movement was radical, even revolutionary, in its tactics.

Until 1965, however, the freedom movement was basically conservative in its goals. Rather than challenge what they considered to be basic American values and institutions the protesters merely sought to purify them of centuries-old encrustations of racism. They did not seek to destroy the law but to fulfill it. At the March on Washington activities in 1963 Martin Luther King eloquently articulated their objectives. His dream, he said, was that "one day this nation will rise up and live out the true meaning of its creed: 'We hold these truths to be self-evident; that all men are created equal.'" He also dreamed that "one day on the red hills of Georgia the sons of former slaves and the sons of former slaveholders will be able to sit down together at the table of brotherhood. . . ."[12]

The movement's early conservatism largely arose out of its middle-class origins. Enjoying an economic and educational status superior to that of a large proportion of the Southern white population, many middle-class blacks were anxious to remove the arbitrary barriers to the enjoyment of middle-class perquisites. Sensitive to the currents sweeping across the world in behalf of human freedom, they acutely resented the offenses to their dignity that Jim Crow signs and practices represented. And as believers in the efficacy of the Protestant ethic as the means of rising in the social order, they chafed at artificial obstacles to their advancement. Moreover, because they were less restricted than their lower-class brothers and sisters by the drudgery of eking out a day-to-day existence, they could find the time and the spirit to engage in protest activities.

Most of the ministers who led the freedom movement were graduates of black colleges and held bachelor of divinity degrees. Although their congregations were usually composed of people of mixed socioeconomic statuses, even the lower-status people among them, "the respectables," shared middle-class values. So too did most of the college students who came from low-income or working-class families. Their presence in college was testimony to their own middle-class aspirations and those of their parents. Thus the dream which King spoke of, though classless in its inspiration and implications, embraced the aspirations and ambitions of the socially mobile within the black population.

Many whites also shared the dream. White college students from Northern and some Southern campuses, nuns, priests, and Protestant ministers from Northern religious communities and institutions, a few labor leaders, some professors, and even a few housewives from aseptic suburban enclaves, ventured into the South in the early 1960s. Singing "We Shall Overcome" and other freedom songs, they joined with blacks in the effort to remove the more obvious barriers to an integrated society. The Congress of Racial Equality (CORE), an interracial Northern-based organization with a predominantly white membership and which had engaged in demonstrations and direct action campaigns against segregated facilities and discrimination in employment in Northern and border state areas in the 1940s, found a new lease on life. Under the leadership of James Farmer, it conducted the celebrated freedom rides in the Deep South in 1961 and joined with other protesters in the full range of protest activities. For the next four years blacks and their white allies worked together in relative harmony in pursuit of the dream.

DISILLUSIONMENT

But there were killers of the dream, literally and figuratively. They included night riders who murdered civil rights workers; Southern policemen who jailed protesters and physically abused them with clubs, water hoses, cattle prods, and police dogs; leading white citizens who presided over the racism embedded in the structural and institutional patterns of life they maintained, and who attempted to mask their atavistic tendencies toward barbarism under the respectable facade of white citizens councils; certain elements within the black community who because of fear, apathy, or economic self-interest consciously or unconsciously refused to challenge the racial status quo; and black and white protesters themselves who were unable to transcend or conquer the effects of centuries of racist assumptions and practices in their relations with each other.

Those who feared to participate in the civil rights struggles had good reasons for their fears. By the 1960s Mississippi blacks still remembered that on May 7, 1955, the Reverend George W. Lee of Belzoni had been killed by a shotgun blast fired from a speeding car simply because he urged blacks to pay their poll taxes and register to vote. Several months later, while FBI agents and local police officials were supposedly still investigating the Lee murder, Gus Courts, Lee's friend and NAACP associate, was wounded by gunshots fired into his store. By the end of the year several prominent black residents of Belzoni and surrounding communities who had been associated with Lee and Courts in civil rights work, including the well-to-do Dr. T. M. Howard of all-black Mound Bayou, were forced by threats or attacks on their lives to leave the state. In the meantime, Lamar Smith was assassinated in broad daylight in front of a Mississippi courthouse for his voter-registration activities.

Herbert Lee, a black farmer in Amite County, Mississippi, was one of the first to die in the freedom struggle of the 1960s, shot in the head on September 25, 1961, by E. L. Hurst, a member of the Mississippi legislature. Lee had been working with SNCC and Robert Moses in a voter-registration project. On the night of June 11, 1963, Medgar Evers, who had been inspired by the work and death of the Reverend George Lee in the mid-1950s, was shot in the back from ambush in the driveway of his Jackson, Mississippi, home. His assailant, Byron De La Beckwith, like the killer of Herbert Lee, was acquitted. Other killings followed. Three months later four little black girls—Addie Mae Collins, Denise McNair, Carole Robertson, and Cynthia Wesley—were killed when their church in Birmingham, Alabama, was bombed. Exactly a year after Ever's death James Chaney and his white companions, Michael Schwerner and Andrew Goodman, were murdered in Philadelphia, Mississippi, in a particularly gruesome crime, by a group of white men including Neshoba County Deputy Sheriff Cecil Price. In February 1965, an Alabama state trooper killed young Jimmie Lee Jackson, a participant in civil rights demonstrations and the youngest deacon in his church in Marion, Alabama. Two weeks later (March 11), the Reverend James J. Reeb, a white Unitarian minister, died of injuries received in a civil rights demonstration in Selma, Alabama. In the same month in the same state, Mrs. Viola Liuzzo, a white housewife from Detroit, was felled by bullets fired by white terrorists.

Five months later a white Episcopal seminary student, Jonathan M. Daniels, was also fatally shot in Alabama.[13] In January 1966 Vernon Dahmer, an NAACP leader in Hattiesburg, Mississippi, died from burns received in the firebombing of his house by white assailants. Finally, on April 4, 1968, the apostle of nonviolence, Martin Luther King, Jr., was assassinated in Memphis, Tennessee. In the meantime other less well-known, even obscure, individuals were victims of violence.

The murder of civil rights workers was only the extreme form of the violence with which Southern whites responded to the freedom movement. White mobs confronted black children in Little Rock, Arkansas; New Orleans, Louisiana; Mansfield, Texas; Clay, Kentucky; Birmingham, Alabama; and other Southern communities in the late 1950s and the early 1960s to prevent integration of the schools; terrorists bombed the homes of civil rights leaders and engaged in an orgy of church bombings and burnings in Alabama, Georgia, and Mississippi; mobs attacked freedom riders, sit-inners, marchers, and other demonstrators in scores of Southern cities; policemen unleashed vicious attacks on demonstrators in Albany, Georgia; Birmingham and Selma, Alabama; and other Southern cities; and Southern governors and politicians fed the spirit of violence by preaching massive resistance and interfering in the execution of federal court decisions. All these actions exacted a heavy price from the protesters for disrupting the Southern way of life.

The morale of the activists was also sorely tried by reactionary and conservative elements and tendencies within the black community. Although large numbers of black Southerners participated in demonstrations and mass meetings, the majority cheered the freedom movement from the sidelines, unable or unwilling to engage in a protracted struggle that would imperil their lives or their livelihoods. Moreover, in a number of communities, the freedom movement was as much a challenge to traditional patterns of leadership and institutional behavior as it was to the racial status quo in the South. In the hands of fearful, apathetic, or confused, ambivalent leaders, community institutions often failed to fulfill their potential as elements of black community power. Too often even those older, traditional, middle-class leaders who initially supported direct-action forms of protests tended to retreat in the face of counterattacks from local white terrorists or the local white establishment.

The preeminence of clergymen among protest leaders could not entirely mask the inertia of many of their ministerial colleagues. Some were inactive out of fear. Others refused to participate in the movement in order to avoid jeopardizing their positions of presumed influence with local whites or to protect their status in conservative black national organizations. During the early 1960s, for example, when activist ministers unsuccessfully challenged the Reverend Joseph H. Jackson of Chicago, a vocal opponent of direct-action forms of protest and a major critic of Martin Luther King, for the leadership of the National Baptist Convention, a number of Southern ministers who held office under Jackson gave him their support.

Nor was the Southern black press unanimous in its support of the freedom movement. The Atlanta *Daily World,* which had been a leader in efforts to abolish the white primary and increase black voter-registration in the 1940s and 1950s, was decidedly cool to the Atlanta student movement in its editorials and refused to give it full coverage in its news columns. Percy Greene, founder, publisher, and editor of the Jackson, Mississippi *Advocate,* and a civil rights leader in the 1940s and early 1950s, was even more conservative. A persistent critic of Martin Luther King, CORE, and SNCC, Greene contended that their activities were responsible for a worsening of race relations. He opposed passage of the Public Accommodations Act of 1964 on the ground that it dealt with "rights of voluntary association which, even if misused, need to be preserved as a part of the system of law by which the nation is governed." As whites from the North prepared to come to Mississippi to participate in the freedom summer of 1964, the *Advocate* warned them to stay away and "leave the solution of the Negro problem in the south to the various states and their people." As one observer noted, "Editorially, the *Advocate* did almost as much as the [rabidly racist white] *Daily News* to defend the *status quo* of second-class citizenship for Mississippi blacks and deflate the growing black awareness."[14] It is significant to note that both the Atlanta *Daily World* and the Jackson *Advocate* depended heavily on advertisements from local white businesses for their financial survival. As one member of the Scott family, which owned and edited the *Daily World,* frankly confessed, "they had to depend on the department stores for their blood—advertising."[15]

No traditional leadership group faced a greater dilemma than the presidents of state-supported black colleges in the South. Long accustomed to walking a "racial tightrope" many, nevertheless, found the circumstances created by the student protests to be beyond their ability to manipulate. Their immediate problem was how to retain the support of their black constituency—students, faculty members, alumni, and the general community—while at the same time satisfying the demands of white state officials that the student demonstrations be stopped and the students disciplined.

College presidents responded variously. In February 1962, Dr. Joseph F. Drake, president of Alabama A. and M. College was forced by Governor John Patterson to take a leave of absence until retirement because he had failed to prevent his students from participating in protest activities.[16] On the other hand, H. Council Trenholm, president of Alabama State College at Montgomery, continued to try to walk the "racial tightrope," despite the advice of some of his associates that he "take a stand and openly defy the governor." During the Montgomery bus boycott Trenholm gave covert encouragement to those faculty members of his college who helped to organize and who participated in the movement. During the student sit-ins in 1960, however, he yielded to Governor Patterson's demand that participating faculty members (including Lawrence C. Reddick, chairman of the history department) and students be dismissed. He tried to lessen the effects of his action, however, by secretly helping to secure positions for some of the dismissed faculty members and students in other institutions.[17]

Similarly, the highly respected Felton Clark, president of Southern University in Louisiana, went through several years of crisis in his efforts to comply with the directives of white state officials regarding student demonstrations. Clark expelled the first student demonstrators on March 31, 1960. Two years later he was still contending with the problem of protesting students.[18] During the course of these developments his prestige within the black community rapidly eroded. When he died in 1970, he, like Trenholm who died in 1963, was a broken man, a victim in a sense of a transitional period in the Southern social order.

By 1963, many of the younger black activists, assessing the price exacted against the victories won and the changes effected, began to question the tactics and goals of their movement. They increasingly realized that their successes in desegregating public facilities merely constituted the peeling off of the outer layer of racism, the elimination of its most blatant symbols. Underneath lay a hard core of attitudes and institutional arrangements which kept blacks subordinate and which entrapped many within a morass of poverty. As the protest movement moved North and as lower-class blacks assumed influential roles in the movement, it became crystal clear that racism was not simply a mere aberration in an otherwise just society, but that it was structural and institutional, inextricably embedded within the very fabric of American life.

At the same time, the activists became more sensitive to the insidious effects of racism within their own midst. The assumptions of superiority, often unconscious, on the part of white protesters, their skill in organization and expression, their influence with Deep South blacks who were accustomed to look to whites for guidance, and their resultant tendency to assume leadership of the protest movement clashed with centuries of black resentment and feelings of inferiority, and made black-white interpersonal relations difficult. Many of the black activists began to feel that their white allies were exercising too strong an influence in shaping the course and tactics of the movement, and many whites, in response, began to feel unappreciated. Estrangement between the two groups developed.[19]

THE ROAD TO BLACK POWER—
POLITICAL AND ECONOMIC

From the welter of these influences, young activists, particularly those in SNCC, were openly expressing as early as 1963 growing doubt of the efficacy of nonviolence as a philosophy and tactic and integration as an immediate goal. When the Freedom Democratic Party of Mississippi, a product of several months of hard and dangerous work by black and white civil rights workers, was betrayed (in minds of the workers) by white liberals who refused to seat its full delegation at the Democratic National Convention in Atlantic City in 1964, the doubts were reinforced. Malcolm X and other vocal leaders of the black masses in the North who preached a philosophy of separatism or black nationalism fed their disillusionment. Malcolm's assassination in 1965 transformed him into a martyr. Many regarded the Watts riot in August of the same year and those of the preceding year in other cities as a rebellion of ghetto residents against colonial rule, and the notion that race relations in America were fundamentally power relations gained increasing currency. The new feeling was summed up by Stokely Carmichael and Willie Ricks on June 6, 1966, when, in the course of marching on Mississippi along with the leaders and followers of SCLC and CORE and the NAACP to protest the shooting of James Meredith, they enunciated the slogan "Black Power," a term which Carmichael had heard Congressman Adam Clayton Powell, Jr., use in a commencement address at Howard University a week earlier.

To black Southerners black power meant many things. To some like Robert Williams of Monroe, North Carolina, and the Deacons Defense for in Louisiana, it included arming oneself in self-defense to resist white aggression. Williams had been driven to this position in the late 1950s. In the summer of 1957, just two weeks before the well-publicized routing of the Ku Klux Klan in Monroe, North Caroina, by the Lumbee Indians, a group of blacks led by Williams, who were guarding the home of Dr. B. F. Perry, president of the Monroe chapter of the NAACP, exchanged gunfire with a motorcade of Klansmen. During the next two years blacks in Monroe suffered a series of indignities at the hands of whites. In October 1958 two little black boys, aged seven and nine, were arrested on the charge of rape and subsequently sentenced to fourteen years in the state reformatory simply because a little white female playmate kissed one of the boys on the cheek. A year later a white man who kicked a black hotel maid down a flight of stairs escaped indictment, and another white man tried on the charge of attempted rape of an eight-month pregnant black woman was acquitted despite the testimony in support of the charge by the black woman's white neighbor. These events led Williams to finally declare that "the Negro in the South cannot expect justice in the courts. He must meet violence with violence, lynching with lynching."[20] Although suspended by the national office of the NAACP for his statement and eventually forced to flee the country to escape arrest on a trumped-up charge of kidnapping a white couple,* Wil-

---

*After losing a six-year court fight in Michigan against extradition, Williams returned to North Carolina in December 1975 to face the charges against him. On January 16, 1976, the kidnapping charges against him were dropped due to the alleged inability of the surviving complainant to testify against him because of ill health. See the *Washington Post,* January 17, 1976.

liams was merely echoing a principle which the NAACP itself had long endorsed—the right of self-defense against assault. It was this principle which inspired the formation in Jonesboro, Louisiana, in 1964 of the Deacons for Defense and Justice, an organization whose avowed purpose was to protect black and white civil rights workers and the black community in general from attack.[21]

To some blacks, including Williams, black power meant the desire to overthrow the capitalistic and racist order through armed struggle. Most native Southern activists, however, tended to interpret the concept in more conservative and pragmatic terms. As Joyce Ladner pointed out, local activists in Mississippi who embraced the concept visualized the acquisition of power through relatively traditional means. Merging the philosophies and programs advanced previously by Booker T. Washington and W. E. B. Du Bois, they advocated racial solidarity and self-help economic projects to upbuild the black community coupled with use of the electoral process—"registering to vote, running for political office, and building political parties"—to establish political control over their own communities and to capture power in the larger arenas of county, state, and national politics.[22] Thus, despite their setback at Atlantic City, the members of the Mississippi Freedom Democratic party continued to pursue black political power as did civil rights workers in other states of the Deep South. They were aided immeasurably by the passage of the Voting Rights Act of 1965, which their own efforts helped to inspire. While less dramatic than sit-ins and freedom rides, such political activities in the rural areas of the Deep South could nevertheless be considered as direct action. One white civil rights worker recalled in 1973 that: "For those of us who worked on voter registration as part of CORE's task force in Louisiana, there was virtually no distinction between the two; both involved enormous risks for the local people and for ourselves, and this feeling was shared by all other civil rights groups in the South."[23]

The risks which local participants in the Deep South freedom movement incurred as well as the pervasive poverty which marked life in so many black communities led a number of civil rights workers to conclude by the mid-1960s that before any real change in the lives of blacks would be forthcoming the pattern of economic relationships between oppressed blacks and dominant whites had to be altered. Consequently, in 1965 the Mississippi Freedom Democratic party formed the Mississippi Freedom Labor Union, the first union of black sharecroppers since the 1930s. In May 1965 sharecroppers in Leland, Mississippi, struck in support of their demand for an eight-hour day and a minimum wage of $1.25 per hour. Like their predecessors in the 1930s, the sharecroppers met determined resistance from the planters who, with the aid of sheriff's deputies, evicted the strikers from the plantations. Failing to get support from the leaders of the labor movement in the United States despite the pleas of the Mississippi Freedom Democratic party, the sharecroppers, facing starvation, were unable to continue the strike.

To provide victims of white retaliation like the Leland sharecroppers with alternate means of making a living as well as to bring a measure of economic independence to black rural and urban workers, SNCC, CORE, and SCLC field workers joined with local residents in Alabama, Mississippi, Louisiana, and Tennessee to form a number of production, marketing, and consumer cooperatives. Several of these cooperative enterprises eventually received moral, technical, and financial assistance from private foundations, religious denominations, established cooperative organizations, and agencies of the federal government. Established in 1965 by SNCC field workers, the Poor People's Corporation of Mississippi, a federation of cooperatives engaged primarily in the production and marketing of handicrafts, was one of the more venturesome of these enterprises. In 1968 it provided employment for about 200 former black sharecroppers. Civil rights workers and black farmers were equally daring and ambitious in forming the Southwest Alabama Cooperative Association in Selma, Alabama, in 1966. A marketing and supply cooperative, it claimed a membership in 1970 of 1,800 black farm families in ten contiguous Alabama counties. Among other important cooperatives formed during the mid- or late-1960s by or with the assistance of civil rights workers were the Grand Mare Vegetable Producers Cooperative covering several parishes in Louisiana; the West Batesville Farmers Cooperative in Panola County, Mississippi; the Freedom Quilting Bee in Wilcox County, Alabama; and the Mid-South Oil Consumers Cooperative in Whiteville, Tennessee. As somewhat conservative expressions of black power, these enterprises were reminiscent of similar endeavors during the Populist and New Deal eras.

DISSOLUTION OF THE FREEDOM COALITION

While black Southerners sought to acquire a measure of power through a variety of means, the emergence of the black power slogan nevertheless signaled the end of the coalition of civil rights groups which had waged the freedom struggle under the banner of integration. The NAACP continued to seek the goal of integration through nonviolent means as did the SCLC. Nevertheless, the SCLC increasingly addressed itself to economic issues. When King was assassinated in 1968 in Memphis while assisting black sanitation workers and their supporters within the black community and among labor groups in an eventually successful strike for union recognition against a recalcitrant city administration, he was in the midst of planning a Poor People's March on Washington. The march was later carried out under Ralph Abernathy, King's successor as the leader of SCLC.

Abernathy, with the assistance of Coretta Scott King, also joined SCLC with the cause of black hospital workers in Charleston, South Carolina. Led by twenty-seven-year-old Mary Ann Moultrie, president of Local 1199B of the Drug and Hospital Employees Union, the workers waged a 100-day strike in 1969 in support of their demands for union recognition, machinery for the resolution of grievances, and a raise in pay to the level of the federal minimum wage. In face of the determined opposition of a contemptuous hospital administration that was supported by the Charleston white power structure and the state governor, who dispatched state troopers and some 5,000 national guardsmen to the city during the course of the strike, the SCLC and black Charlestonians participated in a series of demonstrations, boycotts, and picketing activities during which over 900 arrests occurred. Inspired by the great support that the hospital workers received from the Charleston black community, the leaders of other black organizations and officials of several national labor unions also supported the strikers. In June 1969, after an initial doublecross of the striking workers by the Nixon administration in pursuit of its Southern strategy, a federal mediator was successful in negotiating a settlement that gave the strikers the substance of their demands.

CORE, under the leadership of Floyd McKissick, embraced a version of the black power concept, stressing particularly the need for economic power. During the late 1960s the organization withdrew essentially to the North, leaving as its Southern legacy McKissick's then embryonic plans for the establishment of Soul City, a projected predominantly black community of about 50,000 people in Warren County, North Carolina. By 1967 SNCC had practically ceased its direct-action activities in the South and Stokely Carmichael devoted most of his time to articulating the meaning of black power as theory and program to various audiences around the country. By 1970, the organization was moribund, its new theories and legacy being perpetuated by essentially local groups of activists and loose regional and national confederations of student groups centered in the colleges.

THIRTEEN

Symbols of Change

Although unable to bring to full fruition Martin Luther King's dream, or to alter the pattern of economic relationships that kept the black masses oppressed and impoverished, the freedom movement by 1970 had significantly altered the face of the South. Either through direct-action tactics or through federal legislation and court decisions which such tactics inspired, the blatant symbols of Jim Crow were discarded, swiftly in some communities, fitfully in many, and as a last resort in a few. The Civil Rights Act of 1964, which prohibited discrimination in places of public accommodations, and the Voting Rights Act of 1965, which established effective machinery for assuring blacks access to the ballot, reflected a national consensus in favor of basic constitutional rights.

SCHOOL DESEGREGATION

Within this national mood considerable progress was made toward the desegregation of public schools. By 1970 only 14.1 percent of the black children in the South were going to all-black schools, while 39.1 percent were attending schools with majority white enrollments. Two years later the proportion of black students in all-black schools had declined to 7 percent while the ratio of those in white majority schools had risen to 46 percent. By contrast, by 1972, 11 percent of the black students in the North and West attended all-black schools while only 28 percent were enrolled in white majority schools.[1] The eleven states of the ex-Confederacy therefore led the rest of the nation by a wide margin in the degree of school desegregation.

But the price was high, including the loss to the black community of about 31,000 teaching and administrative jobs by 1970 and the disappearance of many all-black schools (often bearing the name of a prominent black historical personality) as a cohesive force within the black community. Black principals, who had served as positive role models for many black students, became an endangered species. As a result of the desegregation process their numbers declined between 1967 and 1971 from 620 to forty in North Carolina, 170 to sixteen in Virginia, 134 to fourteen in Arkansas, and from 210 to fifty-seven in Alabama.[2]

The desegregation process also masked a good deal of resegregation. Through such practices as ability grouping, the establishment of special classes for or the expulsion of students considered disruptive, and the continuation of such white Southern traditions as the playing of "Dixie" and the displaying of the Confederate flag at school functions, many ostensibly desegregated schools remained functionally segregated. In addition, by 1975 the retreat of whites to the suburbs or to private schools left the public school systems in such major cities as Atlanta, Birmingham, Jackson, Memphis, New Orleans, Norfolk, Richmond, and Savannah predominantly black. Nevertheless, because of the extent of desegregation in the smaller cities, towns, and rural areas, the school systems of the Old Confederacy still remained the most desegregated in the nation.

CHANGING PERSPECTIVES

The protest movement also profoundly altered the white South's perception of its black citizens. The myth of the docile and contented Negro was shattered. No longer could reasonably sane Southerners find ready refuge in the term "outside agitators" as the automatic explanation for periodic flare-ups of black resistance to white oppression. Accompanying the destruction of the myth was a decline in the old paternalistic, but corrupt, pattern of friendly interpersonal relations between whites and blacks which rested upon the assumption of white superiority and black subordination.

Symbols of changing white perceptions abound. When the South Carolina Conference of Branches of the NAACP honored its founder, eighty-year-old Levi Byrd, in ceremonies in Byrd's home town of Cheraw on December 19, 1971, the mayor and city council of Cheraw proclaimed the day "Levi Byrd Day." Not only did the mayor attend the ceremonies, at which Roy Wilkins, executive director of the NAACP, was the principal speaker, but an aide of John West, the governor of South Carolina, also attended. Twelve months later a state representative from Chesterfield County introduced Byrd to the South Carolina House of Representatives as "a man who has done more for the Negro in South Carolina than any other man."[3]

These developments were in marked contrast to those of an earlier decade when the political establishment attempted to run the NAACP out of the state.

Of course not all white Southerners reacted positively to their new perceptions of black Southerners. Many saw in the new black assertiveness confirmation of their long-standing fear that if the Jim Crow system were dismantled, blacks would attempt to become dominant in Southern society. Others, while fearing the black thrust for self-definition and political power, nevertheless were pleased to note that the rhetoric of black nationalism seemed to confirm their oft-repeated assertion that blacks did not really wish to associate with whites. Finally, most white Southerners, while yielding to the elimination of the more blatant symbols of the Jim Crow order, retreated to more subtle defenses against racial equality, similar to those that had long prevailed in the North.

The black revolution also produced profound changes within the black community. On the subjective level it gave blacks a sense of pride, power, and achievement. Feelings of inferiority derived from years of physical and psychological victimization were gradually discarded, and although future generations might continue to suffer material deprivation they would nevertheless be spared the pain and humiliation of frequent, even daily confrontations with symbols and signs in public places expressly or implicitly proclaiming that blacks were inferior and therefore were not wanted. Expectations therefore rose, visions enlarged, and fear declined. A traditionally apathetic, sixty-five year-old Alabama farm woman undoubtedly spoke for many of her peers when she confided to a white Northern visitor that "We do see the light a little mo'. . . . Heap o' things we was feared to say and we don't be feared anymo."[4] This more optimistic perception of themselves and their region is responsible, in part, for a decline in the number of blacks leaving the South in recent years and for a rise in the number from other sections of the country who are migrating to the region. Between 1970 and 1974 some 241,000 blacks left the South, but 276,000 from the North and West made the South their home. As a result since 1970 the proportion of blacks in the United States living in the South has stabilized at 53 percent.[5]

INSTITUTIONAL AND LEADERSHIP CHANGES

On the more mundane level, the freedom movement revitalized black institutions. As the church came to realize its potential power as a force for change, church attendance increased and clergymen enjoyed heightened prestige within their communities. Colleges and universities also felt the impact. More flexible relationships developed among administrators, faculty members, and students. Curricular and extracurricular offerings were revised to reflect both the new career opportunities made available as a result of the movement and the pride in a black identity that the protests spawned.

As previously noted, several college presidents who resisted the trends, who sought to prohibit protest activities by their students, or who disciplined those students who did engage in protest, lost their prestige and credibility within the black community and rarely regained them.

Profoundly modified, at least temporarily, by the movement was the leadership structure of the black community. The activists challenged established leaders to become more assertive, and many who failed to meet the challenge were rendered quiescent or replaced. In several cities and towns relations between conservative leaders and protest leaders were marked by continuous conflict and tension. The two types of leaders often agreed on ultimate goals but differed on tactics and strategy. Such discord occasionally paralyzed effective protest action. More often, however, the effects were salutary. Traditional leaders were often able to capitalize on the reluctance of the white establishment to deal directly with activist leaders and thus lend legitimacy to the latter's tactics and demands. The white elites preference for bargaining with the "responsible" black leaders therefore enabled the latter to win concessions from the white community that the activists had wanted all along. In some instances, the two types of black leaders planned together their strategy in order to produce the desired result.

The overall effect was the stepping-up of the traditional leaders' timetable for change and the enlarging of the black leadership establishment through the addition of younger, more assertive men and women. By the late 1960s, for example, the leaders of the black community in Durham, North Carolina, consisted not only of the old Mutual elite, but younger and more assertive members of the same class as well as Howard Fuller, a black nationalist, who founded Malcolm X University in that city. In Mississippi the ranks of the old activists such as Aaron Henry, a pharmacist, were enlarged by people like Mrs. Fannie Lou Hamer, an evicted sharecropper.

Nevertheless, the black leadership elite remained essentially middle class. In a study of 153 black Mississipians who ran for elective office between 1965 and 1970, Lester Salamon found that 53 percent of the thirty-eight candiates who won held such traditional middle-class, white-collar occupations as teacher, minister, and businessman while an additional 19 percent were farm owners. The presence of some artisans, clerical workers, and nonfarm laborers among both the successful and unsuccessful candidates did indicate, however, the emergence of some new elements into the black leadership class. Of more significance, however, was the freedom movement background of many of the successful candidates and their continued commitment to the goal of moderate-to-radical social change.[6]

A SECOND RECONSTRUCTION?

Rising to prominence as leaders in the South in the late 1960s was a growing number of black politicians, the products of the increasing exercise of the franchise by black citizens as barriers to voting were removed. Political power had always been a goal of the older protest organizations. As the newer organizations observed a corollary between the number of registered black voters in a community and the degree of success of their demonstration tactics and boycotts, they too devoted much of their effort to the removal of franchise restrictions and to voter-registration drives.

The results were phenomenal. In 1940, in eleven Southern states only about 250,000 black people were registered voters, comprising only 5 percent of the adult black population in those states. A decade later nearly a million and a half blacks throughout the South were on the voting rolls. By 1968, indicative of the impact of the protest movement of the 1960s and the Voting Rights Act of 1965, the number had increased to 3,107,000, which comprised 60 percent of the black voting-age population in the region. Five years later an additional 454,000 blacks had registered to vote.[7]

As the number of black voters increased, more blacks ran for elective office. In the process the fact and aura of white monopoly of the political process, which many black Southerners had come to regard as natural, and even legitimate, began to break down. Even when black candidates lost, their running for office had a salutary psychological effect on the black community.

Increasingly, however, black candidates ran and won. In 1969 fourteen blacks sat in the Georgia legislature while sixteen others were distributed among the legislatures of other Southern states, including Louisiana and Mississippi. On the local level about 400 blacks, including Charles Evers as mayor of Fayette, Mississippi, and Lucius Amerson as sheriff of Macon County, Alabama held elective office. By early 1971 the number of black state legislators in the South had increased to forty, and political control of four Southern counties was in black hands. In the eleven states of the old Confederacy, 721 blacks held elective office on all levels. Three years later the number had climbed to 1,314. Barbara Jordan of Texas and Andrew Young of Georgia represented their districts in the U.S. Congress. Sixty blacks sat in state legislatures; forty-six served as mayors; 798 were county commissioners and city councilmen and councilwomen; and eleven were sheriffs or marshalls. Symbolic of the new state of affairs was the election in 1974 of Chris McNair, father of one of the young girls slain in the bombing of a black church in Birmingham in 1964, as chairman of the twenty-one-member Jefferson County delegation to the Alabama House of Representatives. By May 1975 the number of black elected officials in the ex-Confederate states had risen to 1,388, and Representative Harold Ford of Tennessee had joined Jordan and Young in Congress.[8]

Through political organizations such as the Mississippi Freedom Democratic party, the National Democratic party of Alabama, and other independent offshoots of the two major parties, and through more aggressive penetration of the major parties themselves, black Southerners sought to expand and consolidate their gains. In September 1975 voters in Montgomery, Alabama, elected four blacks to the nine-member city council. In November, voters in Jackson, Mississippi, elected three blacks to the state legislature, bringing the number of blacks in that body to four and the total number of black elected officials in that state to 225. And in December the election of four blacks to the city council of Charleston, South Carolina, placed blacks on an equal footing with whites in that body. In neither community, however, were blacks satisfied with the progress that had been made. A Montgomery councilman, who was also the chairman of the Alabama Democratic Conference, a black organization, vowed to continue the struggle for greater black representation in both the municipal and state governments, while such black political leaders in Mississippi as Aaron Henry, Charles Evers, and the newly elected state legislators spoke of forming a coalition with the white Democrats of the state in a way that would assure that black interests would be protected and promoted.[9]

These political leaders desired to consolidate and expand their advances because they realized that although there were more black officeholders in the South in 1975 than at any time since Reconstruction, black Southerners were still far from the threshold of a political millennium. Despite their gains, they still comprised only a small proportion of all Southern officeholders and served mostly towns and rural areas with small populations. By the summer of 1975, sixty-two of the eighty-two black mayors in sixteen Southern and border states and the District of Columbia headed communities of fewer than 5,000 people, forty-two administered political areas of less than 1,000 residents, and only twelve headed cities of more than 25,000 people. Similarly, nearly two-thirds of those in local legislative bodies throughout the region served communities of less than 5,000 residents while in the great majority of the cities having populations in excess of 25,000 where blacks were members of city councils, the black community was not proportionally represented.[10] Thus in the Southern region as a whole, blacks were still grossly underrepresented in the political process by members of their own race, a situation offset, in part, however, by the increasing responsiveness of white officials to an enlarged black electorate.

Upon assuming office black officials have discovered that they must contend with a miscellany of problems, some requiring no more than normal service to their constituents, others posing fundamental challenges to the values and institutional arrangements of the existing social order. A sizable proportion of the black population in the South has made substantial economic progress in recent years. The ratio of Southern black families earning $10,000 or more rose from 14 percent in 1965 to 31 percent in 1974, and the median income of two-parent black families whose heads were under thirty-five years of age increased from 55 percent of that of similar white families in 1959 to 87 percent in 1973.[11] For families such as these the role of black politicians is to help assure that the gains won will not be lost and that future prospects remain bright.

On the other hand the median income of all black families by 1974 was only 56 percent of that of white families, a mere increase of 10 percent over that of 1959. One-half of the black families received less than $6,730 and about one-third were in the low-income category.[12] Since most black local officials serve small towns and rural communities, a disproportionate number of the latter constitute their constituents. In a study of thirty-nine communities headed by black mayors in seven Deep South states and North Carolina, the Joint Center for Political Studies found that the per capita income in thirty-four of these communities in 1970 ranged from $833 to $2,208, while the per capita income range of the five most prosperous towns was from $2,411 to $3,311. It is therefore not surprising that the chief complaints of the mayors of these communities concerned substandard housing, inadequate sewage facilities, insufficient or nonexistent social services and recreational facilities, and high rates of unemployment and underemployment.[13]

The ability of local officials to ameliorate these conditions is limited by a grossly inadequate tax base, lack of cooperation and sometimes resistance from the local white economic elite, an insufficient number of public employees to assist in securing federal funds and in planning and administering programs, and the restrictions which their full-time occupations as craftsmen, industrial workers, ministers, physicians, businessmen, lawyers, and farmers place on the amount of time they can devote to the duties and opportunities inherent in their offices.[14]

Despite the handicaps, many black officials are attacking problems of their constituents with vigor, and with some degree of success. Some, like those in Fayette and Greene County, Mississippi, and Roosevelt City and Tuskegee, Alabama, have been able to obtain federal and private foundation grants for economic and social welfare programs and projects for their communities. Even the presence of blacks in local and state legislative bodies where they may comprise a small minority of the membership has often had a salutary effect. At the least, white members of these organs of government have felt constrained to moderate their consideration of measures that are clearly designed to affect blacks adversely. At the most, in response to the initiative of black members, such bodies have occasionally legislated deliberately in favor of black interests. The four black members of the Virginia legislature, for example, played a major role in that state's enactment in 1973 of the first open-housing law in the South.[15]

TRAVAIL AND TRIUMPH

If, as novelist Ernest Gaines has his centenarian heroine, Miss Jane Pittman assert, "People and time bring forth leaders," then the reemergence of black politicians as leaders and their activities in behalf of the black community may be seen as promising indices of black progress. In a larger sense, however, these developments symbolize the continuation of a historical process whose significance cannot be exclusively or even primarily evaluated in terms of the material advances of the black community.

If, as Samuel Dubois Cook suggests, the history of the South is viewed as tragedy, defined as the pursuit of evil "for the sake of an alleged good," and personified in the commitment of white Southerners to "the systematic, persistent and institutionalized negation of the Negro's meaning and values on the grounds of ethical *desirability and necessity,*"[16] then the historical experience of the black South almost naturally assumes the character of the transcendence of tragedy. As indicated by the vision and the spirit of determination expressed in such songs as "No Man Can Hinder Me," a favorite hymn of the freedmen of the Sea Islands of South Carolina in the 1860s, and "We Shall Overcome," the theme song of the freedom movement generation of the 1960s, since the Civil War black Southerners have rejected on both conscious and subconscious levels the white South's normative consensus. In continuing to develop a community life and culture which, despite its flaws and contradictions, enabled them "to squeeze from life outlets of individuality and particles of meaning and satisfaction," and (as J. Saunders Redding observed in 1940 in traveling through the South under a mandate to observe black life in the region) in holding on to such "intangibles in the scale of human values" as "integrity of spirit, love of freedom, courage, patience, hope,"[17] black Southerners transformed the travail of living under the imperatives of the white South's tragedy into a triumph of the human spirit.

NOTES

CHAPTER 1

1. Quoted in James M. McPherson, *The Negro's Civil War: How American Negroes Felt and Acted During the War for the Union* (New York: Pantheon Books, 1965), p. 291.

2. Herbert Aptheker, ed., *A Documentary History of the Negro People in the United States* (New York: Citadel Press, 1955), p. 535.

3. John Richard Dennett, *The South As It Is 1865-1866,* ed. with an Introduction by Henry M. Christman (New York: Viking Press, 1965), p. 14.

4. George P. Rawick, ed., *The American Slave: A Composite Autobiography,* vol. 7: *Oklahoma and Mississippi Narratives* (Mississippi Narratives) (Westport, Conn.: Greenwood Press, 1972), p. 41. Hereafter material from the volumes of the WPA slave narrative collection edited by Rawick will be cited as Rawick, followed by the name of the state, the volume number of the Rawick edition, the part number, if any, and the page—for example, Rawick, *Texas Narratives,* IV (2), 25.

5. Ibid., p. 118.

6. Quoted in Martin Abbott, "Voices of Freedom: The Response of Southern Freedmen to Liberty," *Phylon* 34 (December 1973): 399.

7. Ibid.; Aptheker, *History of the Negro People,* p. 537.

8. Abbott, "Voices of Freedom," p. 402.

9. Dennett, *The South As It Is,* pp. 53, 73-82, 110-111, 125, 222, 270.

10. Ibid., p. 194.

11. Ibid., p. 361.

12. John H. Franklin, *Reconstruction: After the Civil War* (Chicago: University of Chicago Press, 1963), pp. 51-52.

13. Quoted in Joel Williamson, *After Slavery: The Negro in South Carolina During Reconstruction* (Chapel Hill: University of North Carolina Press, 1965), p. 75.

14. Thomas Holt, "The Emergence of Negro Political Leadership in South Carolina During Reconstruction" (Ph.D. dissertation, Yale University, 1973), p. 49.

15. Dennett, *The South As It Is,* pp. 151-152.

16. Quoted in Williamson, *After Slavery,* p. 337.

17. Joseph M. St. Hilaire, "The Negro Delegates in the Arkansas Constitutional Convention of 1868: A Group Profile," *Arkansas Historical Quarterly* 33 (Spring 1974): 42; Richard L. Hume, "The Black and Tan Constitutional Conventions of 1867-1869 in Ten Former Confederate States: A Study of Their Membership" (Ph.D. dissertation, University of Washington, 1969), pp. 668-669; Holt, "Negro Political Leadership in South Carolina," p. 119.

18. Hume, "Black and Tan Constitutional Conventions," p. 668; Holt, "Negro Political Leadership in South Carolina," p. 56; Edward Magdol, "Local Black Leaders in the South, 1867-75: An Essay Toward the Reconstruction of Reconstruction History," *Societas—A Review of Social History* 4 (Spring 1974): 81-110.

19. William McKee Evans, *Ballots and Fence Rails: Reconstruction on the Lower Cape Fear* (Chapel Hill: University of North Carolina Press, 1967), p. 165; Thomas B. Alexander, *Political Reconstruction in Tennessee* (Nashville: Vanderbilt University Press, 1950), p. 155. See also Carl N. Degler, *The Other South: Southern Dissenters in the Nineteenth Century* (New York: Harper & Row, 1974), p. 234.

20. Scholars differ in their estimates of the number of blacks in the constitutional conventions of the various states. For South Carolina, Hume puts the number at seventy-two while Holt, "after exhaustive checking and cross checking of numerous primary sources," lists seventy black members. Franklin, in the above table, lists the number as seventy-six. Hume, "Black and Tan Constitutional Conventions," p. 673; Holt, "Negro Political Leadership in South Carolina," p. 48. Franklin's figures are somewhat outdated.

21. Aptheker, *History of the Negro People,* pp. 567, 578.

22. Holt, "Negro Political Leadership in South Carolina," pp. 90-92.

23. Ibid., pp. 183-185.

24. Richard N. Current, ed., *Reconstruction (1865-1877)* (Englewood Cliffs, N.J.: Prentice-Hall, 1965), p. 74.

CHAPTER 2

1. Allen W. Trelease, *White Terror: The Ku Klux Klan Conspiracy and Southern Reconstruction* (New York: Harper & Row, 1971), pp. 130, 192.

2. William McKee Evans, *Ballots and Fence Rails: Reconstruction on the Lower Cape Fear* (Chapel Hill: University of North Carolina Press, 1967), pp. 98-101; Trelease, *White Terror,* p. 95.

3. Trelease, *White Terror,* p. 31.

4. *New York Times,* January 10, 1868, cited in Joel Williamson, *After Slavery: The Negro in South Carolina During Reconstruction* (Chapel Hill: University of North Carolina Press), p. 265.

5. U.S. Congress, *Testimony Taken by the Joint Select Committee to Inquire into the Condition of Affairs in the Late Insurrectionary States, Alabama,* House Report No. 22; Senate Report No. 41; 42d Cong., 2d sess., 1871-1872, 13 vols. Washington,

D.C.: Government Printing Office, 1872), X, 1666-1667. Cited hereafter as *KKK Reports* followed by name of state (except for volume I which is the Joint Committee's report), the number of the volume, and the page number.

6. Ibid., VIII, 375; Williams, *After Slavery,* p. 265.

7. *KKK Reports, South Carolina,* III, 1582; Trelease, *White Terror,* pp. 365-366.

8. Trelease, *White Terror,* pp. 291-293.

9. *KKK Reports, South Carolina,* III, 15.

10. *KKK Reports,* I, 563.

11. Trelease, *White Terror,* pp. 337, 364.

12. Ibid., p. 194; *KKK Reports, Mississippi,* XI, 482-484.

13. *KKK Reports, South Carolina,* III, 327.

14. J. Morgan Kousser, *The Shaping of Southern Politics: Suffrage Restriction and the Establishment of the One-Party South, 1880-1910* (New Haven: Yale University Press, 1974), pp. 14-15.

15. Carl N. Degler, *The Other South: Southern Dissenters in the Nineteenth Century* (New York: Harper & Row, 1974), p. 280.

16. James T. Moore, "Black Militancy in Readjuster Virginia, 1789-1883," *Journal of Southern History* 41 (May 1975): 167-186.

17. For a contemporary black acknowledgement of the contributions of the Readjusters to the black community, see Herbert Aptheker, ed., *A Documentary History of the Negro People in the United States* (New York: Citadel Press, 1955), pp. 731-734.

18. For a fuller discussion of the Colored Farmers' Alliance, see pp. 90-91.

19. Aptheker, *History of the Negro People,* pp. 807-809. For a further suggestion that the priorities of black Populists in the South, like those in Kansas, may have been different from those of white Populists, see Jack Abramowitz, "The Negro in the Populist Movement," *Journal of Negro History* 38 (July 1953): 257-289; Robert Saunders, "Southern Populists and the Negro 1893-1895," *Journal of Negro History* 54 (July 1969): 240-261; and William H. Chafe, "The Negro and Populism: A Kansas Case Study," *Journal of Southern History* 34 (August 1968): 402-419.

20. Quoted in Jack Abramowitz, "John B. Rayner—A Grass Roots Leader," *Journal of Negro History* 36 (April 1951): 165. See also Abramowitz, "The Negro in the Populist Movement," p. 270.

21. Kousser, *Southern Politics,* pp. 246-261.

22. Lawrence C. Goodwyn, "Populist Dreams and Negro Rights: East Texas as a Case Study," *American Historical Review* 76 (December 1971): 1444-1447.

23. Kousser, *Southern Politics,* pp. 51-56.

24. Saunders, "Southern Populists and the Negro," pp. 248, 259.

25. Quoted in National Association for the Advancement of Colored People, *Thirty Years of Lynching in the United States* (New York: National Association for the Advancement of Colored People, 1919), p. 13.

26. Walter White, "The Work of a Mob," *Crisis* 16 (September 1918): 222.

27. Quoted in Francis W. Simpkins, "Ben Tillman's View of the Negro," *Journal of Southern History* 3 (May 1937): 164.

28. Southern Commission on the Study of Lynching, *Lynchings and What They Mean* (Atlanta: Southern Commission on the Study of Lynching, 1931), p. 19.

29. Quoted in Rayford W. Logan, *The Negro in American Life and Thought,*

1877-1901 (New York: Dial Press, 1954), p. 91. See also Simkins, "Ben Tillman's View of the Negro," p. 167; and the *Congressional Record,* 56th Cong. 1st sess., February 26, 1900, p. 2245; March 23, 1900, p. 3233; 59th Cong. 2d sess., January 21, 1907, p. 1440.

CHAPTER 3

1. Louis Harlan, ed., *The Booker T. Washington Papers,* 4 vols. (Urbana: University of Illinois Press, 1972-1975), II, 108-109.

2. Quoted in Paul Lewinson, *Race, Class and Party: A History of Negro Suffrage and White Politics in the South* (New York: Oxford University Press, 1932), pp. 84-85.

3. Quoted in Ann Field Alexander, "Black Protest in the New South: John Mitchell, Jr., 1863-1929, and the Richmond *Planet,*" (Ph.D. dissertation, Duke University, 1973), p. 269.

4. Quoted in George B. Tindall, *South Carolina Negroes, 1877-1900* (Baton Rouge: Louisiana State University Press, 1966), p. 154.

5. For representative statements by the bishop, see August Meier, *Negro Thought in America, 1880-1915: Racial Ideologies in the Age of Booker T. Washington* (Ann Arbor: University of Michigan Press, 1963), p. 66; and Edwin Redkey, *Black Exodus: Black Nationalist and Back-to-Africa Movements, 1890-1910* (New Haven: Yale University Press, 1969), pp. 32-40.

6. Herbert Aptheker, ed., *A Documentary History of the Negro People in the United States* (New York: Citadel Press, 1955), pp. 715-721.

7. Ibid., pp. 720-721.

8. Hollie I. West, "Boley, Oklahoma: Once A Town of Hope, Now A Fading Dream," *Washington Post,* February 9, 1975.

9. Alfreda M. Duster, ed., *Crusade for Justice: The Autobiography of Ida B. Wells* (Chicago: University of Chicago Press, 1970), pp. 53-58.

10. Meier, *Negro Thought in America,* pp. 110-114; August Meier, "Toward A Reinterpretation of Booker T. Washington," *Journal of Southern History* 23 (May 1957): 220-227; Louis R. Harlan, *Booker T. Washington, The Making of a Black Leader, 1856-1901* (New York: Oxford University Press, 1972), pp. 288, 296-298, 302-303.

11. For Du Bois's own account of his conflict with the NAACP see, W. E. B. Du Bois, *The Autobiography of W. E. B. Du Bois* (New York: International Publishers, 1969), pp. 295-299.

12. Benjamin E. Mays, *Born to Rebel: An Autobiography of Benjamin E. Mays* (New York: Scribner's Sons, 1971), pp. 214-215.

13. Ibid., pp. 215-218.

14. Ibid., p. 220.

15. Milton Meltzer, ed., *In Their Own Words: A History of the American Negro, 1865-1916* (New York: Thomas Y. Crowell Co., 1965), p. 92.

16. Quoted in Tindall, *South Carolina Negroes,* p. 247.

17. Quoted in August Meier and Elliot Rudwick, *From Plantation to Ghetto: An Interpretive History of Negro American Negroes* (New York: Hill and Wang, 1966), p. 251.

18. Quoted in I. B. Newby, *Black Carolinians: A History of Blacks in South Carolina from 1895 to 1968* (Columbia: University of South Carolina Press, 1973) pp. 54-55.

19. Herbert Aptheker, ed., *The Correspondence of W. E. B. Du Bois: Selections, 1877-1934* (Amherst: University of Massachusetts Press, 1973), I, 233-234.

20. Norfolk *Journal and Guide,* August 2, 1919; see also Robert T. Kerlin, *The Voice of the Negro* (New York: E. P. Dutton, 1920; reprint ed., New York: Arno Press and the *New York Times,* 1968), p. 18.

21. Savannah *Tribune,* March 29, 1945, quoted in Paul D. Bolster, "Civil Rights Movements in Twentieth-Century Georgia," (Ph.D. dissertation, University of Georgia, 1972), p. 108.

CHAPTER 4

1. Rawick, *Texas Narratives,* VI (3), 192.

2. U.S. Bureau of the Census, *Census of Agriculture, 1964,* Vol. II: Ch. 8, *Color, Race, and Tenure of Farm Operators* (Washington, D.C.: Government Printing Office, 1968), p. 765; U.S. Bureau of Census, *Census of Agriculture,* 1969, Vol. II, Ch. 3., *Farm Management, Farm Operators* (Washington, D.C.: Government Printing Office, 1973), p. 102.

3. Hortense Powdermaker, *After Freedom: A Cultural Study in the Deep South* (New York: Viking Press, 1939), p. 104.

4. Ibid., pp. 91, 94-95, 108-110.

5. Theodore Rosengarten, ed., *All God's Dangers: The Life of Nate Shaw* (New York: Alfred A. Knopf, 1974), pp. 494-496. (The name Warren Jencks is a pseudonym); Charles S. Johnson, *Growing Up in the Black Belt* (New York: Shocken Books, 1967), p. 7.

6. William H. Holtzclaw, *The Black Man's Burden* (New York: Neale Publishing Co.; reprint ed., New York: Negro Universities Press, 1970), p. 18.

7. Powdermaker, *After Freedom,* p. 106.

8. Holtzclaw, *Black Man's Burden,* pp. 32-38.

9. Arthur F. Raper and Ira De A Reid, *Sharecroppers All* (Chapel Hill: University of North Carolina Press, 1941), pp. 63-64.

10. U.S. Bureau of Census, *Color, Race and Tenure of Farm Operators, 1964,* p. 765; U.S. Bureau of Census, *Farm Management, Farm Operators, 1969,* p. 102.

11. C. Vann Woodward, *Origins of the New South, 1877-1913* (Baton Rouge: Louisiana State University Press, 1971), p. 207.

12. Hosea Hudson, *Black Worker in the Deep South* (New York: International Publishers, 1972), pp. 15-18.

13. Pete Daniel, *The Shadow of Slavery: Peonage in the South,* 1901-1969 (New York: Oxford University Press, 1973), p. xiv.

14. Rawick, *Texas Narratives,* V (3), 179; *South Carolina Narratives,* III (3), 213; Powdermaker, *After Freedom,* p. 104; Rosengarten, ed., *All God's Dangers,* p. 499.

15. Booker T. Washington, *Working with the Hands* (New York: Doubleday Page & Co., 1904), pp. 64, 116, 153, 162; Booker T. Washington and W. E. B. Du Bois, *The Negro in the South* (Philadelphia: George W. Jacobs and Co., 1907; reprint ed., Northbrook, Ill.: Metro Books, 1972), p. 52.

16. Vernon Johns, "An Agrarian Negro Culture," *Opportunity* 11 (November 1933): 336-339.

17. W. E. B. Du Bois, "Behold the Land," *New Masses,* January 11, 1947, pp. 18-20. See also his "The Economic Future of the Negro," *Publications of the American Economic Association,* 3rd Series, 11 (February 1906): 219-242.

18. Booker T. Washington, *Up from Slavery: An Autobiography* (New York: Doubleday, 1963), pp. 80-83.

19. W. E. B. Du Bois, *Souls of Black Folk* (Chicago: A. C. McClurg and Co., 1903; reprint ed., New York: Blue Heron Press, 1953), p. 135.

20. W. E. B. Du Bois, ed., *The Negro American Family,* Atlanta University Publications, No. 13 (Atlanta: Atlanta University Press, 1908), pp. 130-132.

21. Ibid., pp. 134-142.

22. Washington, *Working with the Hands,* pp. 119-129, 135-150.

23. Thomas M. Campbell, *The Movable School Goes to the Negro Farmer* (Tuskegee Institute: Tuskegee Institute Press, 1936; reprint ed., New York: Arno Press and *New York Times,* 1969), pp. 79-146. See also Felix James, "The Tuskegee Institute Movable School, 1906-1923," *Agricultural History* 45 (July 1971): 201-209.

24. Washington, *Working with the Hands,* pp. 129-134.

25. Several Tuskegee alumni wrote autobiographies. See, for example, William J. Edwards, *Twenty-five Years in the Black Belt* (Boston: Cornhill Co.; reprint ed., New York: Negro Universities Press, 1970), pp. 35-62, 111-114; Henry D. Davidson, *Inching Along: An Autobiographical Study of the Life and Work of Henry Damon Davidson* (Nashville: National Publication Co., 1944); and Holtzclaw, *Black Man's Burden,* pp. 67-152, 159-166, 218-225.

26. Thomas Calhoun Walker, *The Honey Pod Tree: The Life Story of Thomas Calhoun Walker* (New York: John Day Co., 1958), pp. 78, 118.

27. Robert Russa Moton, *Finding a Way Out: An Autobiography* (New York: Doubleday, Page & Co., 1920), pp. 172-178. See also selected issues of the *Southern Workman* from 1913 to 1939.

28. R. L. Smith, "An Uplifting Negro Cooperative Society," *World's Work* 16 (July 1908): 10462-10466.

29. Washington, *Working with the Hands,* p. 141.

30. Thomas C. Walker, "Negro Property Holding in Tidewater Virginia," *Southern Workman* 42 (November 1913): 622-625.

31. Campbell, *The Movable School,* p. 149.

32. Rosengarten, *All God's Dangers,* pp. 79, 447.

33. Howard Kester, *Revolt Among the Sharecroppers* (New York: Covici Friede Publishers, 1936; reprint ed., New York: Arno Press and the *New York Times,* 1969). p. 56.

34. Quoted in Mark Naison, "Black Agrarian Radicalism in the Great Depression; The Thread of a Lost Tradition," *Journal of Ethnic Studies* 1 (Fall 1973): 60.

CHAPTER 5

1. Robert Starobin, *Industrial Slavery in the Old South* (New York: Oxford University Press, 1970), pp. 10-34. See also James H. Brewer, *The Confederate Negro: Virginia's Craftsmen and Military Laborers, 1861-1861* (Durham, N.C.: Duke University Press, 1969).

2. Paul B. Worthman and James R. Green, "Black Workers in the New South," in Nathan I. Huggins et al., eds., *Key Issues in the Afro-American Experience* (New York: Harcourt Brace Jovanovich, 1971), II, 52-53.

3. Ibid., p. 53.

4. Booker T. Washington, "The Negro and the Labour Unions," *Atlantic Monthly* 111 (June 1913): 756-767.

5. W. E. B. Du Bois, ed., *The Negro Artisan,* Atlanta University Publications No. 7 (Atlanta University Press, 1902), pp. 158-176.

6. Philip Foner, *Organized Labor and the Black Worker, 1619-1973* (New York: Praeger Publishers, 1974), pp. 115-119.

7. Angelo Herndon, *Let Me Live* (New York: Arno Press and *New York Times,* 1969), pp. 193-241.

8. Hosea Hudson, *Black Worker in the Deep South* (New York: International Publishers, 1972), pp. 36-110.

9. Foner, *Organized Labor and the Black Worker,* p. 337.

10. U.S. Bureau of the Census, Current Population Reports, Special Studies, Series P-23, No. 54, *The Social and Economic Status of the Black Population in the United States, 1974* (Washington, D.C.: U.S. Government Printing Office, 1975), pp. 73-74. Hereafter referred to as U.S. Bureau of the Census, *Black Population in the United States, 1974.*

11. Ibid., pp. 25-27; U.S. Bureau of the Census, Census of Population, Subject Reports: Negro Population 1970, PC (2)-IB, Table 7; U.S. Bureau of the Census, Current Population Reports, Special Studies, Series P-23, No. 38, *The Social and Economic Status of Negroes in the United States, 1970* (Washington, D.C.: U.S. Government Printing Office, 1971), pp. 27-43.

12. W. E. B. Du Bois, ed., *The Negro in Business,* Atlanta University Publications No. 4 (Atlanta: Atlanta University Press, 1899), pp. 56-60.

13. Ibid., pp. 6-9.

14. Quoted in Walter B. Weare, *Black Business in the New South: A Social History of the North Carolina Mutual Life Insurance Company* (Urbana: University of Illinois Press, 1973), p. 181.

15. *Ebony Handbook* (Chicago: Johnson Publishing Co., 1974), pp. 246-251; North Carolina Mutual Life Insurance Company, *76th Annual Statement, December 31, 1974* (Durham, [1975].

16. Andrew Brimmer, "The Negro in the National Economy," in John P. Davis, ed., *American Negro Reference Book* (Englewood Cliffs, N. J.: Prentice-Hall, 1966), p. 251.

CHAPTER 6

1. Horace Mann Bond, *The Education of the Negro in the American Social Order* (Englewood Cliffs, N.J.: Prentice-Hall, 1954), p. 23.

2. Booker T. Washington, *The Story of the Negro: The Rise of the Race from Slavery,* Vol. II (New York: Outlook Company, 1909; reprint ed. New York: Peter Smith, 1940), pp. 136-138.

3. Ibid., pp. 115-116.

4. Quoted in Clara M. De Boer, "The Role of Afro-Americans in the Origin and

Work of the American Missionary Association,'' (Ph.D. dissertation, Rutgers University, 1973), p. 295.

5. See the remarks of Laura M. Towne regarding Southern white teachers in Rupert S. Holland, ed., *Letters and Diary of Laura M. Towne, 1865-1884, Written from the Sea Islands of South Carolina* (Cambridge: Riverside Press, 1912), p. 178.

6. Quoted in Howard N. Rabinowitz, "Half a Loaf: The Shift from White to Black Teachers in the Negro Schools of the Urban South, 1865-1890," *Journal of Southern History* 40 (November 1974): 557.

7. W. E. B. Du Bois, ed., *The Negro Common School,* Atlanta University Publication No. 6 (Atlanta: Atlanta University Press, 1901; reprint ed. New York: Octagon Books, 1968), pp. 89-92.

8. Holland, ed., *Letters and Diary of Laura M. Towne,* p. 281.

9. Quoted in Henry Allen Bullock, *A History of Negro Education in the South from 1619 to the Present* (Cambridge: Harvard University Press, 1967), p. 76.

10. Stephen J. Wright, "The Development of the Hampton-Tuskegee Pattern of Higher Education," *Phylon* 10 (Fourth Quarter 1949): 338.

11. Booker T. Washington, *Up from Slavery: An Autobiography* (New York: Doubleday, 1963), p. 161.

12. W. E. B. Du Bois, "The Talented Tenth," in Booker T. Washington et al., *The Negro Problem* (New York: James Pott and Co., 1903; reprint ed., New York: AMS Press, 1970), pp. 33-34.

13. William J. Simmons, *Men of Mark, Eminent, Progressive and Rising* (Cleveland, Ohio: Geo. M. Rewell & Co., 1887; reprint ed., Chicago: Johnson Publishing Co., 1970), pp. 12-14.

14. Quoted in William J. Walls, *Joseph Charles Price: Educator and Race Leader* (Boston: Christopher Publishing House, 1943), pp. 199-200.

15. D. W. Culp, ed., *Twentieth Century Negro Literature or a Cyclopedia of Thought on the Vital topics Relating to the American Negro . . .* (Toronto: J. L. Nichols & Co., 1902; reprint ed., New York: Arno Press and *New York Times,* 1969), pp. 72-75.

16. Kelly Miller, *Race Adjustment: Essays on the Negro in America* (New York: Neale Publishing Co., 1908; reprint ed. Miami, Fla.: Mnemosyne Publishing Co., 1969), pp. 19, 267.

17. Bullock, *A History of Negro Education in the South,* p. 189.

18. Quoted in Raymond Wolters, *The New Negro on Campus: Black College Rebellions of the 1920s* (Princeton: Princeton University Press, 1975), p. 195.

19. Quoted in James M. McPherson, "White Liberals and Black Power in Negro Education, 1865-1915," *American Historical Review* 75 (June 1970): 1361.

20. Culp, ed., *Twentieth Century Negro Literature,* pp. 125-126.

21. Ibid., pp. 139-141.

22. Quoted in Wolters, *New Negro on Campus,* p. 27.

23. Carter G. Woodson, *The Mis-education of the Negro* (Washington, D.C.: Associated Publishers, 1933), pp. 27, 30.

CHAPTER 7

1. Horace C. Hamilton and John M. Ellison, *The Negro Church in Rural Virginia.* Virginia Agricultural Experiment Station Bulletin, No. 273, June 1930. p. 12.

2. Ibid., pp. 33-35.

3. Quoted in ibid., p. 12.

4. H. Shelton Smith, *In His Image But . . . Racism in Southern Religion, 1780-1910* (Durham, N.C.: Duke University Press, 1972), pp. 226-251.

5. Benjamin E. Mays, *The Negro's God as Reflected in His Literature* (Boston: Chapman and Grimes, 1938), pp. 84-85.

6. Henry N. Mitchell, *Black Preaching* (Philadelphia and New York: J. P. Lippincott, 1970), pp. 72-74.

7. James Weldon Johnson, *Gods Trombones: Some Negro Sermons in Verse* (New York: Viking Press, 1927), pp. 27-30.

8. I. Garland Penn and J. W. E. Bowen, eds., *The United Negro: His Problems and Progress* (Atlanta: D. E. Luther Publishing Co., 1902; reprint ed., New York: Negro Universities Press, 1969), pp. 10-12, 149-152.

9. Ibid., pp. 153-155.

10. Walter B. Weare, *Black Business in the South: A Social History of the North Carolina Mutual Life Insurance Company* (Urbana; University of Illinois Press, 1973), p. 193.

11. Miles Mark Fisher, *Friends: Pictorial Report of Ten Years Pastorate* (1933-1943) (Durham, N.C.: White Rock Baptist Church, 1943), pp. 13, 27-33.

12. E. Franklin Frazier, *The Negro Church in America* (New York: Schocken Books, 1964), pp. 31-34.

13. See below, p. 177; see also, W. E. B. Du Bois, ed., *Some Efforts of American Negroes for Their Social Betterment,* Atlanta University Publications, No. 3 (Atlanta: Atlanta University Press, 1898), pp. 6-12, and W. E. B. Du Bois, ed., *Efforts for Social Betterment Among Negro Americans,* Atlanta University Publications, No. 14 (Atlanta: Atlanta University Press, 1909), pp. 16-29, 65-87.

14. Mitchell, *Black Preaching,* p. 91.

15. Ella E. Cotton, *A Spark for My People: The Sociological Autobiography of a Negro Teacher* (New York: Exposition Press, 1954), pp. 221-230.

16. Harry W. Roberts, "The Rural Negro Minister: His Educational Status," *Journal of Negro Education* 17 (Fall 1948): 478-481.

17. Hamilton and Ellison, *The Negro Church in Rural Virginia,* p. 18.

18. Harry W. Roberts, "The Rural Negro Minister: His Work and Salary," *Rural Sociology* 12 (September 1947): 285-287, 294-297.

CHAPTER 8

1. Elizabeth Hyde Botume, *First Days Amongst the Contrabands* (Boston: Lee and Shepard Publishers; 1893; reprint ed., New York: Arno Press and *New York Times,* 1968), p. 158.

2. Rawick, *Oklahoma Narratives,* VII, 175.

3. Norman Yetman, ed., *Life under the Peculiar Institution: Selections from the Slave Narrative Collection* (New York: Holt, Rinehart & Winston, 1970), p. 102.

4. Botume, *First Days Amongst the Contrabands,* p. 158.

5. William McKee Evans, *Ballots and Fence Rails: Reconstruction on the Lower Cape Fear* (Chapel Hill: University of North Carolina Press, 1967), p. 92n.

6. Botume, *First Days Amongst the Contrabands,* pp. 153-156.

7. Ibid., 161.

8. Ibid., p. 165.

9. Rawick, *Oklahoma Narratives,* VII, 297.

10. Botume, *First Days Amongst the Contrabands,* p. 179.

11. Ibid., pp. 159-160.

12. U.S. Bureau of Census, *Ninth Census of the United States, 1870,* National Archives, Record Group 120, Microfilm 593, Roll 1658. *Tenth Census, 1880,* T9, R 1375. Peter Kolchin, *First Freedom: The Responses of Alabama's Blacks to Emancipation and Reconstruction* (Westport, Conn.: Greenwood Press, 1972), pp. 67-72; John Blassingame, *Black New Orleans* (Chicago and London: University of Chicago Press, 1973), pp. 90-105; John Blassingame, "Before the Ghetto: The Making of the Black Community in Savannah, Georgia, 1865-1880," *Journal of Social History* 6 (Summer 1973): 475; Herbert G. Gutman, "Persistent Myths about the Afro-American Family," *Journal of Interdisciplinary History* 6 (Autumn 1975): 195-197.

13. See W. E. B. Du Bois, ed., *The Negro American Family,* Atlanta University Publications, No. 13 (Atlanta: Atlanta University Press, 1908), pp. 26-30. Allison Davis and Burleigh and Mary Gardner, *Deep South: A Social Anthropological Study of Caste and Class* (Chicago: University of Chicago Press, 1941), pp. 409-411; Charles S. Johnson, *Shadow of the Plantation* (Chicago: University of Chicago Press, 1934), pp. 71-80.

14. U.S. Bureau of the Census, *Black Population in the United States, 1974,* p. 107.

15. Rawick, *Texas Narratives,* VI, 18, 151, 204.

16. Rawick, *Oklahoma Narratives,* VI, 18, 151, 204.

17. Theodore Rosengarten, ed., *All Gods Dangers: The Life of Nate Shaw* (New York: Alfred A. Knopf, 1947), pp. 453-454.

18. Rupert S. Holland, ed., *Letters and Diary of Laura M. Towne, 1865-1884. Written from the Sea Islands of South Carolina* (Cambridge: Riverside Press, 1912), p. 184.

19. Blassingame, *Black New Orleans,* pp. 87-90; see also comments by Mary Church Terrell, Rosa D. Bowser, and Sarah D. Petty in D. W. Culp, ed., *Twentieth Century Negro Literature or a Cyclopedia of Thought on the Vital Topics Relating to the American Negro . . .* (Toronto: J. L. Nichols & Co., 1902, reprint ed., New York: Arno Press and *New York Times,* 1969), pp. 172-185.

20. Rosengarten, *All God's Dangers,* pp. 120-121, 535-536.

21. W. E. B. Du Bois, ed., *Morals and Manners Among Negro Americans,* Atlanta University Publications, No. 18 (Atlanta: Atlanta University Press, 1914), p. 71.

22. U.S. Bureau of the Census, *Negroes in the United States, 1920-1932* (Washington, D.C.: Government Printing Office, 1935), pp. 297-309.

23. U.S. Bureau of the Census, *Black Population in the United States, 1974,* pp. 60-61.

24. Ibid., pp. 39-40.

25. Virginia Heyer Young, "Family and Childhood in a Southern Negro Community," *American Anthropologist* 72 (April 1970): 270-272.

26. Ibid., 271-272.

27. For a critique of some of the literature on this subject, see Robert Staples, "Towards a Sociology of the Black Family: A Theoretical and Methodological Assessment," *Journal of Marriage and the Family* 33 (February 1971): 129-132. See also Herbert H. Hyman and John S. Reed, "Black Matriarchy Reconsidered: Evi-

dence from Secondary Analysis of Sample Surveys," *Public Opinion Quarterly* 33 (Fall 1969): 346-354; Joseph W. Maxwell, "Rural Negro Father Participation in Family Activities," *Rural Sociology* 33 (March 1968): 80-83.

28. Reynolds Farley, *Growth of the Black Population: A Study of Demographic Trends* (Chicago: Markham Publishing Co., 1970), p. 175.

29. U.S. Bureau of the Census, *Negroes in the United States, 1970,* p. 107; U.S. Bureau of the Census, *Black Population in the United States, 1974,* p. 107.

30. U.S. Bureau of the Census, *Black Population in the United States, 1974,* p. 108.

31. Blassingame, *Black New Orleans,* p. 94; Kolchin, *First Freedom,* pp. 62-63.

32. Kelly Miller, *Race Adjustment: Essays on the Negro in America* (New York: Neale Publishing Co., 1908; reprint ed., Miami, Fla.: Mnemosyne Publishing Co., 1969), pp. 169-171; Du Bois, ed., *The American Negro Family,* pp. 36-37; Oliver C. Cox, "Sex Ratio and Marital Status Among Negroes," *American Sociological Review* 5 (December 1940): 937-947; Jacqueline Jackson, "But Where Are the Men," *Black Scholar* 3 (December 1971): 30-41.

33. See, for example, U.S. Bureau of the Census, *Negroes in the United States, 1920-1932,* pp. 78-86.

34. U.S. Bureau of the Census, *Black Population in the United States, 1974,* pp. 38-40, 43-45.

35. Davis and Gardner, *Deep South,* pp. 411-412.

36. Allison Davis and John Dollard, *Children of Bondage: The Personality Development of Negro Youth in the Urban South* (Washington, D.C.: American Council on Education, 1940), pp. 59-60.

37. Rawick, *Oklahoma Narratives,* VI, 108.

38. Rawick, *Mississippi Narratives,* VI, 13-15.

39. John Richard Dennett, ed., *The South As It Is, 1865-1866* (New York: Viking Press, 1965), p. 125.

40. Ibid., pp. 79-82.

41. Kolchin, *First Freedom,* pp. 64-67.

42. D. E. Emerson, "Home Life of the Negroes," *First Mohonk Conference on the Negro Question . . . June 4, 5, 6, 1890,* ed. by Isabel Bowers (Boston: George H. Ellis, 1890-1891; reprint ed., New York: Negro Universities Press, 1969), p. 61.

43. Rossa B. Cooley, *Homes of the Freed,* with an introduction by J. H. Dillard (New York: New Republic, Inc., 1926; reprint ed., New York: Negro Universities Press, 1970), pp. 100-101.

44. Hortense Powdermaker, *After Freedom: A Cultural Study in the Deep South* (New York: Viking Press, 1939), p. 202.

45. Blassingame, *Black New Orleans,* pp. 169-171; W. E. B. Du Bois, ed., *Some Efforts of American Negroes for Their Own Social Betterment,* Atlanta University Publications, No. 3 (Atlanta: Atlanta University Press, 1898), pp. 28-31, 60-61; W. E. B. Du Bois, ed., *Efforts for Social Betterment Among Negroes,* Atlanta University Publications, No. 14 (Atlanta: Atlanta University Press, 1909), pp. 77-78.

46. Herbert Aptheker, ed., *A Documentary History of the Negro People in the United States, 1910-1932* (Secaucus, N.J.: Citadel Press, 1973), p. 47.

47. Du Bois, *Social Betterment Among Negroes* (1909), pp. 119-120, 126-127.

48. Levi Jones, "The Black Family: Its Process of Survival," (Ph.D. dissertation, Vanderbilt University, 1974), pp. 69-75.

49. Benjamin E. Mays, *Born to Rebel: An Autobiography of Benjamin E. Mays* (New York: Scribner's Sons, 1971), pp. 35-38; William H. Holtzclaw, *The Black Man's Burden* (New York: Neale Publishing Co.; reprint ed., New York: Negro Universities Press, 1970), p. 36.

50. Du Bois, *Morals and Manners Among Negro Americans,* pp. 82-90; Rosengarten, *All God's Dangers,* pp. 14, 15, 17, 18-22; Dennett, *The South As It Is,* pp. 79-81.

51. Aptheker, *History of the Negro People . . . 1910-1932,* p. 49.

52. Cooley, *Homes of the Freed,* p. 109.

53. Powdermaker, *After Freedom,* pp. 182-183.

54. W. E. B. Du Bois, *Darkwater: Voices From Within the Veil* (New York: Harcourt Brace, 1921), p. 172; Robert Russa Moton, *What the Negro Thinks* (Garden City, N.Y.: Doubleday, Doran & Co., 1932), pp. 34-35: Rosengarten, *All God's Dangers,* pp. 553-554. Expressing sentiments similar to those of Ned Cobb, a Mississippi man told Allison Davis in the 1930s that: "I can't stan' dese white men gittin' cullud girls. It steams me up, I guess. I gits mad all ovuh." Quoted in Davis and Gardner, *Deep South,* p. 38.

55. Robert F. Eng, "The Development of Black Culture and Community in the Emancipation Era: Hampton Roads, Virginia, 1861-1870" (Ph.D. dissertation, Yale University, 1972), p. 95; Eliza F. Andrews, *The War-time Journal of a Georgia Girl,* ed. by Spencer B. King, Jr. (New York: D. Appleton and Co., 1908; reprint ed., Macon, Ga.: Ardivan Press, 1960), p. 349; also see above, p. 26.

56. Powdermaker, *After Freedom,* pp. 191-192.

57. Aptheker, *History of the Negro People . . . 1910-1932,* p. 49; Ely Green, *Ely: An Autobiography,* with an Introduction by Lillian Smith (New York: Seabury Press, 1966), pp. 69-73; Davis and Dollard, *Children of Bondage,* p. 246.

58. St. Clair Drake, "In the Mirror of Black Scholarship: W. Allison Davis and Deep South," in *Education and the Black Struggle: Notes from the Colonized World,* ed. by the Institute of the Black World (Cambridge: Harvard Educational Review, 1974), p. 51.

59. Davis and Dollard, *Children of Bondage,* p. 52.

60. Charles S. Johnson, *Patterns of Negro Segregation* (New York: Harper & Row, 1943), pp. 148-149.

61. W. E. B. Du Bois, *Souls of Black Folk* (Chicago: A. C. McClurg and Co., 1903; reprint ed., New York: Blue Heron Press, 1953), p. 9.

CHAPTER 9

1. J. C. Price, "Does the Negro Seek Social Equality?" *Forum* 10 (January 1891): 563.

2. James Bryce, *The American Commonwealth,* 3rd ed. (New York: Macmillan, 1895), II: 508.

3. August Meier, "Negro Class Structure and Ideology in the Age of Booker T. Washington," *Phylon* 23 (Fall 1962): 261-262: August Meier and David Lewis, "History of the Negro Upper Class in Atlanta, Georgia, 1890-1958," *Journal of Negro Education* 28 (Spring 1959): 128-139.

4. U.S. Bureau of the Census, *The Black Population in the United States, 1974,* pp. 26-27.

5. *Saturday Review* 54 (January 16, 1971): 53. See also below, p. 254.

6. E. Franklin Frazier, *Black Bourgeoisie* (New York: Free Press, 1957); Nathan Hare, *The Black Anglo-Saxons* (New York: Marzani & Munsell, 1965). Hare's critique is against blacks of all classes who unthinkingly subscribe to white values and forms of behavior.

7. Thomas Holt, "Radical Blacks and Conservative Browns: The Seeds of Failure in South Carolina's Reconstruction," (Unpublished manuscript in possession of the author), pp. 10-12.

8. John Blassingame, *Black New Orleans* (Chicago and London: University of Chicago Press, 1973), pp. 152-153; Peter Kolchin, *First Freedom: The Responses of Alabama's Blacks to Emancipation and Reconstruction* (Westport, Conn.: Greenwood Press, 1972), p. 143; Perdue, *The Negro in Savannah 1865-1900* (New York: Exposition Press, 1973), pp. 90-91.

9. Different portions of Bruce's manuscript entitled "Washington's Colored Society" in the Schomburg Collection, New York Public Library, are reprinted in Frazier, *Black Bourgeoisie,* p. 197, and in Hollis Lynch, *The Black Urban Condition: A Documentary History, 1865-1971* (New York: Thomas Y. Crowell Co., 1973), pp. 37-39.

10. Langston Hughes, "Our Wonderful Colored Society: Washington," *Opportunity,* 5 (August 1927): 226-227, and excerpted in Lynch, *The Black Urban Condition,* pp. 164-167.

11. Allison Davis, "The Negro Deserts His People," *Plain Talk* 4 (January 1929): 49-54.

12. E. Franklin Frazier, *The Negro Family in the United States,* rev. and abrg. ed. (Chicago: University of Chicago Press, 1966), p. 308; E. Franklin Frazier, *The Negro in the United States,* rev. ed. (New York: Macmillan Co., 1957), pp. 287-291.

13. Many of the new men were quick to take advantage of the changed social realities. During the era of World War I, a dark-skinned Charleston schoolteacher, in referring to the refusal of upper-class mulatto women to allow men of his complexion to cross their thresholds, remarked humorously: "I could collect books—I like them; but first I am going to collect thresholds." Quoted in Laura Beam, *He Called Them by the Lightning* (New York: Bobbs-Merrill, 1967), p. 90.

14. Charles S. Johnson, *Growing Up in the Black Belt* (New York: Schocken Books, 1967), pp. 272-273.

15. Clifton R. Jones, "Social Stratification in the Negro Population: A Study of South Boston, Virginia," *Journal of Negro Education* 15 (Winter 1946): 4-12.

16. Johnson, *Growing Up in the Black Belt,* p. 15; Hortense Powdermaker, *After Freedom: A Cultural Study in the Deep South* (New York: Viking Press, 1939), pp. 176, 180; John Dollard, *Caste and Class in a Southern Town* (Garden City, N.Y.: Doubleday, 1957), pp. 89-90.

17. Marjorie F. Irwin, *The Negro in Charlottesville, Virginia and Albermarle County,* publications of the University of Virginia Phelps-Stokes Fellowship Papers, No. 9 (Charlottesville, Va.: University of Virginia, 1929).

18. Allison Davis and Burleigh and Mary Gardner, *Deep South: A Special Anthropological Study of Caste and Class* (Chicago: University of Chicago Press, 1941), pp. 472-473.

19. Samuel D. Proctor, "Survival Techniques and the Black Middle Class," in Rhoda L. Goldstein, ed., *Black Life and Culture in the United States* (New York: Thomas Y. Crowell Co., 1971), pp. 280-294.

20. Sidney Kronus, *The Black Middle Class* (Columbus, Ohio: Charles E. Merrill Publishing Co., 1971), pp. 38-39.

21. Quoted in David M. Tucker, *Black Pastors and Leaders: Memphis, 1819-1972* (Memphis: Memphis State University Press, 1975), p. 86.

22. Oliver C. Cox, "Leadership Among Negroes in the United States," in Alvin W. Gouldner, ed., *Studies in Leadership: Leadership and Democratic Action* (New York: Harper and Row, 1950), pp. 258-259.

23. Ibid., pp. 259-260.

24. Quoted in Raymond Gavins, "Gordon B. Hancock: A Black Profile from the New South," *Journal of Negro History* 59 (July 1974): 224.

25. Herbert Aptheker, ed., *A Documentary History of the Negro People in the United States,* 1910-1932, (Secaucus, N.J.: Citadel Press, 1973), pp. 759-760.

CHAPTER 10

1. Houston A. Baker, *Long Black Song: Essays in American Literature and Culture* (Charlottesville: University of Virginia Press, 1972), p. 26.

2. *Encyclopaedia Brittanica,* 1973 ed., s.v. "Chesnutt, Charles," by Sylvia L. Render; Sylvia L. Render, ed., *The Short Fiction of Charles W. Chesnutt* (Washington: Howard University Press, 1974).

3. Nathan I. Huggins, *Harlem Renaissance* (New York: Oxford University Press, 1971), p. 238.

4. Nick Aaron Ford, ed., *Black Insights: Significant Literature by Black Americans:1760 to the Present* (Waltham, Mass.: Ginn, 1971), p. 165.

5. Reprinted in Sterling A. Brown et al., *The Negro Caravan* (New York: Dryden Press, 1941), pp. 54-65.

6. Margaret Walker, *How I Wrote Jubilee* (Chicago: Third World Press, 1972), p. 25.

7. Reprinted in Edward Margolies, ed., *A Native Sons Reader* (Philadelphia and New York: J. B. Lippincott, 1970), pp. 58-75.

8. Reprinted in Whit Burnett, ed., *Black Hands on a White Face* (New York: Dood, Mead, 1971), pp. 301-334.

9. Darwin T. Turner, "The Negro Novelist and the South," *Southern Humanities Review* 1 (Winter 1967): 24-26.

10. Reprinted in Alain Locke, ed., *Plays of Negro Life* (New York: Harper and Brothers, 1927; reprint ed., Westport, Conn.: Negro Universities Press, 1970), pp. 187-204.

11. Ibid., pp. 165-186.

12. Thomas C. Dent et al., eds., *The Free Southern Theatre by the Free Southern Theatre* (Indianapolis: Bobbs-Merrill, 1969), p. 4.

CHAPTER 11

1. James Weldon Johnson, *Fifty Years and Other Poems* (Boston: Cornhill Company, 1917, reprint ed., New York: AMS Press, 1975), pp. 6-8.

2. These poems may be found in William H. Robinson, Jr., ed., *Early Black American Poets* (Dubuque, Ia.: Wm. C. Brown Co., 1969), pp. 20-24.

3. Paul Lawrence Dunbar, *The Complete Poems of Paul Lawrence Dunbar* (New York: Dodd, Mead, 1913), p. 71.

4. Reprinted in Langston Hughes and Arna Bontemps, eds., *The Poetry of the Negro, 1740-1970* (Garden City, N.Y.: Anchor Press/Doubleday, 1970), pp. 20-24.

5. James Weldon Johnson, ed., *The Book of American Negro Poetry* (New York: Harcourt Brace, 1922), pp. 41-42.

6. Langston Hughes, *Selected Poems of Langston Hughes* (New York: Alfred A. Knopf, 1970), pp. 157-174, 276-279.

7. Reprinted in Arnold Adoff, ed., *The Poetry of Black America: Anthology of the Twentieth Century* (New York: Harper & Row, 1973), pp. 98-102.

8. Margaret Walker, *For My People* (New Haven: Yale University Press, 1942), pp. 13-14; and *Prophets for a New Day* (Detroit: Broadside Press, 1970), pp. 22-23.

9. Several of Spencer's poems are reprinted in Hughes and Bontemps, *The Poetry of the Negro,* pp. 60-65.

10. Reprinted in Stephen Henderson, *Understanding the New Black Poetry: Black Speech and Black Music as Poetic References* (New York: William Morrow, 1973), pp. 235-236.

11. Reprinted in ibid., pp. 233-234.

12. Ibid., p. 184.

13. Reprinted in Hughes and Bontemps, *The Poetry of the Negro,* pp. 418-422.

14. Reprinted in ibid., pp. 424-428.

15. Reprinted in Adoff, *The Poetry of Black America,* p. 450.

16. Reprinted in Hughes and Bontemps, *The Poetry of the Negro,* p. 306.

17. Eileen Southern, *The Music of Black Americans: A History* (New York: W. W. Norton, 1971), p. 380.

CHAPTER 12

1. Quoted in David L. Lewis, *King: A Critical Biography* (New York: Praeger Publishers, 1970), p. 58.

2. Paul D. Bolster, "The Civil Rights Movement in Twentieth Century Georgia" (Ph.D. dissertation, University of Georgia, 1972), pp. 108-109.

3. Norfolk *Journal and Guide,* August 1, 1970; for other incidents of black protest in North Carolina during the 1940s, see Durham *Morning Herald,* February 9, May 3, 1944; March 18, April 4, April 21, 1948.

4. For King's evolving philosophy, see Martin Luther King, Jr., *Stride Toward Freedom: The Montgomery Story* (New York: Harper & Brothers, 1958); *Strength to Love* (New York: Harper & Row, 1963); and *Where Do We Go From Here: Chaos or Community* (New York: Harper & Row, 1967).

5. Miriam Feingold, review of *CORE: A Study in the Civil Rights Movement, 1946-1968,* by August Meier and Elliot Rudwick, in *Reviews in American History* 2 (March 1974): 159.

6. Henry Allen Bullock, *A History of Negro Education in the South from 1619 to the Present* (Cambridge: Harvard University Press, 1967), pp. 160-166, 194-195.

7. Bernice Reagon, "Songs of the Civil Rights Movement, 1955-1965: A Study in Culture History" (Ph.D. dissertation, Howard University, 1975), pp. 64-89.

8. *Birmingham World,* December 23, 1955; June 15, 1966.

9. For examples of the evolution in the *Guide's* position, see Norfolk *Journal and Guide,* February 13, 27, March 12, 26, 1960; July 8, 1961; June 22, July 27, August 3, September 7, 28, 1963.

10. Norfolk *Journal and Guide,* August 6, 1966; *Birmingham World,* June 22, 1966; *Tri-State Defender,* June 18, 1966, cited in Hugh Davis Graham, *Crisis in Print: Desegregation and the Press in Tennessee* (Nashville, Tenn.: Vanderbilt University Press, 1967), p. 265.

11. Joseph S. Himes, "A Theory of Racial Conflict," *Social Forces* 50 (September 1971): 53-60. See also his "Functions of Racial Conflict," ibid., 45 (September 1966): 3-5.

12. Quoted in Lewis, *King,* pp. 228-229.

13. For a summary of the circumstances surrounding the deaths of civil rights workers before 1966, see Jack Mendelsohn, *The Martyrs: Sixteen Who Gave Their Lives for Racial Justice* (New York: Harper & Row, 1966).

14. Robert Hooker, "Race and the Mississippi Press," *New South* 26 (Winter 1971): 55-69. For Greene's views see, Jackson *Advocate* July 28, 1962; April 13, 1963; May 16, 1964.

15. Quoted in Gloria Blackwell, "Black-Controlled Media in Atlanta, 1960-1970: The Burden of the Message and the Struggle for Survival" (Ph.D. dissertation, Emory University, 1973), p. 77.

16. *New York Times,* February 14, 1962.

17. Albert N. D. Brooks, "H. Council Trenholm: Martyr on Alabama Racial Tightrope," *Negro History Bulletin* 26 (May 1963): 230-231; see also *New York Times,* April 2, June 16, 1960; December 5, 1961.

18. *New York Times,* March 31, April 1, 2, 3, 11, 1960; December 17, 1961; January 19, 27, 28, 31, February 2, 1962.

19. For the varying pespectives of some of the participants on the black-white estrangement, see James Foreman, *The Making of Black Revolutionaries* (New York: Macmillan Co., 1972), pp. 413, 420-422, 449-452; Cleveland Sellers, *River of No Return* (New York: William Morrow, 1973), p. 157; and Debbie Louis, *And We Are Not Saved: A History of the Movement as People* (Garden City, N.Y.: Doubleday, 1970), pp. 187-247.

20. Robert Williams, *Negroes with Guns* (Chicago: Third World Press, 1973), pp. 54-64.

21. See statement by Charles Sims, leader of the Deacons, in Joanne Grant, ed., *Black Protest* (New York: Fawcett, 1968), pp. 357-365.

22. Joyce Ladner, "What 'Black Power' Means to Negroes in Mississippi," *Trans-Action Magazine* 5 (November 1967): 7-15.

23. Feingold, Review of *CORE,* by Meier and Rudwick, p. 153.

CHAPTER 13

1. John Buggs, "School Desegregation, North and South," *Integrated Education* 13 (May-June 1975): 116-121.

2. Johnny S. Butler, "Black Educators in Louisiana—A Question of Survival,"

Journal of Negro Education 43 (Winter 1974): 9-24; Robert Hooker, "Displacement of Black Teachers in the Eleven Southern States," *Afro-American Studies* 2 (December 1971): 165-180.

3. *The Cheraw Chronicle,* December 23, 1971; The Columbia *State,* March 1, 1973.

4. Quoted by Josephine Carson, *Silent Voices: The Southern Negro Woman Today* (New York: Delacorte Press, 1969), p. 202.

5. U.S. Bureau of the Census, *The Black Population in the United States, 1974,* p. 13.

6. Lester M. Salamon, "Leadership and Modernization: The Emerging Black Political Elite in the American South," *Journal of Politics* 35 (August 1973): 603-635.

7. U.S. Bureau of the Census, *The Black Population in the United States, 1974,* p. 146.

8. Ibid., pp. 151-152; *New York Times,* December 1, 1974.

9. *Washington Post,* December 14, 1975; *New York Times,* December 11, 1975, January 4, 1976.

10. U.S. Bureau of the Census, *The Black Population in the United States, 1974,* p. 153; David Campbell and Joe R. Feagin, "Black Politics in the South: A Descriptive Analysis, *Journal of Politics* 37 (February 1975): 142-144.

11. U.S. Bureau of the Census, *The Black Population in the United States, 1974,* pp. 27, 40.

12. *Ibid., p. 25.*

13. Kenneth S. Colburn, *Southern Black Mayors: Local Problems and Federal Responses* (Washington: Joint Center for Political Studies, 1973), pp. 2-11, 41.

14. Ibid., pp. 13-16, 42.

15. Campbell and Feagin, "Black Politics in the South," pp. 153-155.

16. Samuel D. Cook, "The Tragic Conception of Negro History," *Journal of Negro History* 45 (October 1960): 17-28.

17. J. Saunders Redding, *No Day of Triumph* (New York and London: Harper and Brothers, 1942), pp. 340-341.

BIBLIOGRAPHICAL ESSAY

The literature in the various disciplines covering the subjects discussed in this book is too vast to include in the bibliography of a single book. Consequently, I have limited the works that follow to some of the representative books, articles, and some primary source material which I have found useful. In conjunction with the references cited in the notes, this literature should provide the reader with the more significant works on the various topics discussed. For additional references readers should consult the bibliographies listed below.

BIBLIOGRAPHIES AND GENERAL WORKS

The best and most comprehensive listing and description of works from several disciplines dealing with black Americans, which also includes bibliographies, general reference works, collections of documentary sources, and anthologies of reprinted articles and essays, is James M. McPherson et al., *Blacks in America: Bibliographical Essays* (Garden City, N.Y.: Doubleday, 1971). A good supplement to this work, listing books and articles published between 1954 and 1969, is Elizabeth W. Miller and Mary L. Fisher, comps., *The Negro in America: A Bibliography,* rev. ed. (Cambridge, Mass.: Harvard University Press, 1970). Extremely useful is Dwight L. Smith, ed., *Afro-American History: A Bibliography* (Santa Barbara, Calif.: American Bibliographical Center-Clio Press, 1974), which consists of abstracts of some 3,000 articles published in various journals from 1953 to 1972. Dorothy B. Porter, comp., *The Negro in the United States: A Selected Bibliography* (Washington, D.C.: Library of Congress, 1970) is a listing of some of the works on blacks in the Library of Congress. For literature concerning blacks published prior to 1928, Monroe N. Work, ed., *A Bibliography of the Negro in Africa and America* (New York: H. W.

Wilson Co., 1928; reprint ed., New York: Octagon Books, 1965) is a useful resource. A bibliography of autobiographies of many relatively obscure Afro-Americans, who, however, provide much information about and insights into black life, is Russell C. Brignano's *Black Americans in Autobiography* (Durham, N.C.: Duke University Press, 1974).

Many of the topics covered in this book are also treated in Gunnar Myrdal, *An American Dilemma: The Negro Problem in Modern America* (New York: Harper & Row, 1944), which contains notes for each chapter as well as a bibliography.

John Hope Franklin's *From Slavery to Freedom: A History of Negro Americans,* 4th ed. rev. (New York: Alfred A. Knopf, 1974) is the best and most comprehensive single-volume history of Afro-Americans to date. It contains an excellent bibliography. Among its numerous competitors are August Meier and Elliot Rudwick, *From Plantation to Ghetto,* 3d ed. rev. (New York: Hill and Wang, 1976); Rayford Logan and Michael Winston, *The Negro in the United States,* 2 vols. (New York: Van Nostrand Reinhold, 1970-1971); and Benjamin Quarles, *The Negro in the Making of America* (New York: Collier books, 1969).

Among the documentary collections which I've found most useful for this study are Herbert Aptheker, ed., *A Documentary History of the Negro People in the United States,* 2 vols. (Secaucus, N.J.: The Citadel Press, 1951, 1973); Milton Metzler, ed., *In Their Own Words: A History of the American Negro,* 3 vols. (New York: Thomas Y. Crowell Co., 1964-1967); and Francis Broderick and August Meier, eds., *Negro Protest Thought in the Twentieth Century,* rev. ed. (Indianapolis: The Bobbs-Merrill Co., 1971). For other very useful documentary collections, readers should consult McPherson et al., eds., *Blacks in America* (previously cited).

CHAPTER 1

The bleak portrait of the Radical Reconstruction regimes in the South as agencies of corruption, extravagance, and ignorance that characterized the work of the Dunning school of historians has been largely discredited. Today, the basic findings in the pioneering revisionist works of such black scholars as W. E. B. Du Bois, "Reconstruction and Its Benefits," *American Historical Review,* 15 (July 1910) and *Black Reconstruction in America, 1860-1880* (New York: Harcourt Brace, 1935); and Alrutheus A. Taylor, *The Negro in South Carolina During Reconstruction* (Washington: The Association for the Study of Negro Life and History, 1924), *The Negro in the Reconstruction of Virginia* (Washington: The Association for the Study of Negro Life and History, 1926), and *The Negro in Tennessee, 1865-1880* (Washington: Associated Publishers, 1941) to the effect that the Radical regimes were hardly more corrupt than the governments which preceded or followed them and that under these regimes much beneficial legislation of enduring significance was enacted have been confirmed in such recent syntheses as John H. Franklin, *Reconstruction: After the Civil War* (Chicago: University of Chicago Press, 1963); Kenneth Stampp, *The Era of Reconstruction* (New York: Alfred A. Knopf, 1965); Robert L. Cruden, *The Negro in Reconstruction* (Englewood Cliffs, N.J.: Prentice-Hall, 1969); and Lerone Bennett, Jr., *Black Power, U.S.A.: The Human Side of Reconstruction, 1866-1877* (Chicago: Johnson Publishing Co., 1967). Monographs on individual states which reach similar conclusions include Vernon L. Wharton, *The Negro in Mississipi, 1865-1890* (Chapel Hill: University of North Carolina Press, 1947); Joe M. Richardson, *The Negro in the Reconstructon of Florida, 1865-1877* (Tallahassee: Florida State University, 1965); Joel Williamson, *After Slavery: The Negro in South Carolina Reconstruction, 1861-1877* (Chapel Hill: University of North Carolina Press, 1965); Jerrell F. Shofner, *Nor Is It Yet Over: Florida in the Era of Reconstruction, 1863-1877* (Gainesville: The University Presses of Florida, 1974); and Joe Gray Taylor, *Louisiana Reconstructed 1863-1877* (Baton Rouge: Louisiana State University Press, 1974). A convenient sampling of the various issues in Reconstruction historiography from a revisionist perspective is provided in Kenneth Stampp and Leon Litwack, eds., *Reconstruction: An Anthology of Revisionist Writings* (Baton Rouge: Louisiana State University Press, 1969).

Nearly all of the above works discuss in varying degrees the freedmen's reaction to their impending or eventual emancipation and their visions of the future. Other secondary works which treat the subject at some length include Willie Lee Rose, *Rehearsal for Reconstruction: The Port Royal Experiment* (Indianapolis: The Bobbs-Merrill Co., 1964); Bell I. Wiley, *Southern Negroes, 1861-1865* (New Haven: Yale University Press, 1938); Henderson Donald, *The Negro Freedman: Life Conditions of the American Negro in the Early Years After Emancipation* (New York: H. Schuman Co., 1952); Benjamin Quarles, *The Negro in the Civil War* (Boston: Little Brown, 1953); Peter Kolchin, *First Freedom: The Responses of Alabama's Blacks to Emancipation and Reconstruction* (Westport, Conn.: Greenwood Press, 1972); and Martin Abbott, "Voices of Freedom: The Response of Southern Freedmen to Liberty," *Phylon,* 34 (December 1973).

For firsthand accounts and reminiscences of the freedmen themselves, readers should consult such readily accessible, published primary sources as the WPA and Fisk University slave narrative collections, which have been reproduced without change in George P. Rawick, eds., *The American Slave: A Composite Autobiography,* 19 vols. (Westport, Conn.: Greenwood Press, 1972). Excerpts and selections from these collections, arranged topically, have been published in Benjamin A. Botkin, ed., *Lay My Burden Down: A Folk History of Slavery* (Chicago: University of Chicago Press, 1945); Norman R. Yetman, ed., *Life Under the "Peculiar Institution": Selections from the Slave Narrative Collection* (New York: Holt, Rinehart & Winston, 1970); and in several other collections. James M. McPherson's *The Negro's Civil War: How American Negroes Felt and Acted During the War for Union* (New York: Pantheon Books, 1965) contains a number of excerpts from Southern black newspapers and other primary sources. Among the eyewitness accounts of travelers, Northern schoolteachers, and other observers, I found the most informative on the freedmen's reaction to be Elizabeth Hyde Botume, *First Days Amongst the Contrabands* (Boston: Lee and Shepard Publishers, 1893; reprint ed., New York: Arno Press and the *New York Times,* 1968); John Richard Dennett, *The South As It Is 1865-1866,* ed. with an Introduction by Henry M. Christman (New York: Viking Press, 1965); Ray Allen Billington, ed., *The Journal of Charlotte L. Forten* (New York: Dryden Press, 1953); and Laura M. Towne, *Letters and Diary of Laura M. Towne, Written from the Sea Islands of South Carolina, 1862-84,* Rupert S. Holland, ed. (Cambridge, Mass.: Riverside Press, 1912; reprint ed., New York: Negro Universities Press, 1969).

Theodore B. Wilson, *The Black Codes of the South* (University, Ala.: University of Alabama Press, 1965); Eric Mckitrick, *Andrew Johnson and Reconstruction* (Chicago: University of Chicago Press, 1960); Lawanda Cox and John H. Cox, *Politics, Principle and Prejudice, 1865-1866: Dilemma of Reconstruction America* (New York: Free Press, 1963); and John A. Carpenter, "Atrocities in the Reconstruction Period," *Journal of Negro History,* 47 (October 1962) are among the works, in addition to the monographs, syntheses, and eyewitness accounts listed above, which describe the official, attitudinal, and physical obstacles that the freedmen encountered in attempting to make freedom real.

Henry A. Bullock's *A History of Negro Education in the South from 1619 to the Present* (Cambridge, Mass.: Harvard University Press, 1967) synthesizes much of the literature on the educational efforts and attainments of black Southerners and those working in their behalf during the periods of slavery, the Civil War, and the early years of Reconstruction. Readers should consult the bibliography for Chapter 5 for additional references.

Profiles of black Reconstruction leaders may be found in most of the previously cited monographs devoted specifically to black Reconstruction as well as in Franklin, *Reconstruction: After the Civil War* (also previously cited). Emma Lou Thornbrough, ed., *Black Reconstructionists* (Englewood Cliffs, N. J.: Prentice-Hall, 1972) provides a convenient compilation of biographical excerpts from other works. Recently, several full-length biographies have been completed which fill out and, in some cases, correct errors in other biographical accounts. The most scholarly of these recent works are Okon E. Uya, *From Slavery to Public Service: Robert Smalls, 1839-1915* (New York: Oxford University Press, 1971) and Peggy Lamson, *The Glorious Failure: Black Congressman Robert Brown Elliot and the Reconstruction in South Carolina* (New York: W. W. Norton, 1973). James S. Haskins, *Pinckney Benton Stewart Pinchback* (New York: Macmillan, 1973), a biography of a Louisiana black leader, is less scholarly. Among biographies of other black Reconstruction leaders which remain unpublished are Peter David Klingman, "Josiah Walls: Florida's Black Congressman of Reconstruction" (Ph.D. dissertation, University of Florida, 1972) and Julius Eric Thompson, "Hiram R. Revels, 1827-1901: A Biography" (Ph.D. dissertation, Princeton University, 1973).

Recent studies which examine black leaders as a group include Edward Magdol, "Local Black Leaders in the South: An Essay Toward the Reconstruction of Reconstruction History," *Societas,* 4 (Spring 1974); David C. Rankin, "The Origins of Black Leadership in New Orleans During Reconstruction," *The Journal of Southern History,* 40 (August 1974); Joseph M. St. Hilarie, "The Negro Delegates in the Arkansas Constitutional Convention of 1868: A Group Profile," *Arkansas Historical Quarterly,* 33 (Spring 1974); and Richard L. Hume, "The Black and Tan Constitutional Conventions of 1867-1869 in Ten Former Confederate States: A Study of Their Membership" (Ph.D. dissertation, University of Washington, 1969). Two monographs deserve special mention: Thomas Holt, "The Emergence of Negro Political Leadership in South Carolina During Reconstruction" (Ph.D. dissertation, Yale University, 1973), scheduled to be published in revised form by the University of Illinois Press as *Black Over White: Negro Political Leadership in South Carolina During Reconstruction,* has the virtue of treating black officeholders, not as a monolithic entity, but as individuals whose performance and positions on issues reflected a variety of diverse influences in the black community (such as class and ideology) as well as their own personal ambitions and interests. Charles Vincent's *Black Legislators in Louisiana During Reconstruction* (Baton Rouge: Louisiana State University Press, 1976), which "traces the progress of many of Louisiana's black legislators from the Civil War through the Reconstruction Act of 1867," has similar virtues.

In addition to many of the works already cited, William McKee Evans, *Ballots and Fence Rails: Reconstruction on the Lower Cape Fear* (Chapel Hill: University of North Carolina Press, 1967); Thomas B. Alexander, *Political Reconstruction in Tennessee* (Nashville: Vanderbilt University Press, 1950); and Carl N. Degler, *The Other South: Southern Dissenters in the Nineteenth Century* (New York: Harper & Row, 1974) recount striking examples of the determination of freedmen to exercise the franchise and, in the case of Degler, the willingness of certain white Southerners as early as 1865 to accord blacks the vote.

CHAPTER 2

Virtually all of the book-length secondary works covering the Reconstruction period listed for the previous chapter treat the demise of Radical Reconstruction and the tactics employed by the white Conservatives in returning to power. However, Allen W. Trelease, *White Terror: The Ku Klux Klan Conspiracy and Southern Reconstruction* (New York: Harper & Row, 1971), provides the most comprehensive, scholarly treatment of the role of white violence in this development. Frankly anti-Ku Klux Klan in orientation, it contrasts sharply with Stanley F. Horn's *Invisible Empire: The Story of the Ku Klux Klan, 1866-1871* (Boston: Houghton Mifflin, 1939). Trelease also gives some attention to black resistance to Klan violence, as does Herbert Shapiro, "Afro-American Responses to Race Violence During Reconstruction," *Science and Society,* 36 (Summer 1972); Otis Singletary, *Negro Militia and Reconstruction* (Austin: University of Texas Press, 1957); and such previously cited works as Williamson, *After Slavery,* and Evans, *Ballots and Fence Rails.* An adequate, systematic study of the black response to white violence during the Reconstruction period still needs to be made, however.

In suggesting that class divisions within the black community may have contributed to the end of Radical rule in South Carolina, Thomas Holt's *Black Over White* previously cited) adds a new dimension to the historiography of Southern redemption. The complicated story of the initial Northern acquiescence in redemption is covered in such works as C. Vann Woodward, *Reunion and Reaction: The Compromise of 1877 and the End of Reconstruction* (Boston: Little, Brown, 1951), whose thesis of a bargain between Southern Conservatives and Hayes' supporters is disputed by Allan Peskin, "Was There a Compromise of 1877?" *The Journal of American History,* 60 (June 1973) and modified by K. Ian Polakoff, *The Politics of Inertia: The Election of 1976 and the End of Reconstruction* (Baton Rouge: Louisiana State University Press, 1973). Other studies dealing with this issue but covering a longer chronological period include Vincent P. De Santis, *Republicans Face the Southern Question, 1877-1897* (Baltimore: Johns Hopkins University Press, 1959); Stanley P. Hirshon, *Farewell to the Bloody Shirt: Northern Republicans and the Southern Negro, 1877-1893* (Bloomington: Indiana University Press, 1962); and Rayford W. Logan, *The Betrayal of the Negro: From Rutherford B. Hayes to Woodrow Wilson* (New York: Macmillan, 1965).

Among the studies which show that redemption did not immediately end black voting and officeholding in the South are Hampton Jarrell, *Wade Hampton and the Negro: The Road Not Taken* (Columbia: University of South Carolina Press, 1949); George B. Tindall, *South Carolina Negroes, 1877-1900* (Columbia: University of South Carolina Press, 1952); C. Vann Woodward, *The Strange Career of Jim Crow* 3rd ed., rev. (New York: Oxford University Press, 1974); J. Morgan Kousser, *Suffrage Restrictions and the Establishment of the One-Party South, 1880-1910* (New Haven: Yale University Press, 1974) as well as such previously cited studies as Wharton, *The Negro in Mississippi;* Degler, *The Other South;* and Williamson, *After Slavery.* James T. Moore, "Black Militancy in Readjuster Virginia, 1879-1883," *Journal of Southern History,* 41 (May 1975) treats the most successful, albeit temporary, political comeback of blacks in the South between the end of Reconstruction and the beginning of the Populist movement.

Specific studies devoted to blacks and the Populist movement include Jack Abramowitz, "The Negro and the Populist Movement," *Journal of Negro History,* 38 (July 1953); Robert Saunders, "Southern Populists and the Negro, 1893-1895," *Journal of Negro History,* 54 (July 1969); William H. Chafe, "The Negro and Populism: A Kansas Case Study," *Journal of Southern History,* 34 (August 1968); Herbert Shapiro, "The Populist and the Negro: A Reconsideration," in August Meier and Elliot Rudwick, *The Making of Black America: Essays in Negro Life and History,* vol. II (New York: Antheneum, 1969); and Helen Edmonds, *The Negro and Fusion Politics in North Carolina, 1894-1901* (Chapel Hill: University of North Carolina Press, 1951). All of these studies suggest in varying degrees that the priorities of black and white Populists were different and sometimes contradictory, especially on the matter of race. While most of the literature on Southern Populism, including Woodward's *The Strange Career of Jim Crow,* emphasizes the softness of the Populists' commitment to interracial cooperation and black political equality with whites, J. Morgan Kousser, *The Shaping of Southern Politics* (previously cited), attributes the leadership of the movement in the Black Belt areas of the South in the 1890s to disfranchise blacks to "affluent and well-educated" Democrats rather than to Populists. Kousser as well as Degler, *The Other South* (previously cited), and Lawrence C. Goodwyn, "Populist Dreams and Negro Rights: East Texas As a Case Study," *American Historical Review,* 76 (December 1971), point to several white Populist leaders who did not capitulate to racism but remained committed to racial equality and the rights of blacks to the end.

The process by which black Southerners were reduced to a passive political status and a socially proscribed caste in the 1890s and the early 1900s is detailed in several of the works already listed for this chapter. With respect to disfranchisement, Kousser's study should be compared with Paul Lewinson, *Race, Class and Party: A History of Negro Suffrage and White Politics in the South* (New York: Oxford University Press, 1932), with which it purports to differ on some crucial issues. On the issue of the coming of a fully rationalized system of racial segregation in the South, Woodward's conclusions in *The Strange Career of Jim Crow* have been challenged or modified by Joel Williamson, *After Slavery* (previously cited); Roger Fischer, *The Segregation Struggle in Louisiana 1862-1877* (Urbana: University of Illinois Press, 1974); and Charles E. Wynes, *Race Relations in Virginia, 1870-1902* (Charlottesville: The University of Virginia Press, 1961).

Lynching and other barbarities inflicted upon black Southerners and white rationalization of these practices are treated in National Association for the Advancement of Colored People, *Thirty Years of Lynching in the United States, 1889-1918* (New York: NAACP, 1919); Southern Commission on the Study of Lynching, *Lynchings and What They Mean* (Columbia: University of South Carolina Press, 1952); Walter White, "The Work of a Mob," *Crisis,* 16 (September 1918); Francis W. Simkins, "Ben Tillman's View of the Negro," *Journal of Southern History,* 3 (May 1937); Charles Crowe, "Racial Massacre in Atlanta, September 22, 1906," *Journal of Negro History,* 54 (April 1969); and Lawrence J. Friedman, *The White Savage: Racial Fantasies in the Postbellum South* (Englewood Cliffs, N.J.: Prentice-Hall, 1970). The role of the national government in contributing to and endorsing Southern apartheid can be followed in the commentary and documents in Richard Bardolph, ed., *The Civil Rights Record: Black Americans and the Law, 1849-1970* (New York: Thomas Y. Crowell, 1970) as well as in Logan, *The Betrayal of the Negro* (previously cited); Seth M. Scheiner, "President Theodore Roosevelt and the Negro, 1901-1908," *Journal of Negro History,* 47 (July 1962); August Meier and Elliot Rudwick, "The Rise of Segregation in the Federal Bureaucracy, 1900-1930," *Phylon,* 28 (Summer 1967); and Nancy Weiss, "The Negro and the New Freedom: Fighting Wilsonian Segregation," *Political Science Quarterly,* 84 (March 1969).

CHAPTER 3

Much of the literature on blacks and Populism listed for Chapter 2 discusses the political response of black Southerners to the developing disfranchisement and segregation of the 1890s and early 1900s. August Meier, "The Negro and the Democratic Party, 1875-1915," *Phylon* 17 (Second Quarter, 1956), treats the efforts of some blacks to seek an alliance with the Democrats. Verbal protests, demonstrations, boycotts, and other forms of direct-action protest are detailed in Clarence Bacote, "Negro Proscriptions, Protests, and Proposed Solutions in Georgia, 1880-1908," *Journal of Southern History,* 25 (November 1959), and August Meier and Elliot Rudwick, "The Boycott Movement Against Jim Crow Streetcars in the South, 1900-1906," *Journal of American History,* 55 (March 1969). Roger A. Fischer, "A Pioneer Protest: The New Orleans Street-car Controversy of 1867," *Journal of Negro History,* 52 (July 1968), shows that direct-action forms of protest against segregation occurred during the Reconstruction period. The protest activities of newspaper editor John Mitchell, Jr., and his Richmond, Virginia, associates around the turn of the century are discussed in Ann Field Alexander, "Black Protest in the New South: John Mitchell, Jr., 1863-1929, and the Richmond Planet," (Ph.D. dissertation, Duke University, 1973); James H. Brewer, "Editorials from the Damned, (Constitutional Convention to Disfranchise the Virginia Negro)," *Journal of Southern History,* 28 (May 1962) and "The War Against Jim Crow in the Land of Goshen," *The Negro History Bulletin,* 24 (December 1960); and to a lesser extent in Andrew Buni, *The Negro in Virginia Politics, 1902-1965* (Charlottesville: The University Press of Virginia, 1967).

The migration of black Southerners to the West to escape white violence and Southern proscriptions and the resultant evolution of all-black communities in the West are treated in the study by Bacote cited above and in Roy Garvin, "Benjamin 'Pap' Singleton and His Followers," *Journal of Negro History,* 33 (January 1949); Glen

Schwedmann, "St. Louis and the 'Exodusters' of 1879," *Journal of Negro History,* 46 (January 1961); Morgan D. Peoples, "'Kansas Fever' in North Louisiana, *Louisiana History,* 2 (Spring 1970); William E. Bittle and Gilbert Geis, "Racial Self-fulfillment and the Rise of an All-Negro Community in Oklahoma," *Phylon,* 18 (Third Quarter 1957); and Mozelle C. Hill, "The All-Negro Communities in Oklahoma: The National History of a Social Movement," *Journal of Negro History,* 31 (July 1946). The subject is also given considerable coverage in such broader works as Alfreda M. Duster, ed., *Crusade for Justice: The Autobiography of Ida B. Wells* (Chicago: University of Chicago Press, 1970); William I. Hair, *Bourbonism and Agrarian Protest: Louisiana Politics, 1877-1900* (Baton Rouge: Louisiana State University Press, 1969); Frenise Logan, *The Negro in North Carolina, 1876-1894* (Chapel Hill: University of North Carolina Press, 1964); and in the previously cited George B. Tindall, *South Carolina Negroes* and Vernon L. Wharton, *The Negro in Mississippi.* With the exception of Duster, the works just cited also treat back-to-Africa schemes and movements, but the fullest discussion of this subject are provided by William Bittle and Gilbert Geis, *The Longest Way Home: Chief Alfred Sam's Back to Africa Movement* (Detroit: Wayne State University Press, 1964) and Edwin S. Redkey, *Black Exodus: Black Nationalist and Back-to-Africa Movements, 1890-1910* (New Haven: Yale University Press, 1969).

The complex motives behind the migration of Southern blacks to the North before and during the World War I era are explored in Charles S. Johnson, "How Much of the Migration Was a Flight from Persecution?" *Opportunity,* I (September 1923), whose stress on economic motivation is belied by the complex motivation observable in Emmett J. Scott, ed., "Letters of Negro Migrants of 1916-1918," *Journal of Negro History,* 4 (July, October 1919). Florette Henri, *Black Migration: Movement North 1900-1920* (Garden City, N. Y.: Anchor Press/Doubleday, 1975) provides the most recent synthesis of the vast literature on forces behind, the nature of, and the consequences for the black community of the northward migration. George W. Groh's *The Black Migration: The Journey to Urban America* (New York: Wright and Talley, 1972) covers a longer period, is largely sociological, and devotes much attention to conditions in Northern and Southern black communities in the 1960s.

The most systematic treatment of the varying philosophies of racial advancement enunciated by Afro-Americans around the turn of the century, with emphasis upon the Booker T. Washington-W. E. B. Du Bois controversy, is August Meier's, *Negro Thought in America, 1880-1915: Racial Ideologies in the Age of Booker T. Washington* (Ann Arbor: University of Michigan Press, 1963). The complex role which Washington played as overt accommodationist and surreptitious protester, which Meier first recounted in "Toward a Reinterpretation of Booker T. Washington," *Journal of Southern History,* 23 (May 1957), is retold. Washington's formative years as a leader is covered in Louis R. Harlan, *Booker T. Washington: The Making of a Black Leader, 1856-1901* (New York: Oxford University Press, 1973). Firsthand accounts of these early years, which include Washington's autobiographical writings as well as much of his correspondence, are provided in Louis R. Harlan, ed., *The Booker T. Washington Papers,* 4 vols. (Urbana: University of Illinois Press, 1972-1975). Biographies of Du Bois include Francis L. Broderick, *W. E. B. Du Bois: Negro Leader in a Time of Crisis* (Stanford, Calif.: Stanford University Press, 1959), and Elliot M. Rudwick, *W. E. B. Du Bois: A Study of Minority Group Leadership* (Philadelphia: University of Pennsylvania Press, 1960). For Du Bois' own perspective on events, readers should consult his autobiographies—*Dusk of Dawn: An Essay Toward an*

Autobiography of a Race Concept (New York: Harcourt Brace & World, 1940) and *The Autobiography of W. E. B. Du Bois* (New York: International Publishers, 1969)—as well as Herbert Aptheker, ed., *The Correspondence of W. E. B. Du Bois: Selections, 1877-1934* (Amherst: University of Massachusetts Press, 1973).

The persistence of protest thought and action in the South from the death of Booker T. Washington to the Supreme Court school desegregation decision of 1954 is discussed in a number of studies, the chief of which are: Charles Flint Kellogg, *NAACP: A History of the National Association for the Advancement of Colored People, 1909-1920* (Baltimore: Johns Hopkins Press, 1967); Robert Brisbane, *The Black Vanguard: Origins of the Negro Social Revolution, 1900-1960* (Valley Forge, Pa.: Judson Press, 1970); Edward Peeks, *The Long Struggle for Black Power* (New York: Charles Scribner's Sons, 1971); Paul D. Bolster, "Civil Rights Movements in Twentieth-Century Georgia," (Ph.D. dissertation, University of Texas at Austin, 1972) as well as in the previously cited Ann Field Alexander, "Black Protest in the New South."

Although the resorting of Southern blacks to violence in self-defense or in retaliation during the late nineteenth and the first half of the twentieth century has not yet received thorough study, the following works provide some information on the subject: August Meier and Elliot Rudwick, "Negro Retaliatory Violence in the Twentieth Century," *New Politics,* 5 (Winter 1966); Robert Kerlin, *The Voice of the Negro* (New York: E. P. Dutton, 1920); Ann J. Lane, *The Brownsville Affair: National Crisis and Black Reaction* (Port Washington, N. Y.: Kennikat Press, 1971); I. B. Newby, *Black Carolinians: A History of Black South Carolina from 1895 to 1968* (Columbia: University of South Carolina Press, 1973); and Arthur I. Waskow, *From Race Riot to Sit-In, 1919 and the 1960s* (Garden City, N.Y.: Doubleday, 1966). Two studies that cover events in which blacks put up stiff resistance to white attacks are William Ivy Hair, *Carnival of Fury: Robert Charles and the New Orleans Race Riot of 1900* (Baton Rouge: Louisiana State University Press, 1976), and Robert W. Haynes, *A Night of Violence: The Houston Riot of 1917* (Baton Rouge: Louisiana State University Press, 1976).

Southern white participation in programs of interracial cooperation in behalf of black rights are discussed in Wilma Dykeman and James Stokely, *Seeds of Southern Change: The Life of Will Alexander* (Chicago: University of Chicago Press, 1962); Thomas A. Krueger, *And Promises to Keep: The Southern Conference for Human Welfare, 1938-1948* (Nashville: Vanderbilt University, 1967); Henry E. Barber, "The Association of Southern Women for the Prevention of Lynching, 1930-1942," *Phylon,* 34 (December 1973); Edward F. Burrows, "The Commission of Interracial Cooperation in the South," (Ph.D. dissertation, University of Wisconsin, 1955); and Martin P. Sosna, "In Search of the Silent South: White Southern Racial Liberalism, 1920-1950," (Ph.D. dissertation, University of Virginia, 1972). Benjamin Mays, *Born to Rebel* (New York: Charles Scribner's Sons, 1971); Raymond Gavins, "Gordon Blaine Hancock: A Black Profile from the South," *Journal of Negro History,* 59 (July 1974); and Henry Lewis Suggs, "P. B. Young and the Norfolk *Journal and Guide, 1910-1954,*" (Ph.D. dissertation, University of Virginia, 1976) depict the lives of black leaders who were active in the movement for interracial cooperation.

CHAPTER 4

In addition to the bibliographies by McPherson and Smith cited at the beginning of this essay, readers will also find Joel Schor and Cecil Harvey, comps., *A List of References for the History of Black Americans in Agriculture, 1919-1974* (Davis: Agricultural History Center, University of California, Davis, 1975) useful.

The freedmen's dream of land and the extent to which they realized their dream during the Reconstruction and post-Reconstruction years is discussed in most of the book-length syntheses on Reconstruction in general and in the studies on specific states cited for Chapter 1. For firsthand accounts of the freedmen's expectations of land and their later disappointment, readers should peruse the previously cited WPA slave narrative collection compiled by Rawick. Studies which give considerable attention to the land expectations and acquisitions of Sea Island blacks and their eventual betrayal by the federal government include Edwin D. Hoffman, "From Slavery to Self-Reliance," *Journal of Negro History,* 41 (January 1956), and the previously cited Willie Lee Rose, *Rehearsal for Reconstruction.* While LaWanda Cox, "The Promise of Land for the Freedmen," *Mississippi Valley Historical Review,* 45 (December 1958), attests to the sincerity of early Congressional desires to promote black landownership in the South, William S. McFeely, "Unfinished Business: The Freedmen's Bureau and Federal Action in Race Relations," in Nathan I. Huggins et al., *Key Issues in the Afro-American Experience,* vol. I (New York: Harcourt Brace Jovanovich, 1971): Christie Farham Pope, "Southern Homesteads for Negroes," *Agricultural History,* 44 (April 1970); and Warren Hoffnagle, "The Southern Homestead Act: Its Origins and Operations," *Historian,* 36 (August 1970) demonstrate how the inadequate federal efforts were sabotaged on the anvils of prejudice, maladministration, and corruption. Carol K. R. Blesur, *The Promised Land: The History of the South Carolina Land Commission, 1869-1890* (Columbia: University of South Carolina Press, 1969), shows how ineffectual were the efforts of the one state which seriously attempted to deal with the problem.

For statistical data on black farm tenure, readers may find it necessary to go to the appropriate publications of the U.S. Census Bureau, some of which are cited in the notes. However, largely on the basis of census data, Calvin L. Beale, "The Negro in American Agriculture," in John P. Davis, eds., *The American Negro Reference Book* (Englewood Cliffs, N. J.: Prentice-Hall, 1966), provides an informative survey on the tenure, economic conditions,. and social characteristics of black farmers since the Civil War, with greater emphasis on the 1950s and the early 1960s. Representative of similar studies which focus upon specific periods or areas are James A. Russell, "Rural Economic Progress of the Negro in Virginia," *Journal of Negro History,* 11 (October 1926); Ernest E. Neal and Lewis W. Jones, "The Palce of the Negro Farmer in the Changing Economy of the Cotton South," *Rural Sociology,* 15 (March 1950); Seize C. Mayo and Horace Hamilton, "The Rural Negro Population in the South in Transition," *Phylon* 24 (Summer 1963); and James S. Fisher, "Negro Farm Ownership in the South," *Annals of the Association of American Geographers,* 63 (December 1973).

The plight of sharecroppers and farm laborers from the 1880s through the Great Depression is detailed in such general histories of the South as C. Vann Woodward, *Origins of the New South, 1877-1913* (Baton Rouge: Louisiana State University Press, 1951), and George B. Tindall, *Emergence of the New South, 1913-1945* (Baton Rouge: Louisiana State University Press, 1967) and in such Depression era accounts as Arthur Raper, *Preface to Peasantry* (Chapel Hill, University of North Carolina Press, 1936);

Arthur Raper and Ira De A Reid, *Sharecroppers All* (Chapel Hill: University of North Carolina Press, 1941); and Charles S. Johnson, Edwin R. Embree, and Will W. Alexander, *The Collapse of Cotton Tenancy* (Chapel Hill: University of North Carolina Press, 1935). Booker T. Washington, *Up from Slavery: An Autobiography* (New York: Doubleday, Page, 1901; reprint ed., Doubleday 1963), and W. E. B. Du Bois, *The Souls of Black Folk* (Chicago: A. C. McClurg, 1903; reprint ed., New York: Blue Horizon Press, 1953), contain graphic eyewitness descriptions of rural black life in the late nineteenth and early twentieth centuries. The plight of black farmers during these same years and beyond, from the perspective of eyewitness participants who engaged in individual and collective efforts to uplift the farmers in accordance with the tenets of Booker T. Washington's philosophy, are described in William H. Holtzclaw, *The Black Man's Burden* (New York: Neal Publishing Co., 1915; reprint ed., Westport, Conn.: Negro Universities Press, 1970); William J. Edwards, *Twenty-Five Years in the Black Belt* (Boston: The Cornhill Co., 1918; reprint ed., Westport, Conn.: Negro Universities Press, 1970); Henry D. Davidson, *Inching Along: An Autobiographical Study of the Life and Work of Henry Davom Davison* (Nashville: National Publications Co., 1944); and Thomas Calhoun Walker, *The Honey Pod Tree* (New York: John Day Co., 1958). While most of the foregoing autobiographies contain explicit or implicit expressions of the agrarian ideal, the most explicit enunciation of the value of rural life can be found in Booker T. Washington, *Working with the Hands* (New York: Doubleday, Page, 1904); Kelly Miller, "The Farm—The Negro's Best Chance," *Opportunity,* 13 (January 1924); and Vernon Johns, "An Agrarian Negro Culture," *Opportunity,* 11 (November 1933). Expressions by black farmers of the agrarian ideal may be found in Theodore Rosengarten, ed., *All God's Dangers: The Life of Nate Shaw* (New York: Schocken Books, 1957) and in the WPA slave narrative collection compiled by Rawick.

William F. Holmes, "Whitecapping in Mississippi: Agrarian Violence in the Populist Era," *Mid America,* 55 (April 1973) and "Whitecapping: Agrarian Violence in Mississippi, 1902-1906," *Journal of Southern History,* 35 (May 1969) describe the use of violence to force black farmers from the land, while Pete Daniel, *The Shadow of Slavery: Peonage in the South, 1901-1969* (Urbana: University of Illinois Press, 1969) and William Cohen, "Negro Involuntary Servitude in the South, 1865-1950: A Preliminary Analysis," *Journal of Southern History,* 42 (February 1976) provide striking evidence of economic and legal practices reminiscent of slavery which posed special barriers to black realization of the agrarian ideal.

Two articles by William F. Holmes, "The Arkansas Cotton Pickers Strike of 1891 and the Demise of the Colored Farmers' Alliance," *Arkansas Historical Quarterly,* 32 (Summer 1973) and "The Leflore County Massacre and the Demise of the Colored Farmers' Alliance," *Phylon,* 34 (September 1973), as well as Arthur I. Waskow, *From Race Riot to Sit-In, 1919 and the 1960's: A Study in the Connection Between Conflict and Violence* (Garden City, N. Y.: Doubleday, 1966) discuss organized protest movements by black farmers before 1930. Protests movements by black farmers during the 1930s are detailed in Donald H. Grubbs, *Cry from the Cotton: The Southern Tenants Farmer's Union and the New Deal* (Chapel Hill: The University of North Carolina Press, 1971); Louis Cantor, *A Prologue to the Protest Movement: The Missouri Sharecroppers Roadside Demonstration of 1939* (Durham, N. C.: Duke University Press, 1969); and Mark Naison, "Black Agrarian Radicalism in the Great

Depression, The Thread of a Lost Tradition," *Journal of Ethnic Studies,* 1 (Fall 1973). Accounts by participant-observers include Howard Kester, *Revolt Among the Share-croppers* (New York: Covici Friede Publishers, 1936; reprint ed., New York: Arno Press and The *New York Times,* 1969); John Williams, "Struggles in the Thirties in the South," *Political Affairs,* 44 (February 1965); and Ned Cobb's description in the previously cited Rosengarten, ed., *All God's Dangers.* In addition to the studies by Grubb and Cantor, the response of the New Deal administration to the plight of black farmers is discussed in Raymond Wolters, *Negroes and the Great Depression: The Problem of Economic Recovery* (Westport, Conn.: Greenwood Press, 1970) and debated between Donald Holley, "The Negro in the New Deal Resettlement Program," *Agricultural History,* 45 (July 1971) and Robert E. Nipp, "The Negro in the New Deal Resettlement Program: A Comment," *Agricultural History,* 45 (July 1971). Whatever the immediate impact of New Deal programs on the black farmer, some thirty years later black tenant farmers in the Mississippi Delta made clear in Ernest Dunbar, *Our Land Too* (New York: Pantheon Books, 1971), that their plight still left much to be desired.

CHAPTER 5

The central, even dominant role which Southern slaves and freedmen played as skilled artisans and craftsmen as well as unskilled workers in the antebellum and postbellum Southern economy is described by Robert Starobin, *Industrial Slavery in the Old South* (New York: Oxford University Press, 1971); James H. Brewer, *The Confederate Negro: Virginia's Craftsmen and Military Laborers, 1861-1865* (Durham, N.C.: Duke University Press, 1969); and Paul B. Worthman and James R. Green, "Black Workers in the New South," in Nathan I. Huggins et al., *Key Issues in the Afro-American Experience,* vol. II (New York: Harcourt Brace Jovanovich, 1971). Evidence of the decline in the proportion of blacks in the South's skilled labor force and the suppressed status of unskilled black workers during most of the twentieth century is provided in W. E. B. Du Bois, ed., *The Negro Artisan,* Atlanta University Publications No. 7 (Atlanta: Atlanta University Press, 1902); Herbert Northrup et al., *Negro Employment in Southern Industry: A Study of Racial Policies in Five Industries* (Philadelphia: Industrial Research Unit, Wharton School of Finance, University of Pennsylvania, 1970); and Stephan H. Roebuck, "The Negro in the Industrial Development of the South," *Phylon,* 14 (Fall 1953). Two personal accounts of their experiences as laborers and union organizers in the South during the 1920s and 1930s are Hosea Hudson, *Black Worker in the Deep South* (New York: International Publishers, 1972) and Angelo Herndon, *Let Me Live* (New York: Random House, 1937; reprint ed., New York: Arno Press and The *New York Times,* 1969). Charles H. Martin, *The Angelo Herndon Case and Southern Justice* (Baton Rouge: Louisiana State University Press, 1976) is a detailed account of the legal and political history of the Herndon case. General studies of blacks and labor unions in which the Southern black worker is discussed include Denhard S. Spero and Abram Harris, *The Black Worker: The Negro and the Labor Movement* (New York: Columbia University Press, 1931); F. Ray Marshall, *The Negro and Organized Labor* (New York: John Wiley & Sons, 1965); and Philip Foner, *Organized Labor and the Black Worker,*

1619-1973 (New York: Praeger Publishers, 1974). Paul B. Worthman, "Black Workers and Labor Unions in Birmingham, Alabama, 1897-1904," in Milton Cantor, ed., *Black Labor in America* (Westport, Conn.: Negro Universities Press, 1969), provides an example of a successful, but temporary interracial labor movement in the South around the turn of the century.

August Meier, *Negro Thought in America* (previously cited), provides the best analysis of the rationales offered in support of the capitalistic impulse within the black community during the era of Booker T. Washington. Studies of black capitalistic enterprises largely in the South include W. E. B. Du Bois, ed., *The Negro in Business,* Atlanta University Publications No. 4 (Atlanta: Atlanta University Press, 1899); Abram L. Harris, *The Negro as Capitalist: A Study of Banking and Business Among American Negroes* (Philadelphia: The American Academy of Political and Social Science, 1936); Vishnu V. Oaks, *The Negro's Adventure in General Business* (Yellow Springs, Ohio: The Antioch Press, 1949); M. S. Stuart, *An Economic Detour: A History of Insurance in the Lives of American Negroes* (New York: Wendell Mallett and Co., 1940); and Simeon Booker. "Black Business Is Tops in South," *Ebony,* 26 (August 1971). *The Ebony Handbook* (Chicago: Johnson Publishing Co., 1974) provides a convenient compilation of statistics on black business enterprises for the early 1970s.

The best study of a single black business institution, which the author purports to be "Less a business history than . . . a social and intellectual history of a black business," is Walter B. Weare, *Black Business in the New South: A Social History of the North Carolina Mutual Life Insurance Company* (Urbana: University of Illinois Press, 1973). A recent study of another black insurance company in the South is Alexa B. Henderson, "A Twentieth Century Black Enterprise: The Atlanta Life Insurance Company, 1905-1975," (Ph.D. dissertation, Georgia State University—School of Arts and Sciences, 1975).

The overall economic status of blacks in the South as well as in the nation in recent years is analyzed in Andrew Brimmer, "The Negro in the National Economy," in John P. Davis, ed., *The American Negro Reference Book* (Englewood Cliffs, N. J.: Prentice-Hall, 1966) and in such U.S. Census Bureau publications as *The Social and Economic Status of Negroes in the United States, 1970* (Washington: Government Printing Office, 1971) and *The Social and Economic Status of the Black Population in the United States 1974* (Washington: Government Printing Office, 1975).

CHAPTER 6

The most comprehensive history of black education on all levels in the South, which concentrates on the rise and fall of Jim Crow education in the region, is Henry Allen Bullock, *A History of Negro Education in the South from 1619 to the Present* (Cambridge, Mass.: Harvard University Press, 1967). For the Reconstruction era only, readers should consult William Preston Vaughn, *Schools for All: The Blacks and Public Education in the South, 1865-1877* (Lexington: University Press of Kentucky, 1974). The freedmen's thirst for knowledge and the efforts of governmental agencies and private individuals and organizations to meet their demand are recounted in such firsthand accounts as Booker T. Washington, *The Story of the*

Negro: The Rise of the Race from Slavery, vol. II (New York: The Outlook Co., 1909; reprint ed., New York: Peter Smith, 1940); and in the previously cited Elizabeth Botume, *First Days Amongst the Contrabands;* Rupert S. Holland, ed., *The Letters and Diary of Laura M. Towne;* and Ray Allen Billington, ed., *The Journal of Charlotte F. Forten.* Historical monographs and articles covering the same subject include Horace Mann Bond, *The Education of the Negro in the American Social Order* (Englewood Cliffs, N. J.: Prentice-Hall, 1954); John W. Blassingame, "The Union Army As an Educational Institution for Negroes, 1862-1865," *Journal of Negro Education,* 34 (Spring 1965); and Clara M. De Boer, "The Role of Afro-Americans in the Origin and Work of the American Missionary Association," (Ph.D. dissertation, Rutgers University, 1973).

The only known successful integration of public schools during the Reconstruction period is discussed in Louis R. Harlan, "Desegregation in New Orleans Public Schools During Reconstruction," *American Historical Review,* 67 (April 1962) and Roger Fischer, *The Segregation Struggle in Louisiana* (previously cited). John Hope Franklin's "Jim Crow Goes to School: The Genesis of Legal Segregation in Southern Schools," *South Atlantic Quarterly,* 58 (Spring 1959) shows how unique (and temporary) the New Orleans' experiment was. Howard N. Rabinowitz, "Half a Loaf: The Shift from White to Black Teachers in the Negro Schools of the Urban South, 1865-1890," *Journal of Southern History,* 40 (November 1974), discusses the desire of blacks to control their own public schools, while James M. McPherson, "White Liberals and Black Power in Negro Education, 1865-1915," *American Historical Review,* 75 (June 1970), assesses similar sentiment concerning black colleges.

Bullock, *A History of Negro Education in the South* (cited above), contends that in the process of creating a system of segregated education, the white South unwittingly created the instruments for the downfall of the Jim Crow order. The acquiescence of Northern philanthropists in the creation of the system is discussed in Louis R. Harlan, *Separate and Unequal: Public School Campaigns and Racism in the Southern Seaboard States, 1901-1915* (Chapel Hill: University of North Carolina Press, 1958). Most studies of black education during this period treat the debate within the black community over industrial versus liberal arts education, but August Meier's *Negro Thought in America* (previously cited) provides the fullest analysis of the subject. For representative contemporary expressions on the subject, most of which refuse to take an either-or position on the issue, students should read Kelly Miller, *Race Adjustment: Essays on the Negro in America* (New York: Neale Publishing Co., 1908; reprint ed., Miami, Fla.: Mnemosyne Publishing Co., 1969); William J. Walls, *Joseph Charles Price: Educator and Race Leader* (Boston: Christopher Publishing House, 1943); the appropriate sections of William J. Simmons, *Men of Mark, Eminent, Progressive and Rising* (Cleveland: George M. Revill, 1887; reprint ed., Chicago: Johnson Publishing Co., 1970); and the answers by several black intellectuals to the question, "Should the Negro Be Given an Education Different from That Given to the White?" in D. W. Culp, ed., *Twentieth Century Negro Literature or a Cylopedia of Thought on the Vital Topics Relating to the American Negro . . .* (Toronto: J. J. Nichols, 1909; reprint ed., New York: Arno Press and the New York Times, 1969). However, Raymond Wolters, *The New Negro on Campus: Black College Rebellions of the 1920s* (Princeton: Princeton University Press, 1975), shows that the industrial education-liberal arts debate was by no means the only issue concerning college education which animated the black community during the early decades of the twentieth century.

Historical and contemporary assessments of black colleges include Dwight O. W. Holmes, *The Evolution of the Negro College* (College Park, Maryland: McGrath Publishing Co., 1934); Tilden J. LeMelle and Wilbert J. LeMelle, *The Black College: A Strategy for Relevance* (New York: Frederick A. Praegar, 1969); and Earl McGrath, *The Predominantly Negro Colleges and Universities in Transition* (New York: Teachers College, Columbia University, 1965). Histories of individual colleges include Clarence A. Bacote, *The Story of Atlanta University: A Century of Service, 1865-1965* (Atlanta: Atlanta University, 1969); Edward A. Jones, *A Candle in the Dark: A History of Morehouse College* (Valley Forge, Pa.: Judson Press, 1967); Leedell W. Neyland and John W. Riley, *The History of Florida Agricultural and Mechanical University* (Gainesville: University of Florida Press, 1963); Rayford W. Logan, *Howard University, 1867-1967* (New York: New York University Press, 1969); George R. Woolfolk, *Prairie View: A Study in Public Conscience, 1878-1946* (New York: Pageant Press, 1962). Unpublished histories of lesser known institutions include Alandus C. Johnson, "The Growth of Paine College, A Successful Interracial Venture, 1903-1946" (Ph.D. dissertation, University of Georgia, 1970), and Frederick Richardson, "A Power for Good in Society: The History of Benedict College," (Ph.D. dissertation, The Florida State University, 1973).

Vigorous attacks on black college education in general and certain colleges in particular have been levied by such black scholars as Carter G. Woodson, *The Mis-Education of the Negro* (Washington: The Associated Publishers, 1933) and J. Saunders Redding, *No Day of Triumph* (New York: Harper & Row, 1942). Perhaps the most damaging attack on black colleges came from two white scholars: Christopher Jencks and David Reisman, "The American Negro College," *Harvard Educational Review,* 37 (Winter 1967) and *The Academic Revolution* (Garden City, N. Y.: Doubleday, 1968). However, Stephen J. Wright et al., "'The American Negro College': Four Responses and a Reply," *Harvard Educational Review,* 37 (Summer-Fall 1967), and John Sebora, "Our Negro Colleges: A Reply to Jencks and Reisman," *Antioch Review,* 28 (Spring 1968), contain persuasive arguments in defense of these institutions.

While there is no general study of the collective contributions of black scholars at black institutions, Jessie P. Guzman, "Monroe Work and His Contributions," *Journal of Negro History,* 34 (October 1949), and Valien Preston, "Sociological Contributions of Charles Johnson," *Sociology and Social Research,* 42 (March-April 1958), treat two of the more important scholars of black life. Johnson's scholarly contributions are also assessed in Patrick J. Gilpin, "Charles S. Johnson: An Intellectual Biography" (Ph.D. dissertation, Vanderbilt University, 1973). Essays on several black sociologists are contained in James E. Blackwell and Morris Janowitz, eds., *Black Sociologists: Historical and Contemporary Perspectives* (Chicago: University of Chicago Press, 1974). Black historians have naturally evoked study by historians. Although Earle E. Thorpe's *Black Historians: A Critique* (New York: W. W. Morrow, 1971) is a study of nonacademic as well as academic historians, the great majority of the latter spent all or the major portion of their careers at black colleges. Patricia W. Romero, "Carter G. Woodson: A Biography" (Ph.D. dissertation, Ohio State University, 1971), and Janet Harris, "Charles Harris Wesley: Educator and Historian, 1891-1947," (Ph.D. dissertation, Howard University, 1975), are studies of two of the most prolific pioneer professional historians. The social views of several black intellectuals who served on black college faculties are treated in James O. Young, *Black Writers of the Thirties* (Baton Rouge: Louisiana State University Press, 1973), while the social backgrounds of black academicians in several disciplines are discussed in Horace Mann Bond, *Black American Scholars: A Study of Their Beginning* (Detroit: Balamp Publishers, 1972).

CHAPTER 7

A very useful listing of books, articles, and manuscript collections pertaining to black religion in Africa and the Americas is Ethel L. Williams and Clifton F. Brown, comps., *Howard University Bibliography of African and Afro-American Religious Studies: With Locations in American Libraries* (Wilmington, Del.: Scholarly Resources, 1977).

Two general histories of the black church in America which attribute its rapid growth after the Civil War to the desire of the freedmen to be independent of white control are Carter G. Woodson, *The History of the Negro Church,* 2d ed. (Washington: The Associated Publishers, 1945) and E. Franklin Frazier, *The Negro Church in America* (New York: Schocken Books, 1964). However, H. Shelton Smith's *In His Image But . . . Racism in Southern Religion* (Durham, N. C.: Duke University Press, 1972) suggests that the withdrawal of blacks from some white churches was not always purely voluntary. The political roles which many of the ministers of the new black churches played during the Reconstruction period is discussed in several of the works on black Reconstruction cited for Chapter 1.

Among the works which describe black religious beliefs and expressions are Benjamin E. Mays, *The Negro's God as Reflected in His Literature* (Boston: Chapman and Grimes, 1938), which stresses both the otherworldly and secular bases of black belief; Ruby F. Johnston, *The Development of Negro Religion* (New York: New Philosophical Library, 1954) and *The Religion of Negro Protestants: Changing Religious Attitudes and Practices* (New York: Philosophical Library, 1956), which examine the diversities as well as the uniformities in black religious expression, practices, and expectations; Joseph R. Washington, Jr., *Black Religion: The Negro and Christianity in the United States* (Boston: Beacon Press, 1964), which analyzes black religion within the context of mainstream Protestant Christianity in the United States; and Newell N. Puckett, "Religious Folk Beliefs of Whites and Negroes," *Journal of Negro History,* 16 (January 1931), which emphasizes similarities between black religious beliefs and practices and earlier white forms.

Books which best capture the rhythm and imagery of the traditional black sermon are James Weldon Johnson, *God's Trombones: Some Negro Sermons in Verse* (London: George Allen & Unwin, 1929), which contains Johnson's poetic rendering of several themes traditional in black sermons; William H. Pipes, *Say Amen, Brother! Old-Time Negro Preaching: A Study in American Frustration* (New York: William Frederick Press, 1951; reprint ed., Westport, Conn.: Negro Universities Press, 1970), which contains transcriptions and analyses of sermons delivered by seven "old-time" black preachers in Macon County, Georgia, in the 1940s; and Henry N. Mitchell, *Black Preaching* (Philadelphia: J. P. Lippincott Co., 1970), which in addition to analyzing the themes and imagery in both folk and literary sermons, also discusses the secular role of the black minister.

Works which give primary attention to the secular role of the black church include W. E. B. Du Bois, ed., *The Negro Church,* Atlanta University Publications No. 8 (Atlanta: Atlanta University Press, 1903), which also gives considerable attention to the African roots of black religion; E. Franklin Frazier, *The Negro Church in America* (New York: Schocken Books, 1964), which downplays the African heritage while emphasizing the church's role as the guardian of the community's morals and conscience; Miles Mark Fisher, *Friends: Pictorial Report of Ten Years (1933-1943)* (Durham, N. C.: The White Rock Baptist Church, 1943), which is a personal account of a Social Gospel ministry; and Harry V. Richardson, *Dark Glory: A Picture of the Church Among Negroes in the Rural South* (New York: Friendship Press, 1947), which compares the functioning of the black church in three Deep South counties with those in one county in the upper South during the 1940s. Three articles by Harry W. Roberts, "The Rural Negro Minsiter: His Educational Status," *Journal of Negro Education,* 17 (Fall 1948); "The Rural Negro Minister: His Personal and Social Characteristics," *Social Forces,* 27 (March 1949); "The Rural Negro Minister: His Work and Salary," *Rural Sociology,* 12 (September 1947); and articles by Wilbur E. Bok, "Decline of the Negro Clergy: Changes in Religious Leadership in the United States in the Twentieth Century," *Phylon,* 29 (Spring 1968); Glenn M. Sisk, "Churches in the Alabama Black Belt," *Church History,* 23 (June 1954); and Charles H. Wesley, "The Religious Attitudes of Negro Youth—A Preliminary Study of Opinion in an Urban and Rural Community," *Journal of Negro History,* 21 (October 1936), point up the socioeconomic factors which not only militated against a protest role for black churches but also limited their ability to carry out other community functions.

On the other hand, Benjamin E. Mays and Joseph W. Nicholson, *The Negro's Church* (New York: Institute of Social and Religious Research, 1933; reprint ed., New York: Negro Universities Press, 1969), while duly noting the problems and defects of the black church in the early 1930s, were nevertheless optimistic about its contemporary and prospective role as a vital force in the lives of black people. Such studies as Howard H. Harlan, *John Jasper—A Case History in Leadership,* Publications of the University of Virginia, Phelps-Stokes Papers, No. 14 (1936); Horace C. Hamilton and John M. Ellison, *The Negro Church in Rural Virginia,* Virginia Agricultural Experiment Station Bulletin, No. 273 (June 1930); Ralph A. Felton, *Go Down Moses: A Study of 21 Successful Negro Rural Pastors* (Madison, N. J.: Department of Rural Church, Drew Theological Seminary, 1952); David M. Tucker, *Black Pastors and Leaders: Memphis, 1819-1972* (Memphis: Memphis State University Press, 1975); and Harry Richardson, *Dark Glory* (cited above), all of which highlight the accomplishments of Southern black churches when under competent and sometimes inspired leadership, tend to support the optimism of Mays and Nicholson. Gayraud S. Wilmore, *Black Religion and Black Radicalism* (Garden City, N. Y.: Doubleday, 1972), examines the paradox of black religion serving as both a reactionary force and a force for liberation.

CHAPTER 8

Until recently, the study of the black family was almost the exclusive province of sociologists, most of whom evaluated life-styles and institutional arrangements on the basis of white, middle-class norms. As a consequence, much of the literature perceived the black family from the perspective of pathology and deviance. For an analysis of this literature and the recent revolt against such a perspective, students should read Robert Staples, "Towards a Sociology of the Black Family: A Theoretical and Methodological Assessment," *Journal of Marriage and the Family,* 33 (February 1971). For an attempt to provide a new perspective from which to study the black family, Charles Rollo Turner's "Some Theoretical and Conceptual Considerations for Black Family Studies," *Black Lines,* 2 (Summer 1972) should be read. Most traditional studies of black family life have taken their cues from E. Franklin Frazier, *The Negro Family in the United States* (Chicago: University of Chicago Press 1939), which emphasized the impact of slavery, racial oppression, urbanization, and economic deprivation as barriers to a stable family life among blacks. Daniel P. Moynihan's *The Negro Family: The Case for National Action* (Washington: Government Printing Office, 1965), which portrayed the modern black family as pathological, borrowed heavily from Frazier's earlier analysis. Works which have considerably modified the Frazier framework and conclusions and rejected those of Moynihan include Andrew Billingsley, *Black Families in White America* (Englewood Cliffs, N. J.: Prentice-Hall, 1968), which emphasizes the variety and complexity of black family patterns and the interdependence of the black family with other institutions in American society, and Robert E. Hill, *The Strengths of Black Families* (New York: Emerson Hall Publishers, 1972), which pays tribute to the social health and viability of the bulk of lower-class as well as middle-class families.

Studies of black family life by historians have been precipitated by the revived interest in slavery. While differing on the degree to which the integrity of the slave family was respected and preserved, such students of slavery as John Blassingame, *The Slave Community* (New York: Oxford University Press, 1972); George Rawick, *From Sundown to Sun up! The Making of the Black Community* (Westport, Conn.: Greenwood Press, 1972); Robert W. Fogel and Stanley Engerman, *Time on the Cross: The Economics of Negro Slavery* (Boston: Little, Brown, 1974); Eugene Genovese, *Roll Jordan Roll: The World the Slaves Made* (New York: Pantheon Books, 1974), and Leslie H. Owens, *This Species of Property: Slave Life and Culture in the Old South* (New York: Oxford University Press, 1976) all agree that the slaves had a strong sense of family which they sustained in the passage from slavery to freedom. Such Reconstruction studies as Robert Azbug, "The Black Family During Reconstruction," in the previously cited Nathan I. Huggins et al., *Key Issues in the Afro-American Experience,* vol. II; John Blassingame, *Black New Orleans, 1860-1880* (Chicago: University of Chicago Press, 1973); Peter Kolchin, *First Freedom: The Responses of Alabama's Blacks to Emancipation and Reconstruction* (previously cited); and such eyewitness accounts as the previously cited Elizabeth Botume, *First Days Amongst the Contrabands;* the WPA slave narrative collection by Rawick, *The American Slave: A Composite Autobiography;* and selections from the narrative collection by Yetman, ed., *Life Under the Peculiar Institution,* support the findings in Herbert Gutman, "Persistent Myths about the Afro-American Family," *Journal of Interdisciplinary History,* 6 (Autumn 1975), that nuclear families, either as a continuation of the slave family or as a conscious creation preference of the freedmen, were the prevailing family types during the Reconstruction era. Whatever the nature of the black family under slavery, William Harris, "Work and Family in Black Atlanta," *Journal of Social History,* 9 (Spring 1976), suggests that the heritage of slavery had little adverse influence upon the structure of the post-Civil War black family.

Sociological and anthropological treatises depicting the black family in the South during the first four decades of the twentieth century, such as W. E. B. Du Bois, ed., *The Negro American Family,* Atlanta University Publications, No. 13 (Atlanta: Atlanta University Press, 1908); Allison Davis, Burleigh Gardner, and Mary Gardner, *Deep South: A Social and Anthropological Study of Caste and Class* (Chicago: University of Chicago Press, 1941); Charles S. Johnson, *Shadow of the Plantation* (Chicago: University of Chicago Press, 1934) and *Growing Up in the Black Belt: Negro Youth in the Rural South* (New York: The American Council on Education, 1941); Hortense Powdermaker, *After Freedom: A Cultural Study in the Deep South* (New York: Viking Press, 1939), and Allison Davis and John Dollard, *Children of Bondage: The Personality Development of Negro Youth in the Urban South* (New York: American Council on Education, 1940), while tending to emphasize illegitimacy and family disorganization among blacks, nevertheless confirmed the existence of the nuclear family as the black family norm. Among recent sociological studies which have refuted the image of the typical black family as unstable, disorganized, and matriarchal are Reynolds Farley, "Trends in Marital Status Among Negroes," in Charles V. Willie, ed., *The Family Life of Black People* (Columbus, Ohio: Charles E. Merrill Publishing Co., 1970); Herbert H. Hyman and John S. Reed, "Black Matriarchy Reconsidered; Evidence from Secondary Analysis of Sample Surveys," *Public Opinion Quarterly,* 33 (Fall 1969); Joseph W. Maxwell, "Rural Negro Father Participation in Family Activities," *Rural Sociology,* 33 (March 1968); Warren D. Tenhouten, "The Black Family: Myth and Reality," *Psychiatry,* 22 (May 1970); Virginia Heyer Young, "Family and Childhood in a Southern Negro Community," *American Anthropologist,* 72 (April 1970); and Levi Jones, "The Black Family: Its Process of Survival" (Ph.D. dissertation, Vanderbilt University, 1974).

The existence of female-headed families among blacks has been attributed to a host of factors. John Blassingame, *Black New Orleans* (previously cited) and Jacqueline Jackson, "But Where Are the Men," *Black Scholar,* 3 (December 1971), have recently revived interest in the sex ratio among blacks, a factor which such earlier black scholars as Kelly Miller, *Race Adjustment* (previously cited); Du Bois, ed., *The Negro American Family* (cited above); and Oliver C. Cox, "Sex Ratio and Marital Status Among Negroes," *American Sociological Review,* 5 (December 1940), gave considerable attention. Cox elaborates more fully on the subject in "Factors Affecting the Marital Status of Negroes in the United States" (Ph.D. dissertation, University of Chicago, 1938).

Representative of studies which deny, respectively, that the black community takes a casual view toward illegitimacy, and that children in female-headed families suffer unduly from the absence of a male image are Hilda Hertz and Sue Warren Little, "Unmarried Negro Mothers in a Southern Urban Community: A Study of Attitudes Toward Illegitimacy," *Social Forces,* 23 (October 1944), and Donald Nobers, "The Effects of Father Absence and Mother's Characteristics on the Identification of Adolescent White and Negro Males" (Ph.D. dissertation, St. Louis University, 1968). Contemporary observers such as D. E. Emerson, "Home Life of the

Negroes," *First Mohonk Conference on the Negro Question . . . 1890,* ed. by Isabel Bowers (Boston: George H. Ellis, 1890-1891; reprint ed., New York: Negro Universities Press, 1969), and Rossa B. Cooley, *Homes of the Freed* (New York: New Republic, 1926; reprint ed., New York: Negro Universities Press, 1970), and the sociological and anthropological studies of black communities in the South during the 1930s cited above for this chapter suggest that the problems of single parenthood and illegitimacy have been eased considerably by the tendency of black families to care for children not their own. In addition to several studies already cited for this chapter, the special problems, including the effects of the Jim Crow sex code, which black families faced in rearing their children under Southern apartheid are mentioned or discussed in W. E. B. Du Bois, *Darkwater: Voices from Within the Veil* (New York: Harcourt Brace, 1921); Robert R. Moton, *What the Negro Thinks* (Garden City, N. Y.: Doubleday, Doran, 1932); Ely Green, *Ely: An Autobiography* (New York: Seabury Press, 1966); and St. Clair Drake, "In the Mirror of Black Scholarship: W. Allison Davis and Deep South," in *Education and the Black Struggle: Notes from the Colonized World,* ed. by the Institute of the Black World (Cambridge, Mass.: Harvard Educational Review, 1974).

CHAPTER 9

Studies by historians of social stratification within Southern black communities are even rarer than historical studies of the black family. The best treatment of the subject is found in the recent histories of black slavery and the several studies of black communities in the South during the Reconstruction and immediate post-Reconstruction periods that are cited for the previous chapters. To this list should be added such studies of the antebellum free black community as John H. Franklin, *The Free Negro in North Carolina, 1790-1860* (Chapel Hill: University of North Carolina Press, 1943); Martha Wikramanayake, *A World in Shadow: The Free Black in Antebellum South Carolina* (Columbia: University of South Carolina Press, 1973); and Ira Berlin, *Slaves Without Masters: The Free Negro in the Antebellum South* (New York: Pantheon Books, 1974). To the list of works on Reconstruction and post-Reconstruction communities should be added Robert Perdue, *The Negro in Savannah, 1865-1900,* (New York: Exposition Press, 1973), which relies upon John Blassingame, "Before the Ghetto: The Making of the Black Community in Savannah, Georgia, 1865-1880," *Journal of Social History,* 6 (Summer 1973) for much of the discussion on social stratification; August Meier, "Negro Class Structure and Ideology in the Age of Booker T. Washington," *Phylon,* 23 (Fall 1962); and August Meier and David Lewis, "History of the Negro Upper Class in Atlanta, Georgia, 1890-1958," *Journal of Negro Education,* 28 (Spring 1959). The latter two studies owe much to the suggestive findings of E. Franklin Frazier whose works, *The Negro Family in the United States* (previously cited); *The Negro in the United States,* rev. ed. (New York: Macmillan, 1957); and *Black Bourgeoisie* (New York: The Free Press, 1957), treat black social stratification from an historical as well as a sociological perspective.

The several studies of black life in Southern communities during the 1930s and early 1940s by such social scientists as Charles S. Johnson, Hortense Powdermaker, Allison Davis and Burleigh and Mary Gardner, John Dollard, and Davis and Dollard that are listed for the chapter on the black family also give considerable attention to social stratification among rural and urban black Southerners. Paul B. Foreman, "Negro Lifeways in the Rural South: A Typological Approach to Social Differentiation," *American Sociological Review* 13 (August 1948), should also be noted. Most of these studies point to color as one of the indices of social status. An extreme example of a community set off from both blacks and whites by its mulatto, Catholic character is presented in Sister Francis Jerome Woods, *Marginality and Identity: A Colored Creole Family Through Ten Generations* (Baton Rouge: Louisiana State University Press, 1972). On the other hand, Clifton R. Jones, "Social Stratification in the Negro Population: A Study of South Boston, Virginia," *Journal of Negro Education,* 15 (Winter 1946); Marjorie F. Irwin, *The Negro in Charlottesville, Virginia and Albemarle County,* Publications of the University of Virginia Phelps-Stokes Fellowship Papers, No. 9 (Charlottesville: The University of Virginia, 1929); and Hylan Lewis, *Blackways of Kent* (Chapel Hill: University of North Carolina Press, 1955), a study of the community of York, South Carolina, found color to be of little or no significance as a determinant of social status. Mozelle C. Hill and Bevode C. McCall, "Social Stratification in 'Georgia Town,'" *American Sociological Review,* 14 (December 1950), notes the lack of social stratification in an all-black town.

The attack on the black middle class by Frazier, *Black Bourgeoisie* (cited above), and Nathan Hare, *The Black Anglo-Saxons* (New York: Marzani and Munsell, 1965), has recently been countered by Samuel D. Proctor, "Survival Techniques and the Black Middle Class," in Rhoda L. Goldstein, ed., *Black Life and Culture in the United States* (New York: Thomas Y. Crowell, 1971) and Sidney Kronus, *The Black Middle Class* (Columbus, Ohio: Charles E. Merrill, 1971).

While there are many leadership typologies, the one used in this study was borrowed from Oliver C. Cox, "Leadership Among Negroes in the United States," in Alvin W. Gouldner, ed., *Studies in Leadership: Leadership and Democratic Action* (New York: Harper & Row, 1950). Since, however, much black leadership has rested upon an institutional base, readers should consult the bibliography for Chapters 3, 6, and 7. Also since the black press has often played a leadership role, such previously cited works as Ann Field Alexander, "Black Protest in the New South: John Mitchell, Jr., 1863-1929, and the Richmond *Planet*," and Henry Lewis Suggs, "P. B. Young and the Norfolk *Journal and Guide*" should be consulted for the activities of two influential Virginia newspaper editors. Other studies along the same line include Gloria Blackwell, "Black Controlled Media in Atlanta, 1960-1970: The Burden of the Message and the Struggle for Survival" (Ph.D. dissertation, Emory University, 1973); Charles W. Grose, "Black Newspapers in Texas, 1868-1970" (Ph.D. dissertation, The University of Texas at Austin, 1972); and George L. Slaven, "A History of the Missouri Negro Press" (Ph.D. dissertation, University of Missouri, Columbia, 1969) and "The Missouri Negro Press, 1875-1920," *Missouri Historical Review,* 64 (July 1970). In addition to the works on black scholars cited for the chapter on education, readers should turn to Benjamin Mays, *Born to Rebel* (previously cited); Ridgely Torrence, *The Story of John Hope* (New York: Macmillan, 1948); and Raymond Gavins, "Gordon Blaine Hancock: A Black Profile from the New South," *Journal of Negro History,* 59 (July 1974) and his forthcoming *Perils and Prospects of Southern Black Leadership: Gordon Blaine Hancock, 1884-1970* (Durham, N. C.: Duke University Press) for insights into the careers of three Southern intellectuals as leaders. David M. Tucker, *Lieutenant Lee of Beale Street* (Nashville: Vanderbilt University Press, 1971), and the previously cited Walter Weare, *Black Business in the New South,* explore the role of black businessmen as community leaders. Elaine M. Burgess, *Negro Leadership in a Southern City* (Chapel Hill: University of North Carolina Press, 1962), examines essentially the same leadership group as does Weare. Everett C. Ladd, Jr., *Negro Political Leadership in the South* (Ithaca, N. Y.: Cornell University Press, 1966), analyzes the leadership structure of the black communities in Winston-Salem and Greenville, North Carolina, during the early 1960s, while Daniel C. Thompson, *The Negro Leadership Class* (Englewood Cliffs, N. J.: Prentice-Hall, 1963), does the same for New Orleans for a slightly earlier period. Joyce E. Williams, *Black Community Control: A Study of Transition in a Texas Ghetto* (New York: Praeger Publishers, 1973), is a study of leadership functioning within a black community in Fort Worth, Texas, in 1969 and 1970. Floyd Hunter, *Community Power Structure: A Study of Decision-makers* (Chapel Hill: University of North Carolina Press, 1953), and Andrew Buni, *The Negro in Virginia Politics* (previously cited), contain information on black political leadership in Atlanta, Georgia, and Richmond, Virginia, respectively, during the late 1940s and early 1950s. For the impact of the black protest movement of the 1950s and 1960s on black leadership in the South, readers should consult the bibliographical references for Chapters 12 and 13.

CHAPTER 10

For this chapter, readers should go directly to the novels, short stories, and plays mentioned in the text. Much of this material, however, especially the short stories and plays, is more accessible in literary anthologies.

Recently, in their search for or affirmation of a black aesthetic, black writers and literary critics have been reemphasizing the folk roots of Afro-American literature. Many of the folk themes and motifs which have influenced Afro-American writers are included in such collections of folklore as J. Mason Brewer, ed., *American Negro Folklore* (Chicago: Quadrangle Books, 1968); Richard M. Dorson, comp., *American Negro Folktales* (Greenwich, Conn.: Fawcett Publishing Co., 1967); Langston Hughes and Arna Bontemps, eds., *The Book of Negro Folklore* (New York: Dodd, Mead and Co., 1958); and Langston Hughes, ed., *The Book of Negro Humor* (New York: Dodd, Mead and Co., 1966). Essays devoted primarily to the folklore theme in literary works are found in Houston A. Baker, Jr., *Long Black Song: Essays in American Literature and Culture* (Charlottesville: University of Virginia Press, 1972) and Addison Gayle, Jr., ed., *Black Expression: Essays by and About Black Americans in the Creative Arts* (New York: Weybright and Talley, 1969). Three representative interpretations of the folklore motif are provided by Nancy B. McGhee, "The Folk Sermon: A Facet of the Black Literary Heritage," *CLA Journal,* 13 (September 1969); Newbell Niles Puckett, *The Magic and Folk Beliefs of the Southern Negro* (Chapel Hill: University of North Carolina Press, 1926; reprint ed., New York: Dover Publications, 1969); and Sterling Stuckey, "Through the Prism of Folklore: The Black Ethos in Slavery," *Massachusetts Review,* 9 (Summer 1968). In *How I Wrote Jubilee* (Chicago: Third World Press, 1972), Margaret Walker frankly accnoweldges the folk roots of her novel *Jubilee.*

Among the numerous anthologies of black fiction, most of which contain other literary forms as well, is Alain Locke, *The Negro* (New York: Albert and Charles Boni, 1925; reprint ed., New York: Atheneum, 1967), which is a mélange of fiction, poetry, drama, and literary, historical, and social essays supposedly representing the early years of the Harlem Renaissance. Still the best anthology of various forms of black literary expression up to the time of its publication is Sterling Brown, Arthur P. Davis, and Ulysses Lee, eds., *The Negro Caravan* (New York: Dryden Press, 1941). Good recent anthologies of black fiction and other literary works are Houston A. Baker, Jr., ed., *Black Literature in America* (New York: McGraw-Hill, 1971); Richard Barksdale and Kenneth Kinnamon, eds., *Black Writers of America: A Comprehensive Anthology* (New York: Macmillan, 1972); Abraham Chapman, ed., *Black Voices: An Anthology of Contemporary Afro-American Literature* (New York: New American Library, 1968) and *New Black Voices: An Anthology of Contemporary Afro-American Literature* (New York: New American Library, 1971); Arthur P. Davis and Saunders Redding, eds., *Calvacade: Negro American Writing from 1760 to the Present* (Boston: Houghton Mifflin, 1971); James A. Emanuel and Theodore Gross, eds., *Dark Symphony: Negro Literature in America* (New York: Free Press, 1968); Nick Aaron Ford, ed., *Black Insights: Significant Literature by Black Americans—1760 to the Present* (Waltham, Mass.: Ginn & Co., 1971); Edward Margolies, ed., *A Native Sons Reader* (Philadelphia: J. B. Lippincott Co., 1970); and Ruth Miller, ed., *Black American Literature, 1760—Present* (Beverly Hills, Calif.: Glencoe Press, 1971). Among the collections of works of individual authors who wrote about the South are Paul Laurence Dunbar, *The Best Stories of Paul Laurence Dunbar,* ed. by Benjamin Brawley (New York: Dodd, Mead and Co., 1938); and Sylvia Render, ed., *The Short Fiction of Charles W. Chesnutt* (Washington: Howard University Press, 1974). The latter contains a long, informative critical essay on Chesnutt and his works.

While some plays are included in the general anthologies above, readers should consult Alain Locke, ed., *Plays of Negro Life* (New York: Harper and Bros., 1927) for the works of both black and white dramatists written during the early years of the Harlem Renaissance. Darwin T. Turner, ed., *Black Drama in America: An Anthology* (Greenwich, Conn.: Fawcett Publications, 1971), contains plays selected as representative of the history of black drama, while William T. Couch, ed., *New Black Playwrights: An Anthology* (Baton Rouge: Louisiana State University Press, 1968), contains selected works of five black dramatists that were first produced in the 1960s. Woodie King and Ronald Milner, eds., *Black Drama Anthology* (New York: Negro American Library, 1971), is a selection of twenty-three plays only two of which, however, are set in the South.

Works of drama, history, and criticism include Doris E. Abramson, *Negro Playwrights in the American Theatre, 1925-1959* (New York: Columbia University Press, 1969); Thomas C. Dent, Richard Schechner, and Gilbert Moses, eds., *Free Southern Theatre by the Free Southern Theatre* (Indianapolis: Bobbs-Merrill, 1969); Loften Mitchell, *Black Drama: The Story of the American Negro in the Theatre* (New York: Hawthorne Books, 1967); and Floyd L. Sandle, *The Negro in the American Educational Theatre; An Organizational Development, 1911-1964* (Ann Arbor, Mich.: Edwards Bros., 1964). Lindsay Patterson, ed., *Anthology of the American Negro in the Theater: A Critical Approach* (New York: Publishers Co., 1969), is a collection of essays on black drama, playwrights, actors, the dance, and blacks in film, radio, and television.

Among the several works which discuss black literature within the context of social and cultural history are Benjamin Brawley, *The Negro Genius: A New Appraisal of the Achievement of the American Negro in Literature and the Fine Arts* (New York: Dodd, Mead, and Co., 1937); Margaret Butcher, *The Negro in American Culture,* 2d ed. (New York: Alfred A. Knopf, 1971); and Nathan I. Huggins, *Harlem Renaissance* (New York: Oxford University Press, 1971). Works of literary history and criticism which discuss several Southern black writers as well as others include Robert A. Bone, *The Negro Novel in America,* rev. ed. (New Haven: Yale University Press, 1965), which appraises black writers from the presumption of a distinction between art and politics; Arthur P. Davis, *From the Dark Tower, Afro-American Writers, 1900-1960* (Washington: Howard University Press, 1974), which contains critical sketches of black writers and their works; Roger Rosenblatt, *Black Fiction* (Cambridge, Mass.: Harvard University Press, 1974), which argues that virtually all black fiction has been based upon a cyclical conception of Afro-American history; and other studies lacking an overarching thesis such as Hugh M. Gloster, *Negro Voices in American Fiction* (Chapel Hill: University of North Carolina Press, 1948); Carl Milton Hughes, *The Negro Novelist: A Discussion of the Writings of American Negro Novelists, 1940-1950* (New York: Citadel Press, 1953); and Edward Margolies, *Native Sons: A Critical Study of Twentieth-Century Negro American Authors* (Philadelphia: J. P. Lippincott, 1968).

Works which insist upon the existence of a black aesthetic in literature and deny a dichotomy between literature and politics include Addison Gayle, Jr., *The Way of the New World: The Black Novel in America* (Garden City, N. Y.: Anchor Press/ Doubleday, 1975); the previously cited Houston A. Baker, *Long Black Song;* Margaret Wade, "The Black Aesthetic in the Black Novel," *Journal of Black Studies,* 2 (June 1972); and the essays in Addison Gayle, Jr., ed., *The Black Aesthetic* (Garden City, N. Y.: Doubleday, 1971). Perceptive comments on leading black writers are contained in Donald B. Gibson, ed., *Five Black Writers: Essays on Wright, Ellison, Hughes, and Leroi Jones* (New York: New York University Press, 1970). Among the rare essays which specifically discuss the treatment of the South in black fiction is Darwin T. Turner, "The Negro Novelist and the South," *Southern Humanities Review,* 1 (Winter, 1967).

CHAPTER 11

Several of the anthologies listed for Chapter 10 contain selections of poetry. James Weldon Johnson, ed., *The Book of American Negro Poetry* (New York: Harcourt Brace and Co., 1922, 1968), is a pioneer collection of the works of twenty-one poets (including Johnson), most of whom were Johnson's contemporaries. William H. Robinson, ed., *Early Black American Poets* (Dubuque, Iowa: William C. Brown Co., 1969), contains the works produced by poets between 1746 and 1915. One of the most comprehensive poetry anthologies is Langston Hughes and Arna Bontemps, eds., *The Poetry of the Negro, 1746-1970,* rev. ed. (Garden City, N. Y.: Doubleday, 1970), which contains poems by 110 black poets and fifty-two "Tributary Poems by Non-Negroes." For twentieth-century black poetry, readers should consult Arnold Adoff, ed., *The Poetry of Black America: Anthology of the Twentieth Century* (New York: Harper & Row, 1973), and Dudley Randall, *The Black Poets* (New York: Bantam

Books, 1971). Anthologies which primarily reflect the black consciousness of the 1960s include Gwendolyn Brooks, ed., *A Broadside Treasury* (Detroit: Broadside Press, 1971); Woodie King, ed., *Black Spirits: A Festival of New Black Poets in America* (New York: Random House, 1972); and Don E. Lee, *Dynamite Voices: Black Poets of the 1960s* (Detroit: Broadside Press, 1971).

In a class by itself as an anthology is Stephen Henderson, *Understanding the New Black Poetry: Black Speech and Black Music as Poetic References* (New York: William Morrow, 1973), which is organized around the concept of an interactive relationship, structurally, thematically, and experientially, between oral tradition and formal poetic expression. Other interpretive studies of black poetry include Sterling Brown, *Negro Poetry and Drama* (Washington: Associates in Negro Folk Education, 1937); Donald Gibson, ed., *Modern Black Poets: A Collection of Critical Essays* (Englewood Cliffs, N. J.: Prentice-Hall, 1973); and Jean Wagner, *Black Poets of the United States: From Paul Laurence Dunbar to Langston Hughes,* trans. by Kenneth Douglas (Urbana: University of Illinois Press, 1973). The two black poets writing on Southern themes who have received the most attention are Paul Laurence Dunbar and Langston Hughes. For varying interpretations of the works of Dunbar, readers should see Jay Martin, ed., *A Singer in the Dawn: Reinterpretations of Paul Laurence Dunbar* (New York: Dodd, Mead and Co., 1975), and Darwin T. Turner, "Paul Laurence Dunbar: Rejected Symbol," *Journal of Negro History,* 52 (January 1967). A collection of interpretative essays on Hughes is Therman B. O'Daniel, ed., *Langston Hughes, Black Genius: A Critical Evaluation* (New York: William Morrow, 1971).

The literature on black music is extensive. Eileen Southern's *The Music of Black Americans: A History* (New York: W. W. Norton and Co., 1971), which traces the development of the various forms of black music from their African origins through the 1960s, synthesizes much of the primary and secondary literature on the subject, largely through a study of the lives of the performers and the historical and social milieu in which they lived. Of the specific types of black music, the spirituals have, perhaps, received the greatest study. John Lovell's *Black Song: The Forge and the Flame* (New York: Macmillan, 1972), is the most intensive study to date of the origins and nature of the spirituals and of their interpretation by scholars and other listeners around the world. Among the interpretations of the spirituals, Sterling Brown, "Negro Folk Expression: Spirituals, Ballads, and Songs," *Phylon,* 14 (Spring 1953), stresses their commonness with other forms of music as folk literature; Miles Mark Fisher, *Negro Slave Songs in the United States* (Ithaca, N. Y.: Cornell University Press, 1953), emphasizes their African origins; and Howard Thurman, *Deep River: Reflections on the Religious Insight of Certain of the Negro Spirituals* (New York: Harper & Row, 1955), examines them for their theological and eschatological content. For a collection of the spirituals, readers should consult James Weldon Johnson and James Rosamond Johnson, eds., *The Books of American Negro Spirituals* (New York: Viking Press, 1956), originally published in 1925 and 1926 as *The Book of American Negro Spirituals and the Second Book of Negro Spirituals.* A useful scholarly study of gospel music is George H. Ricks, "Some Aspects of the Religious Music of the United States Negro: An Ethnomusicological Study with Special Emphasis on the Gospel Tradition," (Ph.D. dissertation, Northwestern University, 1960).

Studies of the blues include Sterling A. Brown, "The Blues," *Phylon,* 8 (Winter 1952); Samuel B. Charters, *The Country Blues* (New York: Rinehart and Co., 1959);

Paul Oliver, *Blues Fell This Morning: The Meaning of the Blues* (New York: Horizon Press, 1960) and *The Story of the Blues* (Philadelphia: Chilton Book Co., 1969). Leroi Jones, *Blues People: The Negro Experience in White America and the Music That Developed from It* (New York: William Morrow, 1963), contends that as a conscious expression of the Afro-American historical experience, the blues theme is present in all forms of black music. Harold Courlander, *Negro Folk Music U.S.A.* (New York: Columbia University Press, 1963), includes the blues among the various forms of black folk music, which he regards as oral literature expressive of a religious view of life. Frederic Ramsey, Jr., *Been Here and Gone* (New Brunswick, N.J.: Rutgers University Press, 1960), is an attempt to integrate blues lyrics with photographs of the social settings in the Deep South of the 1950s, out of which they emerged. The autobiography of a leading blues composer is W. C. Handy, *Father of the Blues,* ed. by Arna Bontemps (New York: Macmillan, 1941).

On the history and interpretation of jazz, major studies are Gunther Schuller, *Early Jazz: Its Roots and Musical Development* (New York: Oxford University Press, 1968); Marshall Stearns, *The Story of Jazz,* rev. ed. (New York: Oxford Unviersity Press, 1962); and the essays in Nat Hentoff and Albert McCarthy, eds., *Jazz* (New York: Rinehart and Co., 1959).

CHAPTER 12

Previously cited studies such as Robert Brisbane, *The Black Vanguard,* and Edward Peeks, *The Long Struggle for Black Power,* as well as Thomas R. Brooks, *The Walls Come Tumbling Down: A History of the Civil Rights Movement, 1940-1970* (Englewood Cliffs, N. J.: Prentice Hall, 1974), and Loren Miller, *The Petitioners: The Story of the Supreme Court of the United States and the Negro* (New York: Pantheon Books, 1966), clearly suggest that the black protest movement of the late 1950s and 1960s had been building for some time. Richard Kluger, *Simple Justice: The History of Brown v. Board of Education and Black America's Struggle for Equality* (New York: Alfred A. Knopf, 1976), discusses the black struggle for legal equality with emphasis on the drama inherent in the actions of the participants.

While the literature on the freedom movement of the 1950s and 1960s is abundant, scholarly histories of the phenomenon are just appearing. One of the first histories of the entire movement is Robert Brisbane, *Black Activism: Racial Revolution in the United States 1954-1970* (Valley Forge, Pa.: Judson Press, 1974). In *Core: A Study in the Civil Rights Movement, 1942-1968* (New York: Oxford University Press, 1973), August Meier and Elliot Rudwick provide the only full-length historical treatment of one of the four most important protest organizations active during the period. Howard Zinn's *SNCC: The New Abolitionists* (Boston: Beacon Press, 1964), is a contemporary history of the student organization before it became committed to the concept of black power. For the story of the transition of the organization to black power, readers should see Allen Matusow, "From Civil Rights to Black Power: The Case of SNCC, 1960-1966," in Barton J. Bernstein and Allen J. Matusow, eds., *Twentieth Century America: Recent Interpretations* (New York: Harcourt Brace Jovanovich, 1969).

Contemporary analyses and descriptions of the freedom movement abound. Joseph H. Himes, "The Functions of Racial Conflict," *Social Forces,* 45 (September 1966) and "Theory of Racial Conflict," *Social Forces,* 50 (September 1971), as well as August Meier, "On the Role of Martin Luther King," *New Politics,* 4 (Winter 1965), perceived the civil rights movement in terms of the dynamics of power. James A. Geschwender, ed., *The Black Revolt* (Englewood Cliffs, N. J.: Prentice-Hall, 1971), is a useful anthology of some thirty-two essays assessing the movement from the perspective of leadership changes, social structure, student participation, and general results.

In studying the movement from the viewpoint of the participants, readers should first consult the several books by Martin Luther King, especially *Stride Toward Freedom: The Montgomery Story* (New York: Harper & Bros., 1958); *Strength to Love* (New York: Harper & Row, 1963); and *Where Do We Go from Here: Chaos or Community* (New York: Harper & Row, 1967). Books by other participants in the movement include Daisy Bates, *The Long Shadow of Little Rock, A Memoir* (New York: David McKay, 1962); James Forman, *The Making of Black Revolutionaries* (New York: Macmillan, 1972); and Cleveland Sellers, *The River of No Return* (New York: William Morrow, 1973). Sally Belfrage's *Freedom Summer* (New York: Viking Press, 1965) is a participant's description of the Mississippi Summer Project of 1964, while Debbie Louis, *And We Are Not Saved: A History of the Movement as People* (Garden City, N. Y.: Doubleday, 1970), is a participant's analysis of the role of students in the movement during the 1960s.

The role of local black community institutions in the South in the freedom movement has not yet been thoroughly studied. Although the leadership activities of certain ministers has been highly publicized, the overall response of local black churches to the movement is much less known. However, Bruce Hilton, *The Delta Ministry* (New York: Macmillan, 1969), does describe the relatively unsung community action and voter registration activities of black (and some white) church people in Mississippi during the 1960s, while Hart M. Nelsen and Anne K. Nelsen, *Black Church in the Sixties* (Lexington: The University of Kentucky Press, 1975), sees the religiosity of the black church as a potent force in the protest movement. David M. Tucker, *Black Pastors and Leaders* (previously cited), devotes two chapters to the protest activities of church leaders in Memphis during the 1950s and 1960s. Little has been done on the role of college administrators and faculties in the freedom movement. Albert N. D. Brooks, "H. Council Trenholm: Martyr on Alabama Tightrope," *Negro History Bulletin,* 26 (May 1963), is essentially a eulogy of a college president who was caught up in the movement.

Despite suggestive information in Robert Hooker, "Race and the Mississippi Press," *New South,* 26 (Winter 1971); Gloria Blackwell, "Black Controlled Media in Atlanta, 1960-1970: The Burden of the Message and the Struggle for Survival" (Ph.D. dissertation, Emory University, 1973); Andrew W. Secrest, "In Black and White: Press Opinion and Race Relations in South Carolina, 1954-1964" (Ph.D. dissertation, Duke University, 1972); and Hugh D. Graham, *Crisis in Print: Desegregation and the Press in Tennessee* (Nashville: Vanderbilt University Press, 1967), there is no systematic exploration of the overall response of the Southern black press to the freedom movement. Hopefully this gap will be filled with the completion of a doctoral dissertation on the subject by a student in the history department at Howard University.

Of the works on the role of songs in the freedom movement, Guy Carawan and

Candide Carawan, eds., *Freedom Is a Constant Struggle: Songs of the Freedom Movement* (New York: Oak Publications, 1968), is a collection of songs of the movement, while Bernice Reagon, "Songs of the Civil Rights Movement, 1955-1965: A Study of Culture History" (Ph.D. dissertation, Howard University, 1975), is a study of the origin, evolution, and social usage of several of the principal songs by a participant in the movement and a talented singer in her own rights.

A summary of the circumstances in which several activists were killed is provided by Jack Mendelsohn, *The Martyrs: Sixteen Who Gave Their Lives for Racial Justice* (New York: Harper & Row, 1966). A more detailed accounting of the life and death of a student activist is James Forman, *Sammy Younge, Jr.: The First Black College Student to Die in the Black Liberation Movement* (New York: Grove Press, 1968).

Several of the studies already cited for this chapter discuss the emergence of the black power concept and movement. Stokely Carmichael and Charles Hamilton, *Black Power: The Politics of Liberation in America* (New York: Random House, 1967), is an attempt to provide a systematic explication of the slogan and movement after the term had caused considerable confusion among both blacks and whites; interpretations of the term had ranged from the revolutionary nationalism articulated by Robert Williams in *Negroes with Guns* (Chicago: Third World Press, 1973) to a commitment to traditional politics in order to effect change which was discovered [among blacks in the Mississippi Delta by Joyce Ladner "What 'Black Power' Means to Negroes in Mississippi," *Trans-Action Magazine,* 5 (November 1967). Efforts to achieve a modicum of black power through such economic means as the formation of cooperatives and the staging of workers strikes are treated in the previously cited Bruce Hilton, *The Delta Ministry;* Philip Foner, *Organized Labor and the Black Worker;* and in Ray Marshall and Lamond Godwin, *Cooperatives and Rural Poverty* (Baltimore: Johns Hopkins Press, 1971).

CHAPTER 13

Several recent studies depict the changes occurring in the South as a whole that can be attributed, in part, to the civil rights movement of the 1950s and 1960s. Earl Black, *Southern Governors and Civil Rights: Racial Segregation as a Campaign Issue in the Second Reconstruction* (Cambridge, Mass.: Harvard University Press, 1976) analyzes the changing significance of segregation as an issue in gubernatorial campaigns in the South from 1950 to 1973. Through an analysis of county and precinct election returns from 1944 to 1972, Numan V. Bartley and Hugh D. Graham, *Southern Politics and the Second Reconstruction* (Baltimore: Johns Hopkins University Press, 1975), find that although it is expressed in new political alignments, the traditional political and social conservatism of the South remains basically unshaken by the destruction of disfranchisement, Jim Crow, the one-party system, and malapportionment—the basic pillars of the pre-World War II Southern political order. Much broader in scope is Charles P. Roland, *The Improbable Era: The South Since World War II* (Lexington: The University of Kentucky Press, 1975), which describes the political, economic, social, and cultural changes which have occurred in the South over the past thirty years, but notes the region's continued attachment to the traits derived from its historical past. Ernest M. Lander, Jr., and Richard J. Calhoun, eds., *Two Decades of*

Change: The South Since the Supreme Court Desegregation Decision (Columbia: University of South Carolina Press, 1975), is a collection of essays with comments on such aspects of recent Southern life as politics, literature, the effects of the Brown decision, black employment, and a number of ironic manifestations of Southern change.

While John Buggs, "School Desegregation, North and South," *Integrated Education,* 13 (May-June 1975), shows the public schools in the South to be the most desegregated in the nation, Johnny S. Butler, "Black Educators in Louisiana—A Question of Survival," *Journal of Negro Educaiton,* 43 (Winter 1974); Robert Hooker, "Displacement of Black Teachers in the Eleven Southern States," *Afro-American Studies,* 2 (December 1971); Robert Coles, *Children of Crisis* (Boston: Little, Brown, 1967); and Betty Fancher, *Voices from the South: Black Students Talk About Their Experiences in Desegregated Schools* (Atlanta: Southern Regional Council, 1970), show that the desegregation process was not without economic, social, and psychological costs to segments of the black community.

In addition to the three books cited at the beginning of this chapter, Henry Holloway, *The Politics of the Southern Negro: From Exclusion to Big City Politics* (New York: Random House, 1969); Donald R. Matthews and James W. Prothro, *Negroes and the New Southern Politics* (New York: Harcourt Brace and World, 1966); and Pat Watters and Reese Cleghorn, *Climbing Jacobs Ladder: The Arrival of Negroes in Southern Politics* (New York: Harcourt Brace and World, 1967) explore the rise in black political participation during the freedom movement. More recent studies which analyze the character, consequences, and leadership pattern of the increasing participation of blacks in the politics of the South include Joe R. Feagin, "Black Politics in the South: A Descriptive Analysis," *Journal of Politics,* 37 (February 1975), and Lester M. Salamon, "Leadership and Modernization: The Emerging Black Political Elite in the American South," *Journal of Politics,* 37 (August 1973). Kenneth S. Colburn's *Southern Black Mayors: Local Problems and Federal Responses* (Washington: Joint Center for Political Studies, 1973) reveals the current limits to black politics as a means for bringing about substantive economic changes in the status of black Southerners, while Charles S. Bullock, III, and Harrell R. Rodgers, Jr., *Racial Equality in America: In Search of an Unfulfilled Goal* (Pacific Palisades, Calif.: Goodyear Publishing Co., 1975); Sar A. Levitan, William B. Johnston, and Robert Taggart, *Still a Dream: The Changing Status of Blacks Since 1960* (Cambridge, Mass.: Harvard University Press, 1975); and the U.S. Bureau of the Census, *The Social and Economic Status of the Black Population in the United States 1974* (Washington, D.C.: Government Printing Office, 1975), clearly show that blacks throughout the nation still have far to go to reach the socioeconomic level of the majority of white Americans.

INDEX

ABOUT THE AUTHOR

Arnold H. Taylor, professor of history at Howard University, has published in such journals as the *Pacific Historical Review* and *The South Atlantic Quarterly.* A previous book, *American Diplomacy and the Narcotics Traffic: A Study in International Humanitarian Reform, 1900-1939,* was published in 1969.